NEW PERSPECTIVES ON AFRICAN CHILDHOOD

Constructions, Histories, Representations
and Understandings

Edited by

De-Valera N.Y.M. Botchway
University of Cape Coast, Ghana

Awo Sarpong
University of Cape Coast, Ghana

Charles Quist-Adade
Kwantlen Polytechnic University, Canada

Series in Sociology

VERNON PRESS

www.vernonpress.com

In the Americas:	*In the rest of the world:*
Vernon Press	Vernon Press
1000 N West Street,	C/Sancti Espiritu 17,
Suite 1200, Wilmington,	Malaga, 29006
Delaware 19801	Spain
United States	

Series in Sociology

Library of Congress Control Number: 2018964963

ISBN: 978-1-62273-712-3

Also available:

Hardback: 978-1-62273-534-1

E-book: 978-1-62273-587-7

Table of Contents

List of Tables

Introduction

De-Valera N.Y.M. Botchway

Background and Focus of Study

This edited volume, titled *New Perspectives on African Childhood: Constructions, Histories, Representations and Understandings*, contains multidisciplinary works of scholars in the humanities and social sciences that interpret and present accounts, ideas, notions and portrayals about African childhood constructions, histories, representations and understandings. The focus of the studies includes analyses of the depictions of African children and their lived childhood experiences in wars and movies, especially Western-made ones; interpretation of conceptions of creative writers and novels, both African and non-African, about African children and nuances in African childhood; and reinterpretation of the meanings of being an African child and living the life of one in the context of indigenous cosmologies and knowledge systems and how such meanings are similar to or different from certain universalised Western-spawned notions. Other concerns of the studies include the articulated ideas, creativity and agency of children in relation to labour; notions of African health and wellbeing lifeways and their interrelations with African children and their childhood experiences; and representations of the postcolonial African childhood. Despite the fact that each study is not an exhaustive coverage of the subject, a synthesis of the views that they present offers a rich addition to the burgeoning area of childhood studies especially within and for the African context and needs.

The academic inquiry into the area of children and their experiences in social settings and the aetiology and ontology of the notion and state called childhood is steadily and encouragingly attracting various conceptualisations, interpretations and reinterpretations, historicisations and case studies. Thus, research is becoming internationalised, expressed through international conferences, research cooperation and transnational projects which have yielded monographs, anthologies, journal articles and visual and performing arts products such as paintings, poems, songs and drama. Some strands of the interrogation have manifested in different chronological frames or revolved around interesting thematic poles or proceeded from novel theoretical perspectives. Also, others have either explained issues within a single geo-cultural space or comparatively analysed them within geo-cultural spaces. Despite this process, it is apparent that Africa, which hegemonic discourse arbitrarily considers as part of the so-called "Global South", in comparison with the so-called "Global North" of European and North American societies, has not received a lot of attention in the global context of investigative works in childhood studies. In other words, research has been conducted on childhood globally but there is still opportunity and ample room for a higher level of studies to be conducted to bring out more of the contours of the area and stories as they apply to the African historical and contemporary contexts. Indubitably, the several important works that have been produced from childhood studies for the Western terrain – European and North American societies – help to deepen academic and public understanding about children and their lived experience and how adults define and categorise them in the West. Relatively, the case for and in Africa is not so despite the fact that the continent has a large youth population, with a significant percentage of that demography being children. Thus, the need for extensive production and amplification of works that probe into aspects of African childhood, such as childhood belongings and the cultures of childhood, is important.

The scarcity of such works in the African context should not exist because African childhood is real, and as Agya Boakye-Boaten has shown and argued, there is childhood in Africa.[1] The concept and state of childhood can be found in what he calls "traditional Africa, which is the unadulterated Africa, that is prehistoric Africa, and contemporary Africa, that is Africa after the period of slavery, colonialism, and post-independent Africa."[2] Within the cosmology of traditional Africa, children were seen as spiritual beings who had reincarnated after living and dying in previous generations. Thus, they were accorded respect by members of the society; however, children were also deemed human beings who were biologically vulnerable and in need of help and direction, protection and proper socialization to perpetuate their family and cultural legacies. This trapped the childhood period and its political and social spaces and meanings in a socializing mode.[3] However, as he shows, the delicate concept of childhood continues to undergo transformations and redefinitions that even impact society's obligations to its children, because of economic, socio-cultural and political dynamics,[4] including the cultural ef-

---

[1] Agya Boakye-Boaten, "Changes in the Concept of Childhood: Implications on Children in Ghana," *Uluslararası Sosyal Araştırmalar Dergisi, The Journal of International Social Research,* 3 (10), (2010): 114 (104-115).
[2] Ibid. 107.
[3] Ibid. 109.
[4] Boakye-Boaten, "Changes in the concept of Childhood".

fects and forces of colonialism, globalization, HIV/AIDs, corruption, civil and ethnic unrests and neoliberalism and commercialization of children.[5]

It can be concluded from the foregoing that it is important and necessary for attention to be given to Africa's situation through childhood studies. As Benedict Carton has demonstrated in "Africa" in *Encyclopedia of Children and Childhood in History and Society*, where he attempts to briefly trace the rise of scholarship on African childhood, "research on African childhood gathered momentum in the 1980s with the publication of *Maidens, Meals, and Money: [Capitalism and the Domestic Community]*"[6] (1981), by Claude Meillassoux (1925-2005), the renowned French neo-Marxist economic anthropologist and Africanist. According to Carton, Meillassoux's work of anthropology which examined elder and youth interactions in Africa south of the Sahara, similar to *Centuries of Childhood* by Philippe Aries which was a significant work of history about Western family and childhood, offered a good model that depicted the various age shifts and changes within "precapitalist" local environments including simple agrarian communities to "preindustrial" states which world religions and international trade amalgamated.[7] However, as Carton observed, certain crucial questions, such as: "When did adults reckon that children succumbed to 'original sin'?" and "When did parents turn childhood into a stage of indulging innocent individuals?", were not asked or adequately addressed by Meillassoux's work.[8] Thus, African childhood and the multiple ways in which it can be understood required and still requires further explorations as studies like "Beyond Pluralizing African Childhoods: Introduction"[9] and "From the singular to the plural: Exploring diversities in contemporary childhoods in sub-Saharan Africa"[10] have shown. What this means is that inquests which reconsider childhood from multifaceted angles are needed to cause a detour in the trajectory of some of the extant scholarly studies about the lives of African children and African childhood, which have become sterile and repetitive in a tradition that has often looked solely at children as victims of social injustice and exploitation and peripheral subjects of the world

---

[5] Ibid.

[6] Benedict Carton, "Africa," in Paula S. Fass (ed.),*Encyclopedia of Children and Childhood in History and Society*, (New York: Thompson Gale, 2004), 30.

[7] Ibid.

[8] Ibid.

[9] Tatek Abebe and Yaw Ofosu-Kusi, "Beyond Pluralizing African Childhoods: Introduction," *Childhood: A Journal of Global Child Research*, 23 (3), (2016): 303-316.

[10] Afua Twum Danso Imoh, "From the singular to the plural: Exploring diversities in contemporary childhoods in sub-Saharan Africa," *Childhood: A Journal of Global Child Research*, 23 (3), (2016): 455-468.

of adults. What is true, and which the underlined need for a detour supports, is that there are more regions of African childhood, obviously happy and hope-giving ones, worth interrogating. These include, but are not limited to, creative expression in childhood, perceptions of happiness in childhood, childhood versus adultism, childhood spirituality, hijacked childhoods and brave negotiations of safe havens for self-expression, and child(ren) constructed understandings of the African childhood. More especially, opening up discussions about African children and childhood within an interdisciplinary space will enrich the area of childhood studies within the African context. It will offer broader insights into the area from an interdisciplinary perspective where the voices of history, political and social studies and literature, along with visual and performing arts and other subfields of the humanities and social sciences, such as psychology and sociology, and education in combination will use the broader exchange of concepts and ideas to enrich the growing understanding about children and their childhood in the African context. Thus, as Tatek Abebe and Yaw Ofosu-Kusi have also opined aptly, "The future for African scholarship on childhood and children must be hinged on greater collaboration and cooperation on childhood research and studies regardless of which part of the continent takes as a vantage point"[11]

Moreover, there is the need for critical windows, especially scholarly ones, to be opened to the world to have an analytic and broader insight into African childhood to balance the journalistic print and media ones, many of which often provide sensationalist stories about poverty and pain as the characteristics of African children and childhood. This will contribute to bringing forth the understanding that not every child in Africa is hungry, sick and terrorised by civil unrest; for others who have limited views and perceptions about the African situation, such new windows can make them appreciate the fact that African childhood is not static but dynamic and with a long history, a versatile present and negotiable and promising future. They will know that African childhood also manifests aspects that have similarities and differences because of the different geographical regions and cultural zones on the continent.

Childhood can be a happy one and can be a sad one. While chores like fetching water, taking care of younger siblings, herding, gathering firewood or farming to support the family characterise some rural-based childhoods, there are some childhoods that are devoid of these because they manifest in certain urban spaces where such activities do not exist. While some childhoods feature income earning activities like hawking, work in the fields and

---

[11] Abebe and Ofosu-Kusi, "Beyond Pluralizing African Childhoods: Introduction," 314.

prostitution, others are free from such activities. As such, studies like what this volume contains and offers serve as windows and new perspectives into and about aspects of childhood making, representations and understandings in the African situation.

For the African context, Steve Howard has aptly observed and reminded us in his fine seminal and pioneering bibliography of children and childhood in Africa that there generally exists a dearth of reference matter and textbook material on the area under discussion.[12] Boakye-Boaten also laments about "the paucity of research on the concept of childhood in Ghana specifically *and Africa by extension*" (italics mine).[13] In walking us through the few extant works of his bibliographical compilation, Howard explains them as being predominantly works "produced by either intergovernmental agencies or nongovernmental agencies and are often annual statistical compilations", or general summaries of "background, definitions, and social context for discussions of childhood", or works that offer "reviews of literature on a large topic in the field, such as children and work" or provide a sketch "of methodological techniques for researching children".[14]

In making a case for more studies that specifically focus on excavating understanding about the lives and childhoods of children in Africa to be undertaken, Howard was correct with his observation that while a number of anthropological and related studies provide some knowledge about life in rural African society and a sense of the systems that take care of socialisation of children and lead them into adulthood, only a "few" are specifically centred on children. This is because most of them secondarily append children or mortise them into wider contexts of discussions and examinations of "African families, communities, and the wider society."[15] Furthermore, because of an existing privileging of political history and economic history, two areas where children and their lives have not been necessarily foregrounded, much of the literature of historical studies too have not offered in-depth points and facts about the lives of children and childhood.[16] Consequently, we reasonably agree with Howard's implied observation that there is more room for the production of scholarly research and reference and textbook material on the subject of children and childhood in

---

[12] Steve Howard, "Children and Childhood", Oxford Bibliographies, http://www.oxford bibliographies.com/view/document/obo-9780199846733/obo-9780199846733-0045.xml. Accessed on February 19, 2018.

[13] Boakye-Boaten, "Changes in the concept of Childhood".

[14] Howard, "Children and Childhood".

[15] Ibid.

[16] Ibid.

Africa because despite the fact that few scholars have made the historical study of children and slavery a significant field, and some have focused on children basically through the extension of institutions, such as health and education, there exists a dearth of material on the topic.[17] Even the limited-in-circulation literature on socioeconomic development of African children as administered by governmental, nongovernmental, and private-voluntary organizations has an "in-house" nature which makes it difficult to catalogue or collect.[18] Thus, regarding the African terrain and context, it is ultimately time and imperative for more works to be done to showcase the situation and provide insights, views and ideas about it to African and global scholars, policy makers and readers, and enrich, amplify and complement debates about children and childhoods in the corpus of works and researches done globally for intellectual, public and academic consumption.

History of the Evolution and Trajectory of Childhood Studies. A Short Introduction

We can trace the genesis and genealogy of the contemporary academic enterprise known as Childhood Studies to different historical moments. However, it is a product of the academic twists and turns of the so-called West or Western societies. Thus, its origins in the West are anchored in the Enlightenment process and era which promoted a strong interest in understanding human nature and by extension that of "children". Drawing insight from David Kennedy's *The Well of Being: Childhood, Subjectivity, and Education*,[19] Gareth Matthews and Amy Mullin aptly aver in *The Stanford Encyclopedia of Philosophy* that: "But exactly how the conception of childhood has changed historically and how conceptions differ across cultures is a matter of scholarly controversy and philosophical interest".[20] Philippe Ariès, for example, argued, "partly on the evidence of depictions of infants in medieval art, that the medievals thought of children as simply 'little adults.'"[21] By contrast, Shulamith Shahar had evidence-based reason to aver that "some medieval thinkers un-

---

[17] Ibid.

[18] Ibid.

[19] David Kennedy, *The Well of Being: Childhood, Subjectivity, and Education*, (Albany: SUNY Press 2006).

[20] Gareth Matthews and Amy Mullin, "The Philosophy of Childhood", in Edward N. Zalta (ed.), *The Stanford Encyclopedia of Philosophy* (Spring 2015 Edition), https://plato.stanford.edu/archives/spr2015/entries/childhood/. Accessed on 6 February, 2018.

[21] Ibid.

derstood childhood to be divided into fairly well-defined stages".[22] The Age of Enlightenment thinkers like John Locke and Jacques Rousseau, for example, saw – imagined and constructed – the child as an object and a symbol for their "adult" ideas of governance.[23] The romanticized notion and figure of the child took the centre of the intellectual works, political debates and prose, poetry and other literary productions of many thinkers, policy makers and creative writers in the 19th and 20th centuries. Such ideas of the child, produced from the Romantic thought, influenced adult literature such as that of William Wordsworth, the English Poet Laureate from 1843 to 1850. "Often credited with discovering the Romantic child" by creating "a cult of childhood during the Romantic era, which continued well into the Victorian period and beyond", the "Wordsworthian child most often act[ing] as a child of nature" was "the product of the adult's nostalgia and memory as much as he or she is the product of nature."[24] British Romantics often figured children in adult literature and poetry because of their conjured ideas about the child's closeness to nature and innocence. "The child, some Romantic poets believed, had access to a unique worldview, precisely because a child has not yet rationalized and assimilated the workings of society the way an adult has."[25] As Stephanie Metz has aptly observed, the romanticised notions and figure about the child continued and "The literary and political influence of Romanticism retains its potency even today as it still colors our perceptions of children *in European societies and also non-European worlds where European cultural imperialism and colonialism promoted Europeanisation and Westernisation*" (emphasis rendered in italics are mine).[26]

Cultural discussions about children even reified the child as an observable object, a material of inquiry, which could be used to explain racial superiority or inferiority. For example, G. Stanley Hall, the renowned psychologist and

---

[22] Ibid.

[23] John Locke, Two Treatises of Government, from *The Works of John Locke*, Vol. 5, (London: Sharpe and Son, 1823); Jean Jacques Rousseau, *The Social Contract*, trans., Charles Frankel, (New York: Hafner, 1947).

[24] Stephanie Metz, ""The Youth . . . still is Nature's priest": Wordsworth and the Child of Nature," http://web.utk.edu/~gerard/romanticpolitics/wordsworth-and-the-child.html. Accessed on 6 February, 2018.

[25] Stephanie Metz, "Romanticism and the Child: Inventing Innocence," http://web.utk.edu/~gerard/romanticpolitics/childhood.html. Accessed on 6 February, 2018.

[26] Ibid.

arguably the "leader of the 'child study' movement in America",[27] endeavoured to rank "races" according to their supposed advancement alongside an
evolutionary range analogous to individual human development – with some
in childhood, some in adolescence, and some in adulthood – in his opus
magnum *Adolescence: Its Psychology and its Relations to Physiology, Anthropology, Sociology, Sex, Crime, Religion, and Education* (1904). This effort by
Stanley, who held the opinion that "The child and race are each keys to the
other" whereby the adolescent point, a time of "storm and stress", represented also the sprout of promise for the race because it was the significant exem-
plifier of the past of the race, was a form of evolutionary theory. This theory
held the view that the development of races from the supposed primordial
type to the so-called well developed in that progression could be understood
by observing the growth of children.[28] Sigmund Freud's area of psychoanalysis, as Kenneth Kid has concluded, also paid attention to the child only due to
the fact that psychoanalysis obtained some of its growth and insights because
it explored books for children. Arguing that "Freud and Jung make a compelling case for the intimacy of childhood and the fairy tale," Kid reveals that
psychoanalysis then used ideas from children's literature to express and
demonstrate its topics and methods by using folklore and fairy tales, and
materials from psychoanalysis of children and children's literary texts, such as
the classic stories of *Peter Pan* and *Alice's Adventures in Wonderland*.[29] Thus,
children were not actually studied to understand children. Rather, studying
the child was a reification of them into tools and an attempt to theorise, explain and comment on them as subjects of many isolated studies of particular
subjects to elucidate and make sense of the world of adults. Primarily then,
they were not studied to understand them and make sense of their world.
Ignoring prevailing ideas and opinions that understanding children could
shape better relations between adults and children, some early European
scholars in the mid 19th century rather believed that knowledge produced by
academics about children could offer understanding about the genesis and
evolution of human beings. Even Jean Piaget (1896-1980), the Swiss episte-
mologist known for his pioneering work in child development and the formu-
lator of the theory of cognitive development and epistemological view known

[27] Review of G. Stanley Hall, Adolescence: Its Psychology and Its Relations to Physiology, Anthropology, Sociology, Sex, Crime, Religion, and Education, by Alexander F. Chamberlain, American Anthropologist, New Series, 6 (4), (1904): 539, (539-541).
[28] G. Stanley Hall, Adolescence: Its Psychology and its Relations to Physiology, Anthropology, Sociology, Sex, Crime, Religion, and Education, 2 Vols, (New York: Appleton, 1904).
[29] Kenneth Kidd, Freud in Oz: At the Intersections of Psychoanalysis and Children's Literature, (Minneapolis: University of Minnesota Press, 2011).

as "genetic epistemology", was interested in studying children to have knowledge about how we came to comprehend and perceive the world. Still, for some investigators, understanding the development of children was necessary for comprehending development in general than what it could tell us about children. But the interest in children by the turn of the 20th century also produced other aspects of inquiry and interests. Knowledge about children produced an aspect of scholastic concern in which scholars sought to use their lessons to engineer educational, social welfare and management policies and theories. Thus, some scholarship in the humanities, as well as the social and behavioural sciences, became committed to a utilitarian comprehension of children in a quest for an enhanced knowledge of children and their life experiences and a need to engage with the lives of children in order to be able to dictate how such lives should be shaped. This led to the expansion of both the disciplines of child psychology and child development under the umbrella of developmental psychology as dominant providers of defining academic discourses in relation to children.[30] They also largely focused on mining for biology-determined laws of childhood behaviour and using knowledge about genetic formations and conducts to understand the actions and development of children.[31] Nonetheless, other disciplines in the social sciences, namely sociology and anthropology, started to centre children instead of leaving them on the periphery of their epistemic interrogations of family, household and community. This centring was fundamentally driven by a desire to know about how children are prepared for adult life and as adults in society. To the sociologists and anthropologists, this preparation was done through the process of "socialisation" which Talcott Parson's functional structuralist theoretical perspective supported.[32] However, when Anne-Marie Ambert, a sociologist, realised and opined that "socialisation" was not actually about children at all, but was about how adults and their adult society transformed them into adults, and the studying of children was not a major route to becoming famous in sociology,[33] it contributed in making clear the fact that there existed a real, but blurred and camouflaged, lack of interest in children in sociology and even anthropology. Thus, a defining moment for a new academic interest in

---

[30] W. Kessen, *The Rise and Fall of Development,* (Worcester, MA: Clark University Press, 1990).

[31] J. Morss, *The Biologising of Childhood: Developmental Psychology and the Darwinian Myth,* (Hove: Lawrence Erlbaum, 1990).

[32] T. Parsons, *The Social System,* (Glencoe, Illinois: Free Press, 1951).

[33] Anne-Marie Ambert, "Sociology of Sociology: The Place of Children in North American Sociology", in P. A. Adler and P. Adler (eds.), *Sociological Studies of Child Development,* Vol. 1, (Greenwich, CT: JAI Press, 1986), 24 (11-31).

children and childhood started to emerge gradually as Childhood Studies. However, this emergence did not emanate from one specific source, rather through and from a variety of sources and trajectories of thought. The map of the genealogy of Childhood Studies is, therefore, a complex one to read because of the multiple geneses of the inspiration, the variegation in chronology of its beginnings and the numerous pioneers of this interest. For example, *L'enfant et la vie familiale sous l'ancien regime* published in 1960[34], known in English by its 1962 translated version as *Centuries of Childhood: A Social History of Family Life,* by Philippe Ariès,[35] is definitely one of the early decisive works citable as a pioneer initiator that heralded a turning point in promoting a novel academic concern for children and childhood. Ariès was a historian, a social one at that, and not a social scientist per se, who had an interest in the lives of children and their social meanings, characterisations and manifestations in history. For history, Ariès's work mortised the lives of the so-called ordinary person, in this case, the child, into the narratives and concerns of social and cultural history. This fertilised a growing awareness of the historical nature of childhood and promoted the practice and tradition where childhood came to be studied as a state which had different spatial and temporal manifestations and representations in and across history. Some works of non-historians, like anthropologists, energised this awareness with the views that they provided to shades of childhood systems and experiences outside the Western experiences. Such views, which offered more illumination to this awareness about children and childhood, assisted in promoting and sustaining a growing interest in the thought that childhood was not a naturally constructed and determined universal phenomenon as was conceived by many in the West, but relative to and produced and shaped by and from specific historical, cultural and social experiences and circumstances. For example, the earlier ethnographical study done by Margaret Mead in Samoa offered a discourse that suggested that as part of childhood, stress in adolescent girls was induced by "cultural conditions" and not universally-experienced phenomena.[36] Thus, unlike Piaget who claimed that "his subjects [in Europe], Swiss children in the first half of the 20th Century, were animistic in their thinking (Piaget, 1929)",[37] Mead's work which supported the view that the notion of a child is both historically and culturally conditioned "presents

---

[34] Published by Plon, a French book publishing company in Paris.
[35] Philippe Ariès, *Centuries of Childhood: A Social History of Family Life,* trans., Robert Baldick, (New York: Alfred A. Knopf, 1962).
[36] See for example Margaret Mead, *Coming in Age of Samoa: A Psychological Study of Primitive Youth for Western Civilisation,* (William Morrow & Company, 1961).
[37] Matthews and Mullin, "The Philosophy of Childhood".

evidence that Pacific island children were not".[38] Moreover, a work like *Children* of *Their Fathers: Growing up among* the *Ngoni* of *Malawi* by Margaret Read, which aimed to show how adults brought up children to fit into Ngoni society and assimilate and keep alive their cultural values,[39] had demonstrated that the cultural conditions in and of a society and the need by the society to shape, perpetuate or discard them were key factors that determined and gave character to childhood.

Additionally, when earlier staple epistemic normative conclusions and "specialized" assertions of psychology of child development were attacked and deconstructed as domineering and potentially dangerous in the latter half of the 20th century from post modernist perspectives,[40] it also consequently encouraged a new movement of scholars in the UK, Europe and US from the 1980s to engage and interrogate the way scholarship approached and made claims about children and childhood in the areas of sociology, anthropology and child psychology.[41] For example, some scholars charged psychology with the fault of confining childhood within its strong alliance with medicine, education and government agencies,[42] and criticised Piaget's entrenchment of contemporary understandings of the child in positivism and rigid empiricism.[43] Proposing a new childhood sociology, scholars like Alan Prout and Allison James said that childhood should be understood as a social construction which is a variable of social analysis; secondly, children's social relations and cultures should be studied in their own right and their agency in constructing and determining their own lives and those around them recognised; and a new childhood sociology was a necessary response to the process

---

[38] Ibid.

[39] Margaret Read, Children of *Their Fathers: Growing up among* the *Ngoni* of *Malawi*, Case studies in Education *and* Culture, (New York & London: Holt, Rinehart, and Winston, 1968).

[40] S. Greene, "Child Development: Old themes, New directions," in M. Woodhead, D. Faulkner, and K. Littleton (eds.), *Making Sense of Social Development*, (London: Routledge, 1999).

[41] C. Jenks, *The Sociology of Childhood: Essential Readings*, (London: Batsford, 1982); C. Jenks, *Childhood*, (London: Routledge, 1990); A. James and A. Prout, (eds.), *Constructing and Reconstructing Childhood: Contemporary Issues in the Sociological Study of Childhood*, Second Edition, (London: Routledge/Falmer, 1997); B. Mayall (ed.), *Children's Childhoods: Observed and Experienced*, (London: Falmer, 1994).

[42] A. James, C. Jenks, and A. Prout, *Theorizing Childhood*, (Cambridge: Polity Press, 1998), 17.

[43] Ibid. 19.

of reconstructing childhood in society.[44] In this trajectory, they opined that children were active actors and agents instead of passive recipients of socialisation, and that nature did not bequest childhood, rather it was constructed by society. Childhood, therefore, varied in cultural, geographical and time frames. Accordingly, in Europe a scholarly call for a new sociological thought about childhood also emerged and was amplified from the 1980s through the 1990s from the academic views of the Finnish Early Childhood Education scholar Leena Alanen[45] and some sociologists,[46] and it helped to birth the "childhood as a social phenomenon programme", a project whose "task was to map out childhood as a structural form in its own right to illustrate the place children occupy and the roles they play as social actors".[47] Furthermore, some scholars in the US became convinced that children and childhood had to be properly inserted into sociological studies thematically and conceptually. It was in line with this thought and realisation that an essay such as "Is there sufficient interest to establish a sociology of children?" was written in

---

[44] A. Prout and A. James, "A New Paradigm for the Sociology of Childhood? Provenance, promise and problems", in A. James and A. Prout (eds.), *Constructing and Reconstructing Childhood: Contemporary Issues in the Sociological Study of Childhood,* Second Edition, (London: Routledge/Falmer, 1997), 8.

[45] See, for example, Leena Alanen, "Rethinking childhood," *Acta Sociologica,* 31(1), (1988):53-67; Leena Alanen and Marjatta Bardy, *Childhood as a Social Phenomenon: National Report, Finland,* (Vienna: European Centre for Social Welfare Policy and Research, [1990], 1991).

[46] J. Qvortrup, M. Bardy, G. Sgritta, and H. Wintersberger, *Childhood Matters: Social Theory, Practice and Politics,* (Aldershot: Avebury Press, 1994). Additionally, a work like J. Qvortrup, W.A. Corsaro, and M-S Honig (eds.), *The Palgrave Handbook of Childhood Studies,* (London: Palgrave Macmillan, 2009) will also sustain the momentum of interest in Childhood Studies.

[47] See, for example, Anne-Marie Ambert's book reviews of *Childhood as a Social Phenomenon,* and *Childhood Matters: Social Theory, Practice and Politics* edited by Jens Qvortrup, Marjatta Bardy, Giovanni Sgritta and Helmut Wintersberger, in *Journal of Marriage and Family,* 56 (4), (1994):1043-1045. Ambert explains that the Childhood as a Social Phenomenon project was initiated in 1987. The project was sponsored by the European Centre for Social Welfare Policy and Research in Vienna. It was characterised by "meetings and collaboration among scholars from 19 European and North American countries". *Childhood as a Social Phenomenon* (16 National Reports and Statistical Compendium), constituting a key publication of the project, was published between 1987 and 1994. Additionally, *Childhood Matters: Social Theory, Practice and Politics* was published in 1994.

1991. The writer, Gertrud Lenzer, also argued for "a genuinely interdisciplinary multidisciplinary new field of study".[48]

The radical views of sociologists and other scholars in the UK, Europe and the US about childhood and children did acknowledge children holistically as persons with agency, advocated for the study of the plurality of childhoods, and pushed for the study of childhood in cultural contexts. Yielding the fledging disciplinary perspective which became labelled by many as the " 'new sociology' or 'new social studies' of childhood"[49], this radical conviction and advocacy added more verve to the materialization of "Childhood Studies" as a new disciplinary viewpoint that gives children conceptual independence and expressly centres them as the principal personages of study. Having been produced primarily from efforts in Western academia, its orbit and function were mainly concerned with children and childhoods in Europe, North America, UK, Australia and New Zealand. Thus, its current status and plans for its future trajectory have largely been subjected to the historical, social and political needs, movements and environment of the academy in the European and American areas.

Childhood Studies, in both the global "North" and "South" now, is, thus, a fairly burgeoning multidisciplinary endeavour that spans various epistemologies and methodologies. There have been several recent reflections and groundbreaking studies from this field such as the papers included in Sheila Greene and Diane Hogan (eds.), *Researching Children's Experience: Approached and Methods* (2005),[50] Ginger Frost's *Victorian Childhoods* (2009),[51] and articles included in J. Qvortrup et al.'s *Palgrave Handbook of Childhood Studies* (2009).[52] Others are B. Mayall's *A History of the Sociology of Childhood* (2013),[53] David Oswell's *The Agency of Children: From Family to Global Hu-*

---

[48] Gertrud Lenzer, "Is there sufficient interest to establish a sociology of children?," *Footnotes of the American Sociological Association*, 19 (8), (1991): 8.

[49] P. Christensen and A. Prout, "Anthropological and Sociological Perspectives on the study of children," in Sheila Greene and Diane Hogan (eds.), *Researching Children's Experience: Approaches and Methods*, (London/California/New Delhi: SAGE, 2005), 42 (42-60); M. Woodhead, *The Case for Childhood Studies*, (Dublin: Children's Research Centre, Trinity College Dublin, 2003).

[50] Sheila Greene and Diane Hogan (eds.), *Researching Children's Experience: Approached and Methods*, (London/California/New Delhi: SAGE, 2005).

[51] Ginger Frost, *Victorian Childhoods*, (Westport, CT/London: Praeger, 2009).

[52] Qvortrup, et al. (eds.), *The Palgrave Handbook of Childhood Studies*.

[53] B. Mayall, *A History of the Sociology of Childhood*, (London: Institute of Education, 2013).

man Rights (2013)[54] and Markus P.J. Bohlmann's *Misfit Children: An Inquiry into Childhood Belongings* (2017).[55] They offer us varying degrees of understanding about transformations of children and childhood in society as well as methodological and theoretical approaches to the study of children and their childhoods from the 19th to the 21st century through historical, theoretical and interdisciplinary lenses and perspectives. Additionally, the list of venues for the promotion of research findings and studies that produce seamless analyses, interesting histories, novel research methods and approaches, and rethink staple narratives and theories about childhood studies in the non-African world has continued to grow. These include *Childhood: A Journal of Global Child Research, Childhoods Today, Journal of the History of Childhood and Youth, Children's Literature Association Quarterly, The Lion and the Unicorn,* and *Red Feather Journal.*

A Brief Overview of the Scope of Works on Childhood Studies in Africa

Contrarily, except for a few cases, the research focus on children and childhood in Africa are not clearly and profoundly situated and labelled under the scholarly and academic category called Childhood Studies. Apart from *Childhood in Africa: An Interdisciplinary Journal* (2009) whose clear-cut mandate is about encouraging holistic approaches to the understanding of issues impacting children and childhood in Africa, which is published online on a bi-annual basis by The Institute for the African Child at Ohio University, only a small number of journals exist in Africa with mandates that are clearly marked out for the subject like that of the journal *Childhood in Africa.* We can extract from the bibliographical compilation of Howard the fact that "academic journals on the subject of children and childhood in Africa are few". These include *The Journal of Tropical Pediatrics and African Child Health,*[56] *Mwana: Africa Region Newsletter for Early Childhood Care and Education,*[57] *Defi des EJT,*[58] *African Journal of Farm Child and Youth Development,*[59] *Child*

---

[54] David Oswell, *The Agency of Children: From Family to Global Human Rights,* (Cambridge: Cambridge University Press, 2013).

[55] Markus P.J. Bohlmann (ed.), *Misfit Children: An Inquiry into Childhood Belongings,* (Lanham, Maryland: Lexington Books Rowman and Littlefield, 2017).

[56] Offers medical and health reports on children in Africa.

[57] This bulletin offers professional reports of educational facilities and their impact on communities.

[58] Produced annually by African Movement of Working Children and Youth, which is based in Dakar, Senegal, it offers news about projects that are linked to education and protection for children in the workplace.

Abuse Research: A South African Journal,[60] *South African Child Gauge*[61] and *South African Journal of Child Health.*[62] However, due to lack of funding and being under-researched, some of "these journals have had short lifespans in many cases".[63]

Furthermore, the majority of other few extant works that deal with African children and their lives and agency and their culture emanate from different disciplines and research interests. Such works, which mainly consist of individual and scattered studies from the fields of education, culture, sports, public health, economics, social geography, psychology, labour rights, ethics and education, are largely books, book chapters, memoirs, and journal articles. By engaging with popular and dominant themes related to children and childhood such as children and health,[64] children and education or schooling,[65] problems

---

[59] The Research and Development Network of the Children-In-Agriculture Programme (CIAP) in Africa produces this annually to focus on child labour issues in African agriculture and education and training initiatives for child workers.

[60] Encouraging multidisciplinary professional education on topics of relevance in the field of child abuse, it also promotes research and exchange of information among professionals involved in the field of child abuse.

[61] Focusing on a different theme each year it reports and monitors the situation of children in South Africa, especially the realisation of their rights.

[62] A medical journal *devoted* to child health.

[63] Howard, "Children and Childhood".

[64] Mario J. Azevedo, Gwendolyn S. Prater, and Daniel N. Lantum, "Culture, Biomedicine and Child Mortality in Cameroon," *Social Science & Medicine* 32(12), (1991): 1341–1349; Barthélémy K. Defo, "A real and Socioeconomic Differentials in Infant and Child Mortality in Cameroon," *Social Science & Medicine* 42 (3), (1996): 399–420; Victor Lotter, "Childhood Autism in Africa," *Journal of Child Psychology and Psychiatry* 19(3), (1978): 231–244; Robert W. Snow, Jean-Francois Trape, and Kevin Marsh, "The Past, Present and Future of Childhood Malaria Mortality in Africa," *Trends in Parasitology* 17(12), (2001): 593–597; A. van Rie, N. Beyers, R. P. Gie, M. Kunneke, L. Zietsman, and P. R. Donald, "Childhood Tuberculosis in an Urban Population in South Africa: Burden and Risk Factor," *Archives of Disease in Childhood* 80(5), (1999): 433–437; Johan P. Velema, Eusèbe M. Alihonou, Timothé Gandaho, and Félicien H. Hounye, "Childhood Mortality among Users and Non-users of Primary Health Care in a Rural West African Community," *International Journal of Epidemiology* 20(2) (1991): 474–479; Hilary N. Fouts and Robyn A. Brookshire, "Who Feeds Children? A Child's-Eye-View of Caregiver Feeding Patterns among the Aka Foragers in Congo," *Social Science and Medicine* 69(2), (2009): 285–292; John K. Anarfi and Phyllis Antwi, "Street Youth in Accra City: Sexual Networking in a High-Risk Environment and Its Implications for the Spread of HIV/AIDS," *Health Transition Review* 5 suppl. (1995): 131–151; Catherine Campbell, Andy Gibbs, Sbongile Maimane, Yugi Nair, and Zweni Sibiya, "Youth Participation in the Fight against AIDS in South Africa: From Policy to Practice," *Journal of Youth Studies* 12(1),

of the African Girl Child,[66] children and labour,[67] children and media, popular culture and sports,[68] children and politics,[69] children and social development,[70]

(2009): 93–109; Joseph L. P. Lugalla, and Colleta G. Kibassa (eds.), *Poverty, AIDS, and Street Children in East Africa*, Studies in African Health and Medicine 10, (Lewiston, NY: Edwin Mellen, 2002); Frederick Mugisha and Eliya M. Zulu, "The Influence of Alcohol, Drugs and Substance Abuse on Sexual Relationships and Perception of Risk to HIV Infection among Adolescents in the Informal Settlements of Nairobi," *Journal of Youth Studies* 7(3), (2004): 279–293; Arvind Singhal and W. Stephen Howard (eds.), *The Children of Africa Confront AIDS: From Vulnerability to Possibility*. Research in International Studies, Africa Series 80, (Athens, OH: Ohio University Press, 2003).

[65] Gina Porter, Kate Hampshire, Michael Bourdillon, et al. "Children as Research Collaborators: Issues and Reflections from a Mobility Study in Sub-Saharan Africa," *American Journal of Community Psychology* 46(1–2), (2010): 215–227; Andrew I. Epstein, "Education Refugees and the Spatial Politics of Childhood Vulnerability," *Childhood in Africa: An Interdisciplinary Journal* 2(1), (2010): 16–25; Ali A. Abdi, "Education in Somalia: History, Destruction, and Calls for Reconstruction," *Comparative Education* 34(3), (1998): 327–340; Nathan Chelimo, "Transitions in Pastoral Communities in Uganda: Classes under the Trees," *Early Childhood Matters* 107 (2006): 36–37; Nardos Chuta, "Conceptualizations of Children and Childhood in Bishoftu, Oromia," in Eva Poluha (ed.), *The World of Girls and Boys in Rural and Urban Ethiopia*, (Addis Ababa, Ethiopia: Forum for Social Studies, 2007),119–156; Alan Pence and Jessica Schafer. "Indigenous Knowledge and Early Childhood Development in Africa: The Early Childhood Development Virtual University," *Journal for Education in International Development* 2(3) (2006): 1–17.

[66] Saheed Aderinto, "'The Girls in Moral Danger': Child Prostitution and Sexuality in Colonial Lagos, Nigeria, 1930s to 1950," *Journal of Humanities & Social Sciences* 1(2) (2007): 1–22; Seema Agarwal, Memunatu Attah, Nana Apt, Margaret Grieco, E. A. Kwakye, and Jeff Turner, "Bearing the Weight: The Kayayoo, Ghana's Working Girl Child," *International Social Work* 40(3), (1997): 245–263; Susan S. Davis, "Growing Up in Morocco," in Donna L. Bowen and Evelyn A. Early (eds.), *Everyday Life in the Muslim Middle East*, (Indiana Series in Middle East Studies. Bloomington: Indiana University Press, 2002); 24–35; Uché U. Ewelukwa, "The Girl Child, African States, and International Human Rights Law—Toward a New Framework for Action," in Obioma Nnaemeka and Joy N. Ezeilo (eds.), *Engendering Human Rights: Cultural and Socioeconomic Realities in Africa*, (New York: Palgrave Macmillan, 2005), 131–156.; Doris D. Khalil, "Abuses of the Girl Child in Some African Societies: Implications for Nurse Practitioners," *Nursing Forum* 41(1), (2006): 13–24; Elizabeth M. King and M. Anne Hill (eds.), *Women's Education in Developing Countries: Barriers, Benefits, and Policies*, (Baltimore: Johns Hopkins University Press, 1993); Shula Marks (ed.), *Not Either an Experimental Doll: The Separate Worlds of Three South African Women*, (Bloomington: Indiana University Press, 1988); Simeon H. Ominde, *The Luo Girl: From Infancy to Marriage*, Custom and Tradition in East Africa, (London: Macmillan, 1952); Elizabeth H. Boyle, *Female Genital Cutting: Cultural Conflict in the Global Community*, (Baltimore: Johns Hopkins University Press, 2002); Grace Osakue, "Violence against Women and Girls: Breaking the Culture of Silence," *Exchange on HIV/AIDS, Sexuality and Gender* 2 (2006): 1–4; Lidwien

Kapteijns and Maryan M. Boqor, "Memories of a Mogadishu Childhood, 1940–1964: Maryan Muuse Boqor and the Women Who Inspired Her," *International Journal of African Historical Studies* 42(1), (2009): 105–116.

[67] For example, see G. André and M. Godin, "Child labour, agency and family dynamics: The case of mining in Katanga (DRC)", *Childhood*, 21(2), (2014): 161–74; Loretta E. Bass, *Child Labor in Sub-Saharan Africa*, (Boulder, CO: Lynne Rienner, 2004); Sandra Burman and Pamela Reynolds (eds.), *Growing Up in a Divided Society: The Contexts of Childhood in South Africa*, (Johannesburg: Ravan, 1986); Assefa Admassie, "Explaining the High Incidence of Child Labour in Sub-Saharan Africa," *African Development Review* 14 (2), (2002): 251–275; Osita Agbu (ed.), *Children and Youth in the Labour Process in Africa*, Codesria Book Series, (Dakar, Senegal: CODESRIA, 2009); Jens C. Andvig, "Child Labour in Sub-Saharan Africa—An Exploration," *Forum for Development Studies* 25(2), (1998): 327–362; Morten Bøås and Anne Hatløy, "Child Labour in West Africa: Different Work—Different Vulnerabilities," *International Migration* 46(3), (2008): 3–25; Eftetan O. Farrag, "Working Children in Cairo: Case Studies," in Elizabeth W. Fernea (ed.), *Children in the Muslim Middle East* (Austin: University of Texas Press, 1995), 239–249.; I. M. Jimu, "An Exploration of Street Vending's Contribution towards Botswana's Vision of Prosperity for All by 2016," *Pula: Botswana Journal of African Studies* 18(1), (2004): 19–30;

[68] Awo Sarpong and De-Valera, N.Y.M. Botchway, "Freaks in Procession? The Fancy Dress Masquerade as Haven for Negotiating Eccentricity during Childhood. A Study of Child Masqueraders in Cape Coast, Ghana," in Markus P.J. Bohlmann (ed.), *Misfit Children: An Inquiry into Childhood Belongings*, (Lexington Books (Rowman and Littlefield), 2017), 175-196; De-Valera, N.Y.M. Botchway, "Gyama Songs in Ghanaian Schools: A Note on a Students' Musical Creativity," in Tobias Robert Klein (ed.), *Schools and Schooling as a Source of African Literary and Cultural Creativity*, (LuKA (Literaturen und Kunst Akrikas) Series 9, (Trier: Wissenschaftlicher Verlag Trier (WVT), 2017), 3-31; Nicholas Argenti, *The Intestines of the State: Youth, Violence, and Belated Histories in the Cameroon Grassfields*, (Chicago: University of Chicago Press, 2007); Gary Armstrong, "The Lords of Misrule: Football and the Rights of the Child in Liberia, West Africa," *Sport in Society: Cultures, Commerce, Media, Politics* 7(3), (2004): 473–502; Nongenile M. Zenani, *The World and the Word: Tales and Observations from the Xhosa Oral Tradition*, ed. Harold Scheub, (Madison: University of Wisconsin Press, 1992); Bernard van Leer Foundation, "South Africa: Hey Mum, That's Me on the Radio!," *Early Childhood Matters* 103 (2004): 48–49; Muluembeat Kiar, "Children in Ethiopian Media and School Textbooks," in Eva Poluha (ed.), *The World of Girls and Boys in Rural and Urban Ethiopia*, (Addis Ababa, Ethiopia: Forum for Social Studies, 2007), 157–180; Francis B. Nyamnjoh, "Children, Media and Globalisation: A Research Agenda for Africa," in Cecilia von Feilitzen and Ulla Carlson (eds.), *Children, Young People and Media Globalisation*, (Gothenburg, Sweden: Nordicom, Gothenburg University, 2002), 43–52.; Norma O. Pecora, Enyonam Osei-Hwere, and Ulla Carlson (eds.), *African Media, African Children*, (Gothenburg, Sweden: International Clearinghouse on Children, Youth and Media, Nordicom, 2008).

[69] G. André and M. Hilgers, "Childhood in Africa between Local Powers and Global Hierarchies," in L. Alanen, et al. (eds.), *Childhood with Bourdieu. Studies in Childhood and Youth*, (Palgrave Macmillan, London, 2015), 120-141; United Nations Children's

children and war[71] and children in the productions of African literary arts,[72] and childhood and streetism,[73] welfare and future of children in society,[74] such

---

Fund, *Children on the Front Line: The Impact of Apartheid, Destabilization and Warfare on Children in Southern and South Africa* Second Edition, (New York and Geneva, Switzerland: United Nations Children's Fund, 1988).

[70] See, for example, Lorenzo I. Bordonaro, "'Culture Stops Development!': Bijagó Youth and the Appropriation of Developmentalist Discourse in Guinea-Bissau," *African Studies Review* 52(2), (2009): 69–92; Mamadou Diouf, "Engaging Postcolonial Cultures: African Youth and Public Space," *African Studies Review* 46(2), (2003): 1–12; Jude Fokwang, "Youth Subjectivities and Associational Life in Bamenda, Cameroon," *Africa Development* 28(3), (2008): 157–162; Eric Gable, "The Culture Development Club: Youth, Neo-tradition, and the Construction of Society in Guinea-Bissau," Special Issue: Youth and the Social Imagination in Africa, Part 2, *Anthropological Quarterly* 73(4), (2000): 195–203; Stephen O. Gyimah, "Polygynous Marital Structure and Child Survivorship in Sub-Saharan Africa: Some Empirical Evidence from Ghana," *Social Science & Medicine* 68(2), (2009): 334–342; Awan Abdulwasie, "Conceptualizations of Children and Childhood: The Case of Kolfe and Semen Mazegaja, Addis Ababa," in Eva Poluha (ed.), *The World of Girls and Boys in Rural and Urban Ethiopia*, (Addis Ababa, Ethiopia: Forum for Social Studies, 2007), 39–66; Martha Kamwendo, "Constructions of Malawian Boys and Girls on Gender and Achievement," *Gender and Education* 22(4), (2010): 431–445; Marjorie Shostak, "A !Kung Woman's Memories of Childhood," in Richard B. Lee and Irven DeVore (eds.), *Kalahari Hunter-Gatherers: Studies of the !Kung San and Their Neighbors*, (Cambridge, MA: Harvard University Press, 1998), 246–277; Misty L. Bastian, "Young Converts: Christian Missions, Gender and Youth in Onitsha, Nigeria 1880–1929," Special Issue: Youth and Social Imagination in Africa, Part 1, *Anthropological Quarterly* 73(3), (2000): 145–158; Paul La Hausse, "'The Cows of Nongoloza': Youth, Crime and Amalaita Gangs in Durban, 1900–1936," *Journal of Southern African Studies* 16(1), (1990): 79–111.

[71] Susan McKay, "Reconstructing Fragile Lives: Girls' Social Reintegration in Northern Uganda and Sierra Leone," in Ahmad A. Sikainga and Ousseina Alidou (eds.), *Postconflict Reconstruction in Africa*, (Trenton, NJ: Africa World Press, 2006), 149–168; K. Amone-P'Olak, N. Garnefski, and V. Kraaij, "The Impact of War Experiences and Physical Abuse on Formerly Abducted Boys in Northern Uganda," *South African Psychiatry Review* 10(2) (2007): 76–82; Theresa S. Betancourt, Jessica Agnew-Blais, Stephen E. Gilman, David R. Williams, and B. Heidi Ellis, "Past Horrors, Present Struggles: The Role of Stigma in the Association between War Experiences and Psychosocial Adjustment among Former Child Soldiers in Sierra Leone," Special Issue: Conflict, Violence, and Health, *Social Science & Medicine* 70(1), (2010): 17–26; Pamela D. Couture, "Victims, Perpetrators, or Moral Agents: Children and Youth Survivors of the War in the Democratic Republic of Congo," *Journal of Childhood and Religion* 2(2), (2011): 1–17; James Garbarino, Kathleen Kostelny and Nancy Dubrow, "Mozambique's Children: Dying Is the Easy Part," in James Garbarino, Kathleen Kostelny, and Nancy Dubrow, *No Place to Be a Child: Growing Up in a War Zone*, (San Francisco: Jossey-Bass, 1998), 60–82; Alcinda M. Honwana, *Child Soldiers in Africa*, (Philadelphia: University of Pennsylvania

Press, 2005); Carol B. Thompson, "Beyond Civil Society: Child Soldiers as Citizens in Mozambique," *Review of African Political Economy* 26(80), (1999): 191–206.

[72] Camara Laye, *The Dark Child,* trans.,James Kirkup (New York: Noonday, 1994); Mark Mathabane, *Kaffir Boy: The True Story of a Black Youth's Coming of Age in Apartheid South Africa,* (New York: Macmillan, 1986); Wole Soyinka, *Aké: The Years of Childhood,* (London: Methuen, 2000); Uwem Akpan, *Say You're One of Them,* (New York: Little, Brown, 2008); Tsitsi Dangarembga, *Nervous Conditions: A Novel,* (Banbury, UK: Ayebia Clarke, 2004); Athol Fugard, *My Children! My Africa!* (New York: Theatre Communications Group, 2010); Uzodinma Iweala, *Beast of No Nation,* (London: John Murray, 2005); Cheikh Hamidou Kane, *Ambiguous Adventure,* (Brooklyn, NY: Melville House, 2012); Sindiwe Magona, *To My Children's Children,* (Claremont, South Africa: David Philip, 1990).

[73] Agya Boakye-Boaten, "Street Children: Experiences from the Streets of Accra," *Research Journal of International Studies* 8 (2008): 76–84; Judith Ennew, "Difficult Circumstances: Some Reflections on 'Street Children' in Africa," *Children, Youth and Environments* 13(1), (2003): 1–18; Paula Heinonen, *Youth Gangs and Street Children: Culture, Nurture and Masculinity in Ethiopia,* Social Identities 7, (New York: Berghahn, 2011); Philip L. Kilbride, "A Cultural and Gender Perspective on Marginal Children on the Streets of Kenya," *Childhood in Africa: An Interdisciplinary Journal* 2(1), (2010): 38–47; Macalane J. Malindi and Linda C. Theron, "The Hidden Resilience of Street Youth," *South African Journal of Psychology* 40(3) (2010): 318–326.

[74] For example, see Tatek Abebe, "Interdependent rights and agency: The role of children in collective livelihood strategies in rural Ethiopia," in K. Hanson and O. Nieuwenhuys (eds.), *Reconceptualizing Children's Rlights in International Development: Living Rights, Social Justice, Translations,* (Cambridge: Cambridge University Press, 2013), 71–92; Manzoor Ahmed, *Within Human Reach: A Future for Africa's Children,*(New York: United Nations Children's Fund, 1985); Kofi Marfo, Alan Pence, Robert A. LeVine, and Sarah LeVine, "Strengthening Africa's Contributions to Child Development Research: Introduction," *Child Development Perspectives* 5(2) (2011): 104–111; Pamela Reynolds, *Childhood in Crossroads: Cognition and Society in South Africa,* (Cape Town: Eerdmans, 1989); Alan R. Pence and A. Bame Nsamenang, *A Case for Early Childhood Development in Sub-Saharan Africa,* Working Papers in Early Childhood Development 51, (The Hague: Bernard van Leer Foundation, 2008); Leslie Swartz, and Ann Levett, "Political Repression and Children in South Africa: The Social Construction of Damaging Effects," *Special Issue: Political Violence and Health in the Third World. Social Science & Medicine* 28(7), (1989): 741–750; Kristen E. Cheney, "'Village Life Is Better Than Town Life': Identity, Migration, and Development in the Lives of Ugandan Child Citizens," *African Studies Review* 47(3), (2004): 1–22; Jude Fokwang, "Ambiguous Transitions: Mediating Citizenship among Youths in Cameroon," *Africa Development* 23(1–2), (2003): 173–201; Jill R. Brown, "Child Fosterage and the Developmental Markers of Ovambo Children in Namibia: A Look at Gender and Kinship," *Childhood in Africa: An Interdisciplinary Journal* 1(1), (2009): 4–10; Kristen E. Cheney, "Expanding Vulnerability, Dwindling Resources: Implications for Orphaned Futures in Uganda," *Childhood in Africa: An Interdisciplinary Journal* 2(1) (2010): 8–15; Nancy Kendall, "Gendered Moral Dimensions of Childhood Vulnerability," *Childhood in Africa: An Interdisciplinary Journal* 2(1) (2010): 26–37; Philip L. Kilbride and Janet C. Kilbride, *Chang-*

works provide some light on different aspects of the life experiences of African childhood. From these emerge strands of degrees of comprehension of the meanings that adults place on children's innocence or competence, and from that can extractions of understandings of the notion of childhood as a social category be made. Nevertheless, there are many other areas, themes and issues that can receive broader attention for further enlightenment. These include Childhoods Constructed around given Names; Childhoods of Unnamed Children; Experience of Birth and Coming to a Family; Body Experience in Childhood; Childhood belonging mediated by Languages and Cultures; Creative Negotiation of Harmonious Co-existence of Divergent Beliefs of the Individual Child and Convergent Group Beliefs; and Play, Worlds of Play and Social Learning. Other areas that can attract inquiry are Childhoods Marked and Unmarked by Ritual and Rites of Passage; Eccentric, Ill-adjusted, Misfit and Evil Childhoods; the Disabled and Vulnerable Childhood; Sexual Identification and Confrontations with Sex; Digital Technologies and Conceptions of Self and Community in African Childhood; Health and Wellness in Spirit, Mind, Soul and Body; Childhood around Secret Societies and Forbidden Associations; Children's Notions of Childhood; Hijacked Childhoods and Confrontations with Adultism and Games-shaped Childhoods and Creativity. For example, the inquiry into the area of childhood and creativity in the African context recently received a fine addition from the anthology of Tobias Robert Klein (2017), which gathered writings that explored the peculiar significance of schools and schooling in Anglophone African countries as a trigger of literary and cultural creativity animated by African children as part of their childhood. This includes the creation of the popular music genre of Djama (Jama or Gyama) by students in Ghana, and the writing of novels, poetry and autobiographies from childhood memories and experiences about schools in Ghana, Nigeria, Tanzania and Zimbabwe.[75] Anoth-

---

ing Family Life in East Africa: Women and Children at Risk, (University Park: Pennsylvania State University Press, 1990); Alice Lamptey, "Children Creating Awareness about Their Rights in Ghana," in Victoria Johnson, Edda Ivan-Smith, Gill Gordon, Pat Pridmore, and Patta Scott (eds.), *Stepping Forward: Children and Young People's Participation in the Development Process*, (London: Immediate Technology Publications, 1998), 86–87; Anthony Hodges (ed.), *Children's and Women's Rights in Nigeria: A Wake-Up Call; Situation Assessment and Analysis, 2001*, (Abuja, Nigeria: National Planning Commission, 2001); Sahaya G. Selvam, "Capabilities Approach to Youth Rights in East Africa," *International Journal of Human Rights* 12(2), (2008): 205–214; Laurent Fourchard, "Lagos and the Invention of Juvenile Delinquency in Nigeria, 1920–60," *Journal of African History* 47(1), (2006): 115–137.

[75] Tobias Robert Klein (ed.), *Schools and Schooling as a Source of African Literary and Cultural Creativity*, (LuKA (Literaturen und Kunst Akrikas) Series 9, (Trier: Wissenschaftlicher Verlag Trier (WVT), 2017).

er interesting addition is Awo Abena Sarpong and De-Valera Botchway's study of the history of child masqueraders in Cape Coast and interrogation of how the children, using their creativity and agency,[76] "escaped entrapment and socio-cultural pressures to conform to childhood that may not be theirs". The study shows how the children use the masquerade parades to acquire a licence to demonstrate their freakishness and eccentricities which are prohibited from their lives on "normal" days by adults. It shows how the wearing of the mask, strangely enough, allows the child masqueraders "to tap into the multiple facets of their selfhoods that the mask of childhood innocence forbids them to wear."[77] Additionally, the area of childhood and agency has lately been fertilised by papers in Yaw Ofosu-Kusi's edited volume, *Children's Agency and Development in African Societies*, in 2017. The work does not, as Ofosu-Kusi argues, hold the view that the African situation can be dissociated from the global context of childhood studies because it is a futile exercise; however with the conviction that it is imperative to anchor emerging discourse on African specificities of children's agency and development, the book, made up of sixteen chapters (some written in English and others in French) that are "steeped in research around the continent, variously examines issues like children's agency, the inherent contradiction and vulnerabilities, their search for identity and representations and development".[78] The chapters also throw various illuminations on the competencies, skills and creativity of children to respond to experiential and existential needs in spheres of activities such as migration, urban working, rural farming, and schooling. Additionally, we get a sense from the study that regardless of the plethora of challenges that African children face, these persons steadfastly strive to resolve them by applying and utilising their hardiness, discernment of economics and politics and dynamic competence to undertake challenging responsibilities above their chronological age.

Furthermore, a study like M. Bourdillon and G.M. Mutambwa's edited *The Place of Work in African Childhoods* (2014)[79] not long ago illuminated the complex topical terrain of childhood and work. It provided interesting ideas and viewpoints on how work enters and affects the lives of children and

---

[76] Sarpong and Botchway, "Freaks in Procession?"

[77] Markus P.J. Bohlmann, "Introduction," in Markus P.J. Bohlmann (ed.), *Misfit Children: An Inquiry into Childhood Belongings*, (Lexington Books (Rowman and Littlefield), 2017), xxvii.

[78] Yaw Ofosu-Kusi, "Introduction: Children's Agency and Development in African Societies," in Yaw Ofosu-Kusi (ed.), *Children's Agency and Development in African Societies*, (Dakar: CODESRIA, 2017), 2, (1-14).

[79] Michael Bourdillon and Georges M. Mutambwa (eds.), *The Place of Work in African Childhoods*, (Dakar: CODESRIA, 2014),1-20.

young people in Africa taking not for granted neither the traditional values surrounding children's work, nor international standards against it.[80] The fourteen chapters in the book offered empirical studies of the lives of African children, the work that they did and its place in their lives and what the children said about it from places like Accra (Ghana), Kisangani and Lubumbashi (Democratic Republic of the Congo), Addis Ababa (Ethiopia), Cameroon, Brazzaville (Republic of Congo), Abidjan (Cote d'Ivoire), Lome (Togo), Kalaban-Coro (Mali), Central Kenya and Saint Louis (Senegal). Still, G. Spittler and M. Bourdillon's edited *African Children at Work* (2012) also offered a collection of ethnographical studies that paid attention to children's own experience of work and their views about it.[81] Lately, Mwenda Ntarangwi and Guy Massart's edited *Engaging Children and Youth in Africa* (2015), offered a fair analysis of empirical data and methodological and phenomenological issues in African-centred research on children and youth. Drawing on representations of researches from East, Central, West and Southern Africa, the study helps us to consider how our perceptions about African childhood and youth should be made to transcend the common limiting non-African conceptions and ideas, especially Western ones, "of vulnerability and innocence (especially for children)". It also reminds us to consider how ongoing technological advancements, strengthening of global processes and weakening of the nation-state "provide a valuable lens through which to study social change . . . and new and complex ways to be children and youth in Africa *or being an African child*" (Italics are mine).[82]

These researches and works help to unveil understandings and notions of childhood in the African context. Any work that purports to contribute to knowledge about African childhoods should, therefore, focus on Africa's children with the view to finding and understanding their agency in constructing their own world, comprehending the cultural narratives of the adult world about the independence or dependence of the children, and knowing how the so-called dependent child is an imagined being. As Markus P.J. Bohlmann said of the child, "The child is the product of the adult". Drawing on his experiences and knowledge in the history of childhood in the West, he opined that adult

[80] Bourdillon and Mutambwa (eds.), "Introduction," *The Place of Work in African Childhoods*, 2.
[81] G. Spittler and M. Bourdillon (eds.), *African Children at Work: Working and Learning in Growing Up for Life*, (Berlin: LIT Verlag, 2012).
[82] Mwenda Ntarangwi and Guy Massart (eds.), "Introduction," *Engaging Children and Youth in Africa: Methodological and Phenomenological Issues*, (Bamenda, Cameroon: Langaa RPCIG, 2015), 2-3 (1-30).

thoughts, symbolizations and typifications rather than existing conditions or facts motivated it. Consequently, he averred that with the inherited Romantic notion of the "innocent child", "children are [thus] professed to be angels and to possess a purity that adults have lost. Children have come to embody the potentiality and the futurity of humankind. They are its cherished future, but also its venerated past".[83]

Can such views be imagined in and about our knowledge about children and childhood in the African context?

Consequently, this volume seeks to once again expand what we know of African children and their childhood. It takes a diversion from the traditional examination of the child solely to the exploration of childhood in the African context. It explores the manifestations of African childhood and depictions and understandings of it. It offers a congregation of chapters that present original research from African and Africa-centred and Africa-friendly perspectives, rationalisations and conceptions about the psychology, sociology and history of aspects, ramifications and conditions of childhood in the African world. The analysis and interpretations and stories and case studies about various aspects of childhood and the child(ren) actor(s) that are at the centre and across the different stages of personhood development and community life and times within the African continent and African world spaces in this volume emanate from scholars of the humanities and social sciences who focus on African society, culture, education and history.

Organisation of the Volume

In terms of structure, this book is organized into ten chapters, excluding this Introduction and the Conclusion. The volume enters into the conversation with Chapter One, that is Mofeyisara Oluwatoyin Omobowale and Olukemi K. Amodu's paper titled "*Omo boti* and *Omo pako*: Social Construction of Childhood, Livelihood and Health in Southwestern Nigeria", to explore the social construction of the privileged (*omo boti*) and vulnerable (*omo pako*) childhood among the Yoruba of southwestern Nigeria. It provides a contribution to the growing understanding about the issue of childhood formation. Omo boti and Omo pako are two ends of socially structured divides that emanate from social perceptions of people on what is considered as ideal childhood norms, values, symbols and imagery, in relation to the prevailing circumstances and times. In all this, the chapter shows how livelihood determines different categories of childhood in the Yoruba society. Centring and emphasising the social

---

[83] Bohlmann, "Introduction," xv.

constructions of livelihood, childhood and health in the discussion, the paper argues and points out that in the case of the Yoruba, the constructed Omo boti and Omo pako childhoods and child beings are associated with certain constructed dietary lifeways that potentially exert health and ill-health impacts. They may predispose the Omo boti and Omo pako to health problems, like obesity and malnutrition respectively.

Following the discussion about how the social construction of livelihood and childhood pattern revolves around certain Yoruba value systems, and how, over the years, this has had implications on the health status of children and government health policy in Nigeria, Samuel Bewiadze and Richard Awubomu's paper, which constitutes Chapter Two, takes us to Ghana to interrogate an aspect of childhood there. Titled as "Our Stones, our Livelihood: Urban Working Children's Survival Strategy and its Implications in the Daglama Quarry Site in the Ho Municipality of Ghana", the paper's argument revolves around a childhood that is framed by economic production which is animated by and through children's agency for their survival and that of their families, even in the face of certain health dangers. Bewiadze and Awubomu introduce the area of stone quarrying as one field of economic activity for children in Ho, Ghana. While the authors argue that this economics-determined childhood is one which is not animated by passive and inactive children, they, nevertheless, point out that despite the fact that the children are agents in their own right, the economic activity at the quarry affects their health and education immensely. This "endangered childhood" has implications for the future development of the municipality and the country as a whole.

Chapter three and four and five deal with representations and misrepresentations of childhood. In Chapter Three, which is titled "Childhood in Africa: Health and Wellness in Body, Mind, Soul, and Spirit", Waganesh A. Zeleke, Tammy Hughes and Natalie Drozda deal with the issue of mischaracterisation and unilinear representation of childhood in Africa. Taking a detour from what it calls "the narrow lenses of Western ideals", the chapter's argument offers a multidimensional perspective on children and childhood in Africa and advances a logic about how it has been possible for an entire continent to thrive given such longstanding adversity. It argues that in the situation where Africa is commonly compared to a Western standard, its childhoods will be singularly understood by deficiency, and descriptions of African childhoods will be without reference to personal, spiritual or creative community richness. Thus, the chapter broadens the conceptualization of Africa's children and their childhood experiences by elaborating on the building blocks of healthy child development and resilience, including how those experiences are discernible in Africa. By reviewing the status of child health and wellness in Africa, describing a theory of health and holistic wellness applicable to the African context, re-conceptualizing African childhood based on a holistic wellness theory, presenting points of resiliency and protective factors, and discussing implications for future research, practitioners and policy-makers, the chapter brings us to a rich engagement with contexts that support African child development and a valuable understanding about African children's strengths.

In Chapter Four, Andrea Y. Adomako engages with questions of how African children discover the meaning of their African identifications in a postcolonial context in her paper "Efua Sutherland and African Children's Literature: Representations of Postcolonial Childhood". She opines that as the field of childhood studies evolves, it demands for more understandings about the varying representations of postcolonial childhood as projected to children through African children's literature. She argues that the postcolonial African child is a subject born into a system that sustains the hierarchies introduced by colonialism and is simultaneously trying to resist such power structures. They are born already as hybrid subjects, collapsing the boundaries between notions of "Western" and "African" yet, interpellated by external systems of White domination. Consequently, she projects the perspective that African children's literature articulates African pedagogy, and it is a unique archive and opportunity to grapple with postcolonialism as it relates to the subjectivity of African children. She explores African children's literature as a sociopolitical tool through the lens of Frantz Fanon's postcolonial framework which turns to literature and calls for stories and texts for Black children to aid them to combat the violence imparted by colonial education and programming, and support them to enunciate their subjectivities and assert their Blackness and social participation. By so doing, Adomako resurrects Efua Theodora Sutherland in the field of postcolonial African children's literature, because her work represents the hybridity of the postcolonial African child while also presenting opportunities for a gender analysis that rarely happens in this space. Efua Theodora Sutherland of Ghana is one of the early and most influential African authors to Africanize the content found in children's literature in Ghana. Adomako engages with Sutherland's *A Voice in the Forest* (1983) which addresses cultural tensions between Western and African values and reflects the impact of White domination on the sociopolitical climate that confronts postcolonial African children. Adomako brings it in dialogue with Fanon's postcolonial theory, amplified in *Black Skin, White Masks,* about how postcolonialism affects Black identity formations and African children's literature. While Adomako's work reveals how *A Voice in the Forest* classically reorients postcolonial African children as subversive figures, it also serves as a cultural product that shows how African adults attempt to make sense of the world for African children. Adomako discusses how the text defies the boundaries and norms created by the colonial society and ideology, and how childlike figures in the text subvert discourses of dominance and power tied to Western patriarchal values. Moreover, Adomako discusses the work as a critical text that provides understanding about diasporic notions and representations of postcolonial Black girlhood. Using a postcolonial and transnational feminist lens, Adomako argues that Sutherland's postcolonial girl character is part of a legacy of Black girls whose hair, body and behaviour have been politicized and policed. However, the analysis of the chapter also highlights and bears witness to how a postcolonial African girl exercises resistance and agency as she negotiates around and against the masculine strains of colonialism. Thus, Adomako asserts that given the historically masculinized nature of the colonial forces that subjugated Ghanaians, the very gendered independence represented in *A Voice in the Forest* symbolises postcolonial African girlhood as an anticolonial function. Moreover, postcolonial African children are complicating pre-existing binaries and necessitating a re-articulation of what African childhoods can entail.

Following Adomako's paper is Debbie Olson's "On the Innocence of Beasts: African Child Soldiers in Cary Fukunaga's *Beasts of no Nation*". Constituting Chapter Five, the paper also focuses on the issue of the adult-mediated process of representing and making meanings of African childhoods and identifications in a postcolonial context. It steps into the area of Western media and examines the issue of depiction of the postcolonial African child, the African child soldier, and their childhood. Olsen analyses and critiques the depiction of the African child soldier in Cary Fukunaga's 2015 adaptation of Uzodinma Iweala's novel *Beasts of No Nation*. Using the adapted *Beast of No Nation* to illustrate her point, she argues and demonstrates how it has commonly become difficult to see positive and meaningful representations of Black children in popular media, particularly Hollywood cinema. Such depictions, as Olsen shows, are linked to long-held Western notions propagated about Black children, mostly males, as "inherently violent", corrupt, "unable to achieve the promise of childhood innocence", and "ultimately unredeemable". Thus, the image of the African child soldier, as Olsen argues, has come out as a "persistent and complex representation of both real-world, war-time atrocities affecting African children", and Western media's detached (lack of positive and meaningful representation of Black children) passive-aggressive relationship with Black children. Olsen's paper gives us an understanding about how the "discursive nature of cinematic images of African children (and childhood) positions them as furthest from the Western ideal of childhood innocence and perfection—the blonde, blue-eyed, wide-eyed, curly-haired, angelic White child". In Olsen's view, this angel-demon dichotomy of children, popularised in the US by Harriet Beecher Stowe's novel *Uncle Tom's Cabin* and the contrast between the Black slave girl Topsy and the White girl Eva, is used to uphold what she, using Marina Bradbury's expression in "Negotiating Identities: Representations of Childhood in Senegalese Cinema",[84] identifies as "West as eternal adult and Africa as eternal child". Olsen depicts how modern "digital media have been used to foster a transnational circulation of disparaging images of Black children", particularly Black males, "from both the Global North and South". She argues that in the end, the Black child image serves as a "temporal mirror that separates projected Western "White childhoods" of the "now" from the "primitiveness" (i.e., backwardness) of Black childhoods". Such a demarcation "distorts the recognition of real Black children as children, an odd reversal of the West's perpetual depiction of Africa and its adults as "children" incapable of handling their own affairs". A common feature in many "coming of age" narratives is that White children are depicted as easily transcending to "adulthood through knowledge acquisition, something the Black child is both historically and cinematically rarely allowed to achieve". "The Black child is often cinematically frozen in the interstice between child and adult—an oscillation rooted in the racist discourse of the colonial era". Olsen analyses how the cinematic child soldier, Agu, in Fukunaga's *Beasts of No Nation* is depicted as an entity that "elicits both *sympathy* and *fear*" and, thus, becomes an example of the "suspended oscillation between child and adult". Olsen argues that in Iweala's novel, Agu navigates and resists events that happen to him and works to reconcile his belief in his own goodness (and innocence) even when forced to commit atrocities. The Agu persona in the film is a radical departure from the one in Iweala's novel. This departure, Olsen argues, "perpetuate[s] the notion that Black children are not like 'real' (White) children at all, and are in fact the 'beasts' the West has always believed them to be". Ultimately, such a postcolonial moment cinematic depiction reinforces the West's historical 'Africa-as-chaos' narrative through the eyes of an 'already-guilty' boy soldier name Agu". Olsen's paper, therefore, offers a new critical perspective that ultimately challenges cinematic myopic views and depictions of the African child and childhood that lack political correctness.

Komlan Agbedahin's paper "Boys and Girls in the Bush, Bosses in Post-conflict: Liberian Young Veterans Rising to Power", which produces a discussion in Chapter Six, moves away from depictions and representations of African childhood in media to real-life situations of Liberian children in the post-conflict moment in Liberia. The chapter examines the place of agency in Liberian young veterans (children formerly associated with armed forces and groups) rise to power. Accordingly, the chapter contributes to the debate on the nature of involvement of children in post-war reconstruction and reinte-

---

[84] Marina Bradbury, "Negotiating Identities: Representations of Childhood in Senegalese Cinema," *Journal of African Media Studies* 2(1), (2010): 13.

gration in African war-torn countries. It argues that the Liberian civil war (1989 to 2003) saw a massive involvement of child soldiers playing various roles. Owing to the manipulative recruitment and induction ceremonies and subsequent war experiences, former child soldiers predictably were expected to become social misfits in the post-conflict society. Some failed to overcome the post-conflict predicaments despite humanitarian assistance offered by local, national and international agencies; however, there were young veterans who were able to create for themselves some survival space. Based on their own stories and within an Interpretive Phenomenological Analysis (IPA) framework, this chapter offers a new perspective about Liberian childhood by highlighting how young veterans' agency immensely contributed to altering power relations with their former jungle bosses. The chapter argues that, whether in a war context or not, opportunities can be made available to young veterans, but if they fail to exercise agency to seize such opportunities, their living conditions may remain the same or worsen. Cases of young veterans who emerge as counsellors, creators of NGOs, and peace campaigners in Liberia, attest to this. While the available body of writing has acknowledged the agency of such children during the war, the debate on their agency towards the post-conflict reconstruction has been underemphasised and at times unduly overshadowed by skewed discourses of humanitarianism. Ultimately, the chapter offers positive accounts of the involvement of young veterans to rectify such epistemic imbalances.

In Chapter Seven, Ivo Mhike's work "White Poverty, State Paternalism and Educational Reforms in Southern Rhodesia in the 1930s" offers a contribution to the histories of African childhood by examining childhood issues which the Great Depression of the 1930s produced in Southern Rhodesia (now Zimbabwe). It analyses how child citizenship and belonging became predicated on the (re)embracing of particular educational values promoted by the state. According to the chapter, the emergence of a delinquent class of male juveniles and youth unemployment symbolised a national crisis which threatened to imperil colonial designs because the White male in an African country, transformed into a White settler colony, was set on a pedestal as the breadwinner and defender of the British Empire. The state therefore reformed its youth educational policy to combat the twin "evils" of White poverty and attendant moral decay in Southern Rhodesia. The colonial regime was concerned with the development of White males who were growing to adulthood without a useful education and skills necessary to meet the expectations of White society. Social planners considered this as an ominous sign of the fragility of the White race in the face of the Black race in Africa. Thus, in 1936 St. Pancras Home was set up as a juvenile rehabilitation institution for boys. It became a primary instrument of state social engineering which advanced the emergent social model of child education and child development; the model emphasised the cultivation of a productive masculinity through skills training for blue-collar jobs and the fostering of a "rural mindedness" for agriculture sector jobs. Being an institution which signified a practical step towards separating the White lower class and redefining its role in colonial economic development, St. Pancras Home also represented an aggressive form of state paternalism towards the children of the working class. Thus, Mhike's chapter argues that it reconfigured and shaped social policy and the meanings of childhood during the 1930s and 1940s. Mhike's analysis of the constructions and perceptions of childhood in the settler colony of Southern Rhodesia offers an enhanced appreciation of the rich diversity of childhoods in colonial settings and how the interaction between the different races constantly transformed the meanings of childhood in Africa.

Chapter Eight takes us from childhood issues of the colonial South Rhodesia period to one of both the colonial period and "post-apartheid" era in South Africa. In the chapter, Zethu Cakata offers some interesting perspectives about aspects of African childhoods that are characterised and shaped by language and land. Her paper, which is titled "Childhoods Rooted in the Land: Connecting Child Development to Land Using Cultural Practices of the IsiXhosa Speaking People of South Africa", argues that in all cultures life begins with childhood but for colonized lands in Africa, citing those of the AmaXhosa to illustrate and support her point and argument, an understanding of what childhood is has been distorted and diluted with enforced colonial and neo-colonial understandings. This disruption is because of the foregrounding and idealisation of social-cultural systems of the colonisers, such as language, on one hand, and the peripheralisation of those of the colonised on the other.[85] However, language, as Zethu argues, is resistant, for as long as it is alive its knowledge and the cosmologies and keys to the comprehension of practices and know-hows and know-whys that it carries to bind people to their lands can be reclaimed. Thus, Zethu's paper explores childhood formulations by the speakers of isiXhosa language in South Africa and the imperativeness of land possession to child-human development.

In Chapter Nine, Awo Sarpong and De-Valera N.Y.M. Botchway bring an interesting perspective on African childhood from Ghana. Their chapter, "'Adults are just Obsolete Children . . .': Child Fancy Dress Parades as a Carnivalesque Suspension of Adultism in Winneba, Ghana", unveils an urban space-based "power" politics between children and adult residents in Winneba, a littoral town and

---

[85] See, for example, Russell H. Kaschula, "The Oppression of IsiXhosa Literature and the Irony of Transformation," *English in Africa* 35 (1), (2008): 117-32.

the capital of Effutu Municipal District in the Central Region of southern Ghana, through their shared artistic medium of Fancy Dress. Winneba is nationally acclaimed as one of the six powerhouses and citadels of the Fancy Dress culture in Ghana. It holds annual interclub Fancy Dress competitive parades; these parades and national and popular celebrations in Ghana feature the Fancy Dress spectacle, with active child participation. The Fancy Dress masquerade act, which synthesises "special" fashion, music and dance, evolved during the colonial era, c. 18th century, within a patriarchal cultural terrain. It was first an adult male only dramatic merry-making parade; however, by the mid-20th century the adult monopoly had been dissolved by a revolutionary enrolment of children into clubs and a burgeoning wresting of the adult's control and sole ownership of artistic self-expression in the masquerade parades by children. This chapter examines the politics of change and the cultural ramifications it has exerted on the terrain of adult and child power relations in the urban life of Winneba. It discusses the agency of children in Fancy Dress art expression to dissolve adultism and mediate a town that thrives on the input of children. It argues that children performers of Fancy Dress easily slide into the adult category even though they are not adults, and that makes them, and by implication confers on children in Winneba, the status and right to be co-owners of the present and not just a mass of persons whom traditionally adults have dismissively thought and said of as future leaders.

In Chapter Ten, Mawuloe Koffi Kodah's paper "Mending the Broken Fences: A Study of the Socialized and De-socialized Child in Laye's *The African Child* and Kourouma's *Allah Is Not Obliged*" engages the issues of socialization and de-socialization of the African child and in African childhoods. Kodah does this by examining the depiction of these processes and the impact of the interplay of African and Western child-socialization and de-socialization at work in two works of African literature – Camara Laye's *L'Enfant noir* (1953),[86] translated into English as *The African Child*[87] and *The Dark Child*,[88] and Ahmadou Kourouma's *Allah n'est pas obligé*,[89] translated as *Allah is Not Obliged*[90] (2006).

---

[86] It was published in 1953 and was awarded the Charles Veillon literary prize in 1954. However, in this work references will be made to the following edition: Camara Laye, *L'Enfant Noir*, (Paris: Librairie Plon, 1954) and the translated English versions of the work.
[87] Camara Laye, *The African Child*, trans., J. Kirkup, (London: Collins, Fontana Books, 1959).
[88] Camara Laye, *The Dark Child*, trans., J. Kirkup, (New York: Farrar, Straus & Giroux, 1969).
[89] Ahmadou Kourouma, *Allah n'est pas obligé*, (Paris : Seuil, 2000).

The authorial voice of child-narrators has often been used by African novelists, such as Laye and Kourouma, as a mark of objectivity and value judgment in fiction in African literature, considering the perceived naivety, innocence and mere ignorance narrative stance of a child. Moreover, the authorial narrative is an eye-witness account of events akin to the lived-experiences of the narrator, difficult for anyone to contest the credibility of such an account to a large extent. Consequently, Kodah critically examines the upbringing, roles and character of two authorial child-narrators in the two narrative texts within the framework of socio-critique theory and establishes the significance of African child-socialization in a harmonious African communal social setting in the former text, vis-à-vis that of African child de-socialization in a dysfunctional African individualistic social setting in the latter, in view of mending the broken value-fences around the African child and their childhood. Finally, the Epilogue of this volume is written by Charles Quist-Adade.

Although this volume has endeavoured to contribute ideas to the burgeoning interrogation of African childhood in full light, it cannot declare or has no posturing of grandeur; it has not also aimed at completeness. As for us, we hope that the chapters in this volume will put the reader on the way to a more comprehensive interest in and consideration for the subject of African childhood; that is why we share the thrill of the *new perspectives* in this volume with a broader scholarly and reading audience. Clearly, there is a wide multiplicity of aspects of the African childhood theme to investigate, albeit with the need for many more fresh insights.

Bibliography

Abdi, Ali A. "Education in Somalia: History, Destruction, and Calls for Reconstruction." *Comparative Education* 34(3), (1998): 327–340.

Abdulwasie, Awan. "Conceptualizations of Children and Childhood: The Case of Kolfe and Semen Mazegaja, Addis Ababa." In *The World of Girls and Boys in Rural and Urban Ethiopia*, edited by Eva Poluha. Addis Ababa, Ethiopia: Forum for Social Studies, 2007. 39–66.

Abebe, Tatek, and Yaw Ofosu-Kusi. "Beyond Pluralizing African Childhoods: Introduction." *Childhood: A Journal of Global Child Research*, 23 (3), (2016): 303-316.

Abebe, Tatek. "Interdependent rights and agency: The role of children in collective livelihood strategies in rural Ethiopia." In *Reconceptualizing Children's Rlights in International Development: Living Rights, Social Justice,*

---

[90] Ahmadou Kourouma, *Allah is not obliged*, trans., F. Wynne, (London: Vintage Books, 2006).

Translations, edited by K. Hanson and O. Nieuwenhuys. Cambridge: Cambridge University Press, 2013. 71–92.

Aderinto, Saheed. "'The Girls in Moral Danger': Child Prostitution and Sexuality in Colonial Lagos, Nigeria, 1930s to 1950." *Journal of Humanities & Social Sciences* 1(2), (2007): 1–22.

Admassie, Assefa. "Explaining the High Incidence of Child Labour in Sub-Saharan Africa." *African Development Review* 14 (2), (2002): 251–275.

Agarwal, Seema, Memunatu Attah, Nana Apt, Margaret Grieco, E. A. Kwakye, and Jeff Turner. "Bearing the Weight: The Kayayoo, Ghana's Working Girl Child." *International Social Work* 40(3), (1997): 245–263.

Agbu, Osita (ed.) *Children and Youth in the Labour Process in Africa*. Codesria Book Series. Dakar, Senegal: CODESRIA, 2009.

Ahmed, Manzoor. *Within Human Reach: A Future for Africa's Children*. New York: United Nations Children's Fund, 1985.

Akpan, Uwem. *Say You're One of Them*. New York: Little, Brown, 2008.

Alanen, Leena, and Marjatta Bardy. *Childhood as a Social Phenomenon: National Report, Finland*. Vienna: European Centre for Social Welfare Policy and Research, [1990], 1991.

Alanen, Leena. "Rethinking childhood." *Acta Sociologica*, 31(1), (1988):53-67.

Ambert, Anne-Marie. "Sociology of Sociology: The Place of Children in North American Sociology." In *Sociological Studies of Child Development*, edited by P. A. Adler and P. Adler. Vol. 1. Greenwich, CT: JAI Press, 1986. 11-31.

Ambert, Anne-Marie. Reviews of *Childhood as a Social Phenomenon*, and *Childhood Matters: Social Theory, Practice and Politics*, edited by Jens Qvortrup, Marjatta Bardy, Giovanni Sgritta and Helmut Wintersberger. *Journal of Marriage and Family*, 56 (4), (1994):1043-1045.

Amone-P'Olak, K., N. Garnefski, and V. Kraaij. "The Impact of War Experiences and Physical Abuse on Formerly Abducted Boys in Northern Uganda." *South African Psychiatry Review* 10(2) (2007): 76–82.

Anarfi, John K., and Phyllis Antwi. "Street Youth in Accra City: Sexual Networking in a High-Risk Environment and Its Implications for the Spread of HIV/AIDS." *Health Transition Review* 5 suppl. (1995): 131–151.

André, G., and M. Godin. "Child labour, agency and family dynamics: The case of mining in Katanga (DRC)." *Childhood*, 21(2), (2014): 161–74.

André, G., and M. Hilgers. "Childhood in Africa between Local Powers and Global Hierarchies." In *Childhood with Bourdieu. Studies in Childhood and Youth*, edited by L. Alanen, et al. Palgrave Macmillan, London, 2015, 120-141.

Andvig, Jens C. "Child Labour in Sub-Saharan Africa—An Exploration." *Forum for Development Studies* 25(2), (1998): 327–362.

Argenti, Nicholas. *The Intestines of the State: Youth, Violence, and Belated Histories in the Cameroon Grassfields*. Chicago: University of Chicago Press, 2007.

Ariès, Philippe. *Centuries of Childhood: A Social History of Family Life*. Translated by Robert Baldick. New York: Alfred A. Knopf, 1962.

Armstrong, Gary. "The Lords of Misrule: Football and the Rights of the Child in Liberia, West Africa." *Sport in Society: Cultures, Commerce, Media, Politics* 7(3), (2004): 473–502.

Azevedo, Mario J., Gwendolyn S. Prater, and Daniel N. Lantum. "Culture, Biomedicine and Child Mortality in Cameroon." *Social Science & Medicine* 32(12), (1991):1341–1349.

Bass, Loretta E. *Child Labor in Sub-Saharan Africa.* Boulder, CO: Lynne Rienner, 2004.

Bastian, Misty L. "Young Converts: Christian Missions, Gender and Youth in Onitsha, Nigeria 1880–1929." Special Issue: Youth and Social Imagination in Africa, Part 1, *Anthropological Quarterly* 73(3), (2000): 145–158.

Bernard van Leer Foundation. "South Africa: Hey Mum, That's Me on the Radio!." *Early Childhood Matters* 103 (2004): 48–49.

Betancourt, Theresa S., Jessica Agnew-Blais, Stephen E. Gilman, David R. Williams, and B. Heidi Ellis. "Past Horrors, Present Struggles: The Role of Stigma in the Association between War Experiences and Psychosocial Adjustment among Former Child Soldiers in Sierra Leone." Special Issue: Conflict, Violence, and Health, *Social Science & Medicine* 70(1), (2010): 17–26.

Boakye-Boaten, Agya. "Changes in the Concept of Childhood: Implications on Children in Ghana." *Uluslararası Sosyal Araştırmalar Dergisi, The Journal of International Social Research* 3 (10), (2010):104-115.

Boakye-Boaten, Agya. "Street Children: Experiences from the Streets of Accra." *Research Journal of International Studies* 8 (2008): 76–84.

Bøås, Morten, and Anne Hatløy. "Child Labour in West Africa: Different Work—Different Vulnerabilities." *International Migration* 46(3), (2008): 3–25.

Bohlmann, Markus P.J. (ed.) *Misfit Children: An Inquiry into Childhood Belongings.* Lanham, Maryland: Lexington Books (Rowman and Littlefield), 2017.

Bohlmann, Markus P.J. "Introduction." In *Misfit Children: An Inquiry into Childhood Belongings,* edited by Markus P.J. Bohlmann. Lanham, Maryland: Lexington Books (Rowman and Littlefield), 2017), xiii-xxxi.

Bordonaro, Lorenzo I. "'Culture Stops Development!': Bijagó Youth and the Appropriation of Developmentalist Discourse in Guinea-Bissau." *African Studies Review* 52(2), (2009): 69–92.

Botchway, De-Valera, N.Y.M. "Gyama Songs in Ghanaian Schools: A Note on a Students' Musical Creativity." In *Schools and Schooling as a Source of African Literary and Cultural Creativity,* (LuKA (Literaturen und Kunst Akrikas) Series 9, edited by Tobias Robert Klein. Trier: Wissenschaftlicher Verlag Trier (WVT), 2017. 3-31.

Bourdillon, Michael, and Georges M. Mutambwa (eds.) *The Place of Work in African Childhoods.* Dakar: CODESRIA, 2014. 1-20.

Boyle, Elizabeth H. *Female Genital Cutting: Cultural Conflict in the Global Community.* Baltimore: Johns Hopkins University Press, 2002.

Bradbury, Marina. "Negotiating Identities: Representations of Childhood in Senegalese Cinema." *Journal of African Media Studies* 2(1), (2010): 9-24.

Brown, Jill R. "Child Fosterage and the Developmental Markers of Ovambo Children in Namibia: A Look at Gender and Kinship." *Childhood in Africa: An Interdisciplinary Journal* 1(1), (2009): 4–10.

Burman, Sandra, and Pamela Reynolds (eds.) *Growing Up in a Divided Society: The Contexts of Childhood in South Africa.* Johannesburg: Ravan, 1986.

Campbell, Catherine, Andy Gibbs, Sbongile Maimane, Yugi Nair, and Zweni Sibiya. "Youth   Participation in the Fight against AIDS in South Africa: From Policy to Practice." *Journal of Youth Studies* 12(1), (2009): 93–109.

Carton, Benedict. "Africa." In *Encyclopedia of Children and Childhood in History and Society,* edited by Paula S. Fass. New York: Thompson Gale, 2004, 29-33.

Chamberlain, Alexander F. Review of G. Stanley Hall, *Adolescence: Its Psychology and Its Relations to Physiology, Anthropology, Sociology, Sex, Crime, Religion, and Education. American Anthropologist.* New Series, 6 (4), (1904): 539-54.

Chelimo, Nathan. "Transitions in Pastoral Communities in Uganda: Classes under the Trees." *Early Childhood Matters* 107, (2006): 36–37.

Cheney, Kristen E. "'Village Life Is Better Than Town Life': Identity, Migration, and Development in the Lives of Ugandan Child Citizens." *African Studies Review* 47(3), (2004): 1–22.

Cheney, Kristen E. "Expanding Vulnerability, Dwindling Resources: Implications for Orphaned Futures in Uganda." *Childhood in Africa: An Interdisciplinary Journal* 2(1) (2010): 8–15.

Christensen, P., and A. Prout. "Anthropological and Sociological Perspectives on the study of children." In *Researching Children's Experience: Approaches and Methods,* edited by Sheila Greene and Diane Hogan. London/California/New Delhi: SAGE, 2005. 42-60.

Chuta, Nardos. "Conceptualizations of Children and Childhood in Bishoftu, Oromia." In *The World of Girls and Boys in Rural and Urban Ethiopia,* edited by Eva Poluha. Addis Ababa, Ethiopia: Forum for Social Studies, 2007.119–156.

Couture, Pamela D. "Victims, Perpetrators, or Moral Agents: Children and Youth Survivors of the War in the Democratic Republic of Congo." *Journal of Childhood and Religion* 2(2), (2011): 1–17.

Dangarembga, Tsitsi. *Nervous Conditions: A Novel.* Banbury, UK: Ayebia Clarke, 2004.

Davis, Susan S. "Growing Up in Morocco." In *Everyday Life in the Muslim Middle East,* edited by Donna L. Bowen and Evelyn A. Early. Indiana Series in Middle East Studies. Bloomington: Indiana University Press, 2002. 24–35.

Defo, Barthélémy K. "A real and Socioeconomic Differentials in Infant and Child Mortality in Cameroon." *Social Science & Medicine* 42 (3), (1996): 399–420.

Diouf, Mamadou. "Engaging Postcolonial Cultures: African Youth and Public Space." *African Studies Review* 46(2), (2003): 1–12.

Ennew, Judith. "Difficult Circumstances: Some Reflections on 'Street Children' in Africa." *Children, Youth and Environments* 13 (1), (2003): 1–18.

Epstein, Andrew I. "Education Refugees and the Spatial Politics of Childhood Vulnerability." *Childhood in Africa: An Interdisciplinary Journal* 2(1), (2010): 16–25.

Ewelukwa, Uché U. "The Girl Child, African States, and International Human Rights Law—Toward a New Framework for Action." In *Engendering Human Rights: Cultural and Socioeconomic Realities in Africa,* edited by Obioma Nnaemeka and Joy N. Ezeilo. New York: Palgrave Macmillan, 2005. 131–156.

Farrag, Eftetan O. "Working Children in Cairo: Case Studies." In *Children in the Muslim Middle East,* edited by Elizabeth W. Fernea. Austin: University of Texas Press, 1995. 239–249.

Fokwang, Jude. "Ambiguous Transitions: Mediating Citizenship among Youths in Cameroon." *Africa Development* 23(1–2), (2003): 173–201.

Fokwang, Jude. "Youth Subjectivities and Associational Life in Bamenda, Cameroon." *Africa Development* 28(3), (2008): 157–162.

Fourchard, Laurent. "Lagos and the Invention of Juvenile Delinquency in Nigeria, 1920–60." *Journal of African History* 47(1), (2006): 115–137.

Fouts, Hilary N., and Robyn A. Brookshire. "Who Feeds Children? A Child's-Eye-View of Caregiver Feeding Patterns among the Aka Foragers in Congo." *Social Science and Medicine* 69(2), (2009): 285–292.

Frost, Ginger. *Victorian Childhoods.* Westport, CT/London: Praeger, 2009.

Fugard, Athol. *My Children! My Africa!.* New York: Theatre Communications Group, 2010.

Gable, Eric. "The Culture Development Club: Youth, Neo-tradition, and the Construction of Society in Guinea-Bissau." Special Issue: Youth and the Social Imagination in Africa, Part 2, *Anthropological Quarterly* 73(4), (2000): 195–203.

Garbarino, James, Kathleen Kostelny, and Nancy Dubrow. "Mozambique's Children: Dying Is the Easy Part." In *No Place to Be a Child: Growing Up in a War Zone,* by James Garbarino, Kathleen Kostelny, and Nancy Dubrow. San Francisco: Jossey-Bass, 1998), 60–82.

Greene, S. "Child Development: Old themes, New directions." In *Making Sense of Social Development,* edited by M. Woodhead, D. Faulkner, and K. Littleton. London: Routledge, 1999. 250-268

Greene, Sheila, and Diane Hogan (eds.) *Researching Children's Experience: Approached and Methods.* London/California/New Delhi: SAGE, 2005.

Gyimah, Stephen O. "Polygynous Marital Structure and Child Survivorship in Sub-Saharan Africa: Some Empirical Evidence from Ghana." *Social Science & Medicine* 68(2), (2009): 334–342.

Hall, G. Stanley. *Adolescence: Its Psychology and its Relations to Physiology, Anthropology, Sociology, Sex, Crime, Religion, and Education.* 2 Vols. New York: Appleton, 1904.

Heinonen, Paula. *Youth Gangs and Street Children: Culture, Nurture and Masculinity in Ethiopia.* Social Identities 7. New York: Berghahn, 2011.

Hodges, Anthony (ed.) *Children's and Women's Rights in Nigeria: A Wake-Up Call; Situation Assessment and Analysis, 2001.* Abuja, Nigeria: National Planning Commission, 2001.

Honwana, Alcinda M. *Child Soldiers in Africa*. Philadelphia: University of Pennsylvania Press, 2005.

Howard, Steve. "Children and Childhood." Oxford Bibliographies. http://www.oxfordbibliographies.com/view/document/obo-9780199846733/obo-9780199846733-0045.xml.

Imoh, Afua Twum Danso. "From the singular to the plural: Exploring diversities in contemporary childhoods in sub-Saharan Africa." *Childhood: A Journal of Global Child Research*, 23 (3), (2016): 455-468.

Iweala, Uzodinma. *Beast of No Nation*. London: John Murray, 2005.

James, A., and A. Prout (eds.) *Constructing and Reconstructing Childhood: Contemporary Issues in the Sociological Study of Childhood*. Second Edition. London: Routledge/Falmer, 1997.

James, A., C. Jenks, and A. Prout. *Theorizing Childhood*. Cambridge: Polity Press, 1998.

Jenks, C. *Childhood*. London: Routledge, 1990.

Jenks, C. *The Sociology of Childhood: Essential Readings*, London: Batsford, 1982.

Jimu, I. M. "An Exploration of Street Vending's Contribution towards Botswana's Vision of Prosperity for All by 2016." *Pula: Botswana Journal of African Studies* 18(1), (2004): 19–30.

Kamwendo, Martha. "Constructions of Malawian Boys and Girls on Gender and Achievement." *Gender and Education* 22(4), (2010): 431–445.

Kane, Cheikh Hamidou. *Ambiguous Adventure*. Brooklyn, NY: Melville House, 2012.

Kapteijns, Lidwien, and Maryan M. Boqor. "Memories of a Mogadishu Childhood, 1940–1964: Maryan Muuse Boqor and the Women Who Inspired Her." *International Journal of African Historical Studies* 42(1), (2009): 105–116.

Kaschula, Russell H. "The Oppression of IsiXhosa Literature and the Irony of Transformation." *English in Africa* 35 (1), (2008): 117-132.

Kendall, Nancy. "Gendered Moral Dimensions of Childhood Vulnerability." *Childhood in Africa: An Interdisciplinary Journal* 2(1) (2010): 26–37.

Kennedy, David. *The Well of Being: Childhood, Subjectivity, and Education*. Albany: SUNY Press 2006.

Kessen, W. *The Rise and Fall of Development*. Worcester, MA: Clark University Press, 1990.

Khalil, Doris D. "Abuses of the Girl Child in Some African Societies: Implications for Nurse Practitioners." *Nursing Forum* 41(1), (2006): 13–24.

Kiar, Muluembeat. "Children in Ethiopian Media and School Textbooks." In *The World of Girls and Boys in Rural and Urban Ethiopia*, edited by Eva Poluha. Addis Ababa, Ethiopia: Forum for Social Studies, 2007. 157–180.

Kidd, Kenneth. *Freud in Oz: At the Intersections of Psychoanalysis and Children's Literature*. Minneapolis: University of Minnesota Press, 2011.

Kilbride, Philip L. "A Cultural and Gender Perspective on Marginal Children on the Streets of Kenya." *Childhood in Africa: An Interdisciplinary Journal* 2(1), (2010): 38–47.

Kilbride, Philip L., and Janet C. Kilbride. *Changing Family Life in East Africa: Women and Children at Risk.* University Park: Pennsylvania State University Press, 1990.

King, Elizabeth M., and M. Anne Hill (eds.) *Women's Education in Developing Countries: Barriers, Benefits, and Policies.* Baltimore: Johns Hopkins University Press, 1993.

Klein, Tobias Robert (ed.) *Schools and Schooling as a Source of African Literary and Cultural Creativity.* (LuKA (Literaturen und Kunst Akrikas) Series 9. Trier: Wissenschaftlicher Verlag Trier (WVT), 2017.

Kourouma, Ahmadou. *Allah is not obliged.* Translated by F. Wynne. London: Vintage Books, 2006.

Kourouma, Ahmadou. *Allah n'est pas oblige.* Paris : Seuil, 2000.

La Hausse, Paul. "'The Cows of Nongoloza': Youth, Crime and Amalaita Gangs in Durban, 1900–1936." *Journal of Southern African Studies* 16(1), (1990): 79–111.

Lamptey, Alice. "Children Creating Awareness about Their Rights in Ghana." In *Stepping Forward: Children and Young People's Participation in the Development Process,* edited by Victoria Johnson, Edda Ivan-Smith, Gill Gordon, Pat Pridmore, and Patta Scott. London: Immediate Technology Publications, 1998. 86–87.

Laye, Camara. *The Dark* Child. Translated by J. Kirkup. New York: Farrar, Straus & Giroux, 1969.

Laye, Camara. *L'Enfant Noir.* Paris: Librairie Plon, 1954.

Laye, Camara. *The African Child.* Translated by J. Kirkup. London: Collins, Fontana Books, 1959.

Laye, Camara. *The Dark Child.* Translated by James Kirkup. New York: Noonday, 1994.

Lenzer, Gertrud. "Is there sufficient interest to establish a sociology of children?" *Footnotes of the American Sociological Association,* 19 (8), (1991): 8.

Locke, John. *Two Treatises of Government.* From the *Works of John Locke.* Vol. 5. London: Sharpe and Son, 1823.

Lotter, Victor. "Childhood Autism in Africa." *Journal of Child Psychology and Psychiatry* 19(3), (1978): 231–244.

Lugalla, Joseph L. P., and Colleta G. Kibassa (eds.) *Poverty, AIDS, and Street Children in East Africa.* Studies in African Health and Medicine 10. Lewiston, NY: Edwin Mellen, 2002.

Magona, Sindiwe. *To My Children's Children.* Claremont, South Africa: David Philip, 1990.

Malindi, Macalane J., and Linda C. Theron. "The Hidden Resilience of Street Youth." *South African Journal of Psychology* 40(3) (2010): 318–326.

Marfo, Kofi, Alan Pence, Robert A. LeVine, and Sarah LeVine. "Strengthening Africa's Contributions to Child Development Research: Introduction." *Child Development Perspectives* 5(2) (2011): 104–111.

Marks, Shula (ed.) *Not Either an Experimental Doll: The Separate Worlds of Three South African Women.* Bloomington: Indiana University Press, 1988.

Mathabane, Mark. *Kaffir Boy: The True Story of a Black Youth's Coming of Age in Apartheid South Africa*. New York: Macmillan, 1986.

Matthews, Gareth, and Amy Mullin. "The Philosophy of Childhood." In *The Stanford Encyclopedia of Philosophy*, edited by Edward N. Zalta. Spring 2015 Edition. https://plato.stanford.edu/archives/spr2015/entries/childhood/.

Mayall, B. (ed.) *Children's Childhoods: Observed and Experienced*. London: Falmer, 1994.

Mayall, B. *A History of the Sociology of Childhood*. London: Institute of Education, 2013.

McKay, Susan. "Reconstructing Fragile Lives: Girls' Social Reintegration in Northern Uganda and Sierra Leone." In *Postconflict Reconstruction in Africa*, edited by Ahmad A. Sikainga and Ousseina Alidou. Trenton, NJ: Africa World Press, 2006), 149–168.

Mead, Margaret. *Coming in Age of Samoa: A Psychological Study of Primitive Youth for Western Civilisation*. William Morrow & Company, 1961.

Metz, Stephanie. "Romanticism and the Child: Inventing Innocence." http://web.utk.edu/~gerard/romanticpolitics/childhood.html.

Metz, Stephanie. "'The Youth . . . still is Nature's priest': Wordsworth and the Child of Nature." http://web.utk.edu/~gerard/romanticpolitics/words worth-and-the-child.html.

Morss, J. *The Biologising of Childhood: Developmental Psychology and the Darwinian Myth*. Hove: Lawrence Erlbaum, 1990.

Mugisha, Frederick, and Eliya M. Zulu. "The Influence of Alcohol, Drugs and Substance Abuse on Sexual Relationships and Perception of Risk to HIV Infection among Adolescents in the Informal Settlements of Nairobi." *Journal of Youth Studies* 7(3), (2004): 279–293.

Ntarangwi Mwenda, and Guy Massart (eds.) "Introduction." *Engaging Children and Youth in Africa: Methodological and Phenomenological Issues*. Bamenda, Cameroon: Langaa RPCIG, 2015. 1-30.

Nyamnjoh, Francis B. "Children, Media and Globalisation: A Research Agenda for Africa." In *Children, Young People and Media Globalisation*, edited by Cecilia von Feilitzen and Ulla Carlson. Gothenburg, Sweden: Nordicom, Gothenburg University, 2002: 43– 52.

Ofosu-Kusi, Yaw. "Introduction: Children's Agency and Development in African Societies" In *Children's Agency and Development in African Societies*, edited by Yaw Ofosu-Kusi. Dakar: CODESRIA, 2017. 1-14.

Ominde, Simeon H. *The Luo Girl: From Infancy to Marriage*. Custom and Tradition in East Africa. London: Macmillan, 1952.

Osakue, Grace. "Violence against Women and Girls: Breaking the Culture of Silence." *Exchange on HIV/AIDS, Sexuality and Gender* 2 (2006): 1–4.

Oswell, David. *The Agency of Children: From Family to Global Human Rights*. Cambridge: Cambridge University Press, 2013.

Parsons, T. *The Social System*. Glencoe, Illinois: Free Press, 1951.

Pecora, Norma O., Enyonam Osei-Hwere, and Ulla Carlson (eds.) *African Media, African Children*. Gothenburg, Sweden: International Clearinghouse on Children, Youth and Media, Nordicom, 2008.

Pence, Alan R., and A. Bame Nsamenang. *A Case for Early Childhood Development in Sub- Saharan Africa.* Working Papers in Early Childhood Development 51. The Hague: Bernard van Leer Foundation, 2008.

Pence, Alan, and Jessica Schafer. "Indigenous Knowledge and Early Childhood Development in Africa: The Early Childhood Development Virtual University." *Journal for Education in International Development* 2(3), (2006): 1–17.

Porter, Gina, Kate Hampshire, Michael Bourdillon, et al. "Children as Research Collaborators: Issues and Reflections from a Mobility Study in Sub-Saharan Africa." *American Journal of Community Psychology* 46(1–2), (2010): 215–227.

Prout, A., and A. James. "A New Paradigm for the Sociology of Childhood? Provenance, promise and problems." In *Constructing and Reconstructing Childhood: Contemporary Issues in the Sociological Study of Childhood,* edited by A. James and A. Prout. Second Edition. London: Routledge/Falmer, 1997. 7-33.

Qvortrup, J., M. Bardy, G. Sgritta, and H. Wintersberger. *Childhood Matters: Social Theory, Practice and Politics.* Aldershot: Avebury Press, 1994.

Qvortrup, J., W.A. Corsaro, and M-S Honig (eds.) *The Palgrave Handbook of Childhood Studies.* London: Palgrave Macmillan, 2009.

Read, Margaret. *Children of Their Fathers: Growing up among the Ngoni of Malawi.* Case Studies in Education and Culture. New York & London: Holt, Rinehart, and Winston, 1968.

Reynolds, Pamela. *Childhood in Crossroads: Cognition and Society in South Africa.* Cape Town: Eerdmans, 1989.

Rie, A. van, N. Beyers, R. P. Gie, M. Kunneke, L. Zietsman, and P. R. Donald. "Childhood Tuberculosis in an Urban Population in South Africa: Burden and Risk Factor." *Archives of Disease in Childhood* 80(5), (1999): 433–437.

Rousseau, Jean Jacques. *The Social Contract.* Translated by Charles Frankel. New York: Hafner, 1947.

Sarpong, Awo, and De-Valera, N.Y.M. Botchway. "Freaks in Procession? The Fancy Dress Masquerade as Haven for Negotiating Eccentricity during Childhood. A Study of Child Masqueraders in Cape Coast, Ghana." In *Misfit Children: An Inquiry into Childhood Belongings,* edited by Markus P.J. Bohlmann. Lexington Books (Rowman and Littlefield), 2017. 175-196.

Selvam, Sahaya G. "Capabilities Approach to Youth Rights in East Africa." *International Journal of Human Rights* 12(2), (2008): 205–214.

Shostak, Marjorie. "A !Kung Woman's Memories of Childhood." In *Kalahari Hunter-Gatherers: Studies of the !Kung San and Their Neighbors,* edited by Richard B. Lee and Irven DeVore. Cambridge, MA: Harvard University Press, 1998), 246–277.

Singhal, Arvind, and W. Stephen Howard (eds.) *The Children of Africa Confront AIDS: From Vulnerability to Possibility.* Research in International Studies, Africa Series 80. Athens, OH: Ohio University Press, 2003.

Snow, Robert W., Jean-Francois Trape, and Kevin Marsh. "The Past, Present and Future of Childhood Malaria Mortality in Africa." *Trends in Parasitology* 17(12), (2001): 593–597.

Soyinka, Wole. *Aké: The Years of Childhood.* London: Methuen, 2000.

Spittler, G., and M. Bourdillon (eds.) *African Children at Work: Working and Learning in Growing Up for Life*. Berlin: LIT Verlag, 2012.

Swartz, Leslie, and Ann Levett. "Political Repression and Children in South Africa: The Social Construction of Damaging Effects." Special Issue: Political Violence and Health in the Third World, *Social Science & Medicine* 28(7), (1989): 741–750.

Thompson, Carol B. "Beyond Civil Society: Child Soldiers as Citizens in Mozambique." *Review of African Political Economy* 26(80), (1999): 191–206.

United Nations Children's Fund. *Children on the Front Line: The Impact of Apartheid, Destabilization and Warfare on Children in Southern and South Africa*. Second Edition. New York and Geneva, Switzerland: United Nations Children's Fund, 1988.

Velema, Johan P., Eusèbe M. Alihonou, Timothé Gandaho, and Félicien H. Hounye. "Childhood Mortality among Users and Non-users of Primary Health Care in a Rural West African Community." *International Journal of Epidemiology* 20(2), (1991): 474–479.

Woodhead, M. *The Case for Childhood Studies*. Dublin: Children's Research Centre, Trinity College Dublin, 2003.

Zenani, Nongenile M. *The World and the Word: Tales and Observations from the Xhosa Oral Tradition*, edited by Harold Scheub. Madison: University of Wisconsin Press, 1992.

Chapter 1

Omo boti and *Omo pako*: Social Construction of Childhood, Livelihood and Health in Southwestern Nigeria

Mofeyisara Oluwatoyin Omobowale and Olukemi K. Amodu

Introduction

Omo boti and Omo pako[1] represent the ends of two social divides, construct-ed via social perceptions of the Yoruba on what is considered as ideal child-hood norms, values, symbols and imagery, in relation to the prevailing cir-cumstances and times. Although the precise period for emergence of these categories is not known, it is in common knowledge that the demarcation is a post-colonial phenomenon. Despite the fact that childhood is often contest-ed, one cannot deny the fact that childhood is also contextual. The complex chain of social, cultural, economic, political and, even, geographical space in which one lives as a child determines frameworks within which common notions of childhood are produced.[2] This study examines the construction of privilege and vulnerable childhood and its relations to health and ill-health among children of the Yoruba of southwestern Nigeria. The study utilises the idea of contextualised elitism in explaining the construction of childhood among the Yoruba. Locally defined elitism is used in the social construction of hierarchy and class. These are internally generated stratification reproduced by social differences through the dynamics of everyday struggle of everyman to establish their personalities in the society.[3]

---

[1] *Boti and Pako* are two words that can be interpreted as privileged child and vulnerable child respectively. They are used by the Yoruba of southwestern Nigeria to describe the world of a child or the childhood experience of a person.
[2] Peter Kraftl, "Building an idea:the Material Construction of an Ideal Childhood," *Transactions of the Institute of British Geographers* 31 (4), (2006) : 488-504.
[3] K. Barber, *I Could Speak Until Tomorrow: Oriki, Women and the Past in a Yoruba Town,* (London: Edinburgh University Press for the International African Institute, 1991).

Additionally, this study discusses how the means of living of parents, that is, parental livelihood, define the childhood and social construction of a child being among the Yoruba. Consequently, the centrality of livelihood in the social construction of childhood and health is emphasized in this discussion. The primary concern here is the initial social synthesis, which is essentially a matter in the discourse of childhood and health experience. Parental livelihood determines the lifestyle that will be given to a child and experience of his/her childhood, reflected in the provisioning of basic needs of life like clothing, food and shelter, all of which may have long-term implications on the social classification and health status of children. For instance, among the Yoruba, where a child is normally associated with the status of his or her parents, it is not strange that the name of the father or family of a child informs other people's perception about that child and consequently shapes their relationship with him or her. Thus, the Yoruba maxim *ki ri omo oba ka ma ri amin oba lara re* which conveys the idea that "a king's child will always reflect royalty", for example, philosophically articulates and explains the reality of this situation aptly.

The social perception of the reality of what constitutes an ideal privileged and vulnerable child cannot be overemphasised when it comes to the study of childhood development and health.[4] Studying livelihood and childhood social construction implies an examination of how social forces shape social understanding of people and actions toward social ranking, social differentiation, social change, overlapping social group relations, scarcity, abundance, provision, hardship, ill-health and health.[5] It is an exploration of the effects of class, race, gender, language, technology, culture, political economy, institutional and professional structures, norms and values in shaping the knowledge base which produces assumptions about status, and social classification of childhood.[6]

According to Akanmu G. Adebayo[7] in his analysis of grouping among the Yoruba of Nigeria and the Akan of Ghana, the twentieth and twenty-first centuries have witnessed the emergence of newly defined elite and middle classes offered

---

[4] Jocelyn A. Hollander and Hava R. Gordon, "The Processes of Social Construction in Talk," *Symbolic Interaction* 29 (2), (2006):183-212.

[5] P. Brown, "Naming and Framing: The Social Construction of Diagnosis and Illness," *Journal of Health and Social Behaviour*, Extra Issue: Forty Years of Medical Sociology: The state of the Art and Directions for the Future, (1995): 34-52; S. Aderinto, "Researching Colonial Childhoods: Images and Representations of Childhood in Nigeria Newspaper Press, 1925-1950," *History in Africa* 39, (2012): 241-166.

[6] Chiara Saraceno, "The Social Construction of Childhood: Child Care and Education Policies in Italy and the United States," *Social Problem* 31(3), (1984): 351-363.

[7] A.G. Adebayo, "Currency Devaluation and Rank: The Yoruba and Akan Example," *African Studies Review* 50 (2), (2007): 87-109.

by government policies of currency devaluation and Structural Adjustment Programmes (SAPs), all of which have, in a way, led to other types of classifications and constructions in childhood development among the Yoruba, as it is in the case of *omoboti* and *omopako*. The influence of government policies on social hierarchies has received attention from several scholars.[8] They have all analysed social hierarchies and social construction of reality regarding gender, power, space, health, politics, history and economy to mention few perspectives of their analyses. Despite these enormous studies, it is also important to examine the world of the social construction of the privileged and vulnerable childhood among the Yoruba, especially in this era of globalisation.

It will be unproductive discussing childhood outside the livelihood of the parents of children whose childhood is the interest of this study. Livelihood, as it were, comprises capabilities, skills, space, people, income and diet[9] through which a child or family acquire their vital necessities of life. For instance, diet is a vital necessity for child survival; it determines the nutritional status of a child, even its physical and psychological growth and development through a lifetime. A child fed on a diet that is not balanced, and exposed to insanitary and vulnerable conditions in the environment is likely to experience wasting and stunting, and be underweight. The livelihoods of parents largely determine the pattern of childhood development and hierarchy into which their children will be categorised. This also goes a long way in the formation of the perception of the society on the class within the context of childhood. Thus, while pointing out that an imperative paradigm towards the study and understanding of children and their childhood, that is, children's relationships and their cultures, in recent times is the critiquing of the social construction of childhood and peripheralisation of children as beings without agency by adults, Claire O'Kane[10] also states two points aptly. First, children actively participate in constructing and determining their social lives and those of other people and the social environments in which they live. Second,

---

[8] O. B. Lawuyi, *Moral Imaginings of the Nigerian Elite: Playing Satan and God in Performance*, (Ibadan: University Press Ibadan, 2014); G. Clark, *African Market Women: Seven Life Stories from Ghana*, (Bloomington: Indiana University Press, 2010); D. Badejo, "African Feminism: Mythical and social Power of Women of African Descent," *Research in African Literatures* 29 (2), (1998): 94-111.

[9] R. Chambers and G.R. Conway, "Sustainable Rural Livelihoods: Practical Concepts for the 21st century," *IDS Discussion Paper* 296, (1991): 1-105.

[10] C. O'Kane, "Street and Working Children's Participation in Programming for their Rights," *Children Youth and Environments* 13 (10), (2003): 167-183.

because children's experiences of childhood are diverse, childhood as a variable of social analysis can never be entirely separated from other variables such as class, gender, or ethnicity.

The above implies that (in)equalities in families status and the style in which children from different social blocs are raised, socialized and are sustained are historically important in the construction of livelihood and childhood in Africa.[11]

Methodology

This which paper, which contributes some new insights to the discourse on childhood in Nigerian history, draws on salient and relevant information from literature related to childhood, livelihood and health to formulate aspects of its narrative and analysis. Furthermore, qualitative techniques of data collection were used in this study. The qualitative data were generated from January 2015 to June 2016, through observation of social media chats via Facebook, Whatsapp and Instagram. The observation was done to monitor the trend of discussion on the construction of ideal childhood among Yoruba people. In-depth interviews were also conducted in purposively selected areas within the metropolis of Ibadan. This involved two local government areas, namely Ibadan North and North East. Their selection was based on the mixed nature of socio-economic classifications of its population. Newspaper stands[12] and market spaces in the selected areas were also purposively selected for interviews because they are common places of convergence of various people and social consciousness.[13] In all, 21 in-depth interviews and 12 informal interviews were conducted with male and female informants across different social, economic classes and ages. All data were subjected to relational content analysis.

Social Construction of *Omo boti and Omo pako*

Omo boti, as revealed from the data are also called several names among which are: *ajebota* or *ajebo* (butter consumer), *omo-get-inside* (a child restricted to indoors), *mimi pin* (I swallowed pin), *omo-mummy* (mummy's

---

[11] See Saraceno,"The Social Construction of Childhood"; Aderinto, "Researching Colonial Childhoods".

[12] Newspaper stand in Ibadan is a space where different people meet to discuss different social issues. See Footnote 17.

[13] See A.O. Omobowale, M.O. Omobowale, and H.O.J. Akinade, "Newspaper Stands as Centres of Social Consciousness in Nigeria," *Malaysian Journal and Information Sciences* 18 (1), (2013): 79-86.

boy/girl), *adire-goloba*[14] (Glover's cockerel), *agric, golugo* (gullible), *asoo* (western), *foreign, tokunbo* (from over the seas), *omo olowo* (child of the wealthy), *omo torise* (child of the philanthropist) and *omo pampers* (a pampered child). On the other hand, *Omo pako* (a child born with a wooden spoon) also attracts other names like *ajepako* (wood consumer), *paki* (cassava), *lokii* (local), *tiwa-n-ti-wa* (indigenous), *talika* (pauper), *talikuta* (very poor) and *ibile* (traditional). Looking at these names literally and critically, they speak volumes on the social perceptions and expectations of the two divides. These nomenclatures are types of yardsticks for identifying and measuring the pattern of childhood a child possesses. They also signify symbolic framing of childhood among the Yoruba. All these names notwithstanding, this study has adopted the use of *Omo boti and Omo pako* for easy explanation and also because they have gained more popularity than other names that refer to the same issues arising from the data collected.

Boti in Yoruba parlance simply implies butter: a smooth, creamy, edible fat made by churning milk or cream for cooking and table use.[15] It is not indigenous to the Yoruba but it is believed to have been popularised by British colonialists, even though it has always been in Nigeria, especially among the Fulani pastoralists. It became more visible in the early part of the nineteenth century as a special diet among the urban dwellers and elites who had contact with the colonialists and their diets. This was also the period when butter making contributed significantly to the economic development of the world.[16] At this time, butter consumption was almost solely the affair of the colonialists, urban dwellers and elites. It was one of the edible items used as a status symbol by the indigenous elitist class because it was eaten by the colonial masters; it was imported and expensive. Commonly eaten as a spread on pastries, especially bread, it was popularly considered as food for the well-to-do in the urban areas. This perception was partly explained in a Yoruba adage that *omo oko ti yoo je buredi, yoo fi ibepe ranse si ara ile. Bota ki i se onje obo* (a village dweller that wants to eat bread will send pawpaw to those in the city. Butter is not a morsel of food for the poor). The consumption of butter (and also margarine, which at times was referred with the blanket term *butter* by

---

[14] It is generally believed that Western breeds of cockerel were introduced to Nigeria when Sir John Glover was the colonial governor of Lagos Colony from 1863-1872. These foreign breeds were regarded as weak compared to local breeds.

[15] A.G. Adebayo, "Taming the Nomads: The Colonial State, the Fulani Pastoralists and the Production of Clarified Butter Fat (C-B-F) in Nigeria, 1930-1952," *Transafrican Journal of History* 20, (1991):190-212.

[16] J.M. Jensen, "Butter Making and Economic Development in Mid-Atlantic American from 1750 to 1850," *Signs* 13(4), (1988) : 167-168.

some of the masses because of its creamy look and butter-like consistency) in pre-independence Nigerian society increased with its advertisement on television and newspaper.[17] Having inserted itself into the dietary ways of some of the Yoruba since the colonial period, butter became a preferred condiment to bread to those who could acquire it. Consequently, bread and butter have come to be commonly seen as going hand in hand among many Yoruba. This is even reflected in one of the children's rhymes among the Yoruba that goes thus: *Buredi and butter, odu pupo, maje ko gbona, maje ko tutu, omo oloja ki lo mu?* (Bread and butter are delicious. Make it warm. Which one will you opt for?). There are also times when people and things that are gorgeous among the Yoruba are described as *opatarishio* meaning butyraceous. The essence of bringing in this rhyme and these parlances is to show that butter at a time in the colonial history of the Yoruba, in particular, and of Nigeria, in general, was the pride of the elites and the rich and was made popular by the British imperialists. Butter, as gathered through oral interviews, was for a long time the diet of the elites and the rich who could afford to buy it and its other products, like buttered biscuits which were exported from England. However, dry and tough unbuttered biscuits, the *pako* (hard like wood) types of biscuits, were commonly found with the low-income earners and so-called ordinary locals.

Pako in the common knowledge of the Yoruba of southwestern Nigeria is literarily translated as wood, a hard fibrous lignified substance under the bark of a tree; the term also stands for a hard or rugged thing, or an act of being determined, tenacious and relentless; it also symbolises a substance that can withstand uncomfortable situations. Wood is indigenous to the Yoruba physical environment; its usage predates colonialism. For instance, it has been used to construct many different secular and religious objects. For example, its existence and importance are felt in the religious space and belief system of the Yoruba where it is an item for the production of sacred sculptures of deities and other spiritual forces. In the economic space, it is relevant and useful in the construction business of the Yoruba. Furthermore, when wood is burnt it may end up as charcoal, a product of second-hand significance because it is the remains of an incinerated "destroyed" wood; yet the charcoal will still be of both domestic and economic value. This is reflected in one of the informant's statement as stated below:

---

[17] Lawuyi, *Moral Imaginings of the Nigerian Elite:..*

When you are addressed as *Pako,* it simply means that you are rugged, can pass through fire and even when people think you are destroyed you still come out *bouncing* and elastic[18]

Boti and pako as nomenclatures evoke various contextual meanings and imagery – the former representing privilege and the latter signifying vulnerability and marginality. Apart from employing the nomenclatures as a socio-construction, their meanings can be decontextualized and inverted. In other words, one can be referred to as being an *Omo boti* if he or she is in a state of vulnerability because it is a position of softness and physical weakness. There are other yardsticks constructed around the duo, regarding securing major necessities of life such as clothing, shelter, food, water, education and security. The significance of these major necessities to livelihood and formation of childhood will form the central topical platform for our discussion shortly in line with the objective of this study. In the words of an informant:

Boti children are children whose parents are always there for them, they don't allow them to go out, there is a kind of food they eat, there is a kind of school they go, there is a kind of place they live in, there is a way they do their things, they are not very rugged.[19]

This view was further corroborated by another informant as relayed below:

Boti is ignorant of the reality of life. They are born with silver and golden spoons. They are children who do not have a feel of hardship... they are given everything; they are satisfied with all that they are given, they do not know what is happening, they have not had experience of hardship. They wear nice cloth, live in a well-built house, go to good schools, taken in their parents' car to school every day, live in Government Reservation Area, or well planned and fenced neighbourhoods and [have] good hygienic water supply, like borehole.[20]

To further corroborate the social expectations on *Boti,* the informant below added that:

---

[18] Male, Student, 27 years.
[19] Female, Informatics Engineer, 35 years.
[20] Male, Civil Servant, 42 years.

Ajebo children are very sluggish, they act anyhow, though they are usually good-looking, they wear real designer and not fake designer clothes, but they are not very sharp. They are not that strong, even in the heart. They are very smart regarding media, Facebook. You know those social media..., but when it comes to street life they are less smart.[21]

From the above statements, *Boti* (Butter) in social construction and expectations are children who are provided with all necessities of life by their parents. Being *Boti* is defined by material wealth provision, for example, good clothing and access to the latest technological equipment. Regarding non-material provision, they are shadowed about and are trained to be less sensitive to hardship. It is believed that *Boti* children lack the physical and emotional resilience to withstand change, particularly the negative kind. Further explanation to the construction of the privileged and the vulnerable child is reflected in the quality of education received by many children. According to some of the informants:

A *Boti* child will attend private school. Moreover, the kind of skills the child will acquire will be bigger than his age. For example, while a *Boti* child in Nursery 2 can read 2 to 4 letter words, his *Pako* counterpart will still be struggling with ABC to Z.[22]

In another interview, an informant equally enumerated the differences as follows:

You don't need to go far, just call a *Boti* and a *Pako* together, tell them to sing a rhyme. You will begin to hear *twinkle, twinkle little star* being sung in Queen intonation, while *Pako* will sing rhymes with local intonation, like calling airplane *Eropileni*. Then ask them to speak English, you will listen to all manners of *Ibon* (Yoruba argot for grammatical blunders in English) while a true *Boti* will speak correct English. [23]

In another response, the informant revealed that:

A *Boti* will never live in a slum; they live in GRA (Government Reservation Area), well laid out environment, fenced house, with business minding neighbours. Some of them have never witnessed violence. They are set of children that will watch and think cartoons; they also

---

[21] Male, Banker, 31 years.

[22] Female, Teacher, 37 years.

[23] Male, Technologist, 43 years.

watch the news, documentaries and children programmes and not funny home videos, like violence filled *Agbeleku or Koto orun* that an average *omo pako* will watch and act like on a daily basis.[24]

The above responses present the construction of the post-colonial society around being *Boti*, which is about the value systems of access and denial to necessities of life. The preceding transforms into perceptions and actions of ideals and reality. This access and denial of ideals and real value system are also strongly reflected in the construction of health and vitality, as discussed below in the next section.

Pako and Boti in the Context of Child Nutrition and Health

The data revealed that constructing health and nutrition of *Boti and Pako* from societal perspective may be ambiguous. The world of this ambiguity, in itself, reflects a sort of explanation for social realities of childhood and health. In terms of diet, many informants believed that the *omo pako* children were usually physically stronger than *the omo boti* ones. Some of their explanations are written below:

An *ajepako* may eat plenty yam and the stomach will be filled, *ajebota* cannot eat such, he/she will rather eat one or almost two slices of yam with tea. That is why *ajepako* is stronger, aggressive and rugged.[25]

In another interview, the informant hinted that:

Ajepako people may not eat balance diet o, but they eat plenty food, unlike *ajebota* that will be fed three square meals, with balanced diets according to their dictates at times.[26]

Another informant added that:

Ajebota will eat cornflakes, noodles, spaghetti, salad, tomato ketchup with chips and chicken, cereals of different manners, bread with real butter not margarine, correct fried/jollof rice, go to KFC (a fast food restaurant), imported chocolates, sweet, chewing gum, and juice and

---

[24] Male, Taxi Driver, 52 years.
[25] Female, Cleaner, 49 years .
[26] Female, Medical Student, 22 years.

so on. While *ajepako* eats more of eba,[27] amala,[28] rice, ogi,[29] beans, fufu,[30] and other carbohydrate-laden diets. That explains the reason why they are strong and filled with energy. Though many *ajebota* are always very fat due to the fatty and sweet food they eat.[31]

Yet, another informant stated that:

> *Ajebota* does not eat anyhow, they are selective in their food, and that is why they are healthier than *ajepako*. An average *Boti* will look fresher than the finest *ajepako*. They always look chubby and robust, not *topala* (thin).[32]

The contradiction shown here is that the general constructions of "being strong physically" and "being healthy" are not equal to each other. A child may be rough and aggressive, which is not the hallmark of health but the social, environmental disadvantage of the low class. What is obvious from the statements above is that *ajebota* (*omo boti*) and *ajepako* (*omo pako*) diet is one of the socially constructed sharp markers of differentiation. The type of diet that a child is exposed to will determine, in the end, which side of the divide a child will be placed socially. Hence, diet plays a critical role in the development of the child. Going by the general perception of the diet pattern of the duo, *ajepako* is at the risk of malnutrition, while *ajebota* is at the high risk of developing obesity. This is embedded in the interpretation of "fineness". Thus, right from birth, many *ajepako* children may experience stunted growth, and even deformity, due to their diet, while their *ajebota* counterpart will grow normally with all parts of their body well developed. Meanwhile, there are other critical questions raised by these socially constructed views that will be discussed later in the course of this discourse.

Furthermore, the environment in which a child is born and raised is a very significant factor in health and child development. A child born to a "strug-

---

[27] It is a staple food eaten by the Yoruba and other West African ethnic groups. It is made from dried grated cassava flour commonly known as gari.

[28] Indigenous Yoruba food made from cassava and/or yam flour. It is rich source of carbohydrate.

[29] It is a type of fermented pudding from Nigeria. It is traditionally made from maize, sorghum or millet.

[30] This local food is from pounded starchy food crops like cassava, yams or plantains and cocoyams.

[31] Male, Lecturer, 43 years.

[32] Female, Student, 24 years.

gling family" whose parents can hardly afford all necessities of life, like "decent" accommodation, is considered *ajepako* (*omo pako*). Excerpts from the information gathered from informants describe a child living in:

> A crowded neighbourhood...not laid out, with many face-you-and-face-me apartments... slum-like, dirty, waterlogged, all drained blocked with all sort of dirt thrown into the drainage whenever it rained..., high crime-prone neighbourhood, with a high presence of traditionality, impoliteness, and public life that generate unnecessary noise pollution.[33]

According to the statements by informants, any child born and raised in this type of environment is surely an *ajepako*. The implication of this on child health is obvious as a dirty environment will certainly breed illness-causing germs, like bacteria, and raise the incidence of infections, among other afflictions, which may prove very devastating to the health of children growing in such an environment. Another serious health problem is the mass breeding of malaria-causing mosquitos in environments such as the one described above, which poses a danger to the health of both children and adults. This also has its health and economic dimensions in that people or parents in such environments will spend more of their scarce income on treating diseases afflicting their children, instead of investing it in life improvement. This has also given the opportunity to drug abuse, wrong treatments, quack health practitioners, and misuse of herbs to thrive in such environments. All these have a devastating effect on child development in the geographical and cultural space featured by the study. This explains a slow decline in under-5 morbidity and mortality in Nigeria. This is further corroborated by an informant as shown below:

> It is not a good thing to be *ajepako*. It is like a curse; you can never achieve a neat environment. Even when you are neat, people around you are dirty they will frustrate your effort and make sure all is not well. They cannot reason like a normal person; they see thing from the awkward side of life. They will rather blame witches and wizards for their self-inflicted illness, and especially when, through carelessness, they kill their children, and pollute the environment than face the reality of life.[34]

---

[33] Composed from snippets of information from the views of different respondents.
[34] Male, Cook, 48 years.

Another informant observed that:

> *Ajepako* child will grow up in an environment where a child is free to roam around, play with all sorts of dangerous things, eat anything, even *igbe aran and iyepe* (goat dug and sands) and even play a lot with dirty things, while *ajebota* will be raised in clean environment and cannot eat any dirt.[35]

A child exposed to dirt will be prone to the danger of infectious diseases, while a child "over-protected" against germs may lack immunity against infections, all of which are not of positive implication for child development, even though the latter seems better than the former.

A child born into a family of *ajebota* people will be part of the *omo boti* children and will automatically be called *ajebota*. He or she will be expected to live and socialise in a well-built neighbourhood where almost all houses are fenced and residents enjoy utmost privacy in well planned and neatly laid out surroundings where they suffer little or no noise and environmental pollution. As described by all informants, with many giving specific examples, the environment of an *ajebota* child is just the opposite of that of *ajepako*. The health implication for this is not hidden; many parents in the *ajebota* category will spend fewer resources on the treatment of illness and disease during the childhoods of their offspring; they will have more income to invest on other childhood necessities. They are also expected to be more civil in their treatment of illnesses, especially for their children, and many of them may not abuse the drug, or patronise quack and fake herbal doctors, for these undesirables may not even surface in such neighbourhoods.

One important issue to be noted here is that the categorisation of *Boti* and *Pako,* as it were, is not rigid in its classification. There are others who are neither *Pako* nor *Boti*. Such cases may be better appreciated from the class performance angle, that is, those who are especially fighting being classed as low and in reality are not in the middle or upper class, but have, over the years, accumulated material wealth that could place them and their children into a *Boti* classification. The reality is that from the data gathered, no one desired to be *Pako* or raise *pako* children. Every informant claimed and desired to bring their children up as *Boti* with little change in values. The emphasis here is that it is important to recognise that the gap between *Boti* and *Pako* is not empty, but is filled with many performing "being *Boti*", while in the real sense their value system still

---

[35] Male, Civil servant, 44 years.

places them back to the disadvantaged group. Drawing understanding from Marek Ziolkowski's "Individuals and the Social System: Values, Perceptions, and Behavioral Strategies" we are of the opinion that the significance of this is the variance in how the individual adapts to the social system which includes, "values, perceptions, and popular explanations of . . . reality, attitudes towards the system, and declared behavioural strategies... [v]alues [in] images of objects, events, [place and space], state or processes that are considered right, just, moral and desirable...used in measuring the gap between the ideal and the real."[36] Likewise, the state of health of a *Boti and a Pako* child lies within this value system even when they fall within the gaps.

Conclusion

Omo boti and Omo pako, the privileged child and vulnerable child respectively, are largely in the world of the value system of the Yoruba societal construction of the ideal and reality of livelihood and childhood. The categories are largely defined and determined by access to and provision of necessities of life and their utilisation within a value system. Thus, the construction points to internally generated stratification that establishes essences of being. Moreover, this construction also has a way of impacting on the state of child health and ill-health experienced among the Yoruba in southwestern Nigeria. Finally, it is worth mentioning however that childhood among the Yoruba is contextual, its definition and construction are ambiguously applied contextually.

Bibliography

Adebayo, A.G. "Currency Devaluation and Rank: The Yoruba and Akan Example." *African Studies Review* 50 (2), (2007): 87-109.

Adebayo, A.G. "Taming the Nomads: The Colonial State, the Fulani Pastoralists and the Production of Clarified Butter Fat (C-B-C) in Nigeria, 1930-1952." *Transafrican Journal of History* 20, (1991): 190-212.

Aderinto, Saheed. "Researching Colonial Childhoods: Images and Representations of Childhood in Nigeria Newspaper Press, 1925-1950." *History in Africa* 39, (2012): 241-166.

Badejo, D. "African Feminism: Mythical and social Power of Women of African Descent." *Research in African Literatures* 29 (2), (1998): 94-111.

Barber, Karin. *I Could Speak Until Tomorrow: Oriki, Women and the Past in a Yoruba Town*. London: Edinburgh University Press for the International African Institute, 1991.

---

[36] Marek Ziolkowski, "Individuals and the Social System: Values, Perceptions, and Behavioral Strategies," *Social Research: An International Quarterly* 55 (1), (1988): 139-140.

Brown, Phil. "Naming and Framing: The Social Construction of Diagnosis and Illness." *Journal of Health and Social Behaviour* 35 (Extra Issue: Forty Years of Medical Sociology: The State of the Art and Directions for the Future), (1995): 34-52.

Chambers, R., and G. R. Conway. "Sustainable Rural Livelihoods: Practical Concepts for the 21st century." *IDS Discussion Paper* 296, (1991): 127-130.

Female Cleaner. Interview by authors. Ibadan. August 3, 2016.

Female Informatics Engineer. Interview by authors. Ibadan. May 5, 2016.

Female Medical Student. Interview by authors. Ibadan. August 3, 2016.

Female Student. Interview by authors. Ibadan. April 2, 2016.

Female Teacher. Interview by authors. Ibadan. June 28, 2016.

Hollander, Jocelyn A., and Hava R. Gordon. "The Processes of Social Construction in Talk." *Symbolic Interaction* 29(2) (2006): 183-212.

Jensen, J.M. "Butter Making and Economic Development in Mid-Atlantic American from 1750 to 185." *Signs* 13(4), (1988): 813-829.

Kraftl, Peter. "Building An Idea: The Material Construction of an Ideal Childhood." *Transactions of the Institute of British Geographers* 31(4), (2006): 488-504.

Lawuyi, O. B. *Moral Imaginings of the Nigerian Elite: Playing Satan and God in Performance*. Ibadan: University Press Ibadan, 2014.

Male Banker. Interview by authors. Ibadan. May 7, 2016.

Male Civil Servant. Interview by authors. Ibadan. May 28, 2016.

Male Cook. Interview by authors. Ibadan. April 2, 2016.

Male Lecturer. Interview by authors. Ibadan. June 28, 2016.

Male Student. Interview by authors. Ibadan. May, 5 2016.

Male Taxi Driver. Interview by authors. Ibadan. May 10, 2016.

Male Technologist. Interview by authors. Ibadan. August 3, 2016.

Male Civil servant. Interview by authors. Ibadan. August 3, 2016.

O'Kane, C. "Street and Working Children's Participation in Programming for their Rights." *Children Youth and Environments,* 13(1), (2003): 167-183.

Omobowale, A.O, M.O. Omobowale and H.O.J. Akinade, "Newspaper Stands as Centers of Social Consciousness in Nigeria." *Malaysian Journal and Information Sciences* 18(1), (2013): 79-86.

Saraceno, Chiara. "The Social Construction of Childhood: Child Care and Education Policies in Italy and the United States." *Social Problem* 31(3), (1984): 351-363.

Ziolkowski, Marek. "Individuals and the Social System: Values, Perceptions, and Behavioral Strategies." *Social Research: An International Quarterly* 55(1), (1988): 139-177.

Chapter 2

Our Stones, Our Livelihood: Urban Working Children's Survival Strategy and its Implications in the Daglama Quarry Site in the Ho Municipality of Ghana

Samuel Bewiadzi and Richard Awubomu

Introduction

Child labour is a major problem in most countries throughout the world. This problem has become very acute in many so-called developing countries.[1] In most African countries, a large proportion of households live at a minimum level of expenses owing to factors such as weak economic base, high rates of unemployment, and inadequate income of parents, resulting in children's economic production becoming an important aspect of economic survival strategies.[2] Indeed, there is a large body of literature on child labour with polarized viewpoints. One school of thought argues that child labour emanates from the economic conditions facing the household.[3] It argues that as family incomes fall

---

[1] H. Reza, T. Kumar Das, and F. Ahmmed, *Struggle for Survival: A Study on the Needs and Problems of the Street and Working Children in Sylhet City*, Sylhet, (Bangladesh: Department of Social Work, Shahjalal University of Science and Technology (SUST) 2005).

[2] D. Togunde , "Child labor and educational outcomes in urban Nigeria," Conference Paper, 6th Annual Conference of the Institute for the African Child , Ohio University , Athens , Ohio, 2005.

[3] K. Basu, *Child Labour: Cause, Consequence, and Cure, with Remarks on International Labour Standards*, (Washington, D.C.: World Bank, 1998); S. Bhalotra and C. Heady, "Child Farm Labour: The Wealth Paradox," *World Bank Economic Review 17(2)*, (2003): 197-227; K. Basu, and P.H. Van, "The Economics of Child Labor," *The American Economic Review* 88(3), (1998): 412-27; T. Mwebaze, "Extent and Determinant of Child Labour in Uganda," *AERC Research Paper,* (2007): 167; E. Edmonds and C. Turk, *Child Labour in Transition in Vietnam*, (Washington, D.C.: World Bank, 2002); B.C. Okukpara and N. Odurukwe, "Incidence and Determinants of Child Labour in Nigeria: Implica-

below subsistence levels, families tend to rely on their children's income in order to survive. The other school of thought asserts that although economic factors contribute to children's participation in the labour market, non-economic factors are equally important.[4] It cautions further that an overemphasis on economic factors limits the understanding of the reasons for children's involvement in labour market activities. These perspectives, while useful in explaining the demand and supply factors contributing to children's participation in the labour market, tend to portray children as inactive agents, who cannot make rational decisions concerning improvement in their living standards, and as such, are compelled by their parents to participate in economic activities. Beverly Grier attributes the neglect of child workers in African scholarship to the fact that children are perceived as 'invisible workers'.[5] Allison James and Alan Prout point out that when we conceive children as naturally passive, incompetent, incomplete, and defenseless, we foreclose a series of important questions for theory and empirical research.[6] Alebachew A. Nurye adds that children are as much part of the economy as adults, and are affected by the economic and social change, and indeed contribute to it as they struggle to make a living for themselves and their dependents.[7]

The two frameworks discussed above point to the fact that both economic and non-economic factors are critical to consider in any effort that aims at unearthing insight into the phenomenon of children's participation in economic activities since both factors tend to reinforce each other. This paper therefore further argues that children are active and strategic agents in labour market, taking responsibility for their own well-being and that of others. Thus, children work

tions for Poverty," *AERC Research Paper,* (2006): 156; D. Togunde and A. Carter, "In their own Words: Consequences of Child Labour in Urban Nigeria," *Journal of Social Science* 16 (2), (2008):173-181.

[4] R. Ray, "Analysis of Child Labour in Peru and Pakistan: A Comparative Study," *Journal of Social Science* 16 (2), (2000):173-181; A. Adamassie, *Explaining the High Incidence of Child Labour in Sub-Saharan Africa,* (UK: Blackwell Publishers, 2002); S. Bhalotra and C. Heady, "Child Farm Labour: The Wealth Paradox," *World Bank Economic Review* 17 (2), (2003): 197-227; A. De Groot, *Child Labour in Kathmandu, Nepal,* (Amsterdam: IREWOC, 2010).

[5] B. Grier, "Child Labour and Africanist Scholarship: A Critical Overview," *African Studies Review* 47 (2), (2004): 1-25.

[6] A. James and A. Prout, *Constructing and Reconstructing Childhood: Contemporary Issues in Sociological Study of Childhood,* (London: Falmer Press, 1997) cited in Grier "Child Labour and Africanist Scholarship", 16.

[7] A. A. Nurye, "My Shop is my School: Children's Perspectives on Work and School in a Multi-Ethnic town in Southern Ethiopia," 16th International Conference of Ethiopian Students, Trondheim, Norway, 2007.

not only because they are told to do so by their parents or adults, but also because they feel responsible for meeting their own needs and those of their families. The problem is that, although children are active agents in labour market activities, their views have been underrepresented in the literature, since they are assumed to be inactive in decisions relating to their participation in the labour market. Secondly, the effects of children's participation in labour market activities are also partially represented. For this reason, this paper points out that children are active agents in labour market activities; therefore, views about their work and contributions to their families' sustenance, will generate sufficient insights about how complex socio-cultural norms and values, economic environment, as well as need on the part of children contribute to their participation in labour market activities. More importantly, the paper endeavours to ascertain some effects of children's participation in labour market activities on their development. By arguing that children are rational and active participants in labour market activities, this study incorporates children's views into the child labour literature, and thus contribute to filling the noticeable gap which has been overlooked in the literature. The analytical point of departure from previous studies is the availability of data obtained especially from children, thereby giving voice to children whose views on their financial contributions to the family survival strategies have been largely underreported. Thus, this paper addresses three key questions. First, to what extent are children part of the family decision-making process in relation to their participation in stone quarrying at Daglama? Second, what factors underlie children's participation in stone quarrying at the Daglama quarry site? Finally, what are the effects of stone quarrying on the development of these children in relation to health and education?

Operationalising Working Children

According to Hasan Reza and colleagues, working children are children who are mostly involved in different activities for mere survival. They are often deprived of their basic needs and do not have the opportunity to enjoy the basic rights that are supposed to be ensured by the state under which they live. These children are involved in income-generating activities.[8] They argue that children undertaking all kinds of work that may be paid or unpaid should be described as "working children". They further opine that work activities which children engage in that are injurious and hazardous, and which may prevent education, damage health or subject the child to physical, sexual, or emotional abuse or exploitation could be considered as child labour.

---

[8] Reza et al, *Struggle for Survival.*

The International Labour Organization (ILO) emphasizes that child labour hinders children's development and is a violation of fundamental human rights. It makes a distinction between "child work" (or children in employment), child labour and hazardous work by children. According to the ILO standards, "working children" are those engaged in any economic activity for at least one hour during the reference period; work in both the formal and informal economies inside and outside family settings; work for pay or profit (in cash or in kind, part-time or full time), or serve as domestic workers outside their own household for an employer (with or without pay).[9]

In addition, children in child labour, according to the standards of the ILO involve not only children below the minimum age in employment, but those who "engage in work that deprives children of their childhood, their potential and their dignity, and that is harmful to physical and mental development."[10] Furthermore, "[in] its most extreme forms, child labour involves children being enslaved, separated from their families, exposed to serious hazards and illnesses and/or left to fend for themselves on the streets of large cities – often at a very early age."[11] Thus, the children, in such "worst forms of child labour", according to ILO standards, may also be those sold and/or forced into compulsory recruitment into "hazardous" work activities which are likely to harm the health, safety or morals of children such as armed conflict, child prostitution and pornography, and production and trafficking of drugs.[12] Finally, the ILO considers hazardous work as any activity or occupation that, by its nature or type has or leads to adverse effects on the child's safety, health and moral development. Thus, when considered broadly, hazardous work may include night work and long hours of work leading to an exposure of the "worker" to physical, psychological or sexual abuse; and work performed underground or underwater or under noise levels and vibrations that are damaging to the health of the worker. Hazardous work by children is often treated as a proxy for the worst forms of child labour.[13]

---

[9] ILO *Making Progress against Child Labour: Global Estimates and Trends 2000-2012*, (International Labour Office, International Programme on the Elimination of Child Labour (IPEC), Geneva: ILO, 2013).

[10] ILO, "What is child labour," (n.d.), https://www.ilo.org/ipec/facts/lang--en/index.htm. Accessed on September 13, 2018.

[11] Ibid.

[12] ILO, "International Labour Standards on Child Labour," (n.d.), https://www.ilo.org/global/standards/subjects-covered-by-international-labour-standards/child-labour/lang--en/index.htm. Accessed on September 13, 2018.

[13] Ibid; ILO, *Making Progress against Child Labour.*

From the above framework, this study defines "working children" as those involved in the activities which are injurious and hazardous to their life and are deprived of education and health services, and are often subjected to physical, mental and emotional exploitation. In other words, children who have been forced or who voluntarily involve themselves in stone quarrying for earning their own livelihood or helping their family have been described as "working children" in this study.

Working Children and Labour Market Activities in Ghana: the Socio-Cultural Context

In dominant western views, childhood has been categorized as a special and precarious phase of life when one needs protection and care if complete and responsible adulthood is to be achieved. This view conceptualizes child work as detrimental to children's education and unhealthy for their physical, cognitive and emotional development.[14] According to Manfred Liebel, this notion of childhood is widespread in the world today, though by no means universally accepted.[15] In Africa, children have always worked as part of their socialization process, often assuming adult roles.[16] The process of socialization often took place within the extended family, underpinned by the notion that a child belonged to the entire community and not just the nuclear family. As such, the daily lives of children tended to be intertwined with the family collective, where they maintained reciprocal care and support from family members.[17]

In many non-Western (non-Euro-American) countries, especially African ones, including Ghana, children make significant monetary and other contributions to their families' sustenance through their participation in la-

---

[14] H. Cunningham, "Children's Changing Lives from 1800 to 2000," in J. Maybin and M. Woodhead (eds.), *Childhood in Context*, (The Open University/Wiley, Chichester, 2003).
[15] M. Liebel, *A Will of their Own: Cross-Cultural Perspectives on Working Children*, (London: ZED Books, 2004).
[16] G.K. Nukunya, *Kinship and Marriage among the Anlo Ewe*, (New York: Humanities Press Inc., 1969); O. Agbu, "Children and Youth in the Labour Process in Africa", Paper prepared for the Child and Youth Studies Institute on Children and the Youth in the Labour Process, CODESRIA: Dakar, 4-29 October, 2004,; I. Mahama, *History and Traditions of Dagbon*, (Tamale, Ghana: GILLBT Printing Press, 2004); J. Feigben, "Child Labour and Children's Education in Northern Region of Ghana: Case Study of Bunkpurugu-Yunyoo and East Mamprusi District," (Master Thesis, School of Graduate Studies, Kwame Nkrumah University of Science and Technology (KNUST), 2010).
[17] T. Abebe and S. Bussel, "Dominant Discourses, Debates and Silences on Child Labour in Africa and Asia," *Third World Quarterly* 32 (4), (2011): 765-786.

bour market activities.[18] A survey conducted by the Ghana Statistical Service (GSS) found that about 57% of children were engaged in agriculture, forestry and fishing; 21% worked as hawkers and street vendors, with the rest in other sectors of the economy.[19] In spite of cultural diversity in Ghanaian societies, a common strand is that children are initiated into a form of occupation and self-recognized role-plays in order to become responsible members of the community.[20] It was therefore considered normal for a child to play any role that its mental and physical abilities could support. According to Jamon Feigben, a child was considered lazy or having poor upbringing if he or she could not perform basic household chores like fetching water, washing dishes, and sweeping.[21] Among the Anlo Ewe and indeed other ethnic groups in Ghana, children from about ten years of age participated in economic activities by helping their parents, especially on the farm.[22] Child-work served as a platform where children, especially boys, were taught to pursue economic activities which gave them some form of income and greatly alleviated their dependence on their parents. According to Afrifa, cited in Akosua Adomako Ampofo et al., traditionally, since child upbringing was a communal effort, this "insulated children, youth, and even adults from poverty, hunger, malnutrition, waywardness and some of the emotional and psychological problems that afflicted the individualized and alienated societies of the industrialized world."[23] The gradual disappearance of this cohesion and support, Afrifa argues, is as a result of economic necessity that makes it impossible for parents to give children the care they need. This lack of support can make children vulnerable and enter the labour market to support themselves and their families.[24]

---

[18] Bhalotra and Heady, "Child Farm Labour: The Wealth Paradox"; Basu and Van, "The Economics of Child Labor"; ; R. Khanam and R. Russel, "Child Work and Other Determinants of School Attendance and School Attainment in Bangladesh," *MPRA Paper* 9397, (2005); G. Zdunnek, et al., "Child Labour and Children's Economic Activities in Agriculture in Ghana," *SLE Publication Series* S2333, Centre for Advanced Training in Rural Development, (2008).

[19] Ghana Statistical Service, *Ghana Child Labour Survey*, (Accra: Ghana Statistical Service, 2003),

[20] Feigben, "Child Labour and Children's Education in Northern Region of Ghana".

[21] Ibid.

[22] Nukunya, *Kinship and Marriage among the Anlo Ewe.*

[23] A. Adomako Ampofo, O. Alhassan, F. Ankrah, D. Atobrah, and M. Dortey, *Examining the Sexual Exploitation of Children on the Streets of Accra,* (Accra: UNICEF, 2007), 5.

[24] Ibid.

Theoretical Framework: Sustainable Livelihoods Framework
and Quarrying

The Sustainable Livelihoods Approach (SLA) centres on both people and their livelihood; it prioritizes both the tangible and intangible assets that people utilize to achieve their desires. The approach also considers the vulnerable environment which the poor operate in and their ability to withstand shocks and stresses, amidst external forces such as policies that affect the accessibility of the assets upon which people depend.[25] Livelihood, according to Robert Chambers and Gordon R. Conway, comprises capabilities, assets and activities required as a means of living. It is considered sustainable when it can cope with and recover from stress and shocks, maintain and enhance its capabilities and assets, and provide sustainable livelihood opportunities for the next generation.[26] Kristin Helmore and Naresh C. Singh identify sustainable livelihood as one that maintains the ecological integrity of the environment.[27] This approach is founded on the belief that people require a range of assets to achieve positive livelihood outcomes. No single category of assets on its own is sufficient to yield varied livelihood outcomes that people seek; rather, they are utilized synergistically to pursue the different livelihood opportunities which people aspire to have. The relevance of the Sustainable Livelihood Approach lies in the fact that it is people-centred. It seeks to gain an accurate and realistic understanding of people's strengths and how they endeavour to convert these into positive livelihood outcomes. The approach does not perceive the poor to be in "lack of" but it recognizes the inherent potential in individual households and communities, which is used to build positive livelihood outcomes.[28] This approach is relevant to stone quarrying as it aids in the understanding of how urban working children meet their needs using minimal financial input, simple technology and indigenous resources amidst a competitive formal market and restrictive government policy. Indeed, working children use different assets that they have in order to achieve their livelihood outcomes.

---

[25] GLOPP, "DFID's Sustainable Livelihoods Approach and its Framework," (2008), http://www.glopp.ch/B7/en/multimedia/B7_1_pdf2.pdf. Accessed on September 14, 2018.

[26] R. Chambers and G.R. Conway, "Sustainable Rural Livelihoods: Practical Concepts for the 21st Century," *IDS Discussion Paper 296*, Institute of Development Studies, Brighton, (1992).

[27] K. Helmore and N.C. Singh, *Sustainable Livelihoods: Building on the Wealth of the Poor*, (Connecticut: Kumarian Press, 2001).

[28]Ibid.

The Sustainable Livelihoods Framework (SLF), developed by the British Department for International Development (DFID),[29] forms the core of the Sustainable Livelihoods Approach and serves as an instrument for the investigation of financially poor people's livelihoods. The framework is divided into five key components, namely Vulnerability Context, Livelihood Assets, Transforming Structures and Processes (policy, institutions, and processes), Livelihood Strategies and Livelihood Outcomes. The vulnerability context in the framework is viewed as an external environment in which people exist.[30] In relation to quarrying, the vulnerability context encompasses shocks such as accidents, diseases, and death occasioned by the activity. It also includes price fluctuations, loss of stone products and loss of money during business transactions. Seasonality and trends in the framework can also be related to stress, which are predictable events that affect livelihood outcomes attained from a livelihood strategy. Seasonality in relation to stone quarrying can be related to the weather changes that affect productivity at the quarry especially during the rainy season. Seasonality can also be related to price fluctuations that are mainly determined by the demand for stone products. All these may have either temporary or permanent effects on the income flow of an average or poor income household.

The vulnerability context also acknowledges how people cope with stress and shocks associated with their livelihood activity. As for coping strategies, the stone workers would diversify their livelihood portfolios or lean on other family members to survive. Common in informal activities such as stone quarrying is the reliance on social networks such as family and friends for material and immaterial support. Assets, according to the framework, are presented in the asset pentagon, which shows the different assets people use to realize their livelihood outcomes. Frank Ellis defines assets as natural capital (such as land, water and forests), human capital (including skills, knowledge, physical capability and ability of labour), physical capital (infrastructure such as roads), and social capital (such as safety networks, social claims and social relations).[31] The use of these assets and appropriate strategies would yield livelihood outcomes. Assets in relation to stone quarrying are the availability of land, simple tools and equipment, skills and labour that working children offer at the quarry site. This

---

[29] ATHA, Harvard Humanitarian Initiative, "Sustainable Livelihoods Framework," (n.d.), http://atha.se/content/sustainable-livelihoods-framework. Accessed on September 14, 2018.

[30] DFID, *Sustainable Livelihoods Guidance Sheets* 1-4, (London: Department of International Development, 1999),

[31] F. Ellis, *Rural Livelihoods and Diversity in Developing Countries*, (Oxford: Oxford University Press, 2000).

framework largely guides the organization of this current research in the stone quarrying spaces of Daglama.

Research Design and Methodology

This study adopted the qualitative approach. Data for the study was obtained through in-depth interviews with working children and their parents/guardians. The aim of conducting in-depth interviews was to explore the views of informants about decision making that was related to their participation in quarry work, the causal factors for child participation in quarry work and the effects that such factors have on their personal development. The analytical point of departure from previous studies is the availability of data obtained from previous studies on children, thereby giving voice to children whose views on their financial contributions to their family's survival strategies have been largely unreported. Purposive sampling was adopted to select 30 children who were between the ages of 8 and 15. This comprised 18 males and 12 females working at the quarry. Twenty (20) parents/guardians, comprising 8 males and 12 females were also interviewed. The reason for this distribution was that women were more than the men at the quarry site. Permission was sought from parents and guardians at the quarry site before interacting with the children. The interviews were conducted in Ewe, which is the dominant language of the area, and transcribed, translated and analyzed thematically.

Study Site

This study was conducted at Daglama, a stone quarry site in the Ho Municipality of the Volta Region. Daglama is an area in Sokode Lokoe where quarry activities take place. This area is within the permanent campus of the University of Health and Allied Sciences (UHAS). The area is rich in stones, which attracts people from Sokode Lokoe, Ho and Adaklu Kodzobi. On a daily basis, one can count more than 20 tipper trucks, loading stones from the location to construction sites in and around Ho. Daglama is not an inhabited place. But owing to the establishment of UHAS, people are now focusing their attention on developing their plots of land within the area. The area is also fertile for agricultural productivity and has rich vegetation for animal husbandry. For this reason, Fulani herdsmen graze their cattle on some sections of the land. The area is gradually being opened up to different architectural structures as a result of the presence of the university. Furthermore, internal road constructions are underway within the university community, while the dual carriage linking Sokode Etoe to Ho Regional Airport is also under construction. The establishment of new road networks has further intensified quarry work in the area, as there is easy access to the quarry site either through Adaklu Kodzobi or through Voradep Village, a suburb of Ho.

Findings

The literature on children's participation in economic activities is polarized along two schools of thoughts; one focusing on the economic conditions facing the household, and the other on non-economic factors. These two theoretical perspectives, while useful in explaining the factors contributing to children's participation in the labour market activities, portray children as inactive agents and who cannot make rational decisions concerning improvement in their living standards, and as such, are compelled by their parents to participate in economic activities. In contrast to the two perspectives, the study found out that economic and non-economic factors are interrelated, and significantly contribute to children's participation in labour market activities, although economic factors are dominant. Beyond this, it also found out that children's involvement in economic activities both voluntary and involuntary, and finally, their participation in labour market activities affect their personal development in terms of health and education. The next session focuses on the socio-demographic features of the informants. This is important as it gives an overview of the characteristics of people involved in the study.

Socio-demographic Background of Working Children

The socio-demographic background of children in Daglama shows that the average age of working children is 12. This, for example, is interestingly consistent with some studies on child labour carried out elsewhere in Africa such as that of Dimeji Togunde and Arielle Carter on Nigeria.[32] The ILO classifies children's engagement in quarrying as a Worst Form of Child Labour (WFCL), in the light of its potential to negatively affect a child's overall development. This study, however, found that even at the age of 9 years, some children were already engaged in quarry work. Data collected from the field indicated that the majority (85%) of working children were found to live with both parents, while 15% live with only a mother and relatives, whereas none stayed on their own. This finding is in contrast with findings made by Marten van den Berge[33] who argued that the majority of the children working in quarries in Peru belonged to either one-parent households or to families in which the father had migrated.

---

[32] Togunde and Carter, "In their own Words: Consequences of Child Labour in Urban Nigeria".
[33] M. van den Berge, *Rural Child Labour in Peru: A Comparison of Child Labour in Traditional and Commercial Agriculture*, (Amsterdam: IREWOC, 2009).

Table 2.1. Distribution of Daglama Working Children by Sex, Age, and Education.

Sex	Male	Female	Total
Frequency	20	10	30
Percent	**67.0**	**33.0**	**100.0**
Age	**Male**	**Female**	**Total**
8 – 10	3	1	4
11 – 13	7	4	11
12 – 15	10	5	15
Grand Total	20	10	30
Percentage (%)	**67.0**	**33.0**	**100.0**
Education	**Male**	**Female**	**Total**
Primary 1 – 3	3	1	4
Primary 4 – 6	6	3	9
Junior High School (JHS) 1 – 3	11	6	17
Dropped out	-	-	-
Grand Total	20	10	30
Percent (%)	**67.0**	**33.0**	**100.0**

Source: Authors' field work, November 2016 to March 2017

Socio-demographic Features of Parents/Guardians of Working Children

The findings on the socio-demographic background of parents/guardians of Daglama working children indicated that formal education, which is an important tool for human capacity development, was low among parents and guardians of the informants. Noteworthy, this is similar to the findings of some studies on Africa, such as those of Togunde[34] and Edith Osiruemu,[35] which have been reported in the literature. Although the majority of parents/guardians were quarry workers, some of the interviewed children mentioned that their parents

---

[34] Dimeji Togunde and Arielle Carter, "Socioeconomic causes of child labor in urban Nigeria," *Journal of Children and Poverty* 12(1), (2006): 73-89.
[35] E. Osiruemu, "Poverty of Parents and Child Labour in Benin City, Nigeria: A Preliminary Account of its Nature and Implications," *AERC Research Paper 156,* (2007).

were seamstresses, tailors, petty traders, farmers, security men and drivers. According to some of the parents and guardians, their main occupations had suffered some economic setbacks and so, they had to resort to quarrying since the return was fast. For instance, one seamstress argued that there had been an increase in the number of seamstresses in her community. For this reason, she rarely got customers and this had affected her family income. But since quarry products were in high demand in the municipality, she resorted to quarrying to support her family income. In several cases, one or both parents of informants were unemployed. This finding is consistent with views expressed about other similar studies that the socio-economic status of poor parents who subsist at the periphery of the urban economy made children susceptible to participation in labour market activities. [36]

Table 2.2. Age and education distribution of parents/guardians.

Age	Male	Female	Total
20 – 29	2	3	5
30 – 39	4	5	9
40 – 49	2	3	5
50 – 59	-	1	1
60 and above	-	-	-
Grand Total	8	12	20
Percentage	**40.0**	**60.0**	**100.0**
Education	**Male**	**Female**	**Total**
Primary	1	2	3
JHS	4	3	7
Secondary	2	2	4
Never been to school	1	5	6
Grand Total	8	12	20
Percentage (%)	**40.0**	**60.0**	**100.0**

Source: Authors' field work, November 2016 to March 2017

---

[36] See, for example; Osiruemu, "Poverty of Parents and Child Labour in Benin City, Nigeria: A Preliminary Account of its Nature and Implications".

Organization of Daglama Quarry and Activities Performed by Children

It is important to examine the peri-urban nature of Ho in order to understand the reasons why stone quarry emerged in Daglama. In spite of the fact that Ho is the regional capital of the Volta Region, it is characterized by a high level of unemployment. There are many unemployed Junior High School graduates who have not been able to continue with their education to the Senior High School level. There are also many Senior High School graduates who are unemployed. In addition, there are people who have not been to school before and are unemployed. Besides, the peri-urban nature of Ho has attracted many youth from the nearby Republic of Togo to migrate to Ho in search of jobs, thereby intensifying the already existing problem of unemployment. From the Ghana Statistical Service (GSS) findings about the marital status and economic activity of residents of age 12 years and older in the Ho Municipality, this study found that 32.3% of males who had never married were employed; 5.5% were unemployed and 62.2% were economically inactive. Regarding the female population of age 15 years and older, 26.1% who were unmarried were employed, 4.2% were unemployed and 69.8% were economically inactive. The GSS report also showed that these people were workers in the informal sector. In relation to dependency ratio in the Municipality, the GSS further pointed out that the dependency ratio for the Ho Municipality was about 59% (child and old age) for every 100 people working. Making reference to migration, the GSS averred that the migrant population in the Municipality was 74,677 of which 54,677 were born elsewhere in the Volta Region whilst 4,953 were born outside the shores of Ghana.[37]

In the light of the issues presented above, several people facing economic hardships exploit natural resources (agricultural lands, forests, streams, etc) found within the municipality. Before Daglama, stone quarrying originally took place in the Hofedo Electoral Area in an area called Kpedome. Following the increase in the population of the area, however, landowners developed their plots by putting up new structures. This situation forced workers to look for an alternative place for their livelihood, leading to the emergence of quarry work at Daglama. It is interesting to note that in spite of the several hazards involved in quarrying, it is uncommon to find numerous adults and children working at the quarry, since quarries provide regular, instant, and sustainable sources of income vis-à-vis other economic activities in the town.

---

[37] Ghana Statistical Service, *Population and Housing Census 2010: District Analytical Report, Ho Municipality* Accra: Ghana Statistical Service.

Several visits to the quarry site and interviews with quarry workers revealed that the land they were working on originally belonged to individual families in Sokode Lokoe until the government took it for the establishment of the University of Health and Allied Sciences in Ho. But informants argued that because the government was yet to compensate the landowners, the workers had capitalized on that to quarry the land. Some family members of the land-owners were actually involved in the quarrying enterprise. From the field, it was observed that workers were not formally organized as a group, and there were no leaders as such. In fact, there were no rules and regulations governing their operations, but that did not imply that they lived in a state of lawless-ness. A significant observation was that nobody interfered in another person's area of operation. Everybody was independent and chose a particular place to quarry. Quarry activity in Daglama was found to be a family business involv-ing parents/guardians, children, grandparents and grandchildren. The study revealed that activities performed by children were similar to those per-formed by adult workers, even though some physically demanding activities, like the cracking of big stones, were reserved for the adults. Children were involved in carrying stones in head pans/bowls and gathering them into a pile; they were also involved in breaking the stones into small chippings with hammers and were also asked to run certain errands. The next session dis-cusses the role working children play in decision-making relating to their participation in quarry activities in Daglama.

Decision-making Relating to Children's Participation in Quarry Work in Daglama

Scholars such as David Archard[38] and Kwabena Anane Kwarteng[39] are of the view that adults mostly make decisions in the family owing to the unequal power relations existing between adults and children. The above view sug-gests that the ability of children to take decisions relating to their welfare is limited and constrained by the authority and power from the adults. Although the study found that the decisions relating to a child's quarry work in Dagla-ma were sometimes made by parents/guardians, it was often informed by low family incomes. In such cases, parents/guardians negotiated work decisions with their children, instead of compelling them. Evidence from the field sug-gests that some children decided on their own to work at the quarry to sup-

[38] D. Archard, *Children: Rights and Children*, (London: Routledge,1993).
[39] A.K. Kwarteng, "Duties and Responsibilities of Children in Ghana: Perspectives of Children and Adults in Kumasi", (MPhil. Thesis, Norwegian University of Science and Technology (NTNU), 2012).

port their parents to increase the family income. While a study conducted by Prince Ofei Darko[40] has argued that children who worked at the Pokuase quarry in Ghana totally controlled monies they earned, and used it to buy specific items they deemed fit, children at Daglama, on the other hand, as this study found, did not control their money. Both children and parents worked as a team to generate family income. They chose to work owing to the socio-economic context in which they found themselves and the need to support their parents to earn some family income to promote their livelihood. Although work at the quarry posed some challenges to the personal development of these children, it still looked attractive to them to engage in it. Some of the responses derived from interviews with informants on decision-making relating to their participation in quarry work are as follows:

> My parents did not force me to engage in the quarry business. I realized that my parents needed help at the site and that was why I supported them. I do all kinds of work at the quarry including digging, cracking, piling and heaping of stones. When my parents sell the stones, they give me money and also use it for the upkeep of the home" (Veronica: 14-year-old JHS 1 female worker).

> My father is a carpenter and my mother is a trader. I have realized that though they are doing their best for me, the money is not enough. For this reason, I have been following my auntie to this place to assist her to make some money so that I can also buy some things on my own rather than asking my parents all the time. I came here voluntarily especially during weekends when I don't go to school" (Mawuko: a 15-year-old JHS 3 male worker).

From the above statements, it was observed that children were aware of their family's economic situation, and the potential consequences it would have on their welfare. For this reason, children resort to working to support their family incomes and their own welfare. It was also observed that the children were not compelled to work in the quarry but it was rather voluntary. These children exhibited agency in their ability to identify their family's economic challenges and how to support the family to surmount this challenge. This was evident in the work they did in terms of digging or removing stones, cracking

---

[40] P.O. Darko, "Our Daily Bread Comes from Rocks: The Livelihood Struggles of Children at a Quarry in Pokuase, Ghana," *Contemporary Journal of African Studies* 2, (1), (2014): 97-120.

or breaking stones and collection of stones. It was also observed that these children normally went to the site after school and not during school hours. This showed that they are aware of the importance of education in their personal development. The next section interrogates the factors responsible for children's participation in stone quarrying in Daglama.

Factors Responsible for Children's Participation in Quarry Work in Daglama

The findings from the field revealed varied reasons for children's participation in quarrying. The majority of working children and parents/guardians mentioned economic reasons as the main cause of children's participation in quarry work. Parents/guardians indicated that because of economic hardship, they were forced to work in the quarry. Secondly, the returns in the quarry work were very fast and constant, depending on how fast one could produce a trip of stones. Anytime one got a trip, contractors went to buy, hence the need to work hard and make labour efficient by having their children around to support them. The economic reasons given by parents and children were consistent with findings made by scholars such as Sonia Bhalotra and Christopher Heady, Kaushik Basu and P.H. Van,[41] Niels-Hugo Blunch and Dorte Verner,[42] Eric Edmonds and Carrie Turk,[43] and Togunde and Carter[44] in other settings. For instance, these scholars argue that as family incomes fall below subsistence levels, families tend to rely on their children's income in order to survive. Some of the responses derived from the field interviews that reflect the position of these scholars are presented below:

> My parents do not have enough money like other people. This is because they are not gainfully employed. The only work they do is to crack stones here. This makes it difficult for them to take care of myself and my siblings. That is why we come here to work. (Mawunyo: 13-year-old primary 6 female worker)

---

[41] Bhalotra and Heady, "Child Farm Labour: The Wealth Paradox"; Basu and Van, "The Economics of Child Labor".

[42] N-H. Blunch and D. Verner, *Revisiting the Link between Poverty and Child Labour: The Ghanaian Experience*, (World Bank: Washington D.C., 2000),

[43] Edmonds and Turk, *Child Labour in Transition in Vietnam.*

[44] Togunde and Carter, "In their own Words: Consequences of Child Labour in urban Nigeria".

It is because of hardship that is why we are doing this work. Nobody wants to go through this struggle but it is because there is no other means. My children come to help me here every day to remove and crack stones so that I will be able to use the money to cater for them. (Benedicta: 29-year-old mother of a child worker)

Apart from the economic motives, the study further found that socio-cultural norms and values were important reasons mentioned particularly by parents/guardians for their children's involvement in quarry work. In their view, work was part of children's upbringing and served as an important avenue that prepared children for the challenges that they would encounter in the future. It was observed that several young children assisted their parents in any form in the quarry work. Some of them cracked stones into chippings, some collected stones, some piled up stones, and some even cooked for their parents. It is worth noting that because it is a full-time work, parents also normally do cook and eat in with the children in the bush before going home. Thus, the quarry has virtually become their second home.

Some of the parents were of the view that children who participated in the work that their parents did got the chance of being exposed to the life and world of work at an early stage; this, they believed prepared them better for their future. With this, they would be able to survive any difficulty in the future. In the view of Mr. Foli, a 39-year-old father of a child-worker, "work instills in a child the spirit of hard work. In my society, every child is supposed to emulate the father's occupation to enable it to do any kind of work itself in the future". According to Ms. Amanor, a 33-year-old mother of a working child, "laziness is not accepted in our society. For this reason, we train our children to develop the spirit of hard work so that they become responsible in the future".

Findings from the field also indicated that children worked at the quarry because of educational reasons. The basic educational reason was to pay school fees, feeding and teaching and learning materials. The responses from the majority of the working children revealed that they assisted their parents because their parents needed money to pay for their school fees, transportation fees, feeding and education materials such as a pen, bags and mathematical sets. Parents and guardians of working children also expressed similar views in relation to why their children supported them in the quarry business. Below are some responses from the children:

I work here to support my parents to get money so that they will be able to pay my school fees, buy books for me, give me money for transportation and feeding. If I don't support them, my education will suffer. (Enyonam: 14-year-old JHS 1 female worker)

I want to become a teacher in the future. So I help my mother to crack stones so that she will be able to pay my school fees, by books for me and also give me feeding fee. I don't want my mother to continue doing this work the whole of her life. (Gameli: 13-year-old primary 6 male worker)

Dzinyo, a 15-year-old class six male worker, stated that his father is unemployed. So he has to come around to help him daily after school. This was what he had to say: "I come here to help my father every day after school. This helps my father to get money to pay for my school fees. I want to be a government worker in the future". The section below concentrates on the effects of stone quarrying on the development of the working children.

The Effects of Children's Participation in Quarry Work on their Personal Development

The findings from the field revealed that children's participation in quarry work in Daglama had two major effects on the personal development of the children. These effects are health and education.

During a Focus Group Discussion with the working children, they outlined a number of health-related problems that they had been experiencing because of this daunting work. These included fever, malaria, body pains, headache, severe physical injuries on the body, among others. In the view of the children, these were occupational hazards, which affected them, but this did not discourage them from supporting their parents to work. Below are some of the views from the working-children:

I know that this work affects my health. Sometimes, I feel a lot of pains in my body – waist, back, legs, arms; I also experience headache and severe fever. I know that it is because of the hard work that I am doing. (Wisdom: 11-year-old primary 4 male worker)

The quarry work is difficult especially digging and breaking of the stones. I normally break the stones and more often, I end up breaking my fingers with the hammer. Sharp stones often cut other places of my body such as my legs, arm. This is because while cracking, pieces of stones do spread spontaneously. (Dziedzorm: 14-year-old JHS 2 female worker)

It is obvious from these statements that the working children in Daglama are exposed to a variety of health hazards. These affect their overall development in terms of physical and psychological outlook which has a correlation with their output in education. Let us now focus on the effects of children's participation in quarry work on the educational development of these children.

Aside from the health implication, children's participation in quarry work affects their education. Responses from the working children indicated that their participation in the quarry work has some effects on their academic output. This includes poor classroom results, poor examination results, being passive in class discussions, sleeping in class and sometimes absenteeism. Below are some responses from the working children:

> I attend school A in Ho. Sometimes when I go to school, I sleep a lot, especially Mondays. This is because of the hard work that I do on Saturdays and Sundays. This affects my studies on Mondays as I am unable to follow teaching in class. (Mawuli: 10-year-old primary six male worker)

> I know that the work that I do in the quarry affect my academic performance. But I cannot stop since that is where the money comes from. Sometimes I am unable to do my homework since I have to go and help my parents at the quarry. I have adopted a new way of doing my homework not which is doing it in school before going to the quarry site. (Kwame: 14-year-old JHS 1 male worker)

These responses from the working children show vividly that their participation in the quarry business is detrimental to their personal development in terms of health and education. Some other informants also argue that as a result of ill-health, they absent themselves from school, and this affects their academic performance. According to Elikplim, a 13-year-old male worker, "sometimes when I am sick, I don't go to school. I miss a lot of lessons that are taught that day and this makes me lag behind in class. This affects my performance in class." It is therefore obvious that child labour affects the personal development of the working-child.

Conclusion and Recommendations

Contrary to the dominant theoretical perspectives that children are dormant and inactive agents who cannot make rational decisions concerning their participation in labour market activities, it has been identified from this study that children in Africa participate in the labour market voluntarily and that is their personal decision. Secondly, the children are aware of the socio-economic conditions in which their families live and, as a way of helping salvage the problem, they participate in stone quarry activities to enhance their family's income and personal welfare. It is therefore argued that children are active agents in the labour market, who work not only because they are forced to do so, but because they feel responsible for meeting the multiplicity of their needs. The study also shows that economic, social, cultural and educational needs are factors that compel African children to engage in quarry work in the Daglama quarry site in Ghana. Some of the evident adverse effects that the quarry work has on the development of the working children in terms of their school-type educational development are poor academic performance, passiveness in class and absenteeism.

From this study, it is recommended that parents should take their children to hospitals for a regular check-up so that their health would be ensured. It is also recommended that parents and guardians should make sure that their children go to school every day before coming to the quarry site to assist them. This will enable the children to be regular in class and produce good academic results. In addition, it is recommended that parents should not allow their children to do very difficult quarry work like loading vehicles with stones. Finally, it is recommended that the Social Welfare Department should constantly tour the quarry area to make sure that children are in school during school hours.

Bibliography

Abebe, T., and S. Bussel. "Dominant Discourses, Debates and Silences on Child Labour in Africa and Asia." *Third World Quarterly* 32 (4), (2011): 765-786.

Adamassie, A. *Explaining the High Incidence of Child Labour in Sub-Saharan Africa*. UK: Blackwell Publishers, 2002.

Agbu, O. "Children and Youth in the Labour Process in Africa". Paper prepared for the Child and Youth Studies Institute on Children and the Youth in the Labour Process, CODESRIA, Dakar, 4-29 October, 2004.

Ampofo Adomako, A., O. Alhassan, F. Ankrah, D. Atobrah, and M. Dartey. *Examining the Sexual Exploitation of Children on the Streets of Accra*. Accra: UNICEF, 2007.

Archard, D. *Children: Rights and Children*. London, Routeledge, 1993.

ATHA. Harvard Humanitarian Initiative, "Sustainable Livelihoods Framework." http://atha.se/content/sustainable-livelihoods-framework.

Basu, K., and P. H. Van, "The Economics of Child Labor," *The American Economic Review* 88 (3), (1998): 412-27.

Basu, K. *Child Labour: Cause, Consequence, and Cure, with Remarks on International Labour Standards*. Washington, D.C: The World Bank, 1998.

Berge, M. V. D. *Rural Child Labour in Peru: A Comparison of Child Labour in Traditional and Commercial Agriculture*. Amsterdam: IREWOC, 2009.

Bhalotra, S., and C. Heady. "Child Farm Labour: The Wealth Paradox". *World Bank Economic Review* 17(2) (2003): 197-227.

Blunch, N. H., and D. Verner. *Revisiting the Link between Poverty and Child Labour: The Ghanaian Experience*. Washington D.C: The World Bank, 2000.

Chambers, R., and G. R. Conway. "Sustainable Rural Livelihoods: Practical Concepts for the 21st Century". *IDS Discussion Paper 296*. Brighton, UK: Institute of Development Studies, 1992.

Cunningham, H. "Children's Changing Lives from 1800 to 2000". In *Childhood in Context*, edited by J. Maybin, and M. Woodhead. Chichester: John Wiley/Open University Press, 2003.

Darko, O. P. "Our Daily Bread Comes from Rocks: The Livelihood Struggles of Children at a Quarry in Pokuase, Ghana." *Contemporary Journal of African Studies* 2 (1), (2014): 97-120.

De Groot, A. *Child Labour in Kathmandu, Nepal*. Amsterdam: IREWOC, 2010.

DFID. *Sustainable Livelihoods Guidance sheets* 1-4. Department of International Development: London, 1999.

Edmonds, E., and C. Turk. *Child Labour in Transition in Vietnam*. Washington, D.C.: World Bank, 2002.

Ellis, F. *Rural Livelihoods and Diversity in Developing Countries*. Oxford: Oxford University Press, 2000.

Feigben, J. "Child Labour and Children's Education in Northern Region of Ghana: Case Study of Bunkpurugu-Yunyoo and East Mamprusi District." Graduate Thesis. University of Science and Technology, KNUST, Ghana, 2010.

G. Zdunnek et al "Child Labour and Children's Economic Activities in Agriculture in Ghana." *SLE Publication Series*-S2333. Centre for Advanced Training in Rural Development, 2008.

Ghana Statistical Service. *Ghana Child Labour Survey*. Accra: Ghana Statistical Service, 2003.

Ghana Statistical Service. *Population and Housing Census 2010: District Analytical Report, Ho Municipality*. Accra: GSS, 2010.

GLOPP. "DFID's Sustainable Livelihoods Approach and its Framework." http://www.glopp.ch/B7/en/multimedia/B7_1_pdf2.pdf.

Grier, B. "Child Labour and Africanist Scholarship: A Critical Overview," *African Studies Review* 47(2), (2004): 1-25.

Helmore, K., and N Singh. *Sustainable Livelihoods: Building on the Wealth of the Poor*. Connecticut, USA: Kumarian Press, 2001.

ILO. "International Labour Standards on Child Labour." https://www.ilo.org/global/standards/subjects-covered-by-international-labour-standards/child-labour/lang--en/index.htm.

ILO. "What is child labour." https://www.ilo.org/ipec/facts/lang--en/index.htm.

ILO. *Making Progress against Child Labour: Global Estimates and Trends 2000-2012*. Geneva: ILO International Programme on the Elimination of Child Labour (IPEC). 2012.

James, A. and A. Prout. *Constructing and Reconstructing Childhood: Contemporary Issues in Sociological Study of Childhood*. 2nd ed. London: Falmer Press, 1997.

Khanam, R. and R. Russel. "Child Work and Other Determinants of School Attendance and School Attainment in Bangladesh." *MPRA Paper* 9397, 2005.

Kwarteng, A. K. "Duties and Responsibilities of Children in Ghana: Perspectives of Children and Adults in Kumasi." M.Phil. Thesis. Norwegian University of Science and Technology, 2012.

Liebel, M. *A Will of their Own: Cross-Cultural Perspectives on Working Children*. London: Zeb books, 2004.

Mahama, I. *History and Traditions of Dagbon*. Ghana: GILLBT Printing Press, 2004.

Mwebaze, T. "Extent and Determinant of Child Labour in Uganda." *AERC Research Paper* 167, 2007.

Nukunya, G. K. *Kinship and Marriage among the Anlo Ewe*. New York: Humanities Press Inc, 1969.

Nurye, A. A. "My Shop is my School: Children's Perspectives on Work and School in a Multi-Ethnic town in Southern Ethiopia." 16th International Conference of Ethiopian Studies, Trondheim, Norway, 2007.

Okukpara, B.C. and N. Odurukwe. "Incidence and Determinants of Child Labour in Nigeria: Implications for Poverty." *AERC Research Paper* 156, 2006.

Osiruemu, E. "Poverty of Parents and Child Labour in Benin City, Nigeria: A Preliminary Account of its Nature and Implications." *AERC Research Paper* 156, 2007.

Ray, R. "Analysis of Child Labour in Peru and Pakistan: A Comparative Study." *Journal of Social Science* 16(2) (2000): 173-181.

Reza, H., T. Kumar Das, and F. Ahmmed. *Struggle for Survival: A Study on the Needs and Problems of the Street and Working Children in Sylhet City*. Bangladesh: Department of Social Work, Shahjalal University of Science and Technology (SUST), 2005.

Togunde, D. and A. Carter, "In their own Words: Consequences of Child Labour in Urban Nigeria." *Journal of Social Science* 16(2) (2008), 173-181.

Togunde, D., and A. Carter. "Socioeconomic causes of child labor in urban Nigeria." *Journal of Children and Poverty* 12(1), (2006): 73-89.

Togunde, D. "Child labor and educational outcomes in urban Nigeria." Conference Paper at 6th Annual Conference of the Institute for the African Child. Ohio University, Athens, Ohio, 2005.

Chapter 3

Childhood in Africa: Health and Wellness in Body, Mind, Soul, and Spirit

Waganesh A. Zeleke, Tammy Hughes and Natalie Drozda

"Health is a state of complete physical, mental and social well-being
and not merely the absence of disease or infirmity."

World Health Organization (WHO)

Introduction

*On a bright morning, six-year-old Selam is seated on a big rock in front of her
house, a building made of mud walls and a straw roof, in a remote village in
Ethiopia. There is no formal school in her village, nor a playground in her neighbourhood. Next to Selam, her mother mixes leaves and herbs to make a home
remedy for Hana, the seventh of 10 children in the home, who has a serious ear
infection. Also missing from the village is a health centre to go for medical attention. The two youngest children, three-year-old Abel and two-year-old Melaku are
fighting and crying, which is irritating Selam. Although it is already 10:00 in the
morning, breakfast is not yet ready. Nine-year-old Lemelem, the oldest, is cleaning
the house and feeling rushed to cook a brunch for the family. Selam's father and
her two older brothers are on the field working on their farm where they spend
most days in the wheat field returning home as the sun sets.*

The previous scene portrays a familiar representation of the children in Africa. Like most literature and media accounts, the story relies heavily on what
is missing (e.g., Western concepts of schooling, medicine, and family roles); it
gives enough information for the reader to infer distress and perpetuates the
misconception of African culture as fundamentally disadvantaged. The story,
however, actually says little about the child's sense of belonging, family care
and the security in relationships with parents or siblings, or feelings of happiness and satisfaction. This mischaracterization is widely accepted as a fundamental truth of African families and African culture. Even scholarly works

primarily focus on childhood victimization and exploitation and social injustice.[1] Africa is often compared to a Western standard, singularly understood by deficiency, and its descriptions are without reference to personal, spiritual or creative community richness. Reporting on the environmental conditions that children in Africa experience may be an important step in understanding the African context and subsequent child development. However, a unilateral image of the lives of African children is perpetuated when the strengths of the child's family and community that allow generation after generation to survive and overcome documented hardships are not considered. In contrast, Western culture considers influences on the development of children, and there is a commitment to exploring complexity, such as where biopsychosocial influences converge and are examined in interactive ecological systems.[2]

In this chapter, we aim to broaden the conceptualization of Africa's children and their childhood experiences by elaborating on the building blocks of healthy child development and resilience, including how those experiences are discernible in Africa. Specifically, in this chapter we: (a) review the status of child health and wellness in Africa, (b) describe a theory of health and holistic wellness applicable to the African context, (c) re-conceptualize African childhood based on a holistic wellness theory, (d) present points of resiliency and protective factors, and (e) discuss implications for future research, practitioners, and policy-makers. We propose a move away from simplistic conceptualizations to a richer engagement with contexts that support African child development. This effort is consistent with the call of Tatek Abebe and Yaw Ofosu-Kusi for "knowledge that moves away from the 'deficit' models of childhood, intersected and dissected by economic and social class, geography, agency, gender and capacity of children".[3] Knowledge of this kind, they claim, "is either hidden, invisible, unacknowledged or simply non-existent".[4]

---

[1] Oludele Akinloye Akinboade and Segun Adeyemi Adeyefa, "An Analysis of Variance of Food Security by its Main Determinants Among the Urban Poor in the city of Tshwane, South Africa," *Social Indicators Research: An International and Interdisciplinary Journal for Quality-of-Life Measurement* 137(1), (2018): 61-82; Colin Pritchard and Steven Keen, "Child Mortality and Poverty in Three World Regions (the West, Asia and Sub-Saharan Africa) 1988-2010: Evidence of Relative Intra-regional Neglect?," *Scandinavian Journal of Public Health* 44 (8) (2016): 734-741; Lucie Cluver and Mark Orkin, "Cumulative Risk and AIDS-orphanhood: Interactions of Stigma, Bullying and Poverty on Child Mental Health in South Africa," *Social Science & Medicine* 69(8), (2009): 1186-1193.

[2] Urie Bronfenbrenner, *Ecological Models of Human Development* (Oxford: Elsevier, 1994).

[3] Tatek Abebe and Yaw Ofosu-Kusi, "Beyond Pluralizing African Childhoods: Introduction," *Childhood* 23 (3), (2016): 305.

[4] Abebe and Ofosu-Kusi, "Beyond Pluralizing African Childhoods: Introduction," 305.

Children and Childhood in Africa in Review

The recognition of the importance of childhood as a stage in one's life course was officially established in the international context following two pivotal meetings: 1979 International Year of the Child and the United Nations' Convention of the Rights of the Child.[5] These events called for a range of academic disciplines (e.g., psychology, anthropology, history, sociology, social geography, among others) to come together to explore the importance of childhood experiences from a variety of, sometimes even conflicting, vantage points.

Overview of Childhood Research Areas

Table 3.1. Different disciplines and their contributions to the understandings of childhood.

Discipline	Explanations for Child Development
Developmental Psychology	How children develop certain competencies (e.g., language, social interactions, emotional control).
Sociology	Children as social actors (they make their own choices which influence who they become as adults). The role of childhood in the family and social context (e.g., part of the workforce in times of need).
Social Anthropology	Exploring socially constructed definitions of childhood across time and place (e.g., age of child marriages).
Human Geography	Geographies of childhood and "children's geographies."

Credit: Authors

Discussions about children and childhood in different parts of the world are strongly influenced by the areas of study from which research is conducted. Specifically, developmental, political and economical, social and cultural, and human rights evaluations of policies and resources are often detailed. While useful as a starting point, integrated perspectives where complexity and nuance are highlighted are only possible when the literature is well developed and synthesized.

---

[5] United Nations Treaty Collection, *Convention on the Rights of the Child,* (1990), https://treaties.un.org/Pages/ViewDetails.aspx?src=TREATY&mtdsg_no=IV-11&chapter=4&lang=en. Accessed on October 2, 2018.

The processes that move children into adulthood in Africa have been documented through anthropological and sociological research. The dominant discourse surrounding childhood in Africa is characterized by limitations and insufficiency. In much of the available literature, childhood in Africa is understood through reports of poverty and inadequate access to education. There is a tendency to skew the description of children toward low levels of well-being.[6] The research is oversaturated with descriptions of poverty;[7] malaria, Ebola, HIV/AIDS;[8] trauma and violence;[9] food insecurity;[10] poor education;[11] child

---

[6] Keetie Roelen, Emily Delap, Camilla Jones and Helen Karki Chettri, "Improving Child Wellbeing and Care in Sub-Saharan Africa: The Role of Social Protection," *Children and Youth Services Review* 73, (2017): 309-318.

[7] See, for example, Akinboade and Adeyefa, "An Analysis of Variance of Food Security by its Main Determinants Among the Urban Poor in the city of Tshwane, South Africa"; Pritchard and Keen, "Child Mortality and Poverty in Three World Regions (the West, Asia and Sub-Saharan Africa) 1988-2010: Evidence of Relative Intra-regional Neglect?"; Cluver and Orkin, "Cumulative Risk and AIDS-orphanhood: Interactions of Stigma, Bullying and Poverty on Child Mental Health in South Africa".

[8] Tamsen J. Rochat, Joanie Mitchell, Anina M. Lubbe, Alan Stein, Mark Tomlinson, and Ruth M. Bland, "Communication About HIV and Death: Maternal Reports of Primary School-aged Children's Questions After Maternal HIV Disclosure in Rural South Africa," *Social Science and Medicine* 172, (2017): 124-134; Nicola Ansell, "Once Upon a Time: Orphanhood, Childhood Studies and the Depoliticisation of Childhood Poverty in Southern Africa," *Childhood* 23(2), (2016): 162-177; Elona Toska, Lesley Gittings, Rebecca Hodes, Lucie D. Cluver, Kaymarlin Govender, K. Emma Chademana, and Vincent Evans Gutierrez, "Resourcing Resilience: Social Protection for HIV Prevention Amongst Children and Adolescents in Eastern and Southern Africa," *African Journal of AIDS Research* 15 (2), (2016): 123-140; Elise Denis-Ramirez, Katrine Holmegaard Sorensen, and Morten Skovdal, "In the Midst of a 'Perfect Storm': Unpacking the Causes and Consequences of Ebola-related Stigma for Children Orphaned by Ebola in Sierra Leone," *Children and Youth Services Review* 73, (2017): 445-453; Stella N. Anasi, "Access to and Dissemination of Health Information in Africa: The Patient and the Public," *Journal of Hospital Librarianship* 12(2), (2012): 120-134.

[9] Frances Hills, Anna Meyer-Weitz and Kwaku Oppong Asante, "The Lived Experiences of Street Children in Durban, South Africa: Violence, Substance Use, and Resilience," *International Journal of Qualitative Studies on Health and Well-being* 11, (2016): 1-11; Ria Reis, "Children Enacting Idioms of Witchcraft and Spirit Possession as a Response to Trauma: Therapeutically Beneficial, and for Whom?," *Transcultural Psychiatry* 50(5), (2013): 622-643; Kalysha Closson, Janan Janine Dietrich, Busi Nkala, Addy Musuku, Zishan Cui, Jason Chia, Glenda Gray, et al., "Prevalence, Type, and Correlates of Trauma Exposure Among Adolescent Men and Women in Soweto, South Africa: Implications for HIV Prevention," *BMC Public Health* 16(1), (2016): 1-15.

[10] See Akinboade and Adeyefa, "An Analysis of Variance of Food Security by its Main Determinants Among the Urban Poor in the city of Tshwane, South Africa; Mary Bachman

soldiering;[12] death and genocide;[13] and, orphanhood and homelessness.[14] The cumulative effect is an unbalanced, overwhelmingly negative picture of child experiences in Africa, without a proportional number of studies building from African children's strengths. For example, there are many studies describing the experience of war and child soldiers in Africa, despite the fact that the numbers of children engaged in such violence are relatively small.

When it comes to children and childhood in Africa, children are primarily described in the context of their family, social or economic status, or the role they have in society, rather than a focus on the contributors to their suc-

---

DeSilva, Anne Skalicky, Jennifer Beard, Mandisa Cakwe, Tom Zhuwau, Tim Quinlan, and Jonathon Simon, "Early Impacts of Orphaning: Health, Nutrition, and Food Insecurity in a Cohort of School-going Adolescents in South Africa," *Vulnerable Children and Youth Studies* 7(1), (2012): 75-87; Rebecca Fielding-Miller, Kristin L. Dunkle, and Daniel Murdock, "Not Everyone can Afford an Apple a Day: Stigma and Food Insecurity in Rural South African Young Adults," *African Journal of AIDS Research* 14(4), (2015): 361-369.

[11] Mark Orkin, Mark E. Boyes, Lucie D. Cluver, and Yuning Zhang, "Pathways to Poor Educational Outcomes for HIV/AIDS-affected Youth in South Africa," *AIDS Care* 26(3), (2014): 343-450; Beatrice Ifeoma Ajufo, "Challenges of Youth Unemployment in Nigeria: Effective Career Guidance as a Panacea," *An International Multidisciplinary Journal, Ethiopia* 7(1), (2013): 307-321.

[12] Gracie Brownell and Regina T. Praetorius, "Experiences of Former Child Soldiers in Africa: A Qualitative Interpretive Meta-synthesis," *International Social Work* 60(2), (2017): 452-469; Miranda Worthen, Grace Onyango, Mike Wessells, Angela Veale, and Susan McKay, "Facilitating War-affected Young Mothers' Reintegration: Lessons from a Participatory Action Research Study in Liberia, Sierra Leone, and Uganda," *International Journal of Social Science Studies* 1(1), (2013): 145-149; Neil Boothby, "What Happens When Child Soldiers Grow Up? The Mozambique Case Study," *Intervention: International Journal of Mental Health, Psychosocial Work and Counseling in Areas of Armed Conflict* 4)3), (2006): 244-259.

[13] Pritchard and Keen, "Child Mortality and Poverty in Three World Regions (the West, Asia and Sub-Saharan Africa) 1988-2010: Evidence of Relative Intra-regional Neglect?"; Rumishael Shoo, "Reducing Child Mortality: The Challenges in Africa," (2007), https://unchronicle.un.org/article/reducing-child-mortality-challenges-africa.   Accessed on April 28, 2017; Habtamu Dugo and Joanne D. Eisen, "Famine, Genocide and Media Control in Ethiopia," *Journal of Pan African Studies* 9(10), (2016): 334-357.

[14] Hills, Meyer-Weitz and Asante, "The Lived Experiences of Street Children in Durban, South Africa: Violence, Substance Use, and Resilience"; DeSilva, Skalicky, Beard, Cakwe, Zhuwau, Quinlan and Simon, "Early Impacts of Orphaning: Health, Nutrition, and Food Insecurity in a Cohort of School-going Adolescents in South Africa"; Fielding-Miller, Dunkle and Murdock. "Not Everyone can Afford an Apple a Day: Stigma and Food Insecurity in Rural South African Young Adults"; Denis-Ramirez, Sorensen and Skovdal, "In the Midst of a Perfect Storm': Unpacking the Causes and Consequences of Ebola-related Stigma for Children Orphaned by Ebola in Sierra Leone".

cessful development or how the children themselves perceive a childhood lived in Africa. Although it is important to consider how children in Africa are viewed from a standard perspective – that is, from a similar set of empirical standards – in order to contribute to a universal theory regarding the essentials of promoting child development, there is also a need to understand how children view their lived experience. Furthermore, because much of the empirical data focus on measuring the type and quantity of deficits, there is scant documentation of resilience in African children. For example, notions of Western individualism and self-reliance are not always relevant or appropriate for understanding individuals who function within collectivist cultures. Resilience may look vastly different.

African children are often portrayed as passive victims, as there is a hyper focus in the media on the problems they face rather than "how children thrive despite these adversities".[15] The researchers liken this to "Afro-pessimism," or the focus on problems such as AIDS, drought, and starvation, which are major contenders in the life of many Africans. This is exceedingly problematic because "research and scholarship routinely focus on a uniform childhood defined by existential challenges that not only flatten children's varied experiences but also view childhood as a mere site of intervention".[16] Research regarding African children tends to overlook their inner subjective world and takes a more "outside in" than "inside out" approach in describing their experiences.[17] The second depiction of African children is "indigenizing," which romanticizes or exoticizes the children, universalizing their experiences as indigenous, so they are seen as separate from the modern world. This focus on the uniqueness of African childhood may serve to perpetuate the "otherness" often associated with growing up in Africa, rather than acknowledging the commonalities in children growing up in different parts of the world (having friends, sharing experiences, playing outside, etc.). Notably, the hyperfocus on orphanhood and AIDS serves to detract attention from the "structural roots of poverty"[18]

---

[15] Abebe and Ofosu-Kusi, "Beyond Pluralizing African Childhoods: Introduction," 304.
[16] Abebe and Ofosu-Kusi, "Beyond Pluralizing African Childhoods: Introduction".
[17] Ibid.
[18] Ansell, "Once Upon a Time: Orphanhood, Childhood Studies and the Depoliticisation of Childhood Poverty in Southern Africa," 162.

Furthermore, Nicola Ansell calls into question the very association between AIDS, orphanhood, and disadvantage, noting the contradictory associations[19] that result from the application of Western ideals regarding the necessity of a nuclear family, a value she sees as both problematic and irrelevant. Poignantly, Ansell also describes how the orphan is often used as a fairy-tale-like metaphor to simultaneously represent vulnerability and a hero overcoming all odds. This mischaracterization can be dangerous in that it dehumanizes the individual.

There are myriad ways of "othering" individuals in Africa.[20] Again, Western notions of what it means to be a child may not be appropriate markers of childhood in other areas of the world. Age may not be emphasized as much by people in other cultures. In Ethiopia a daughter's age may be estimated when she is ready to be married, tracking her exact age is of less importance.[21] This example shows how applying seemingly straightforward constructs is not always possible or recommendable.

The majority of African societies structure rituals and contemporary institutions around celebrating the lives of children. Across the continent, communities view children as representing generational continuity and success. Rituals are designed to ensure children's survival and prosperity. Africa's children are also regarded as critical to an individual family's survival. Children help to maintain household economies via labour provided in the home, familial agriculture or food-processing activities, or through accomplishments in trade or artisanship.

African standards on child health and wellness are more inclusive; Western conceptualizations may be one useful ideal, yet inadequate for describing African family experiences and priorities. That is, while it is true that African children will have less material items and formal educational opportunities than the average child in the US, there is a developmental path that allows children to thrive and circumvent these adversities. Differences in these developmental paths need to be acknowledged and validated. Working toward

---

[19] Ibid; DeSilva, Skalicky, Beard, Cakwe, Zhuwau, Quinlan, and Simon, "Early Impacts of Orphaning: Health, Nutrition, and Food Insecurity in a Cohort of School-going Adolescents in South Africa".

[20] Patricia Henderson, "South African AIDS Orphans: Examining Assumptions Around Vulnerability from the Perspective of Rural Children and Youth," *Childhood* 13(3), (2006): 303-327.

[21] Abebe and Ofosu-Kusi. "Beyond Pluralizing African Childhoods: Introduction"; P. N. Sorensen and S. Bekele, *Nice Children Don't Eat A Lot of Food: Strained Livelihoods and the Role of Aid in North Wollo, Ethiopia,*(Addis Ababa, Ethiopia: Forum for Social Studies, 2009).

promoting this more inclusive and holistic picture of childhood helps to dispel the concept of childhood development in Africa as stunted or nonexistent. Additionally, such an enterprise has the potential to reveal how differing experiences are important in the developmental process of children from different parts of the world.

Some researchers call for children to be "active participants rather than subjects of research,"[22] arguing that "if a society accepts children as equal human beings then the study of their quality of life should accept that other human beings cannot simply by virtue of age decide what children's well-being consists of, how it should be measured and analyzed".[23] Understanding the experiences of children needs to be a focal point of research, rather than relying so heavily on the environments they function within to give information about them. Including positive aspects of their lives and looking at their experiences will aid in conceptualizing their well-being as more nuanced, rather than simply discussing their survival.[24] In order to study children's well-being, several fundamental questions need to be considered.[25] These can be summarized as including:

- What do children think and feel?

- To whom or what are children connected and related?

- What do children contribute?

Much of the research available today showcases the fact that these questions are largely unanswered.[26] Furthermore, children in Africa seem to be particularly susceptible to being defined by the outside markers of their social contexts rather than their subjective, inner experience.

---

[22] Asher Ben-Arieh, "Where are the Children? Children's Role in Measuring and Monitoring Their Well-being," *Social Indicators Research: An International and Interdisciplinary Journal for Quality-of-Life Measurement* 74(3), (2005): 574.

[23] Ibid., 575.

[24] Ben-Arieh, "Where are the Children? Children's Role in Measuring and Monitoring Their Well-being."

[25] Ibid; Asher Ben-Arieh, Natalie Hevener Kaufman, Arlene Bowers Andrews, Robert M. George, Bong Joo Lee, and L. J. Aber, *Measuring and Monitoring Children's Well-being*, (Netherlands: Kluwer Academic Press, 2001).

[26] Ben-Arieh, "Where are the Children? Children's Role in Measuring and Monitoring Their Well-being".

Our purpose is not to minimize the hardships children in Africa's face, but rather to point out how the literature regarding children in Africa emphasizes tragedy and, in a way, romanticizes the vulnerable child in need. This emphasis is problematic not only because the hardships are only a piece of a child's life and do not define him or her, but also because it gives rise to Western saviour fantasies and actions. It is also important to note that we recognize that some of the studies cited above do attempt to provide a wider context for understanding children's resilience beyond that of Western ideals. Also, we argue that a closer examination continues to be warranted. We seek to uncover, and not suppress, children's subjective experience. We seek to call attention to the paucity of studies focusing on the strengths and resilience of children in Africa.

Some literature has given voice to positive African experiences, highlighting the role social protection programmes and income transfers play in increasing child well-being.[27] Of note, these authors do rely on the role of external aids (e.g., funding sources) rather than identifying the internal strengths, talents, and resources of children. Too few studies focus on child resiliency, although there are some that document cases of overcoming adversity. One case study following child soldiers from Mozambique found that the majority of the participants grew up to be trusted and productive members of society, even though past experiences still haunted them.[28] Miranda Worthen and colleagues found that young females who had experienced war programming were able to successfully reintegrate into society.[29]

There are some studies documenting children's experiences and concerns. For example, Tamsen J. Rochat and colleagues investigated what types of questions children in South Africa had after their mothers disclosed that they had HIV.[30] While researchers hypothesized that greater knowledge would foster child resilience, the mechanisms leading to resilience were not clarified. Results showed child questions centred on understanding the threats

---

[27] Keetie Roelen, Emily Delap, Camilla Jones, and Helen Karki Chettri, "Improving Child Wellbeing and Care in Sub-Saharan Africa: The Role of Social Protection," *Children and Youth Services Review* 73, (2017): 309-318.

[28] Neil Boothby, "What Happens When Child Soldiers Grow Up? The Mozambique Case Study," *Intervention: International Journal of Mental Health, Psychosocial Work and Counseling in Areas of Armed Conflict* 4(3), (2006): 244-259.

[29] Miranda Worthen, Grace Onyango, Mike Wessells, Angela Veale and Susan McKay, "Facilitating War-affected Young Mothers' Reintegration: Lessons from a Participatory Action Research Study in Liberia, Sierra Leone, and Uganda," 145-149.

[30] Rochat, Mitchell, Lubbe, Stein, Tomlinson and Bland, "Communication About HIV and Death: Maternal Reports of Primary School-aged Children's Questions After Maternal HIV Disclosure in Rural South Africa."

(e.g., illness and death) of the disease. In this study, mothers, and not children, were the source of data.

Although there are ethical considerations when researching sensitive topics involving children, we argue that a cautious approach balanced by a curiosity concerning the viewpoint of the child is required to move the literature base from a deficit model to a model that better accounts for the dynamic and (realistic) nuances that characterize the lived experiences of children growing up in this diverse region of the world.[31]

Theoretical Considerations: Theory of Health and Holistic Wellness

There are several health and wellness models described by a variety of theorists defining aspects of human experiences (for example mind, body, spirit, soul, context, society, etc.). Despite variations, one overarching principle is generally used to define and clarify the concept of health and wellness, and that is, holism or wholeness. In a seminal piece by Alfred Adler – a prominent psychologist who introduces the role of social interests in personal adjustment and re-adjustment – the concept of holism is defined as an individual's functioning as an integrated whole where feelings, beliefs, and actions represent a dynamic state of being.[32] This state of being includes physical, mental, emotional, social, and spiritual aspects of life.[33] In most individuals, these aspects are well-crafted, orderly, and in a harmonious flow. If one or more areas are lacking or insufficient, the person will not feel whole and will function in a sub-optimal and less integrated way. In order to understand an individual's health and wellness fully, it is necessary to perceive him or her through the lens of interconnected patterns of functioning. Wellness is a feeling of constant well-being, and a fine-tuning and balance between different aspects of being such as mind, body, soul, and spirit. Wellness refers to "a way of life oriented toward optimal health and well-being in which body, mind, and spirit are integrated by the individual to live life more fully within the human and natural community".[34] Alt-

---

[31] Abebe and Ofosu-Kusi, "Beyond Pluralizing African Childhoods: Introduction"; Hills, Meyer-Weitz and Asante, "The Lived Experiences of Street Children in Durban, South Africa: Violence, Substance Use, and Resilience".

[32] Alfred Adler, *Understanding Human Nature*, trans., W. B. Wolf, (New York: Greenberg, 1927).

[33] Kevin A. Fall, Janice Miner Holden, and Andre Marquis, *Theoretical Models of Counseling and Psychotherapy* Second Edition, (New York, NY: Routledge, 2010).

[34] Jane E. Myers, Thomas J. Sweeney, and J. Melvin Witmer, "The Wheel of Wellness Counseling for Wellness: A Holistic Model for Treatment Planning," *Journal of Counseling and Development* 78(3), (2000): 252.

hough the different aspects of being can be studied separately, they are better conceptualized in relation to each other, because the imbalance of one aspect is reflected through the blockage of energy at all other layers and can emerge as a disease or disorder. Hence, these aspects of being, and concepts related to health and wellness from a holistic approach have long been documented, but need to continue to inform best practices for health and developmental professionals. Modern definitions of holism assume that individual humans should be viewed as unified wholes that are more than the sum of their respective constituent elements.[35]

David Bohm, one of the prominent figures in the theory of wholeness, likens the term wholeness to integrity; he cautions that "man has sensed always that wholeness or integrity is an absolute necessity to make life worth living. Yet, over the ages, he has generally lived in fragmentation".[36] Integrity can be conceptualized as relating to one living genuinely, honestly, and ethically, while being authentically oneself. Wholeness is related to the integration of multiple parts into a whole and recognizing that everything is connected, rather than separate and fragmented; such notions are in line with Eastern traditions.[37] Bohm's important work, *Wholeness and the Implicate Order*, which argues "that fragmentation is the response of this whole to man's action, guided by illusory perception, which is shaped by fragmentary thought …",[38] outlines how functioning in the West, and subsequent traditions of separateness, has led to confusion, fragmentation, and problems. Wholeness, Bohm argues, "is what is real" therefore the human being must consider his or her fragmentary thought, be conscious of it, and consequently end it. In that case, the human "approach to reality …, and … the response will be whole."[39] Furthermore, subscribing to absolute truths leads to fragmentation and works against wholeness, or recognizing that everything is a part of the universe's flux and movement together.[40] He also emphasizes that theories about the nature of reality are just that, theories, and it is important to be mindful that they are not actually representative of reality itself, but rather fluid forms of insight. To this point, he added that what was needed was not

---

[35] David Bohm, *Wholeness and the Implicate Order*, (New York: Routledge, 1980); Thomas J. Sweeney and J. Melvin Witmer, "Beyond Social Interest: Striving Toward Optimum Health and Wellness," *Individual Psychology: Journal of Adlerian Theory, Research and Practice* 47(4), (1991): 527-540.

[36] Bohm, *Wholeness and the Implicate Order*, 4.

[37] Bohm, *Wholeness and the Implicate Order*.

[38] Ibid., 9

[39] Ibid., 9-10.

[40] Bohm, *Wholeness and the Implicate Order*.

just a kind of mundanely imposed unity or integration of thought since that "imposed outlook would itself be merely another fragment". Thus, he illustratively explained this notion that:

> Rather, all our different ways of thinking are to be considered as different ways of looking at the one reality, each with some domain in which it is clear and adequate.[41]

Bohm seems to emphasize that values and ideas are reasonable to have, but it is important to recognize them as such and not privilege certain parts above others. These notions are useful metaphors for human development as considered across a variety of contexts, including the US and African cultures. When applying this idea of wholeness to human development, it seems to follow logically that part of development is to recognize not only the parts of oneself (body, mind, soul, and spirit) and to strike a balance, but also to recognize that an individual is always connected to other individuals and situated in a greater whole (e.g., groups of individuals, nature, the universe, etc), which can be conceptualized as similar to ecology that posits that different areas of life are interconnected and interdependent.[42] The concept of wholeness can be useful when discussing human development: in order to be healthy, one must not only obtain an awareness and integration of body, mind, soul, and spirit, but also apply the concept of wholeness in relationships to others, which can entail emotional intelligence, perspective taking, and so on and so forth. Importantly, "balance between the many factors contributes to health and happiness".[43]

The journey toward wholeness and harmony between parts of self on an individual level begins in childhood. The integration of the different parts of self, while being mindful of contextual factors, is necessary. Scott Shannon names the following seven factors as contributing to the wholeness of a child: proper nutrition, connection (that is, attachment and social competency), sleep, engagement, self-regulation (for example, emotionality, executive functioning, and character), spirituality (for instance, meaning and purpose), and family.[44] Wendy Anne McCarty emphasizes the transcendent nature of humans and asserts "our primary nature is as conscious, sentient, non-physical

---

[41] Ibid., 9-10.
[42] Scott M. Shannon, *Mental Health for the Whole Child: Moving Young Clients from Disease and Disorder to Balance and Wellness,* (New York: W. W. Norton, 2013).
[43] Ibid.,xxv.
[44] Shannon, *Mental Health for the Whole Child.*

beings that exist prior to and beyond physical human existence".[45] In her work *Welcoming Consciousness* she describes cultivating babies' wholeness, drawing on the work of Ken Wilber's *Integral Model* when describing an integrated approach to wholeness and human experience. Visualizing a bullseye with multiple circles (body, mind, soul, and spirit) inside of each other may be of use when thinking of this model because "Each higher level contains all the elements of the junior level while transcending and adding something new to the previous level".[46] What is also noteworthy about this approach, McCarty explains, is that the soul and spirit levels are actually seen as more primary than the body or physical level of experience and existence. These two levels encompass the mind and body and not vice versa.[47] If one is to espouse this view of experience and development, it would be essential then not only to take into account a child's physical surroundings and environment but also their essence as a person, which, as we will demonstrate shortly, is severely lacking in the extant research on children in Africa.

Related to wholeness is the theory of wellness. Jane Myers presents five different domains to describe holistic wellness: the creative self, the coping self, the social self, the essential self, and the physical self, all of which speak to the different pieces that are needed to have an integrated functional whole.[48] These domains serve as a point of reference for researchers considering child development in the African culture.

The Creative Self: this domain is composed of thinking, emotion or feeling, the working self, control or self-efficacy and usefulness, and positive humour or activities that sustain life and facilitate participation in multiple life contexts.[49] The component of the creative self can also be viewed as the building blocks of strength that an individual human relies on in order to contribute to

---

[45] Wendy Anne McCarty, *Welcoming Consciousness: Supporting Babies' Wholeness from the Beginning of Life-An Integrated Model of Early Development*, (Santa Barbara, CA: Wondrous Beginnings Publishing, 2012), 62.

[46] McCarty, *Welcoming Consciousness*, 31.

[47] Ibid.

[48] Jane Myers, "Coping with Care Giving Stress: A Wellness-oriented, Strengths-based Approach for Family Counselors," *The Family Journal: Counseling and Therapy for Couples and Families* 11, (2003): 153-161.

[49] Jane Myers and Thomas J. Sweeney, "The Indivisible Self: An Evidence-based Model of Wellness," reprint, *Journal of Individual Psychology* 61(3), (2005): 269-279.

his or her respective social world and to create the kind of life that he or she finds meaningful.[50]

The Coping Self: this domain includes leisure activities that promote a sense of fun and enjoyment, stress management strategies, a sense of self-worth, and holding realistic beliefs. The coping self helps to maintain balance when different stressors arise by managing stress, maintaining realistic perspectives, and engaging in what one finds enjoyable.

The Social Self: this domain is composed of (a) friendship or social relationships that involve a connection with others individually or in community, (b) having a capacity to trust others, and (c) love, the ability to be intimate, trusting, self-disclosing with another. The ability to connect with others is a cornerstone of holistic wellness, as it emphasizes the interconnectedness of individuals with not only other individuals, but greater wholes (for example, communities, nature, the universe, and so on and so forth).

The Essential Self: this domain includes spirituality, gender identity, cultural identity, and taking responsibility for one's wellness through self-care and safety habits that are preventive in nature. The essential self speaks to living authentically and accepting, embracing, and expressing the constructs that one associates with. This domain also requires self-exploration and insight.

The Physical Self: this domain focuses on nutrition and exercise that refers to engaging in sufficient physical activity to keep in good physical condition. The interconnectedness of the mind and body is difficult to deny, and it would be arduous to cultivate living authentically, for example, when one does not take care of one's body. Put another way, physical health and safety need to be attended to, otherwise spending time and energy nurturing other domains of the self may be more difficult.

While different components are often discussed in theories of wholeness or holistic wellness, every detailed piece fits into the model which integrates body, mind, soul, and spirit. These four core components need nurturing for the well-being of a person. Broadly, the body entails a person's physicality, which includes nerves, bones, and organs; the mind is comprised of a person's consciousness, thoughts, emotions, and imagination; the soul is the non-physical essence of a person, which seeks meaning, purpose, and crea-

---

[50] Myers, "Coping with Care Giving Stress: A Wellness-oriented, Strengths-based Approach for Family Counselors."

tive expression; and the spirit is the universal force that flows throughout all things – some call this pure energy God.[51]

The body factor can incorporate nutrition, sleep, and safety; the mind can incorporate self-regulation, executive functioning, and emotionality; spirituality entails feeling a sense of meaning, purpose, and connection with a higher power; and the soul can be conceptualized as being authentically true to self.

As a point of comparison, it can be argued that while children in general in the US function within a materialistic culture, they may be more disconnected from nature, their authentic selves, and each other, more so than in other cultures. Such disconnection may actually work against wholeness and instead cultivate fragmentation. In contrast, African children are often more connected to the natural environment and foster social connections that would promote a better integration of mind and body connections.

Re-conceptualizing Childhood in Africa Using Holistic Wellness Theory

The studies presented earlier in the chapter conceptualize Africa's children and childhood in the context of socialization and developmental theory. Using that framework, African children are typically perceived as victimized, incompetent, asocial and acultural. All such constructions have consequently contributed to the marginalization of children. Recent theorists have shown, through a process of deconstructing dominant scientific discourses on childhood, how these denigrating concepts function to establish taken-for-granted assumptions about certain children in different cultures. In this section, we attempt to explore the ways in which looking at the whole being of a child can work toward mobilizing more meaningful constructions of childhood in Africa. Specifically, by using the holistic wellness theoretical framework, we aim to reconstruct the meaning and conceptualization of childhood in Africa.

The African context cultivates the pillars of "wholeness." Furthermore, by considering how the body, mind, soul and spirit are developed in African children, it is possible to examine how these children derive meaning from their existence – rather than languish as passive victims of their circumstance. The examples offered are not an exhaustive list, but instead are meant to be illustrative.

Body: The body is the physical aspect of the human being. Recall the vignette sketched at the beginning of this chapter. Selam lives in an area where there are no hospitals, meaning no yearly physicals or wellness checkups for

---

[51] The Sanctuary at Sedona, "Mind, Body, Soul, and Spirit Integration," (2014), http://sanctuary.net/mind-body-soul-spirit-integration/. Accessed on April 4, 2017.

her and her siblings. That is not to say, however, that African children do not meet physical milestones, even though they may be raised with the intuitive knowledge of parents rather than more modern notions of health status. Such intuitive parenting is not without benefit, though it likely is mischaracterized and misunderstood in the Western context.

The stereotypical Western gaze upon African childhood may echo statements like "they have nothing." However, even without a plethora of manufactured toys to choose from, children find their own ways to play, create their own toys, and develop gross motor skills via ample opportunities for running, jumping, hopping and physical games like tag.[52] Researchers qualitatively investigated child living within low socioeconomic status in South Africa and reported that "lack of conventional play equipment in the environment did not hinder play".[53] They also pointed out that "children walked between the garbage, and they played in areas that were surrounded by filth. In no way did it appear to obstruct their willingness and ability to play".[54] Researchers acknowledge the possibility that children would not find ample opportunity to play in all low-income contexts.[55] They also note the importance of examining cognitive and fine motor development in these contexts with the caveat that fine motor skills may be of less importance for some regions. Also, examining children in South Africa, Frances Hills and colleagues qualitatively investigated children living on the streets and found that strength was a source of "pride in their physical prowess".[56] Researchers also noted that while children may need to be physically strong to keep from being victimized, they also found evidence that physical activities such as sports also helped them cope.

As for food relating to the physical body, food not only sustains life and nourishes the body, but food is often a cornerstone of establishing friendship and community[57] in many African contexts and may actually have symbolic

---

[52] Michelle Bartie, Alex Dunnell, Jesse Kaplan, Dianka Oosthuizen, Danielle Smit, Anchen van Dyk, Lizahan Cloete, and Mia Duvenage, "The Play Experiences of Preschool Children from a Low-socio-economic Rural Community in Worcestor, South Africa," *Occupational Therapy International* 23(2), (2015): 91-102.

[53] Ibid. 94.

[54] Ibid. 99.

[55] Bartie, Dunnell, Kaplan, Oosthuizen, Smit, van Dyk, Cloete and Duvenage, "The Play Experiences of Preschool Children from a Low-socio-economic Rural Community in Worcestor, South Africa".

[56] Hills, Meyer-Weitz and Asante, "The Lived Experiences of Street Children in Durban, South Africa: Violence, Substance Use, and Resilience," 6.

[57] Filip de Boeck, "'When Hunger Goes Around the Land': Hunger and Good Among the Aluund of Zaire," *Man* 29(2), (1994): 257-282.

meanings that are not readily apparent if one is not familiar with the culture. The quality and nature of the relationships between friends and family can be expressed through eating.[58] For example, a grandmother may cook a special meal for her grandchild's visit. Likewise, some research has shown that those who experience food insecurity actually emphasize the social and emotional toll rather than just the physical toll.[59]

Mind: The mind is a chemical factory full of neurotransmitters that affect how and what we think and feel, including pain. The mind is the generator of thoughts, feelings, and emotions.

As some ethnographic researches indicate, the culture in Africa influences the development of the mind[60] by allowing the space for children to be creative. In Western culture, parents often subscribe to the notion that childrearing demands a hands-on approach from caregivers until the child is self-sufficient. In Africa, this is not necessarily the case; children are often left to explore freely as a form of self-education that fosters their development. They are mostly left to "find their own way" from a much younger age than Westerners are accustomed. We argue that this approach might validate and acknowledge the child's personhood earlier in the life-cycle, which could help the child build resilience, social skills, autonomy, emotional intelligence, and creativity.

Illustrating African children's creativity and ingenuity, Nigerian children[61] and South African children[62] used creativity to find ways to engage in play. In addition to creating their own toys, as described above, children developed structured and unstructured games. They created their own toys from the materials they had – appreciating and using them even when they became dirty and began to wear out; one girl called her worn out doll "pretty." Chores were sometimes blended with play, and while there was not a lot of direct

---

[58] T. A. Okoror, C. O. Airhihenbuwa, M. Zungu, D. Makofani, D. C. Brown, and J. Iwelunmor, "'My Mother told Me I must not Cook Anymore'—Food, culture, and the Context of HIV-and AIDS-related Stigma in Three Communities in South Africa," *International Quarterly of Community Health Education* 28(3), (2007): 201-213.

[59] Fielding-Miller, Dunkle and Murdock, "Not Everyone can Afford an Apple a Day: Stigma and Food Insecurity in Rural South African Young Adults."

[60] McCarty, *Welcoming Consciousness*.

[61] George Thomas Basden, *Among the Ibos of Nigeria: An Account of the Curious and Interesting Habits, Customs and Beliefs of a Little Known African People by One Who Has for Many Years Lived Amongst Them on Close and Intimate Terms*, (London: Cass, 1966), eHRAF World Cultures Database http://ehrafworldcultures.yale.edu/document?id=ff26-006. Accessed on September 14, 2018.

[62] Ibid.

supervision of the children, they implemented their own safety measures of getting out of the way when cars came by. Interestingly, the researchers noted how parallel play is sometimes conceptualized as signifying a lower level of development, but for these children, parallel play represented their belonging to the group while they were waiting for their turn.[63] This phenomenon is now observed in Western families whereby children watch and wait, while one or two children play video games.

A focus on the positive aspects of life also influences the development of the minds of children in Africa. In a qualitative study interviewing children who live on the streets of South Africa, authors not only identified adversities but also positive experiences youth reported including caring deeply for other street children, persevering through difficult circumstances, and working toward personal autonomy; sometimes children chose to live in the streets because of detrimental familial situations.[64] Social connection is also a staple of development; engaging with peers through play,[65] and even supportive relationships among children who live on the street, contribute to who children become as adults.[66] The difficult times that many children face in Africa can simultaneously highlight their emotional strength and hope.[67]

Soul: The soul is a non-physical aspect of the human being. It is our personal and individuated expression of the divine or spirit. The soul is the part of us that longs to have meaning and seeks answers to the great questions: Who am I? Why am I here? What is my purpose? In Africa, children learn who they are through lived experiences rather than having other people or media tell them who they are. This identity formation lays the groundwork for a richer and more accurate interaction with themselves and nature and may bring them toward a more actualized version of themselves or congruence between the real and ideal self. Learning through experience may yield more accurate self-understanding.[68]

---

[63] Bartie, Dunnell, Kaplan, Oosthuizen, Smit, van Dyk, Cloete, and Duvenage, "The Play Experiences of Preschool Children from a Low-socio-economic Rural Community in Worcestor, South Africa," 100-101.

[64] Chris Myburgh, Moolla Aneesa, and Marie Poggenpoel, "The Lived Experiences of Children on the Streets of Hillbrow," *Curations* 38(1), (2015): 1-8.

[65] Bartie, Dunnell, Kaplan, Oosthuizen, Smit, van Dyk, Cloete, and Duvenage, "The Play Experiences of Preschool Children from a Low-socio-economic Rural Community in Worcestor, South Africa."

[66] Hills, Meyer-Weitz and Asante, "The Lived Experiences of Street Children in Durban, South Africa: Violence, Substance Use, and Resilience."

[67] Ibid.

[68] McCarty, *Welcoming Consciousness.*

The soul is eternal and communicates in the language of creative expression. This expression can include music, art, dance, and various forms of writing like poetry, among many other things. Connecting with nature is also good for the soul, and as outlined above, children in Africa often have ample time to play outside, be one with nature, and subsequently, nature can aid in teaching children about themselves via caring for animals on a farm, for example.

There are many different activities that can be food for the soul; we choose here to elaborate on music. Music speaks to the soul by connecting us with others, leading us to discover who we are, and manifesting better understandings of diverse cultures and human experiences.[69] "Music is a neutral and common ground to displace fears of hegemonic and minority cultures";[70] especially in countries with colonialism in their history, music can be a very powerful and poignant form of self and community expression in which members of a culture can collectively relate. Music can communicate shared experiences, but also be used as an agent for resistance, social commentary, and social change. Some parts of Africa subscribe to a more oral tradition of storytelling, and simply because there may be no written history does not mean that certain cultures or groups of people have no history; the past is often detailed and experienced through music.[71] Music allows individuals not only to explore their social and cultural identities, but also to engage and learn about the history of the traditions they function within.[72]

While it is beyond the scope and purpose of this chapter to include a comprehensive discussion of African art, we thought it was important to include some brief language describing how the art created in Africa, whether the well-known wood sculptures or otherwise, are rich with the diverse legacy of Africa's people. "Contemporary art in Africa is a product of the vast changes that took place when indigenous cultures were invaded by outside ideologies," and "visual art in Kenya, like the art of all sub-Saharan Africa, is a di-

---

[69] Dawn Joseph, "Tertiary Educators' Voices in Australia and South Africa: Experiencing and Engaging in African Music and Culture," *International Journal of Music Education* 33(3), (2015): 290-303; J. Dinham, *Delivering Authentic Arts Education*, (Melbourne: Cengage Learning Australia, 2011).

[70] Dawn, "Tertiary Educators' Voices in Australia and South Africa: Experiencing and Engaging in African Music and Culture," 293.

[71] Justice Stephen Kofi Gbolonyo, "Want the History? Listen to the Music! Historical Evidence in Anlo Ewe Musical Practices: A Case Study of Traditional Song Texts," (PhD Dissertation, University of Pittsburgh, 2005).

[72] Andrea Emberly, "'Mandela Went to China ... and India Too': Musical Cultures of Childhood in South Africa," (PhD Dissertation, University of Washington, 2009).

verse mix of systems, media, and styles, traditional and contemporary".[73] Works of art can tell the stories of the land and people, the relationship between the two, as well as how colonialism literally changed the landscape and attempted to eradicate much of the culture and belief systems that were in place before such a jarring intrusion. Another noteworthy term related to art is that of a historicism, signifying how without specific documentation, sometimes the history of Africa appears to be somewhat absent or flattened. John Peffer argues that "African art historians face formidable challenges when it comes to documentation of the past. These are compounded by the perennial problem that, in the public view, Africa's deep past is conflated with its recent past".[74] We, too, emphasize that art goes beyond mere aesthetic enjoyment and documentation of a time period, and should be further contextualized, and recognized as situated as part of the context in which it was created.

Spirit: The spirit is the vital force within all things and can be a very powerful and healing experience when people feel connected with it. Spirit may be called God or Creator. It can also be called the Quantum Field, the field, or the unmanifest. It is the indescribable organizing principle of the universe and its language is pure energy. One can come into contact with such a divine entity or energy via practicing spirituality or religion. There are many different ways of practicing spirituality and religion in Africa, some of which include Christianity and Islam, while others may subscribe to a more indigenous African spiritual system commonly called African Traditional Religion. Religion can be used as a source of negative or positive coping strategies by children going through difficult times. For example, some may view their circumstances as a punishment from a higher power (negative), or they may use prayer as a coping strategy, recognizing that facing problems does not mean that God is not present (positive).[75] Such positive aspects of religion can foster resilience.[76] Placing faith and hope in a God or ancestors to protect them through hardships is how some children in Africa face the struggles in their lives.[77]

---

[73] Themina Kader, "Contemporary Art of Kenya: A Different Perspective," *Art Education* 59(4), (2006): 25&27.

[74] John Peffer, "Notes on African Art, History, and Diasporas Within," *African Arts* 38(4), (2005): 70 .

[75] Arve Gunnestad and S'lungile Thwala, "Resilience and Religion in Children and Youth in Southern Africa," *International Journal of Children's Spirituality* 16(2), (2011): 169-185.

[76] Ibid.

[77] Hills, Meyer-Weitz and Asante, "The Lived Experiences of Street Children in Durban, South Africa: Violence, Substance Use, and Resilience".

An interesting study regarding the divine dreams of children in South Africa yielded common themes of reassurance, instruction/missionary, and fear of an eternity without God/fear of the devil, among others.[78] Researchers argue that divine dreams of children not only help them learn about themselves but also about religion and spirituality in general. Drawing from the works of researchers like Kate Adams and Ferdinand J. Potgieter, Johannes L. van der Walt, and Charl C. Wolhuter we know that dreams provide a reflection of the spirituality of children in particular, and people in general.[79] Furthermore, the occurrence of dreams implies that children have a mystical centre where a confluence of "cognitive, knowable facts about a particular religion" and their own "internalised, appreciation of spirituality [can] . . . give effect to the 'reality' of a distinct transcendental beyondness that provides direction and meaning to their lives".[80]

The role of religion and spirituality is a very personal journey, and even dreams may offer a gateway for further exploration into the divine, or, at the very least, provide rich discussion for further self-insight.

The body, mind, soul, and spirit are the components that, collectively, comprise and define our species. If we are sick or suffering, we must work holistically to heal completely. If we do not, we are missing the connection and, in all likelihood, will never reach our potential for wellness and vitality. If we do not consider the whole human being, we will most likely work to alleviate the symptoms of a problem and never address the root cause. It is with this in mind that we further implore researchers and consumers of literature to take a more holistic perspective of children in Africa and recognize their capacity for deriving meaning from their experiences as well as their evident strength and resilience.

Resilience and Protective Factors

Regardless of the financial hardship, lack of access to school-type education, water, food, and other such needs, research shows that African children have access to collective social support and relationships with adults, societies, and nature that can help foster resilience. Research also shows that children who

---

[78] Ferdinand J. Potgieter, Johannes L. van der Walt, and Charl C. Wolhuter, "The Divine Dreams of a Sample of South African Children: The Gateway to Their Spirituality," *International Journal of Children's Spirituality* 14(1), (2009): 31-46.

[79] Kate Adams, "God Talks to Me in My Dreams: The Occurrence and Significance of Children's Dreams about God," *International Journal of Children's Spirituality* 6(1) (2001): 99-111; Potgieter, van der Walt and Wolhuter, "The Divine Dreams of a Sample of South African Children: The Gateway to Their Spirituality", 43.

[80] Potgieter, van der Walt and Wolhuter, "The Divine Dreams of a Sample of South African Children: The Gateway to Their Spirituality", 43.

do well despite serious hardships have had at least one stable and committed relationship with a supportive adult. Maurice Place and colleagues[81] indicate that resilient children have protective factors in three broad areas: (a) within themselves, (b) within their families, and (c) within their communities. These relationships buffer children from developmental disruption and can help them develop resilience and the skill sets needed to thrive and respond to adversity. The application of holistic wellness theory to the conceptualization of Africa's children in the African cultural context (for example, addressing children that are able to thrive and excel in spite of their lack of resources, exposure to adversity, and trauma) helps explain resiliency, too.

Resilience is defined as "the process of coping with adversity, change, or opportunity in a manner that results in the identification, fortification, and enrichment of resilient qualities or protective factors".[82] With regard to children, resilience refers to the child's ability to cope and do well in life in spite of difficulties.[83]

In this section, we examine how the health and wellness of the body, mind, soul, and spirit of the child can also serve as a protective factor to develop resilience, health and wellness. Researchers describe protective factors as those within the child and within the environment (for instance, family and community). Internal resiliency (that is, factors within the child), develop from connection to spirituality, cognitive competence, emotional stability, behavioural and social well-being.[84] Examining the child's mental strength, temperamental style, emotional stability and social skills as well as his or her competencies, values and faith will help to understand the child more fully, including their resilience. Additionally, cultural experiences affect the manner in which families are formed and communities are built, and colours how protective factors (e.g., meaning in life, values, and faith) are experienced; the child's soul and spiritual wellness are essential expressions of culture. In examining the process of resilience development, research shows that children

---

[81] Maurice Place, Joanna Reynolds, Anna Cousins, and Shelagh O'Neill, "Developing a Resilience Package for Vulnerable Children," *Child Adolescent Mental Health* 7(4), (2002): 12–167.

[82] Glenn E. Richardson, "The Metatheory of Resilience and Resiliency," *Journal of Clinical Psychology* 58(3), (2002): 308 .

[83] Arve Gunnestad, "Resilience in a Cross-Cultural Perspective: How resilience is generated in different cultures," *Journal of Intercultural Communication* 1, (2006): 1-29.

[84] Richardson, "The Metatheory of Resilience and Resiliency"; Gunnestad, "Resilience in a Cross-Cultural Perspective: How resilience is generated in different cultures"; E. Werner and R. Smith, *Overcoming the Odds: High-Risk Children from Birth to Adulthood,* (New York: Cornell University Press, 1992).

create resilience by building a positive self-image when they become aware of their coping values and the faith they hold. Connections with others are also a large piece of building resilience and a positive self-image. It is the positive self-image that motivates the child to make a greater effort to behave in healthy ways, thus contributing to resilience.

A study by Stephan Collishaw and colleagues highlights how resilience works in African children. These authors, examining orphanhood and mental health resilience among children who lost their parents due to AIDS in urban South Africa, show that food security and physical health predicted sustained mental health resilience.[85] Additionally, orphanhood alone did not equate with child mental health problems; a quarter of the sample showed no signs of mental health issues. These results contradict Western notions of orphanhood being synonymous with dysfunction and tragedy. Also noteworthy is that children rated their own physical health, related to whether they had been unwell in the past year, so their personal perceptions were accounted for in the results of this study.

Proposed Implications for Research, Intervention, and Policy

Not only is holistic wellness theory useful for guiding research efforts, it is also useful when considering culturally informed interventions and policy recommendations. For example, many relief projects, especially of international groups, agencies and institutions, focus on providing children aid through materials, such as toys and other children's supplies. Although these actions are well-intentioned, they run the risk of neglecting to build upon the strengths, skills, and autonomy people in Africa already have. Attention should be given to what is already working as it is viewed from their cultural standard where resilience is promoted. This simple shift could dismantle the near archetype of passive needy children in Africa.

Conclusion

This chapter serves as a call to action for researchers and policy-makers alike. The challenge is to move from a problem-saturated lens to a culturally-informed vantage point when researching and characterizing childhood in Africa. If there is to be a greater focus on enhancing the health and well-being of Africa's children, then researchers must pivot to theories of development that consider the

---

[85] Stephan Collishaw, Frances Gardner, J. Lawrence Aber, and L. Cluver, "Predictors of Mental Health Resilience in Children Who Have Been Parentally Bereaved by AIDS in Urban South Africa," *Journal of Abnormal Child Psychology* 44(4), (2016): 719-730.

holistic contributions to the child's successes, including the capacity for resilience. "A focus on Western notions of age, children's rights and wellbeing might be desirable, but will only yield material significance if they are interpreted and practiced within the context of African children's lives".[86]

If and when there is a consensus regarding the need to focus on African children's strengths, we cannot fail to collaborate with the children themselves. As described by Abebe and Ofosu-Kusi, "The future for African scholarship on childhood and children must be hinged on greater collaboration and cooperation on childhood research and studies regardless of which part of the continent takes as a vantage point".[87] Holding out exemplars of strength and resilience serves to (re) remind the community of this critical need.

Bibliography

Abebe, Tatek, and Yaw Ofosu-Kusi. "Beyond Pluralizing African Childhoods: Introduction." *Childhood* 23 (3), (2016): 303-316.

Adams, Kate. "God Talks to Me in My Dreams: The Occurrence and Significance of Children's Dreams about God." *International Journal of Children's Spirituality* 6(1) (2001): 99-111.

Adler, Alfred. *Understanding Human Nature.* Translated by W. B. Wolf. New York: Greenberg, 1927.

Ajufo, Beatrice Ifeoma. "Challenges of Youth Unemployment in Nigeria: Effective Career Guidance as a Panacea." *An International Multidisciplinary Journal, Ethiopia* 7(1), (2013): 307-321.

Akinboade, Oludele Akinloye, and Segun Adeyemi Adeyefa. "An Analysis of Variance of Food Security by its Main Determinants Among the Urban Poor in the city of Tshwane, South Africa." *Social Indicators Research: An International and Interdisciplinary Journal for Quality-of-Life Measurement* 137(1), (2018): 61-82.

Anasi, Stella N. "Access to and Dissemination of Health Information in Africa: The Patient and the Public." *Journal of Hospital Librarianship* 12(2), (2012): 120-134.

Ansell, Nicola. "Once Upon a Time: Orphanhood, Childhood Studies and the Depoliticisation of Childhood Poverty in Southern Africa." *Childhood* 23(2), (2016): 162-177.

Bartie, Michelle, Alex Dunnell, Jesse Kaplan, Dianka Oosthuizen, Danielle Smit, Anchen van Dyk, Lizahan Cloete, and Mia Duvenage. "The Play Experiences of Preschool Children from a Low-socio-economic Rural Community in Worcestor, South Africa." *Occupational Therapy International* 23(2), (2015): 91-102.

---

[86] Abebe and Ofosu-Kusi. "Beyond Pluralizing African Childhoods: Introduction", 315.
[87] Ibid. 314.

Basden, George Thomas. *Among the Ibos of Nigeria: An Account of the Curious and Interesting Habits, Customs and Beliefs of a Little Known African People by One Who Has for Many Years Lived Amongst Them on Close and Intimate Terms.* London: Cass, 1966. eHRAF World Cultures Database http://ehrafworldcultures.yale.edu/document?id=ff26-006.

Ben-Arieh, Asher, Natalie Hevener Kaufman, Arlene Bowers Andrews, Robert M. George, Bong Joo Lee, and L. J. Aber. *Measuring and Monitoring Children's Well-being.* Netherlands: Kluwer Academic Press, 2001.

Ben-Arieh, Asher. "Where are the Children? Children's Role in Measuring and Monitoring Their Well-being." *Social Indicators Research: An International and Interdisciplinary Journal for Quality-of-Life Measurement* 74(3), (2005): 573-596.

Bohm, David. *Wholeness and the Implicate Order.* New York: Routledge, 1980.

Boothby, Neil. "What Happens When Child Soldiers Grow Up? The Mozambique Case Study." *Intervention: International Journal of Mental Health, Psychosocial Work and Counseling in Areas of Armed Conflict* 4)3), (2006): 244-259.

Boothby, Neil. "What Happens When Child Soldiers Grow Up? The Mozambique Case Study." *Intervention: International Journal of Mental Health, Psychosocial Work and Counseling in Areas of Armed Conflict* 4(3), (2006): 244-259.

Bronfenbrenner, Urie. *Ecological Models of Human Development.* Oxford: Elsevier, 1994.

Brownell, Gracie, and Regina T. Praetorius. "Experiences of Former Child Soldiers in Africa: A Qualitative Interpretive Meta-synthesis." *International Social Work* 60(2), (2017): 452-469.

Closson, Kalysha, Janan Janine Dietrich, Busi Nkala, Addy Musuku, Zishan Cui, Jason Chia, Glenda Gray, et al. "Prevalence, Type, and Correlates of Trauma Exposure Among Adolescent Men and Women in Soweto, South Africa: Implications for HIV Prevention." *BMC Public Health* 16(1), (2016): 1-15.

Cluver, Lucie, and Mark Orkin. "Cumulative Risk and AIDS-orphanhood: Interactions of Stigma, Bullying and Poverty on Child Mental Health in South Africa." *Social Science & Medicine* 69(8), (2009): 1186-1193.

Collishaw, Stephan, Frances Gardner, J. Lawrence Aber, and L. Cluver. "Predictors of Mental Health Resilience in Children Who Have Been Parentally Bereaved by AIDS in Urban South Africa." *Journal of Abnormal Child Psychology* 44(4), (2016): 719-730.

de Boeck, Filip. "'When Hunger Goes Around the Land': Hunger and Good Among the Aluund of Zaire." *Man* 29(2), (1994): 257-282.

Denis-Ramirez, Elise, Katrine Holmegaard Sorensen, and Morten Skovdal. "In the Midst of a 'Perfect Storm': Unpacking the Causes and Consequences of Ebola-related Stigma for Children Orphaned by Ebola in Sierra Leone." *Children and Youth Services Review* 73, (2017): 445-453.

DeSilva, Mary Bachman, Anne Skalicky, Jennifer Beard, Mandisa Cakwe, Tom Zhuwau, Tim Quinlan, and Jonathon Simon. "Early Impacts of Orphaning: Health, Nutrition, and Food Insecurity in a Cohort of School-going Adolescents in South Africa." *Vulnerable Children and Youth Studies* 7(1), (2012): 75-87.

Dinham, J. *Delivering Authentic Arts Education.* Melbourne: Cengage Learning Australia, 2011.

Dugo, Habtamu, and Joanne D. Eisen. "Famine, Genocide and Media Control in Ethiopia." *Journal of Pan African Studies* 9(10), (2016): 334-357.

Emberly, Andrea. "'Mandela Went to China ... and India Too': Musical Cultures of Childhood in South Africa." PhD Dissertation. University of Washington, 2009.

Fall, Kevin A., Janice Miner Holden, and Andre Marquis. *Theoretical Models of Counseling and Psychotherapy* Second Edition. New York, NY: Routledge, 2010.

Fielding-Miller, Rebecca, Kristin L. Dunkle, and Daniel Murdock. "Not Everyone can Afford an Apple a Day: Stigma and Food Insecurity in Rural South African Young Adults." *African Journal of AIDS Research* 14(4), (2015): 361-369.

Gbolonyo, Justice Stephen Kofi. "Want the History? Listen to the Music! Historical Evidence in Anlo Ewe Musical Practices: A Case Study of Traditional Song Texts." PhD Dissertation. University of Pittsburgh, 2005.

Gunnestad, Arve, and S'lungile Thwala. "Resilience and Religion in Children and Youth in Southern Africa." *International Journal of Children's Spirituality* 16(2), (2011): 169-185.

Gunnestad, Arve. "Resilience in a Cross-Cultural Perspective: How resilience is generated in different cultures." *Journal of Intercultural Communication* 1, (2006): 1-29.

Henderson, Patricia. "South African AIDS Orphans: Examining Assumptions Around Vulnerability from the Perspective of Rural Children and Youth." *Childhood* 13(3), (2006): 303-327.

Hills, Frances, Anna Meyer-Weitz, and Kwaku Oppong Asante. "The Lived Experiences of Street Children in Durban, South Africa: Violence, Substance Use, and Resilience." *International Journal of Qualitative Studies on Health and Well-being* 11, (2016): 1-11.

Joseph, Dawn. "Tertiary Educators' Voices in Australia and South Africa: Experiencing and Engaging in African Music and Culture." *International Journal of Music Education* 33(3), (2015): 290-303.

Kader, Themina. "Contemporary Art of Kenya: A Different Perspective." *Art Education* 59 (4), (2006): 25-32.

McCarty, Wendy Anne. *Welcoming Consciousness: Supporting Babies' Wholeness from the Beginning of Life-An Integrated Model of Early Development.* Santa Barbara, CA: Wondrous Beginnings Publishing, 2012.

Myburgh, Chris, Moolla Aneesa, and Marie Poggenpoel. "The Lived Experiences of Children on the Streets of Hillbrow." *Curations* 38(1), (2015): 1-8.

Myers, Jane E., Thomas J. Sweeney, and J. Melvin Witmer. "The Wheel of Wellness Counseling for Wellness: A Holistic Model for Treatment Planning." *Journal of Counseling and Development* 78(3), (2000): 251-266.

Myers, Jane, and Thomas J. Sweeney. "The Indivisible Self: An Evidence-based Model of Wellness." Reprint, *Journal of Individual Psychology* 61(3), (2005): 269-279.

Myers, Jane. "Coping with Care Giving Stress: A Wellness-oriented, Strengths-based Approach for Family Counselors." *The Family Journal: Counseling and Therapy for Couples and Families* 11, (2003): 153-161.

Okoror, T. A., C. O. Airhihenbuwa, M. Zungu, D. Makofani, D. C. Brown, and J. Iwelunmor. "'My Mother told Me I must not Cook Anymore'—Food, culture, and the Context of HIV-and AIDS-related Stigma in Three Communities in South Africa." *International Quarterly of Community Health Education* 28(3), (2007): 201-213.

Orkin, Mark. Mark E. Boyes, Lucie D. Cluver, and Yuning Zhang. "Pathways to Poor Educational Outcomes for HIV/AIDS-affected Youth in South Africa." *AIDS Care* 26(3), (2014): 343-450.

Peffer, John. "Notes on African Art, History, and Diasporas Within." *African Arts* 38(4), (2005): 70-77.

Place, Maurice, Joanna Reynolds, Anna Cousins, and Shelagh O'Neill. "Developing a Resilience Package for Vulnerable Children." *Child Adolescent Mental Health* 7(4), (2002): 12–167.

Potgieter, Ferdinand J., Johannes L. van der Walt, and Charl C. Wolhuter. "The Divine Dreams of a Sample of South African Children: The Gateway to Their Spirituality." *International Journal of Children's Spirituality* 14(1), (2009): 31-46.

Pritchard, Colin, and Steven Keen, "Child Mortality and Poverty in Three World Regions (the West, Asia and Sub-Saharan Africa) 1988-2010: Evidence of Relative Intra-regional Neglect?." *Scandinavian Journal of Public Health* 44 (8) (2016): 734-741.

Reis, Ria. "Children Enacting Idioms of Witchcraft and Spirit Possession as a Response to Trauma: Therapeutically Beneficial, and for Whom?." *Transcultural Psychiatry* 50(5), (2013): 622-643.

Richardson, Glenn E. "The Metatheory of Resilience and Resiliency." *Journal of Clinical Psychology* 58(3), (2002): 307–321.

Rochat, Tamsen J., Joanie Mitchell, Anina M. Lubbe, Alan Stein, Mark Tomlinson, and Ruth M. Bland. "Communication About HIV and Death: Maternal Reports of Primary School-aged Children's Questions After Maternal HIV Disclosure in Rural South Africa." *Social Science and Medicine* 172, (2017): 124-134.

Roelen, Keetie, Emily Delap, Camilla Jones, and Helen Karki Chettri. "Improving Child Wellbeing and Care in Sub-Saharan Africa: The Role of Social Protection." *Children and Youth Services Review* 73, (2017): 309-318.

Shannon, Scott M. *Mental Health for the Whole Child: Moving Young Clients from Disease and Disorder to Balance and Wellness.* New York: W. W. Norton, 2013.

Shoo, Rumishael. "Reducing Child Mortality: The Challenges in Africa." 2007. https://unchronicle.un.org/article/reducing-child-mortality-challenges-africa.

Sorensen, P. N., and S. Bekele. *Nice Children Don't Eat A Lot of Food: Strained Livelihoods and the Role of Aid in North Wollo, Ethiopia.* Addis Ababa, Ethiopia: Forum for Social Studies, 2009.

Sweeney, Thomas J., and J. Melvin Witmer. "Beyond Social Interest: Striving Toward Optimum Health and Wellness." *Individual Psychology: Journal of Adlerian Theory, Research and Practice* 47(4), (1991): 527-540.

The Sanctuary at Sedona. "Mind, Body, Soul, and Spirit Integration." 2014. http://sanctuary.net/mind-body-soul-spirit-integration/.

Toska, Elona, Lesley Gittings, Rebecca Hodes, Lucie D. Cluver, Kaymarlin Govender, K. Emma Chademana, and Vincent Evans Gutierrez. "Resourcing Resilience: Social Protection for HIV Prevention Amongst Children and Adolescents in Eastern and Southern Africa." *African Journal of AIDS Research* 15 (2), (2016): 123-140.

United Nations Treaty Collection. *Convention on the Rights of the Child.* 1990. https://treaties.un.org/Pages/ViewDetails.aspx?src=TREATY&mtdsg_no=IV-11&chapter=4&lang=en.

Werner, E., and R. Smith. *Overcoming the Odds: High-Risk Children from Birth to Adulthood.* New York: Cornell University Press, 1992.

Worthen, Miranda, Grace Onyango, Mike Wessells, Angela Veale, and Susan McKay. "Facilitating War-affected Young Mothers' Reintegration: Lessons from a Participatory Action Research Study in Liberia, Sierra Leone, and Uganda." *International Journal of Social Science Studies* 1(1), (2013): 145-149.

Chapter 4

Efua Sutherland and African Children's Literature: Representations of Postcolonial Childhood

Andrea Y. Adomako

"I've heard a lot of people discussing at conferences the role of the [African] writer--all this rigmarole, well if there's any role, they should write for the children."

Efua Sutherland

Introduction

In B*lack Skin, White Masks* Frantz Fanon states "we are witness to the desperate efforts of a [B]lack man striving desperately to discover the meaning of [B]lack identity."[1] Fanon's words have led to an abundance of scholarly work dedicated to understanding how postcolonialism affects identity formations; however, to fully understand the relationship between postcolonialism, resistance and identity formation it is important to critically engage the unique positioning of the postcolonial child. Understanding representations of postcolonial African childhood, which are rarely incorporated in current discourses around childhood, helps destabilize narrow comprehensions of childhood and understandings around the never-ending effects of colonialism. This essay positions Efua Theodora Sutherland's *A Voice in the Forest* (1983) in dialogue with Frantz Fanon's postcolonial theory and African children's literature. Sutherland's work centres the postcolonial perspectives from which African realities for children are examined or perceived. It is through her characterizations that Sutherland ultimately critiques dominant ways of conceiving African childhood.

---

[1] Frantz Fanon, *Black Skin, White Masks,* (London: Pluto, 2008), xviii.

African children's literature, because of its articulations of African pedagogy, presents a unique archive and opportunity to grapple with postcolonialism as it relates to the subjectivity of African children. These works are cultural products in which African adults attempt to make sense of the world for African children. Often, children cannot represent themselves and must rely on adults to mediate their coming into knowing—in both their Blackness and their social participation. Thus, the enunciation of their subjectivities and liberation must rely on a mediated form. Through a postcolonial lens, the African child is born into a system that sustains the hierarchies introduced by colonialism and is simultaneously trying to resist such power structures. African postcolonial children are born already as hybrid subjects, collapsing the boundaries between notions of "Western" and "African" yet, interpellated by external systems of white domination.[2] As a result, they must navigate an understanding of their Blackness under intersecting conditions. This begs the question of how African children discover the meaning of their African identifications in a postcolonial context. Fanon turns to literature as one tool that can provide a framework within which help for such a discovery could be obtained; he calls for stories and texts for Black children in order to combat the multiple forms of violence imparted by colonial education.

I read Sutherland's *A Voice in the Forest* in line with Fanon's call for action. Despite her groundbreaking work in Ghana, Sutherland remains relatively unknown and under-examined in the world of African children's literature.[3] Tony Simoes Da Silva has noted that,

> to suggest that scholarly research on African women writers pales in comparison to the attention devoted to that of their male counterparts is not too far-fetched a proposition, especially when we consider the sheer weight of critical writing on a few authors, such as [Chinua] Achebe.[4]

---

[2] Interpellation is associated in particular with Louis Althusser who discusses the ways in which ideology interpellates or hails individuals as subjects in his work "Ideology and Ideological State Apparatuses".
[3] Mabel Komasi, "Efua Sutherland: Visionary Pioneer of Ghanaian Children's Literature," in Anne V. Adams and Esi Sutherland-Addy (eds.), *The Legacy of Efua Sutherland: Pan-African Cultural Activism,* (Banbury: Ayebia, 2007), 70.
[4] Tony Simoes da Silva, "Myths, Traditions and Mothers of the Nation: Some Thoughts on Efua Sutherland's Writing," *EnterText* 4(2), (2005): 256.

He goes on to discuss the ways in which Sutherland has often been ignored in conversations around African women's writing despite her literary influence.[5] It is therefore important to resurrect Sutherland in the field of postcolonial African children's literature because her work represents the subjectivity of postcolonial African children while also presenting opportunities for a gender analysis that rarely happens within this space.

I begin this essay by exploring children's literature as a sociopolitical tool through the lens of Fanon's postcolonial framework. Doing so enables me to chart the ways in which the genre of children's literature is an essential political mechanism in understanding and framing conceptions of childhood. After investigating the mobilization of children's literature, I discuss African children's literature specifically, keeping in mind the historical context that necessitated using children's literature as an extension of the nation-building project. I then move on to consider Sutherland's work, *A Voice in the Forest*. This text presents an example of how postcolonial African children's literature reorients African children as subversive figures. *A Voice in the Forest* addresses cultural tensions between Western and African values and reflects the impact of white domination on the socio-political climate that confronts postcolonial African children. It is also a critical text to examine diasporic notions of postcolonial Black girlhood. By defying the boundaries and norms created by the colonial society and ideology, both child-like figures, as presented in the text, Afrum and the Samanta girl, subvert discourses of dominance and power tied to Western patriarchal values. I argue that Sutherland clearly participates in Fanon's project of writing for Black children by writing stories within the context of Ghanaian folktales. Sutherland casts light on how the genre of African children's literature reorients conventional understanding of postcolonial African children and also confirms the political use of the genre.

Children's Literature as a Tool for Identification

From early contact with the white world, most Black children have commonly come to understand themselves through self-hatred and alienation. Fanon argues that the internalization of white supremacy, with its racist representation of the Black other, causes a self-division in the Black subject. From a colonial perspective, the indoctrination of African children in order to keep them docile in the face of their oppression is essential. The colonizer has designed an educational system that "was capable only of improving the lives

---

[5] Ibid.

of the colonizers, not their own".[6] Western idealized notions of knowledge were disseminated throughout the educational system to produce subjugated colonised subjects. As Fanon explains, colonial school children learn early to reject their dialect and traditional language in favour of the coloniser's.[7] In literature and the larger political realm, one of the drives toward identity hinges on this question of language. For the postcolonial subject to speak or write in the coloniser's tongue is to call forth questions of a postcolonial subjectivity. Fanon explains,

> [we] consequently consider the study of language essential for providing us with one element in understanding the [B]lack man's dimension of being-for-others, it being understood that to speak is to exist absolutely for the other.[8]

Colonial education often only equipped students with a language that reflected their subordination, and this was further perpetuated in the storybooks written for colonial children.[9]

As a result, colonial children's literature committed educational violence against the discovery of postcolonial African children by depicting stereotypical Black characters. Anthropologist Paul Bohannon asserts, "savages became a philosophical necessity for the emergence of Europe."[10] Through children's literature, in the form of storybooks, comics, and/or cartoon representations, colonial schools systems represented Black people as savages and villains, and as a result, Black children saw Blackness associated with evil. The continent of Africa and its inhabitants were romanticized as the ultimate "other." This violence is a form that, "does not only have for its aim the keeping of these enslaved men at arm's length; it seeks to dehumanize them. Everything will be done to wipe out their traditions…to destroy their culture."[11] Early depictions of the *Curious George* tales perpetuate a primitive, barbaric version of Africa. *Tarzan*, created by American writer Edgar Rice Burroughs and first published in 1912, is one of the best-known examples of colonial children's literature that

[6] Ernest Emenyonu, "Education and the Contemporary Malaise in Nigeria," in Charles E. Nnolim (ed.), *The Role of Education in Contemporary Africa,* (New York: Professors World Peace Academy, 1988), 37

[7] Fanon, *Black Skin, White Masks*, 4.

[8] Ibid.

[9] Mabel Komasi and Helen Yitah, "Children's Literature in Ghana: A Survey," *Children's Literature* 37, (2009): 242.

[10] Paul Bohannan, *Africa and Africans,* (Garden City: N.Y., 1964), 1.

[11] Frantz Fanon, *Wretched of the Earth,* (New York: Grove, 1963), 16.

portrays Africa as a place inhabited by savages. Sheila S. Walker and Jennifer Rasamimanana state that, "although Burroughs never set foot in Africa, his books, and the films based on them, have constituted the major source of misinformation on Africa for many for generations."[12] Tarzan represents indigenous Africans as "scantily clad spear throwers who are consistently outwitted in their own environment by Whites."[13] These types of children's literature serve as propaganda to portray Western superiority over Africa, and persist to this day.

The African child who seeks to identify with the hero but is categorized as the African experiences a severe mental disconnect. For this reason, Fanon asked for

> the establishment of children's magazines especially for Black children, the creation of songs for Black children, and, ultimately, the publication of history texts especially for them...I believe that if there is a traumatism it occurs during those years.[14]

Fanon understands how education and cultural knowledge can be used against alienation in order to work towards a Black postcolonial subject who has the ability to mobilize resistance over internalization. Children's literature has the possibility of enabling subjects to rearticulate and reconstruct an understanding of themselves. This starts with changing the ways in which children come to understand their Blackness, including their identification as Africans. Bohannon believes that "only if the myth is stripped away can the reality of Africa emerge."[15] As the social process of decolonisation continues, as well as neo-colonialism, conversations regarding culturally relevant material for children are taking place throughout Africa.

Literature of Combat: African Children's Literature

The publication of *A Voice in the Forest* (1983) occurred at a pivotal time in Ghanaian history as well as in Sutherland's career. Exploring this era in Ghanaian history, along with Sutherland's position as a writer, helps us better understand the book through a postcolonial framework.

---

[12] Sheila S. Walker and Jennifer Rasamimanana, "Tarzan in the Classroom: How "Educational" Films Mythologize Africa and Miseducate Americans," *The Journal of Negro Education* 62(1), (1993): 5.
[13] Ibid.
[14] Fanon, *Black Skin, White Masks*, 127.
[15] Bohannan, *Africa and Africans*, 1.

Almost 26 years after Ghana's independence from British rule, 1983 marked a period where "the chickens of the [Kwame] Nkrumah overthrow came home to roost."[16] During this time Ghanaians were being expelled from Nigeria, an estimated 700,000 people, in what was termed the "Ghana Must Go" era. Ghanaians, both those returning from Nigeria and those already residing in Ghana, found themselves under the rule of Flt. Lt. Jerry John Rawlings, during the worst drought and famine in the history of the country. Due to the famine, the term "Rawlings Chain" was coined to "describe the deep gorges formed around people's necks when their emaciated skin exposed protruding collarbones."[17] The economic downfall of the first West African country to gain independence from colonial rule caught the attention of world leaders.

Seung Hong Choi, a representative of the World Bank at the time, stated that "if it can happen in Ghana, it can happen in any African country...1983 Ghana was really a hopeless place – everybody, both Ghanaians and donors, were abandoning the place."[18] At this catastrophic moment, it was clear that the nation needed restructuring and a massive political and social revolution. Defining the term "postcolonial" as one that "designates a time after imperial powers have departed (in one way or another), and that the postcolonial voice is a voice speaking its own authority and identity in confidence of that authority and identity," 1983 marked a time where Ghanaians once again tried to construct their postcolonial voice.[19] Although already hybrid, the attempts at a confident postcolonial voice emerge from an awareness of this positioning and with an attempt to combat conventional colonial subjectivity. Stepping onto the world stage, Ghana had to reconcile its colonial history with its socio-political present, and renegotiate a Ghanaian identity; a negotiation that still lives on today.

This pivotal climate influenced Ghanaian authors who used radical politics and children's literature to reclaim Ghanaian identity and mobilize the figure of the child. During this time Ghanaian cultural affirmation was centred. This moment "ensured the local production of new books that reflect the Ghanaian

---

[16] Kwasi Gyan-Apenteng, "Lest We Forget-1983-Thirty Years Ago," *Ghanaweb,* (13 May 2013) https://www.ghanaweb.com/GhanaHomePage/NewsArchive/Lest-We-Forget-1983 -Thirty-Years-Ago-273736. Accessed on September 17, 2018.

[17] Ibid.

[18] James Brooke, "Ghana, Once 'Hopeless,' Gets at Least the Look of Success," *The New York Times,* 3 January 1989.

[19] Sayed Ahmad Hashemy, Daryoosh Hayati, and Eisa Amiri, "Postcolonialism, Children, and Their Literature," in Azadeh Shafaei (ed.), *Frontiers of Language and Teaching, Vol.2: Proceedings of the 2011 International Online Language Conference,* (Boca Raton: Brown, 2011), 65.

sociocultural environment, which supplemented the foreign ones that the Ghanaian child had been exposed to over the years."[20] In *African's Children's and Youth Literature*, Osayimwense Osa examines the historical context and framework that surrounded the emergence of African children's literature. Osa states that literature must serve a purpose by being relevant to its sociocultural environment; it is not for aesthetic pleasure alone. He writes that "[Literature] is the repository of cultural life of the people and is a major source of education for the young."[21] In conversation with Osa's work, Meena Khorana describes how "seminars and conferences were organized in the 1960s and 1970s by concerned scholars, writers, publishers, and educators; firm directives were outlined to Africanize publishing for children and to take economic, cultural, and ideological control."[22] Out of these seminars and conferences emerged small, independent publishers and authors dedicated to instilling Ghanaian pride within the minds of its youth, especially during the turbulent 1980s.

The methods in which Ghanaian authors participated in writing children's literature varied, but traditional literature played a crucial role in its genesis. For Homi Bhabha, the act of translation from the colonial form of written language into a "native" cultural product produces a new form of knowledge, a symptom particular to the postcolonial condition.[23] This is a contested position within African scholarship, not just for Ghanaians, as the question of language is a crucial one. As cultural products, children's literature reflects the social and global politics of the time. Not only do these texts serve a political function but they also focus on the subjectivity of children, communicating specific ideologies. On the one hand, African writers use the former colonial language for their creative writings and engage in producing works relevant to African children, often through the adaption of African folktale tradition, as a valid form of instruction and entertainment.[24] In opposition, as pioneered by Ngugi wa Thiong'o in his well-known piece *Decolonising the Mind*,[25] some writers participate and encourage the use of indigenous languages for African literature as a whole. However, educational and fictional titles that have the

---

[20] Komasi and Yitah, "Children's Literature in Ghana: A Survey," 236.

[21] Osayimwense Osa, *African Children's and Youth Literature*, (New York: Twayne Publisher, 1995), 136.

[22] Meena Khorana, *Critical Perspectives on Postcolonial African Children's and Young Adult Literature*, (Westport. CT: Greenwood, 1998), 3.

[23] Homi Bhabha, *The Location of Culture*, (London: Routledge, 1994), 336.

[24] Ernest Emenyonu, "Selection and Validation of Oral Materials for Children's Literature: Artistic Resources in Chinua Achebe's Fiction for Children," *Callaloo* 25(2), (2002): 585.

[25] Ngugi wa Thiong'o, *Decolonising the Mind: The Politics of Language in African Literature*, (London: James Currey, 1986).

highest sales tend to be those in English or another colonial language. This underscores that, as in many other African countries, children's books in indigenous African languages are very difficult to promote where, generally speaking, language and instruction policies are still mostly oriented towards former colonial languages, thus affecting people's literacy in their own languages. These conflicts continue to be discussed, as literature is seen as a resource in which African children have the ability to understand their subjectivity and tools of subversion.

African children's literature continuously seeks to find ways to contest the dominant culture, and show children how to transcend such hegemonic discourses and why it is important to do so. Understanding that the postcolonial discourse "places emphasis on the political, economic, social, and cultural subjugation of a nation's spirit of nationalism, freedom, and heroic struggle against foreign oppression," postcolonial African children's literature equips children with the tools necessary to resist.[26] One of the most influential African authors who have taken the call to "Africanize" the content and illustrations found in children's literature in Ghana is Efua Theodora Sutherland, an activist, writer, and pioneer of children's literature.[27]

In Ghana, the beginning of written children's literature emerges with Sutherland's *Playtime in Africa* (1960), three years after the country gained independence. It was the first documentation of children's play culture in Ghana. This book was significant for many reasons. First, it presented the nuances of children's lives to the forefront of society and, second, it ushered in an indigenous movement in writing for children, along with publishing and development through drama for children. Sutherland established the Drama Studio as a workshop for writers who wrote for children. Such workshops sought to create greater awareness of the need to write more culturally appropriate books for Ghanaian children. The idea of an "African personality", something distinct and separate from non-Africanness, had taken over the country during this time and was reflected in the ways authors wrote stories for children. Writers were able to provide Ghanaians with a highly visible cultural identity around which to unite.

---

[26] Hashemy, Hayati and Amiri, "Postcolonialism, Children, and Their Literature," 70.

[27] Efua Theodora Sutherland was born in 1924 in Cape Coast in the Gold Coast (now Ghana). After graduating from St. Monica's Training College, Sutherland moved to England where she studied at Homerton College, Cambridge, and the School of Oriental and African Studies, University of London. She returned to Ghana in 1951 where she co-founded the cultural journal *Okyeame* and worked as a teacher in several schools. She died on January 2, 1996.

As an activist, Sutherland was appointed in the 1980s to lead Ghana to become one of the first countries to ratify the UN Convention on the Rights of the Child (CRC). With her leadership, there was an understanding that childhood was a unique life stage, and the Ghanaian child required specific consideration unique to his or her experiences. Sutherland introduced children's literature that reflected the particular subjectivity of postcolonial African children, calling attention to issues of race, nationality and gender in Ghana. Sutherland's biographers note her importance to the genre of Ghanaian children's literature and recognize that "she was the first Ghanaian writer to take a serious interest in writing for children."[28] In line with Fanon's call for action, her texts address cultural tensions between Western and African values and reflect the impact of white domination on the socio-political climate that confronts postcolonial African children. Sutherland publicly discussed her motives for writing children's books, and has stated that the most important thing an African writer can do is "write for the children."[29]

An Akan proverb states, "*se wo were fi, na wosankofa a yenkyi*", which can be translated as "it is not wrong to go back for what you have forgotten."[30] Sutherland embodies this principle by writing on what is of value from the past. Postcolonial themes emerge in her stories and characters, with "their internalized rebellion, their sense of outrage at being denied freedom, and their helplessness in the face of crushingly superior – often military – forces."[31] Sutherland creates characters that engage in subversive strategies in order to express their hybridity as postcolonial African children. By retaining their past in the present, her characters find moments of resistance in a postcolonial context as exemplified by *A Voice in the Forest*.

The Fool in the Forest: Cultural Subversion

Recognizing the historical context of *A Voice in the Forest* permits a more nuanced critical analysis of the book. Sutherland's text powerfully portrays the political, economic, and social complexity of colonialism and cultural relativism in Ghana in regards to children. The text is a retelling of an Akan folktale and deals with navigating diverse cultural values. It tells the story of a man

---

[28] Mabel Komasi, "Efua Sutherland: Visionary Pioneer of Ghanaian Children's Literature," in Anne V. Adams and Esi Sutherland-Addy (ed.), *The Legacy of Efua Sutherland: Pan-African Cultural Activism*, (Banbury: Ayebia, 2007), 69.

[29] Gay Wilentz, "Writing for the Children: Orature, Tradition, and Community in Efua Sutherland's "Foriwa," *Research in African Literatures* 19(2), (1988): 182.

[30] Andrea Y. Adomako's translation.

[31] Hashemy, Hayati and Amiri, "Postcolonialism, Children, and Their Literature," 72.

named Bempong who unknowingly discovers a Samanta, a wood nymph, and brings her back to his village. Initially, Bempong believes the Samanta is a lost girl, wandering alone through the forest. For the first half of the story, the Samanta refuses to speak. It is not until Bempong cuts off her hair, in an effort to tame her outgrown hair, that Bempong realizes this girl is a Samanta, a wood nymph – "a creature of strange magical powers."[32] Finding her voice in a moment of anger, the Samanta girl curses the village, leaving them with no food until she has her hair back. The hero of the book is Afrum, Bempong's son, who is regarded as the village fool.

Sutherland describes Afrum as someone with an affinity for riddles. He picked up this talent in childhood and never grew out of it. For this reason, "neither his family nor the other villagers could understand him. "Afrum the Fool, they had teased and mocked."[33] Although a disregarded member of the community, Afrum is able to save the village by tricking the Samanta through his riddles. He allows the Samanta girl to play at his home, which happens to be a beach. At sunset, Afrum asks the Samanta girl to return his sand as it was before. When the Samanta is unable to do so, she tells the village they can keep her hair and lifts the curse. Through Afrum's riddle, the Samanta realizes that she cannot undo what she did to the sand, just as the villagers cannot uncut her hair. It is after this encounter that the society realizes that this out-cast has useful skills; "Afrum, 'the Fool' has shown his people that the mind of the sons and daughters of our people has power over the Samanta and all such pesky creatures forever."[34] It is in this time of trouble that Afram's worth is recognized and affirmed, and as a result, he is named chief of the village.

Sutherland's choice to celebrate the redemption of the fool, a childlike figure, speaks to the ways in which colonised subjects of the Gold Coast (who on the attainment of independence will become known as Ghanaians) were seen as fools by the British because of their culture and customs. Like a fool, Afrum represents a set of values that had been rejected by the dominant group, in this case, his affinity for riddles. His family and larger community did not understand him and dismissed what they did not understand. His position is representative of the demeaning dismissal to which colonised Ghanaians have been subjected.

As a result of this colonial gaze, ethnic cultures and customs were ridiculed even within colonised populations. Although Ghanaians were no longer defined

---

[32] Efua Sutherland, *A Voice in the Forest*, (Ghana: Afram Publishing, 1983), 9.
[33] Ibid., 6.
[34] Ibid., 36.

as colonial subjects in 1983, the legacy of devaluing Ghanaian culture remained within "the ruling community". In this sense, the villagers, including Bempong, are representative of colonial, hegemonic ideals. The institution of colonialism implicitly assigned a value system to everyday life, with Western ways of knowing and existing being the most valued. Even after colonial forces had physically vacated, the value system remained for a large part of society. This internalized oppression means that some Ghanaians have oppressed indigenous cultural practices, knowledge systems and traditions. As a result, postcolonial African children have been taught to mistrust their cultural practices including the utilization of riddles. Sutherland's choice to place value on the use of riddles underscores the importance of Ghanaian culture and deemphasizes colonized logic based on Western culture and identity.

In addition, framing Afrum as childish is representative of the demeaning positioning Ghanaians were regarded under colonial forces. Colonised Ghanaians, known then as Gold Coasters, were seen not only as second-class subjects and non-citizens by the British but also as children in need of paternalistic care. Only a small percentage of the colonised population participated in British national affairs. This dynamic was due to the increasing opinion by the British of the unlikelihood that the Africans were capable of being full citizens of their own country. Many Ghanaians internalized this belief and have become convinced that "they have no voice in the nation's affairs, that their actions are useless, that their voice is not heard."[35] This feeling of inadequacy has persisted even after the physical colonial presence ended. Most Ghanaians have turned away from practices marked as "tradition" in an effort to participate in the so-called modern world as it has been presented to them through colonialism. This type of indoctrination was not one that postcolonial authors wanted to pass down to future generations; thus, Sutherland uses Afrum to illustrate that the skills deemed frivolous by the colonial gaze are actually integral aspects of identity that prove useful and fruitful.

Children and "fools" have much in common: they are both dependent, misunderstood members of society who hold little power. It is important to consider the particular subjectivity of postcolonial African children as social beings with a psychic life of their own, in need of liberation. Bhabha states that "for Fanon, the liberatory 'people' who initiate the productive instability of revolutionary cultural change are themselves the bearers of hybrid identity. They are caught in the discontinuous time of translation and negotiation."[36]

---

[35] Albert Memmi, *The Colonizer and the Colonized*, (New York: Orion Press, 1965), 91-92.
[36] Bhabha, *The Location of Culture*, 55.

Postcolonial African children tend to encounter the clash between traditional values and the influence of Western culture, which is often depicted as morally corrupt. However, because the postcolonial African child is a transgressing figure Afrum is able to rearticulate and reposition his identity. The translation and negotiation that Bhabha notes are significant to his concept of the "third space", in which Bhabha examines the subject situated between the I and the You.[37] Afrum enacts subversion through his use of riddles and gains power in a third space that is neither traditional nor colonial.

The village, to which Afrum is named chief of, includes the same villagers but paradoxically is not the same village that rejected him. As Sutherland writes, "a beautiful village grew around Afrum's cottage by the river. His people never returned to the village they had left behind."[38] Afrum creates a literal third space for himself and his community, which he then governs. This liminal space constantly fluctuates, but it is in this nexus that subjects can anchor their identity. Bhabha terms this process a "dialectical reorganization" in which people "construct their culture from the national text translated into modern Western forms of information technology, language, and dress. The changed political and historical site of enunciation transforms the meanings of the colonial inheritance into liberatory signs . . ."[39] These hybrid subjects can then emerge in a space that constitutes a temporal break from white-constructed subject formation. It is in this space that the postcolonial African child can creatively disrupt Western notions of time and self. Afrum showcases how the hybrid nature of the postcolonial child subject demands its construction through subversion of both the colonial discourse and that of the elders in the community. Although Afrum becomes the hero, it is important to note that subversion also exists for the Samanta girl who is also able to position herself as a self-creating agent outside of traditional constraints.

Postcolonial African Girlhood

While the story centres on the heroic figure of Afrum, it is important to also consider the Samanta girl within the context of postcolonial African girlhood. Within postcolonialism, African women writers such as Sutherland are positioning themselves within theories of transnational feminist discourses that have to fight against images of girlhood and "a colonialist discourse that exercises a very specific power in defining, coding, and maintaining existing

---

[37] Ibid., 56.
[38] Sutherland, *A Voice in the Forest*, 35.
[39] Bhabha, *The Location of Culture*, 56.

First/Third World connections."[40] Sutherland's work draws our attention to the "hierarchical relationships among girls as vulnerable, and/or innocent subjects."[41] I examine the Samanta girl in order to understand the important role that gender plays in postcolonial African childhood.

A Voice in the Forest demonstrates what Sara Ahmed defines as "stranger fetishism" in the sense that the book highlights the figure of the exotic girl stranger. The Samanta girl piques Bempong's interest because he sees her as a meek, strange little girl who he might rescue and save. According to Ahmed, "'the stranger' is assumed to be knowable, seeable and hence be-able."[42] The impulse to civilize the Samanta girl feeds into colonial ideologies of controlling and protecting colonised bodies in a way that asserts dominance. This control was essential to the British policy of indirect rule in Ghana that wanted the previous colonised subjects to align themselves with the culture, values and worldview of the coloniser. Specifically contextualizing postcolonialism within transnational girlhood studies, it is important to note how "global capitalist and imperialist dynamics operate within the material practices and representations of 'girlhood' or 'the girl child.'"[43] The narrative of the Samanta girl forces readers to confront the colonial and hierarchal relationships that are symbolized through the Samanta's girl's body.

The little girl in the story is never named, other than being called a Samanta, and therefore only becomes defined through her characteristics: she is beautiful, loves to sing, has dainty legs and a pretty smile. However, her most important feature, which becomes central to the story, is her overgrown curly Black hair as characterized in the text. This feature is important because it signifies that the Samanta girl is a product of global representations of Black girls' bodies as "unruly, spirited, physically active, self-reliant, and when able, unabashedly vocal."[44] Sutherland's postcolonial girl character is a part of a longer legacy of Black girls whose hair, body, and behaviour have been politicized and policed.

---

[40] Chandra Talpade Mohanty, *Feminism without Borders: Decolonizing Theory, Practicing Solidarity,* (Durham: Duke, 2006), 41.

[41] Elizabeth Marshall, "Global Girls and Strangers: Marketing Transnational Girlhood through the Nancy Drew Series," *Children's Literature Association Quarterly* 37(2), (2012): 211.

[42] Sara Ahmed, *Strange Encounters: Embodied Others in Post-Coloniality,* (New York: Routledge, 2000), 133.

[43] Lisa Weems, "'Border Crossing with M.I.A. and Transnational Girlhood Studies," in Roland Sintos (ed.), *Postcolonial Challenges in Education,* (New York: Peter Lang, 2009), 179.

[44] Nazera Sadiq Wright, "Girlhood in African American Literature, 1827-1949," (PhD Dissertation, University of Maryland, College Park, 2010), 28.

Hair for women and girls has always been a visual signifier for class, ethnicity, religion, and respectability. As a result, hair is often linked to social status and ultimately significations of power.[45] Black women and girls have complicated relationships with these significations, because these symbols have been used to place value on their claim to humanity since colonialism. For Black girls, the notion that they are unruly and defiant is tied to the way their "unruly, wild" hair has been positioned in society. In the case of the Samanta girl, concerns of her unruliness and rebellion are implicit in her hair. Bempong sees it as something that needs to be tamed and does so without her permission. Throughout the story, the Samanta girl cries, squirms, or even tries to run away at every mention that her hair is a "problem" to be cut down. It is not until her hair is finally cut that she unleashes her fury and magical powers. With her hair she was a carefree girl; without it she is enraged.

This postcolonial African girl symbolizes anxieties about a mass of politically disruptive colonised subjects. The Samanta girl poses a challenge to the colonial-inspired aesthetic norms that serve as a political mechanism for control. She is a metaphorical form of resistance in her negation of both hegemonic imperatives as well as male figures. For outsiders, her hair indicates an unwillingness to comply, or indifference to cultural and gender norms. Therefore, her resistance to authoritative cultural requirements is seen as a threat to existing power structures. Her disruptive behaviour towards the villagers, after she loses her hair, becomes her way of effecting control and order within the circumstances she encounters.

The postcolonial subjectivity of African children motivates them to create authority out of their positioning. Rather than retreat without a fight, the Samanta girl insists that her presence be acknowledged since a pervasive effect of colonisation has been the erasure of Black girls' presence through the dismissal of conflicts and concerns connected to the displacement experienced by women and girls of African descent. The Samanta girl's function as an anti-colonial figure rests primarily with her assertion of female independence, symbolized primarily by her hair. Given the historically masculinized nature of the colonial forces that have subjugated Ghanaians, the Samanta's very gendered independence represents her anti-colonial function as an aggressive agent against the masculine strains of colonialism.

However, the Samanta girl ultimately loses to the masculine figures in the text, Bempong and Afrum. Her magical powers do not transfer into any real political power and she is left without having her hair restored to her. The Samanta girl's

---

[45] Kobena Mercer, "Black Hair/Style Politics," *New Formations* 3, (1987): 36.

hybridity, both magical and real, leave her vulnerable to the same injustices postcolonial African girls and women often face. In this sense, we see how "'girlhood' becomes a site that consolidates assumptions and practices regarding difference, colonial power, and economic relations between and among gendered subjects in transnational contexts."[46] Due to institutionalized forces, the Samantha girl continues to be marginalized under colonialism and patriarchy while simultaneously asserting her power as much as she can.

Here Sutherland, through transnational feminist theory, represents complexities and possibilities in postcolonial girlhood. We see an African girl exercising resistance and agency as she negotiates around masculine, nationalist discourses. As Lisa Weems writes, "what is at stake in this cultural politics is the extent to which youth (girls and boys) can create, inhabit, and transgress the discursive positions to which they are subject."[47] The figure of the postcolonial African girl is not represented solely as a victim, but as an active and vocal participant who is her own producer of culture and knowledge. She is striving for her freedom and hoping to maintain her independence. As a postcolonial African girl, the Samanta is able to navigate her space while creating new relationships and responses to the "'tense and tender ties' of colonialism."[48] In this sense, Sutherland's narrative strategy and characterization is postcolonial in its assertive re-framing of African girlhood. The Samanta girl is both subversive and embedded in the tradition despite her final defeat by the male protagonists. Sutherland provides a necessary critique of the perpetuations of masculine norms even in this idealized "third space," which allows for a transnational feminist reading in efforts to theorize within postcolonial African girlhood.

Conclusion

Afrum and the Samanta girl are able to defy the boundaries and norms created by their elders, and as a result, they subvert the discourses of dominance and power. These characters showcase the ways in which their subjectivities cannot be explained in terms of oppositional binaries, but rather through their in-betweeness that characterizes their postcolonial subjectivity. Sutherland's use of African children's literature reflects an understanding of the genre as a space in which children can understand their inherited place in history and use imagination as a site to create a new redemptive subjectivity. Hybridity becomes a mechanism to survive and thrive in the postcolonial moment.

---

[46] Weems, ""Border Crossing with M.I.A. and Transnational Girlhood Studies", 179.
[47] Ibid.
[48] Ibid., 186.

In *The Wretched of the Earth*, Fanon emphasizes that with decolonisation comes a complete change from the colonial situation and Black subjectivity by stating that, "decolonization is the veritable creation of new men."[49] This "new man" begins with understanding the child as a self-creating agent. Presently, the push to "decolonise" the African mindset as well as overthrow colonial rule is still very much alive. African nationalists wish to re-educate their youth and give value to African culture. We cannot discuss an education for liberation without speaking of an education that connects and respects hybrid identities without reinforcing exploitative power dynamics.

As the field of childhood studies evolves, it is important to understand the different representations of postcolonial childhood as being presented to children in African children's literature. Looking solely at the numbers, African children occupy a unique position in African society because they are, and will continue to be, an overwhelming majority. As a result, the weight of the nation falls on their shoulders. Although previous generations operate under a particular set of binaries, postcolonial African children are complicating such tensions and necessitating a re-articulation of what African childhood entails. For postcolonial African girls, there needs to be an increasing effort by scholars to decolonise the ahistorical notion of girlhood and to understand it as a site of unequal distributions of power. The goal is for African children to no longer see themselves as inferior to Europeans and the West, and by extension other peoples of non-African descent, but rather to understand that it is possible to exist as a postcolonial subject without alienation from one's own culture.

Sutherland acknowledges and writes against the cultural legacy of Europe and the capitalistic educational system it birthed. In doing so, she creates characters that participate in the disruption of a purely Eurocentric subjecthood. The trajectory of African children's literature, as it stands, is a constant negotiation where authors must reflect the dialectical relationship between the pre-colonial and the colonial, the old and the new – in order to reflect the position of the postcolonial African child accurately and portray the cultural blending these subjects represent. African children's literature exists in what Bhabha defines as a liminal space that "provides the terrain for elaborating strategies of selfhood – singular or communal – that initiate new signs of identity, and innovative sites of collaboration, and contestation, in the act of defining the idea of society itself."[50] Through this literature, conscious adults arm children with strategies for resisting colonial discourses. Notions of an un-

---

[49] Fanon, *The Wretched of the Earth*, 34.
[50] Bhabha, *The Location of Culture*, 2.

knowable and ahistorical Africa still haunt the popular imagination of children and make it necessary for scholars and writers to affirm Africa's cultural relevance. This alternative discourse enables the intellectual and psychic decolonisation that Fanon calls for. The multiple possibilities for negotiation and re-articulation are the most significant signs of African postcolonial children's literature. It refutes boundaries in an effort to participate in a literature of decolonisation, one that destroys previous patterns of alienation and instead calls for postcolonial African children to reconstruct themselves.

Bibliography

Ahmed, Sara. Strange Encounters: Embodied Others in Post-Coloniality. New York: Routledge, 2000.

Bhabha, Homi. The Location of Culture. London: Routledge, 1994.

Bohannan, Paul. Africa and Africans. N.Y: Garden City, 1964.

Brooke, James. "Ghana, Once 'Hopeless,' Gets at Least the Look of Success." The New York Times, Jan. 3, 1989.

Emenyonu, Ernest. "Education and the Contemporary Malaise in Nigeria." In The Role of Education in Contemporary Africa, edited by Charles E. Nnolim. New York: Professors World Peace Academy, 1988. 31-40.

Emenyonu, Ernest. "Selection and Validation of Oral Materials for Children's Literature: Artistic Resources in Chinua Achebe's Fiction for Children." Callaloo 25 (2) (2002): 584-596.

Fanon, Frantz. Black Skin, White Masks. London: Pluto, 2008.

Fanon, Frantz. Wretched of the Earth. New York: Grove, 1963.

Gyan-Apenteng, Kwasi. "Lest We Forget-1983-Thirty Years Ago," Ghanaweb, May 13, 2013. https://www.ghanaweb.com/GhanaHomePage/NewsArchive/Lest-We-Forget-1983-Thirty-Years-Ago-273736.

Hashemy, Sayed Ahmad, Hayati, Daryoosh and Eisa Amiri. "Postcolonialism, Children, and Their Literature." In Frontiers of Language and Teaching, Vol.2: Proceedings of the 2011 International Online Language Conference, edited by Azadeh Shafaei. Boca Raton: Brown Walker Press, 2011: 63-74.

Khorana, Meena. Critical Perspectives on Postcolonial African Children's and Young Adult Literature. Westport. CT: Greenwood, 1998.

Komasi, Mabel and Helen Yitah. "Children's Literature in Ghana: Survey." Children's Literature 37 (2009): 236-255.

Komasi, Mabel. "Efua Sutherland: Visionary Pioneer of Ghanaian Children's Literature." In The Legacy of Efua Sutherland: Pan-African Cultural Activism, edited by Anne V. Adams and Esi Sutherland-Addy. Banbury: Ayebia Clarke, 2007.

Marshall, Elizabeth. "Global Girls and Strangers: Marketing Transnational Girlhood through the Nancy Drew Series." Children's Literature Association Quarterly 37(2) (2012): 210-227.

Memmi, Albert. The Colonizer and the Colonized. New York: Orion Press, 1965.

Mercer, Kobena. "Black Hair/Style Politics." New Formations 3 (1987): 33-54.

Mohanty, Chandra Talpade. Feminism without Borders: Decolonizing Theory, Practicing Solidarity. Durham: Duke University Press, 2006.

Osa, Osayimwense. African Children's and Youth Literature. New York: Twayne Publisher, 1995.

Simoes da Silva, Tony. "Myths, Traditions and Mothers of the Nation: Some Thoughts on Efua Sutherland's Writing." EnterText 4 (2) (2005): 254-270.

Sutherland, Efua. A Voice in the Forest. Ghana: Afram Publishing, 1983.

Walker, Sheila S. and Jennifer Rasamimanana. "Tarzan in the Classroom: How "Educational" Films Mythologize Africa and Miseducate Americans." The Journal of Negro Education 62 (1) (1993): 3-23.

Weems, Lisa. "Border Crossing with M.I.A. and Transnational Girlhood Studies." In Postcolonial Challenges in Education, edited by Roland Sintos. New York: Peter Lang, 2009.

Wilentz, Gay. "Writing for the Children: Orature, Tradition, and Community in Efua Sutherland's "Foriwa." Research in African Literatures 19 (2) (1988): 182-196.

Wright, Nzera Sadiq. "Girlhood in African American Literature, 1827-1949." PhD Dissertation. University of Maryland, 2010.

Chapter 5

On the Innocence of Beasts: African Child Soldiers in Cary Fukunaga's *Beasts of No Nation*

Debbie Olson

"I am not a bad boy. I am not a bad boy."

Beasts of No Nation

Introduction

The image of the African child soldier has emerged as a persistent and complex representation of both real-world, war-time atrocities affecting African children, and Western media's detached, passive-aggressive relationship with Black children. By "detached" I refer to the lack of positive and meaningful representation of Black children in popular media, particularly Hollywood cinema. Most depictions of Black children in mainstream film are so often new interpretations of very old stereotypes—pickaninnies (*Beasts of the Southern Wild*, 2012), violent gangsters (*Fresh*, 1991), hypersexual Jezebels, or nonsexual mammies (*Precious*, 2012). These representations suggest both a passive attitude towards Black children (they are beneath notice) and an aggressive attitude (they are depicted as threats to society and the "American" way of life).

The African child soldier as depicted in Western film is often intimately connected to the historical notions the West propagates about Black children, most often males, as inherently violent and unredeemable. Black children in Western films are often framed as impure and unable to achieve the promise of childhood innocence, therefore affirming cultural notions of "blackness" as inherently corrupt. The discursive nature of cinematic images of African children (and childhood) positions them as furthest from the Western ideal of childhood innocence and perfection – the blonde, blue-eyed, wide-eyed, curly-haired, dimpled, angelic white child. This angel-demon dichotomy[1] of children is used to uphold the "West as eternal adult and Africa as eternal child."[2] Indeed, modern digital media fosters the transnational circulation of disparaging images of Black children that reveal a pattern of misrepresentation regarding the nature of Black children from both the Global North and South, particularly Black males. Maureen Moynagh suggests three ways the child soldier character is popularly interpreted: the "pity at a distance," as representative of a "sentimentality" that is intimately connected to the "material force of global inequalities;" the age-old trope of innocence lost; and as representatives of the loss of "moral order."[3] All of these are part of the cinematic child soldier narrative.

As Robin Bernstein and others argue, the mid-nineteenth century shift from viewing the child as a mini-adult to the "sentimentalized child" changed the way culture perceived children and childhood. Childhood itself became "understood not as innocent but as innocence itself; not as a symbol of innocence, but as its embodiment."[4] But popular representations of innocence favoured, and still favour, white children over children of colour: "popular culture purged innocence from representations of African American children [and] the black child was redefined as a nonchild—a pickaninny."[5] The Black child has never been a part of that cultural shift to the sentimental child, and even more so for African children. In Western popular culture, African children are often depicted as the "other" to the white child. African children are quite often portrayed as transgressive and fractured, as non-children, "perverted from [childhood's] 'natural' course of innocence, fragility, and purity."[6] The African child image is most commonly seen in the West through ads by

---

[1] This dichotomy is most popularized in the US by Harriet Beecher Stowe's novel *Uncle Tom's Cabin* and the contrast between the Black slave girl Topsy and the white girl Eva.

[2] Marina Bradbury, "Negotiating Identities: Representations of Childhood in Senegalese Cinema," *Journal of African Media Studies* 2(1), (2010): 13.

[3] Maureen Moynagh, "Human Rights Child-Soldier Narratives, and the Problem of Form," *Research in African Literatures* 42(4), (2011): 39.

[4] Robin Bernstein, *Racial Innocence: Performing American Childhood from Slavery to Civil Rights,* (New York: New York University Press, 2011), 4. See also Karen Sanchez-Eppler, *Dependent States,* (Chicago: University of Chicago Press, 2005); Viviana Zelizer, *Pricing the Priceless Child,* (New York: Basic Books, 1985); Caroline F. Levander, *Cradle of Liberty,* (Durham: Duke University Press, 2006).

[5] Bernstein, *Racial Innocence: Performing American Childhood from Slavery to Civil Rights,* 34.

[6] Myriam Denov, "Child Soldiers and Iconography: Portrayals and [Mis]Representations," *Children and Society* 26, (2012): 282.

NGO's (non-governmental organizations): "boys and girls with bloated bellies, no parents, and bruised and broken bodies [which] present a compelling image of victimhood."[7] Kate Manzo argues that images of African children are the "means through which NGOs produce themselves as humanitarian."[8] Ultimately, the Black child image functions as a temporal mirror that separates Western white childhoods of the "now" from the "primitiveness" (that is, backwardness) of Black childhoods. This separation functions to distort the recognition of real Black children as children, an odd, contradictory reversal of the West's perpetual depiction of Africa and its adults as "children" incapable of handling their own affairs.

The image of the Black child also presents a temporal contrast to white notions of innocence and purity. Coming of age narratives in cinema commonly feature white children who transcend to adulthood through knowledge acquisition, something the Black child is both historically and cinematically rarely allowed to achieve. As the white child progresses to adulthood, the Black child is often cinematically frozen in the interstice between child and adult – an oscillation rooted in the racist discourse of the colonial era. The child soldier character functions as a counter to the Western narrative of perfect childhood and is often featured in Hollywood films. This cinematic child soldier, who elicits both sympathy and fear, is an example of the African child's suspended oscillation between child and adult.

It is my argument that the African child soldier in Cary Fukunaga's 2015 adaptation of Uzodinma Iweala's *Beasts of No Nation*, is an extension of, and inextricably bound to, Western notions about Black male children as inherently violent, non-innocent, and ultimately unredeemable. In Iweala's novel, Agu navigates, and resists, events that happen to him and works to reconcile his belief in his own goodness (and innocence) even when forced to commit atrocities. In stark contrast, Fukunaga's film sets up Agu as *deserving* the events that happen to him *because of* his flawed character since he was *already* not innocent, which the film establishes at its opening. While Iweala's novel compellingly and convincingly captures Agu's innocence and childlike worldview, the film adaptation makes pointed changes to Iweala's story that work to perpetuate the notion that Black children are not like "real" (white) children at all, and are in fact the "beasts" the West has always believed them to be. Ultimately, the film does not challenge, but rather reinforce the West's

---

[7] Scott Gates and Simon Reich (eds.), *Child Soldiers in the Age of Fractured States*, (Pittsburg: University of Pittsburg Press, 2009), 5

[8] Kate Manzo, "Imagine Humanitarianism: NGO Identity and the Iconography of Childhood," *Antipode* 40(4), (2008): 634.

historical "Africa-as-chaos" narrative through the eyes of an "already-guilty" boy soldier name Agu.

Uzodinma Iweala's Agu

Youth or child characters have emerged as a prominent feature in many contemporary African fictional narratives, such as Helen Oyeyemi's *The Icarus Girl*, Chimamanda Ngozi Adichie's *Purple Hibiscus*, Chris Abani's *Song for Night*, and Emmanual Jal's *Warchild*. According to Madelaine Hron, the child character "occupies a critical position in African . . . literature" in which children "examine mature themes and complex global issues" in a context that raises questions about, among other things, childhood, innocence, and agency.[9] The concept of childhood in Africa is, in some ways, different from the idealized notions of childhood prominent in the West. For instance, children in some parts of Africa are viewed with distrust and suspicion. Speaking about notions of childhood in Sierra Leone, Danny Hoffman explains that children are deemed to straddle both the domains and activities of spirits and the human realm. Thus, "To be born is not to be vested with the fullness of humanity; it is, rather, a stage in a process of movement through a liminal, dangerous, state."[10] In some parts of West Africa, children are often viewed as closer to the spiritual realm and as such are not "fully trusted" by adults.[11] The belief in this "in-between" status of children works in some African literature by allowing child characters to comment on socio-political conditions, to "make ethical demands" of its readers.[12] Thus, while pointing out that "children without visible authority can 'stand where adults do not dare,' and . . . gain access to knowledge that can bring grief to their social superiors",[13] Marianne C. Ferme argues,

> they are able to do so by crisscrossing "boundaries between ordinary and ritual practices" due to the fact that they do not "embody distinct social

---

[9] Madelaine Hron, "Ora na-asu nwa: The Figure of the Child in Third-Generation Nigerian Novels," *Research in African Literatures* 39(2), (2008): 28.

[10] Danny Hoffman, "Like Beasts in the Bush: Synonyms of Childhood and Youth in Sierra Leone," *Postcolonial Studies* 6(3), (2003): 299.

[11] For more on personhood in West Africa, see Charles Piot *Remotely Global: Village Modernity in West Africa*, (University of Chicago Press, 1999).

[12] Allison Mackey, "Troubling Humanitarian Consumption: Reframing Relationality in African Child Soldier Narratives," *Research in African Literatures* 44(4), (2013): 100.

[13] Marianne C. Ferme, *The Underneath of Things*, (University of California Press, 2001), 199.

identities". Consequently, they navigate "between public and secret discursive domains, which adults are more reluctant to transgress."[14]

And so, children are often valued for their insight into adult issues. Children are also greatly loved and cherished by their families. Child characters in film and fiction tend to challenge notions of power, social discourse, and cultural practices in ways that transcend adult norms and expectations. Such is the character of the child soldier, who is "constantly negotiating, questioning or even resisting these cultural constructions, even by virtue of its own constructedness."[15] But for the Western viewer of the child soldier narrative, the challenge to cultural norms functions only to reinforce their historical beliefs about Black children and Africa.

The "constructedness" of the child character is central to the argument of both child agency and child victimhood. Narratives of the child solder become "trapped in a rhetorical effort to restore . . . childhood innocence" to Black children the Western reader always already views as Other. For the West, the rhetorical move back towards innocence in the "lost childhood" narrative is unattainable for the African child soldier because the Black child is assumed to have *more* agency than white children, but no innocence. As Katrina Lee-Koo astutely argues, "the predominance of the African male child as the poster boy of contemporary conflict on the African continent, if not the Global South more broadly . . . reflects and reinforces pre-existing notions of the Global South as a morally defunct zone of tragedy."[16] To the West, Black children are always culpable, even if they are victims – similar to the way Western narratives will often blame a rape victim for her victimization.[17] The constructedness of the child and the "horror of childhood perverted from its 'natural' course of innocence, fragility, and purity"[18] are at the core of the differences between Iweala's and Fukunaga's child soldier, Agu.

Beasts of No Nation (2005) is Nigerian American Uzodinma Iweala's first novel. Iweala was inspired by former child soldiers he met while he was pres-

---

14 Ibid.

15 Hron, "Ora na-asu nwa: The Figure of the Child in Third-Generation Nigerian Novels," 29.

16 Katrina Lee-Koo, "Horror and Hope: (Re)presenting Militarised Children in Global North-South Relations," *Third World Quarterly* 32(4), (2011): 730-731.

17 See Estelle B. Freedman, *Redefining Rape: Sexual Violence in the Era of Suffrage and Segregation*, (Harvard University Press, 2013).

18 Myriam Denov, "Child Soldiers and Iconography: Portrayals and (Mis)representations," 282.

ident of the African Students Association at Harvard. *Beasts of No Nation* was developed from his senior thesis at Harvard and won the Los Angeles Times Art Seidenbaum Award for First Fiction, the Sue Kaufman Prize for First Fiction from the Academy of Arts and Letters, the Young Lions 2006 Fiction Award (New York Public Library), and the 2006 John Llewellyn Rhys Prize. The novel was described by one reviewer as "so scorched by loss and anger that it's hard to hold and so gripping in its sheer hopeless lifeforce that it's hard to put down."[19] Another reviewer noted that it is the "psychological conflict" within Agu that gives the novel its power.[20] However, not all reviewers were impressed with Iweala's novel. Aaron Bady, writing for the LA review of books, felt the novel "not only draws from its predecessors, but is imprisoned by them." Bady suggests that the novel is merely a "sentimental writing in which the piteous spectacle of the tragic child [is] the only point of the exercise." But while Bady misses the complexities of the novel entirely, he is correct to acknowledge that it is the "spectacle of the tragic child" that captures the West's imagination. And it is the West's "consumption of stories of suffering and violence [that] has the potential to confirm preexisting stereotypes about Africa as a savage, inhuman landscape full of unimaginable horrors."[21] There is no shortage of savage acts in *Beasts of no Nation*, as in any war story, yet the primary conflict arises from Agu's struggle to *retain* his humanity, his innocence, and his childhood while being forced to commit the most inhuman acts of violence. As Allison Mackey observes, in Iweala's *Beasts* "the contrast between the figure of the child and the predator are combined in one character."[22] In the novel, Agu is a nine-year-old boy who is conscripted into a rebel group after being separated from his family (he sees his father murdered) during an attack on his village. Thus begins Agu's complex negotiation with morality, innocence, horror, and being a child.

Into the Valley of Death

The novel opens with a symbolic birth scene as Agu lays in a fetal position in the corner of a small building and articulates:

---

[19] Ali Smith, "The Lost Boys," *The Observer*, 3 September 2005, https://www.theguardian.com/books/2005/sep/03/fiction.alismith. Accessed on September 17, 2018.
[20] Noah Deutsch, "The Grim and the Dead–*Beasts of No Nation* by Uzodinma Iweala," (15 January 2007), https://themillions.com/2007/01/grim-and-dead-beasts-of-no-nation-by.html. Accessed on September 17, 2018.
[21] Mackey, "Troubling Humanitarian Consumption: Reframing Relationality in African Child Soldier Narratives," 108.
[22] Ibid. 109.

> . . . I am opening my eye . . . light . . . coming into the dark through hole
> in the roof, crossing like net above my body . . . [M]y body crunched up
> like one small mouse in the corner when the light is coming in.[23]

This seemingly benign scene is shattered when Agu is suddenly being beaten by
another child, Strika, who then drags him out into the road: "he is grabbing my
leg, pulling it so hard that it is like it will be coming apart like meat, and my body
is just sliding slowly from the stall out into the light and onto the mud."[24] Strika
is another child who was conscripted into the rebel group and later becomes
Agu's friend. Strika does not speak, which is his way of dealing with the trauma
of being a soldier. According to Susan J. Song and Joop de Jong, child soldiers
often utilize silence as a survival mechanism: "silence was an indication of stoic
emotional withholding. Showing tears, fear, or sadness were met with extreme
punishments."[25] Between Strika's silence and Agu's Pidgin English, there is a
"complete failure of language"[26] to adequately frame the boy's experience, im-
mersing the reader into their world through the rhythm of Agu's speech and his
childlike observations. In this opening scene, the reader witnesses Agu's paradoxical "birth" into the realm of death – the death of his childhood, of innocence, and the physical death he will learn to inflict on others.

Agu's speech in the novel functions to highlight both his childness (the state of
being a child) and his psychological struggle with the horror he sees, and later,
commits. Iweala's use of Pidgin English, perhaps influenced by Ken Saro-wiwa's
Sozaboy: a Novel in Rotten English,[27] adds to the readers' empathy for both Agu's
helplessness and the trauma he experiences. As Mackey explains, "the helplessness reflected in Agu's language mirrors his sense of being overwhelmed by
outside forces."[28] But Agu's language, particularly his repetition of key descriptive or emotional words – beating beating; slowly slowly; begging begging; killing
killing – foregrounds the surreal aspect of his experience. Indeed, throughout
the novel at key moments of terror or extreme violence Agu embraces the surre-

---

[23] Uzodinam Iweala, *Beasts of No Nation*, (New York: Harper Collins, 2005),1, (hereafter
in notes as BNN).
[24] BNN, 3.
[25] Suzan J. Song and Joop de Jong, "The Role of Silence in Burundian Former Child
Soldiers," *International Journal of Advanced Counseling* 36(1), (2014): 88.
[26] Mackey, "Troubling Humanitarian Consumption: Reframing Relationality in African
Child Soldier Narratives," 109.
[27] Ken Saro-wiwa, *Sozaboy: a Novel in Rotten English*, (Saros International Publishers,
1985).
[28] Mackey, "Troubling Humanitarian Consumption: Reframing Relationality in African
Child Soldier Narratives," 109.

al: "I am floating on top of my body and just watching,"[29] or "I am standing outside myself and watching it all happening."[30] Similar to Strika's silence, this doubling of key words or phrases effectively highlights Agu's childlike negotiation with reality (is this real? is this real?) as his young mind works to resolve the moral conflicts he must constantly face.

In the novel, Agu's first meeting with the Commandant occurs through half-consciousness caused by starvation and thirst. The Commandant offers him water, offers to take care of him, then asks "do you want to be a soldier? . . . If you are staying with me, I will be taking care of you and we will be fighting the enemy that is taking your father." Remembering how his father "just danc[ed] like that because of a bullet," Agu first asks "What am I supposed to be doing?" and then tells the reader "So I am joining. Just like that. I am soldier."[31] That Agu asks himself (and us) "what am I supposed to be doing?" suggests, not agency, but rather a Hobson's choice: fearing they will kill him if he refuses, his only choice is to accept. But his questioning of the choice also allows the reader to clearly position Agu as victim. As Maureen Moynagh explains, it is the "child-*as-victim* – we are meant to connect with, not the child-as-soldier,"[32] and it is this moment of the (false) choice in the novel that reinforces Agu's childness and the many moral conflicts he will face, especially when he is taught to kill.

Agu's first kill in the novel is the most traumatic event he suffers and sets the stage for his eagerness to take the "gun juice" later in the novel. The Commandant calls Agu to him but Agu is frozen by fear: "I am standing in my place and I am just fearing. I am not wanting to be killing anybody today. I am not ever wanting to be killing anybody." But Commandant loses patience, drags Agu to the "enemy soldier" and starts shouting "Do you see this dog? . . . you want to be a soldier, enh? Well – kill him! KILL HIM NOW!"[33] Agu's reaction to this is worth repeating in detail as it reinforces Agu's innocence in the face of such atrocities and differs in significant ways from the film: "I am . . . crying and . . . shaking. . . thinking, if I am killing . . . I am going to hell, so I am just standing there crying crying, shaking shaking, looking looking . . . [34]

Agu mentions how the Commandant tells him to kill the enemy soldier like "a goat" while assisting him to raise his hand with the machete to strike ". . . the enemy's head and I am feeling like electricity . . . through my whole body .

[29] BNN, 8.
[30] BNN, 48.
[31] BNN, 11.
[32] Moynagh, "Human Rights Child-Soldier Narratives, and the Problem of Form," 45.
[33] BNN, 18.
[34] BNN, 19.

. . I am bringing the machete up and down . . . seeing just pink while hearing the laughing KEHI KEHI KEHI all around me."[35]

Strika joins Agu in hitting the man with the machete, but afterwards, Agu vomits and collapses on the road in shock: "and then I am falling down on the road and watching cause they are killing everybody."[36] One of the hallmarks of trauma in children is the sense of being physically and emotionally over-whelmed coupled with their powerlessness to change or escape the situa-tion.[37] In a seminal study of trauma in child soldiers, Fiona Klasen et al., found that former child soldiers suffered from Developmental Trauma Disorder (DTD), a type of Post Traumatic Stress Disorder (PTSD) that is more specific to the developmental stages and unique symptoms in children. Children like Agu who were exposed repeatedly to the most egregious violence suffer from anxiety, dissociative disorders, depression, "massive disruption of affect, bodily and behavioural regulation problems, disturbed attachment patterns, reduced autonomous strivings, aggression against self, peers, or adults, failure to pass developmental tasks, altered schemas of the world, and low self-esteem."[38] For Agu, these ongoing intersections of trauma, survival, and his cognitive immaturity create an ongoing psychological struggle that provides the discursive framework for the rest of the narrative.

As the reader follows Agu's harrowing journey, his young mind tries to rec-oncile his self-image with his actions: "I am not a bad boy. I am not a bad boy. I am telling this to myself because soldier is supposed to be killing killing killing . . . I am hearing too many voice in my head telling me I am bad boy."[39] In "The Representation of Child Soldiers in Contemporary African Fiction," J.A. Kearney suggests that Iweala here hints at the possibility that Agu can be corrupted, despite his moral crisis. Agu is consumed by guilt for his actions, yet he attempts to rationalize his violence as just "being a good soldier"[40] while at the same time wanting to not be a soldier. Significantly, the reader learns that Agu was a diligent student who loved to read, particularly the

---

[35] BNN, 20-21.

[36] BNN, 22.

[37] Michael Bader, "The Breakdown of Empathy and the Political Right in America," (22 December 2016), http://www.alternet.org/print/right-wing/breakdown-empathy-and-political-right-america. Accessed on September 18, 2018.

[38] Fionna Klasen, Johanna Gehrke , Franka Metzner , Monica Blotevogel, and James Okello, "Complex Trauma Symptoms in Former Ugandan Child Soldiers," *Journal of Aggression, Maltreatment, and Trauma* 22(7), (2013): 699-700.

[39] BNN, 23.

[40] J. A. Kearney, "The Representation of Child Soldiers in Contemporary African Fic-tion," *Journal of Literary Studies* 26(1), (2010): 85.

Christian Bible. Agu talks about his favourite stories and his mental images of the armies in David and Goliath, how they are "shining with gold and bronze in the sun." These images entice him: "I am seeing all these thing when she is reading and thinking that I am wanting to be a warrior."[41] Yet he finds that the reality of war is nothing like the gold and bronze of biblical description. Instead, Agu is thrust into living in a liminal state, existing in a "gap between ordered worlds" where he is required to remain "in a stage that is neither childhood nor adulthood in a hierarchy of power relations based entirely on the ability and eagerness to kill and exercise violence."[42] As he constantly oscillates between his childness and adult actions he experiences internal moral conflicts on numerous levels – biblical teachings, fear of going to hell, fear of Commandant killing him, bad boy versus good boy, being a good soldier, and confusion at his own bloodlust when he is taking gun juice. As Kearney argues, Agu experiences "continuous tension between the demands of his sensitive conscience, and the corrupting influences of child-soldier existence."[43] I disagree, however, that Agu is "corrupted" in the way Kearney describes. Kearney argues that Iweala suggests Agu's corruption *is* a possibility. But I believe Agu's mental oscillation between good boy/bad boy clearly demonstrates Agu's resistance to corruption – he insists he is a *good boy* despite having to also be a *good* soldier. As he states throughout the novel: "I want to be telling him I cannot be fighting anymore, that my mind is becoming rotten like the inside of fruit."[44] He would rather be just a "boy" than a soldier. It is Agu's *awareness* of the potential for corruption that *prevents* him from becoming corrupt.

Agu is *always* horrified at the violence he witnesses and later commits. For Agu, his "longing to avoid harm, be blameless" is a constant internal discourse as he attempts to retain his previous innocence. Even when he is high on gun juice, hallucinates and sees everyone as animals, he questions his actions: "I am wanting to kill; I don't know why." He sees Strika as a dog and almost kills him, but then they are "hugging in all of the screaming and the gunfire and I am feeling his head and he is feeling my head and then we are going together through all the changing color to the main house of the com-

---

[41] BNN, 25.

[42] Irina Kyulanova, "From Soldiers to Children: Undoing the Rite of Passage in Ishmeal Beah's *A Long Way Gone* and Bernard Ashley's *Little Soldier*," *Studies in the Novel* 42(1 & 2), (2010): 30.

[43] Kearney, "The Representation of Child Soldiers in Contemporary African Fiction," 88.

[44] BNN, 89.

pound."[45] Agu and Strika clinging to each other while making their way to a "safe" space reinforces Iweala's intentional positioning of Agu (and Strika) as a child-victim, despite the violence he commits: "All of this is really happening to me?"[46] The reader is witness to Agu being forcibly yanked from childhood with "no stable social structure" to protect him.[47] The novel clearly subjects Agu to the most horrendous violence and abuse, yet his core self – his belief in goodness – is a constant presence throughout the narrative. And it is this core, innocent, child-self that allows the reader to believe in Agu's ultimate goodness, despite the horrible things he has done.

One of the fundamental violations of innocence in the West is carnal knowledge. While Agu is witness to many rapes of women by the other soldiers during raids, and is aware that the Commandant has molested some of the other boys, particularly Strika, it is not until Agu himself is raped by the Commandant (repeatedly) that he releases his desperate hold on childhood: "I am knowing I am no more child so if this war is ending I cannot be going back to do child thing."[48] When the Commandant calls for him the first night, he is "thinking as many good thing I can think because if you are thinking good thing then nothing bad is happening to you."[49] His naiveté rings false, however, as his suspicions and fear about the Commandant's intentions demonstrate. But the fact that his first reaction is to "think good thoughts" reinforces Agu's psychologically stubborn hold on being a "good boy." As James Russell Kincaid argues, adults have made children "savages and sinners, but [they] have also maintained their innocence," a condition that Agu has deeply internalized. Indeed, Agu uses innocence and childhood as a form of resistance to the violence he is required to perform.[50] His attempt to "think good things" in this instance suggests he is aware something bad is about to happen, perhaps even suspects what it is; yet he wants to believe in a "goodness" that will save him. Afterwards, Agu stumbles in the dark, "angry and confusing in [his] head," to a stream where he falls in bottom first in an effort to both assuage the pain and wash away the rape. Agu here wishes he were a "brave boy" and could drown himself – he sinks under and holds his breath – but his fear of the Ancestor's rejection if he commits

---

[45] BNN, 46-47.

[46] BNN, 73.

[47] Kyulanova, "From Soldiers to Children: Undoing the Rite of Passage in Ishmeal Beah's *A Long Way Gone* and Bernard Ashley's *Little Soldier*," 29.

[48] BNN, 93.

[49] BNN, 81.

[50] James Russell Kincaid, *Erotic Innocence: The Culture of Child Molesting*, (Durham, NC, Duke University Press, 2000), 53.

suicide stops him.[51] Here Iweala ensures that we see Agu as an innocent child victimized throughout the novel.

At the end of the novel, Agu faces the Western white woman, Amy, "from America who is coming here to be helping people like me."[52] Katrina Lee-Koo argues that the "stereotypical image of the child soldier" is often used to "externalise the rescuer and impl[y] that there is nobody within the child's community who may care for him." Here Agu is positioned at the mercy of The West, represented as the saviour. Indeed, the final chapter opens with Agu describing the place where he now lives: "In heaven, I am thinking it is always morning." Lee-Koo states that, "in terms of global politics this places the Global South as the cause of the child's abandonment, and the Global North as its rescuer."[53] Agu works to come to grips with the horror he survived while trying to regain some semblance of normalcy – which seems an impossibility to his young mind: "I am seeing more terrible thing than twenty thousand men and I am doing more terrible thing than twenty thousand men."[54] But, Agu's final words resonate with hope, and belief in his previous innocence and goodness, as he works to recover his childness: "I am all of this thing. I am all of this thing, but I am also having mother once, and she is loving me."

Fukunaga's Agu

In stark contrast to Iweala's Agu, the film version changes the character so significantly that the viewer's sympathy for the child is challenged from the start. The first sound the viewer hears is of children playing, then singing. The opening shot fades into children playing in a field and a child's voiceover "It is starting like this." The camera pans backward to an extreme long shot and discovers that we are watching the playing children through an empty television set. A cut to three young boys carrying an empty television set then comes into view. We learn that Agu (played by Abraham Atta) has stolen the TV set box in order to get some money (the actual TV tube is still at his home). With this opening, the film

---

[51] BNN, 86. African spirituality often includes a wide variety of forms of ancestor veneration. Agu's fear of offending his ancestor's by committing suicide is an example of the way behaviour can be dictated by a fear of reprisals by the ancestors, or fear that they will stop helping him if he offends them: "I am not wanting to die this way because the ancestor will not be letting you to come and live with them. Instead your spirit will just be living where ever you are leaving your body" (BNN, 86).

[52] BNN, 140

[53] Lee-Koo, "Horror and Hope: (Re)presenting Militarised Children in Global North-South Relations," 736.

[54] BNN, 141.

immediately casts Agu and his friends as thieves and miscreants. This representation, in direct contrast to the novel's depiction of Agu as a good, responsible boy, works to undermine notions of an innocent Black child. At the outset, the film presents Agu and his friends as troublemakers – Agu pees on his older brother who is showering (there is no older brother in the novel); he and his friends place a large tree branch across the road and ask money from drivers to move it; and Agu continually picks on his elderly grandfather, who appears comatose. All of these happen in the first minutes of the film establishing Agu as less than innocent; in fact, as a "naturally" bad boy. This characterization of Agu is disturbingly reinforced by the "witch-woman," who walks by them as they move the tree branch in the road for a motorist. The old woman asks the boys, "Why are you so disrespectful?" She then points to Agu and says "Curse be on you!" as she exclaims that his whole family are thieves and "the devil will bless you one by one." And indeed, further in the film, when the rebels capture Agu's father and other men, they bring the same witch-woman as a "witness" to their "treason" and she self-righteously condemns them all as traitors. The rebels then shoot Agu's father and the village men.

In the novel, this witch's appearance is brief and in a different context altogether, and she has nothing to do with the father's death. Agu tells the reader that he was very upset and shocked to find out that his best friend Dike had left with his family in the night and was not paying attention as he walked home. Agu explains that young people are supposed to acknowledge their elders as they pass by, but Agu did not acknowledge the old woman because he was looking at the ground as he walked (she is made a crazy "witch" woman in the film). The old woman took offense at Agu's seeming lack of respect. She stopped him and says "you are not wanting to greet me? . . . But it is ok, trouble go follow you."[55] She does not "curse" Agu or his family like she does in the film, but rather tells him that "trouble go follow you" because he does not pay attention. It is more an admonition to Agu to pay more attention to what he is doing. The film corrupts the meaning to fit the stereotype of the "witch" woman and to reinforce that Agu and his family are to blame for the tragedy that befalls them. In the novel, Agu apologizes to the woman for forgetting to acknowledge her and continues on his way – that is the only appearance of the old woman in the novel, Yet Fukunaga uses this seemingly benign episode as a way to establish Agu's guilt very early in the film.[56]

---

[55] BNN, 60.

[56] The film here also stereotypes the old African woman as crazy or a "witch." In the book, the episode is hardly more than one paragraph, but Fukunaga uses the "crazy" old woman to point out how "bad" the boys are. Her curse of them comes to fruition by

Of Blood and Goodness

Agu's first kill is a surreal and horror-filled experience in the novel. In the film, however, Agu's first kill visually solidifies the notion of his complicity: "Agu's perceived powerlessness is juxtaposed with the absolute power he has of killing and terrorizing others,"[57] a power the camera emphasizes. The rebels ambush a small caravan of researchers and architects as they pass over a bridge. The Commandant (played by Idris Elba) orders most of them killed and while the soldiers ransack the trucks, Commandant has one of the prisoners brought before him. He calls Agu over and says: "Agu – you are going to kill this man. You are going to kill him today," then hands Agu a machete. The camera cuts to the prisoner, who is begging for his life: "I am supposed to be fixing the bridges. I am not a soldier. I am an engineer from the University. I am supposed to fix the bridges." His words resonate in the cut to Agu's facial expression. Agu's father was a teacher, and his mother lovingly called Agu the "professor" because he loved to read and wanted to go to University. Now he is faced with more than having to kill another human being, he is being asked to symbolically kill his own father, and himself, to "cut" away with the machete the dream of his future, to "kill" knowledge and University.

The Commandant steps behind Agu and takes his hand to show Agu how to hold the machete, how to "chop it" like when he chops wood, or a melon "well well." Then the Commandant steps away as the camera pulls back to a medium shot, and Agu is left alone to hold the machete. The Commandant circles behind Agu, provoking him to chop the man who "killed your family." The irony here is that this prisoner is like his father – educated, a reader of books. The prisoner also represents what Agu wants to be – University educated. The camera cuts to a close-up of Agu's face, clearly distressed, as he struggles internally. The camera seems to caress Agu's face, his conflicted conscience evident and unresolved in his eyes. The music heightens, the man screams louder, Commandant is goading Agu; the camera tracks slowly backwards as Agu raises the machete and quickly brings it down on the man's bald head. We hear the "chop" and the squishy sound as Agu withdraws the blade from the man's head, which then pours blood. But that first chop also kills the extra-diegetic sound: we hear the

---

her own hand as she denounces the town men, a betrayal that leads to their deaths. During her tirade against the boys, she accuses his family of "stealing her land," which is never explained, but works to establish the belief that Agu and his family later "deserve" the misfortune they experience. She also points at the boys and calls on the Devil to curse each one. None of this is in the novel.

[57] Mackey, "Troubling Humanitarian Consumption: Reframing Relationality in African Child Soldier Narratives," 109.

Commandant as if through a tube, a far away and faint echo. All sound is muffled, distant; mimicking the shock wave Agu feels at that first "chop" and the site of blood pouring from the screaming man's head. The camera pans to the left and Strika (played by Emmanual Nii Adom Quaye) comes into view, looking at Agu whose face is frozen in shock at what he has done. Strika then swings his machete and strikes the man a glancing blow, knocking him over into the dirt. The man's cries now fade even further and the extra-diegetic music returns with a steady, soft, base tone accompanying the now low-angle camera, as the boys begin to chop back and forth at the man's head. The scene is surreal; the boys chopping filmed in a slightly slower speed and in near-silhouette, reminiscent of Colonel Kurtz's death scene in *Apocalypse Now*, a 1979 American epic war film directed by Francis Ford Coppola, and Kurtz's last whispered words "the horror, the horror." Strika and Agu take turns, each methodically chopping the man's body. The camera, at the level of the victim, heightens the visual paradox of innocent children viciously killing. Blood spatter flies on the lens with each chop; the camera captures the boys' blank faces, while the Commandant behind them mouths (still muffled) encouragement. As they systematically chop, the camera shifts to focus on the boys' faces in silhouette, chopping, when Agu says, in whispered voice over, "God - I have killed a man. It is the worst sin" followed by, "but I am knowing too, it is the right thing to be doing." By this statement, Fukunaga's Agu articulates the internal "good/bad" boy struggle within a framework of violence that forces the viewer's gaze to reconcile the "frightful and discomfiting agency of the child-soldier figure"[58] with the Western expectation of childhood innocence. That Agu did not resist killing the man underscores the film's subtle move to blame Agu, or at the very least highlight his culpability, despite the fact that we see Agu "traumatized and terrorized"[59] throughout the film. His whispered claim, "it is the right thing to be doing," chillingly reminds the viewer that this child is a product of major social disruption and exhibits an agency that challenges the Global North's mandate of childhood innocence.[60]

This scene in the novel is different in very important ways. In the novel, Agu is physically compelled to kill the man through threat of violence: "He [Commandant] is grabbing my neck and whispering into my ear, 'kill him now because I am no having the time oh. If you are not killing him, enh, Luftenant will be

---

[58] Moynagh, "Human Rights Child-Soldier Narratives, and the Problem of Form," 45.

[59] Hron, "Ora na-asu nwa: The Figure of the Child in Third-Generation Nigerian Novels," 40.

[60] Catarina Martins, "The Dangers of the Single Story: Child-Soldiers in Literary Fiction and Film," *Childhood* 18(4), (2011): 442.

thinking you are a spy. And who can know if he just won't be killing you."[61] Agu here is threatened with death if he does not comply, whereas there is no clear death threat in the film. Significantly, when Commandant orders Agu to kill the man in the novel, the Commandant *holds Agu's hand through the first chops*: "He is squeezing my hand around the handle of the machete . . . He is taking my hand and bringing it down . . . the enemy's head and I am feeling like electricity is running through my whole body." In the film version, Agu kills the man on his own. The question of agency in the novel does not lie with Agu as it is portrayed in the film. However, in the novel Agu *does* continue to chop on his own when Strika joins him. Having Strika join him seems to validate for Agu that it is alright, and he chops following Strika's lead.

One of the often discussed issues within the child-soldier phenomenon is the question of agency. According to Ah-Jung Lee, in "Understanding and Addressing the Phenomenon of 'Child Soldiers,'" global discourse about children tends to follow Western expectations for childhood and the notion of "straight 18" in which childhood lasts until the age of 18. But globally, childhood is a complex condition that varies by region and culture. She argues that in some cultures young children are politically aware and "judged the military struggle as the best and perhaps the only means of effecting social change and thus willingly [fight] on the side of the guerrillas."[62] Perceived from a Western point of view, "the contradiction that arises from the use of children in postcolonial 'new wars' opposes innocence and savagery [not innocence and soldiery]".[63] In the light of this assertion, Catarina Martins echoes Lee's argument by challenging the representation of child soldiers in the West. Invoking the Western perception about the African terrain into her argument, Martins sees in the Western notion of child-soldiering the obvious "oxymoron between innocence and savagery" which meets on one plane "a value whose preservation became a criterion for measuring the degree of civilization, as defined by the West/North;" and confronts "on the other hand, the ultimate 'heart of darkness'. . . : Africa as the intrinsically irrational, primitive, *black* hole, where violence is an inextricable part of nature, and which will eternally be dependent on the North".[64]

---

[61] BNN, 20.

[62] Ah-Jung Lee, *Understanding and Addressing the Phenomenon of 'Child Soldiers': The Gap between the Global Humanitarian Discourse and the Local Understandings and Experiences of Young People's Military Recruitment*, (Oxford: University of Oxford Refugee Studies Centre Working Paper Series, 52, 2009): 20.

[63] Martins, "The Dangers of the Single Story: Child-Soldiers in Literary Fiction and Film," 438.

[64] Ibid., 438.

The film *Beasts of No Nation* works in just such a way by presenting Africans as savage and violent for no apparent cause, and children as having an agency that allows them to commit violence. The film's opening shots of the children as they work to sell the stolen "imagination" TV, and Agu's admission "I am having the ideas and Dike is having the talent," hints at their questionable moral centre. From the outset of the film, the boys are not established as objects of compassion, but rather as suspect, in stark contrast to the novel. For instance, after the first kill scene in the film, Agu steps away and vomits once. In the novel, after the kill, Agu says: "I am vomiting everywhere. I cannot be stopping myself . . . I am feeling hammer knocking in my head and chest. My nose and my mouth is itching."[65] The physical reaction Agu has in the novel emphasizes his horror at committing murder. This reaction is downplayed in the film. When they sell the TV box to a Nigerian guard (one of the few references to an actual place in the film), Dike performs "3-D" and pokes his head through the TV box opening, making growling and barking noises. The close-up of Dike as he pokes through the TV suggests the "framing" of the boys as "animals" who could "come through the screen," thus playing on the Western fear of blackness and Black children as "animals." This contradiction between "innocence and savagery" is on full display when Fukunaga's Agu and Strika chop the man's head freely, without help from Commandant. The scene is filmed in such a way as to privilege a "sensationalist voyeurism of the exotic"[66] – we are horrified, but cannot look away – while at the same time the scene reinforces long-held, colonial-era stereotypes about Africa, Africans, and African children.

"I am not a bad boy"

One of the key differences between Fukunaga's film and Iweala's novel is the internal conflict Agu experiences. In the novel, Agu continually negotiates with his moral centre by saying that he is not a bad boy but: "I am soldier, and soldier is not bad if he is killing. I am telling this to myself . . . how can I be bad boy? Me . . . who is having life like I am having and fearing God the whole time."[67] Agu examines his actions in the context of his belief in his own goodness throughout the novel. He understands that his circumstances challenge what he was taught about moral behaviour, yet he holds on to his innate goodness, rationalizing what he is forced to do with how a soldier should behave. In the novel, the reader experiences Agu's loss of innocence, but not

[65] BNN, 21-22.
[66] Martins, "The Dangers of the Single Story: Child-Soldiers in Literary Fiction and Film," 439.
[67] BNN, 23-24.

necessarily the loss of his childness. The film, however, does not reveal any such inner turmoil. Agu's few, brief voice-overs do little to convince the viewer of his resistance to the violence he is required to perform. In fact, the many images of Agu amidst the gratuitous killing work to the contrary. Indeed, the novel invites the viewer to identify with the innocent child as the victim of brutal rebel fighters, while the film functions more as a cautionary tale about Africa itself – it conflates the notion of savagery with African childhood in a way that "leaves the viewers with an impression of [Africa] . . . not as a region whose problems can be solved . . . but as a place of little hope" and corrupted childhoods.[68] In the film, sympathy for Agu competes with the visual reinforcement of long-established Western myths about Africa as a "menacing, violent, and chaotic" place.[69]

One of Agu's more traumatic experiences is his rape by the Commandant, which happens midway through the film, but nearer the end in the novel. In the film, this event is hinted at only through vague scenes. Agu is in the Commandant's cabin where Commandant gives him a colourful hat, claiming that Agu is his favourite but not to tell the others. Agu is at first happy to be singled out, but then the Commandant moves to the bedroom. He mixes a drug, which he then sniffs, lays back on the bed and motions for Agu to come closer. He asks Agu to kneel down and the close up of Agu's face captures his fear. The Commandant in this scene has his head covered with a scarf, similar to the way women wear a veil. It is a feminization and is the only place in the film that he wears a scarf in such a way, perhaps to appear less intimidating, or to reassure Agu. Though the veil does not cover his face, it does cover his head, functioning as a symbolic mask, hiding the carnal corruption underneath. The next scene shows Strika at the bottom of the stairs waiting, then a cut to Agu, head bowed, clothes dishevelled, gun dragging, as he appears at the top of the stairs. He waivers slightly, then leans against the door frame. Strika runs up the stairs and helps him down. They move to a fire and sit together; Agu rests his head against Strika's shoulder, who offers comfort as the shot fades to dark. The film then cuts to a bright scene of laughter and the boys trying to catch a chicken. While understanding the conservative constraints on the American film industry where sexual imagery is concerned, particularly in relation to children, the film's not-so-subtle omission of the seriousness of the Commandant's sexual abuse of Agu works to diminish the significance of the experience. It also trivializes how a child might deal with

---

[68] Martha Evans and Ian Glenn, "'TIA—This is Africa': Afropessimism in Twenty-First-Century Narrative Film," *Black Camera* 1(2), (2010): 26.

[69] Lee-koo, "Horror and Hope: (Re)presenting Militarised Children in Global North-South Relations," 735.

such a trauma (just go chase a chicken). In contrast, the novel takes the time to emphasize how fully horrific this event was for Agu. We witness the evolution of Agu's childlike naiveté as it devolves into disillusionment with life itself. We see how he openly articulates that in the face of the threat of being molested by the Commandant he thought about "good things", positive things, since he believed that such a mindset would protect him because by keeping such a state of mind "nothing bad is happening to you". Nevertheless, he was defiled by the Commandant who threatened and coerced him to follow an order as a "good soldier" because "it is order for you to let me touch you like this". Agu mentions how in that state of feeling defiled he felt he did not want to be a good soldier at all and could never smile again. He also declares how he had suicidal ideations. Thus, he wanted to sink to the bottom of a stream where "I would just staying forever, but I am not wanting to die this way because the ancestor would not be letting you to come and live with them".[70]

The situations and articulations of Agu expressed above are heavily condensed, of course; the full episodes last for nearly 10 pages. What is significant, however, is how Iweala weaves together real-world effects on children who suffer sexual abuse (suicidal thoughts, feelings of powerlessness, questioning whether or not relatives will love them) with Agu's complex sense of his own goodness. In the novel, it is this event that breaks his spirit. He realizes he can never recover what was lost: "I am knowing I am no more child so if this war is ending I cannot go back to doing child thing . . . I am not happying anymore. I am not happying ever again."[71] For Agu, the assault by the Commandant seems to be the culmination of the horror he has experienced, even beyond the killing.

In some sense, Agu's reaction falls in line with the Western notions of innocence, which requires a lack of carnal knowledge. According to Western ideologies, once there is carnal knowledge, there is no more innocence, no matter what else the child may have experienced. In his mind, Agu can kill and not be a "devil. I am not a bad boy." And Agu has seen rape, and even been the rapist, such as his limited physique would allow, but to be violated himself and by a male parental figure marks a betrayal that his young mind cannot overcome. Agu's rape marks a turning point in the novel that is not present in the film (in the film, it is the death of Strika that marks this turning point.) In the film, the vagueness of Agu's sexual assault renders it almost insignificant; indeed, the film's suggestion of a sexual assault is tamed by the laughter and playfulness of the next scene when they try to catch a chicken. The film never alludes to the assault again, leaving the viewer to wonder why Fukunaga included it at all. Yet,

---

[70] BNN, 81-89.
[71] BNN, 93-94.

in the novel, it is after the rape that we see Agu lose his hold on goodness, on his childness. He no longer kills; he does not kill anyone from that point on, but he also no longer tries to convince himself he is a "good boy," as he had throughout the novel up to that point. The assault also emboldens Agu to *not* defend the Commandant when the boy Rambo shoots and kills him, thus allowing the children to finally escape. In the film, however, there is a drawn-out threat scene between the Commandant, Rambo, and Agu, that leaves the Commandant alive, but alone in the encampment as his soldiers just walk away. At one point in the confrontation, in a reversal of Agu's rape, the Commandant kneels in front of Agu, who points his gun at him. Commandant takes the barrel of Agu's gun and puts it over his heart: "ehn, Agu, you want kill Commander? Put it here!" He shouts for Agu to shoot, but then Commandant puts his own revolver, forcefully, to Agu's head: "Kill Commandant, or surrender!" – in effect showing Agu that killing him will also kill Agu.

After Agu escapes, he hopes to recapture his goodness and his childness, even though he is aware of its corruption. As Myriam Denov has explained the common dichotomous discourse surrounding male child soldiers is that they are dangerous and victims. This, she observes is a representation of certain paradoxical "common sense" Western conceptions about children in general, that is, on one plane, a child is "passive and innocent" and on the other hand, "they are to be feared and dreaded, and their 'deviant' actions must be explained by reference to their inherent duplicity, their taintedness."[72]

It is the notion of an "inherent taintedness" that Fukunaga captures in his depiction of Agu, the other child soldiers, the Commandant, and Africa. Such a notion, conversely, taints viewer sympathy for Agu and his plight. As Denov argues, such depictions are not only "highly racialised and imbued with stereotypes" but they also reveal the erroneous notion and perception about a so-called morally superior North and a "savage" South. Consequently, "[s]uch representations also cement linkages of race, perversity and barbarism, dehumanize child soldiers and their societies, and ultimately present a site where colonial themes are played out."[73] Fukunaga's *Beasts of No Nation* is just such a site.

Conclusion

Speaking about the issue of "child soldier narratives being symptomatic of an arrested historicization in part because they become trapped in a rhetorical effort to restore the childhood innocence of their narrator", Eleni Coundouri-

---

[72] Denov, "Child Soldiers and Iconography: Portrayals and [Mis]Representations," 283-284.
[73] Ibid. 282.

otis observed that they consequently "produce a metaphor of African Child-hood that is politically limiting as a characterization of the historical agency of the continents peoples".[74]

It is well known that any novel-to-film adaptation will change certain story elements to fit the visual medium, and yet the specific *ways* the story is changed can suggest a more deeply ideological rendering that, in the case of *Beasts of No Nation*, Westernizes a specifically non-western narrative in dam-aging ways. The visual denial of innocence to the Black child soldier is ac-complished by the film's early depiction of Agu and his friends as thieves and trouble-makers. The viewer rarely sympathizes with the "brat," yet Fukunaga makes a point of positioning Agu and his friends as just that: brats, bad boys, thieves and miscreants. In fact, the very first shot of the film is *through the opening of the imagination TV* the boys stole. So from the outset, African chil-dren are "framed" by a negation of childhood innocence and "goodness," by an "empty shell" of childhood which functions to Other African children. As the narrative progresses, this established framing works to reinforce the "cau-tionary tale of [not really] innocent childhood gone awry."[75] The children seen through the TV box work as a "distancing mechanism" that "elicits sympathy, on the one hand, but comforts white racial anxieties, on the other. The Black child is culturally positioned as "not innocent" and "not like us" (white chil-dren)"[76] so that when Agu is later conscripted by the Commandant, viewer sympathy is somewhat tempered by the notion that he "deserves" it, just as the witch woman prophesied.

The child soldier as a character seems to fascinate the West. Films such as *Invisible Children* (2006), *Blood Diamond* (2006), *Kassim the Dream* (2008), and *Kony 2012* (2012) all contain narratives of child soldiers as seen through a white Western gaze, which confront the viewer with both the evil of [Black] adults and the potential for the same evil perpetrated by [Black] children. Rarely are white children positioned in such ways, yet for Black children, be-ing a "child-soldier" has become cinematically naturalized. Western-produced child soldier narratives often present a visible fragmentation of the child in such a way that comforts the Western viewer that such things happen to "other[ed]" children who do not fit the narrow confines of childhood any-way. In "An Ethical Perspective on Child Soldiers," Jeff McMahan asks: "Do

---

[74] Eleni Coundouriotis, "The Child Soldier Narrative and the Problem of Arrested His-toricization," *Journal of Human Rights* 9(2), (2010):192.

[75] Denov, "Child Soldiers and Iconography: Portrayals and [Mis]Representations," 280.

[76] Debbie Olson, *Black Children in Hollywood Cinema: Cast in Shadow,* (New York: Palgrave Macmillan, 2017), 162.

conditions of ignorance and duress in which child soldiers normally act ever make their action morally permissible?"[77] The core of this question is the notion of "ignorance" instead of "innocence" in relation to the condition of being a "child." This regressive colonial rhetoric positions African children, and Black children generally, within a framework that always finds them lacking, *not*-innocent, *not*-good. The inevitable result of such beliefs about Black children have far-reaching consequences and are part of the *cause* of recent tragedies in the US like the 2014 shooting death of 12-year-old Tamir Rice. The white officers did not see him *as a child* – they saw him as a threatening "black male."[78] A recent CDC report, published in the journal *Pediatrics*, found that Black male youth are 10 times more likely to be killed by guns than any other juvenile group in the US, accounting for 82% of the deaths.[79] The numbers are sobering and offer a disturbing insight into the ways the notion of the child – and who is and is not a child – can have real-world tragic effects.

In Iweala's novel, Agu ends up at a rehabilitation centre where he struggles to learn to be a child again. The counsellor, Amy, who tries to get him to speak of his experiences, is white, and Agu has trouble confiding in her: "She is white woman from America who is coming here to be helping people like me . . . I am saying to her, if I am telling this to you it will be making you think I am some sort of beast or devil."[80] This scene hints at Iweala's criticism of the colonial-mindset of the West who paternalistically assumes they alone can "fix" Africa's problems. Noteworthy, Lee-Koo has, consequently, observed that the "construction of the 'child-soldier'" has been made to be "a powerful icon" that articulates very little about children and their human rights and insecurities. Rather, it speaks more about "contemporary Global North-South power relations. As a result, children's diversity, the range of their experiences, the complexity of their agency, and their individual needs can be silenced.[81] And with Amy, Agu, following his best friend Strika, chooses silence

---

[77] Jeff McMahan, "An Ethical Perspective on Child Soldiers" in *Child Soldiers in the Age of Fractured States*, edited by Scott Gaines and Simon Reich (Pittsburgh: University of Pittsburgh Press, 2010): 27.

[78] For detailed information about children killed or injured by guns, see http://www.gun violencearchive.org.

[79] Katherine A. Fowler, Linda L. Dahlberg, Tadesse Haileyesus, Carmen Gutierrez, and Sarah Bacon, "Childhood Firearm injuries in the United States," *Pediatrics* 140 (1), (2017): 2, http://pediatrics.aappublications.org/content/pediatrics/early/2017/06/15/peds.2016-3486.full.pdf. Accessed on September 16, 2018.

[80] BNN, 140, 142.

[81] Lee-Koo, "Horror and Hope: (Re)presenting Militarised Children in Global North-South Relations," 740.

– for now. However, Fukunaga did make one significant and powerful change in the film. He replaced the white woman from America with an African woman and man who run the rehabilitation centre and who care for and counsel the former child soldiers. This positive ending offers the hope of redemption for Agu that seems missing in the novel; a redemption that is not mediated by the West at all, but rather is achieved through the strength and love of the African community. And so the film, which began with a group of boys playing ball in a grassy field, comes full circle as we watch Agu run across the sand to join the other boys playing ball in the surf – a renewal, a baptism of sorts. We are left with the promise of, if not a return to innocence, at least a return of the *possibility* of childness, of goodness: "beast or devil . . . I am all of this thing, but I am also having mother once, and she is loving me."[82]

Bibliography

Bader, Michael. "The Breakdown of Empathy and the Political Right in America." *Alternet.org*, December, 22 2016. http://www.alternet.org/print/right-wing/breakdown-empathy-and-political-right-america

Bernstein, Robin. *Racial Innocence: Performing American Childhood from Slavery to Civil Rights*. New York: New York University Press, 2011.

Bradbury, Marina. "Negotiating Identities: Representations of Childhood in Senegalese Cinema." *Journal of African Media Studies* 2(1), (2010): 9-24.

Coundouriotis, Eleni. "The Child Soldier Narrative and the Problem of Arrested Historicization." *Journal of Human Rights* 9 (2) (2010):191-206.

Denov, Myriam. "Child Soldiers and Iconography: Portrayals and [Mis]Representations." *Children & Society* 26 (2012): 280-292.

Deutsch, Noah. "The Grim and the Dead – *Beasts of No Nation* by Uzodinma Iweala." *themillions.com*, January 15, 2007. http://themilions.com/2007/01/grim-and-dead-beasts-of-no-nation-by.html

Diallo, Yolande. *African traditions and Humanitarian Law: Similarities and differences*. Geneva: International Committee of the Red Cross, 1976.

Evans, Martha and Ian Glenn. "'TIA — This is Africa': Afropessimism in Twenty-First-Century Narrative Film." *Black Camera* 1 (2), (2010): 14-35.

Ferme, Marianne C. *The Underneath of Things*. CA: University of California Press, 2001.

Fowler, Katherine A., Linda L. Dahlberg, Tadesse Haileyesus, Carmen Gutierrez, and Sarah Bacon. "Childhood Firearm injuries in the United States," *Pediatrics*, 140 (1) (2017): 1-11. Doi:10.1542/peds.2016-3486.

Freedman, Estelle B. *Redefining Rape: Sexual Violence in the Era of Suffrage and Segregation*. Harvard University Press, 2013.

---

[82] BNN, 142.

Gates, Scott and Simon Reich, eds. *Child Soldiers in the Age of Fractured States*. Pittsburgh: University of Pittsburgh Press, 2009.

Hoffman, Danny. "Like Beasts in the Bush: Synonyms of Childhood and Youth in Sierra Leone." *Postcolonial Studies* 6 (3) (2003): 295-308.

Hron, Madelaine. "Ora na-asu nwa: The Figure of the Child in Third-Generation Nigerian Novels. *Research in African Literatures* 39 (2) (2008): 27-48.

Iweala, Uzodinam. *Beasts of No Nation*. New York: Harper Collins, 2005.

Kearney, J. A. "The Representation of Child Soldiers in Contemporary African Fiction." *Journal of Literary Studies* 26 (1) (2010): 67-94.

Kincaid, James Russell. *Erotic Innocence: The Culture of Child Molesting*. Durhan: Duke University Press, 2000.

Klasen, Fionna, Johanna Gehrke , Franka Metzner, Monica Blotevogel and James Okello. "Complex Trauma Symptoms in Former Ugandan Child Soldiers." *Journal of Aggression, Maltreatment, and Trauma* 22 (7) (2013): 699-700.

Kyulanova, Irina. "From Soldiers to Children: Undoing the Rite of Passage". In Ishmael Beah's *A Long Way Gone* and Bernard Ashley's *Little Soldier*," *Studies in the Novel* 42 (1 & 2) (2010): 28-47.

Lee, Ah-Jung. "Understanding and Addressing the Phenomenon of 'Child Soldiers': The Gap between the Global Humanitarian Discourse and the Local Understandings and Experiences of Young People's Military Recruitment." *University of Oxford. Refugee Studies Centre Working Paper Series* 52 (2009): 1-45.

Lee-Koo, Katria. "Horror and Hope: (Re)presenting Militarised Children in Global North-South Relations." *Third World Quarterly* 32 (4) (2011): 730-731.

Levander, Caroline F. *Cradle of Liberty*. Durhan: Duke University Press, 2006.

Mackey, Allison. "Troubling Humanitarian Consumption: Reframing Relationality in African Child Soldier Narratives." *Research in African Literatures* 44 (4) (2013): 99-122.

Manzo, Kate. "Imagine Humanitarianism: NGO Identity and the Iconography of Childhood." *Antipode* 40 (4) (2008): 632-657.

Martins, Catarina. "The Dangers of the Single Story: Child-Soldiers in Literary Fiction and Film." *Childhood* 18 (4) (2011): 434-446.

McMahan, Jeff. "An Ethical Perspective on Child Soldiers" in *Child Soldiers in the Age of Fractured States*, edited by Scott Gaines and Simon Reich. Pittsburgh: University of Pittsburgh Press, 2010.

Moynagh, Maureen. "Human Rights Child-Soldier Narratives, and the Problem of Form." *Research in African Literatures* 42 (4) (2011): 39-59.

Olson, Debbie. *Black Children in Hollywood Cinema: Cast in Shadow*. New York: Palgrave Macmillan, 2017.

Piot, Charles. *Remotely Global: Village Modernity in West Africa*. Chicago: University of Chicago Press, 1999.

Sanchez-Eppler, Karen. *Dependent States*, Chicago: University of Chicago Press, 2005.

Saro-wiwa, Ken. *Sozaboy: a Novel in Rotten English. Nigeria:* Saros International Publishers, 1985.

Smith, Ali. "The Lost Boys." *The Observer,* September 3, 2005. www.theguardian.com/books/2005/sep/03/fiction.alismith

Song, Suzan J. and Joop de Jong. "The Role of Silence in Burundian Former Child Soldiers," *International Journal of Advanced Counseling* 36 (1) (2014): 84-95.

Zelizer, Viviana. *Pricing the Priceless Child.* New York: Basic Books, 1985.

Chapter 6

Boys and Girls in the Bush, Bosses in Post-Conflict Society: Liberian Young Veterans Rising to Power

Komlan Agbedahin

Introduction

African countries have been (and continue to be) beset by low, medium and high armed conflicts as a result of protracted religious, ethnic, economic and political crises. Contrary to pre-colonial wars where children were absent in African war theatres,[1] recent civil wars have been chiefly characterised by greed and grievance[2] and have seen the active immoral participation of children, playing roles revolving around fighting, logistics and intelligence.[3] For almost the past four decades, there has hardly been a war in Africa where children have not served as fighters. The Liberian two-phase civil war,[4] which actually started in 1989 and ended in 2003, epitomises these predatory armed conflicts. During the war, children (both boys and girls, some as young as six

---

[1] Yolande Diallo, *African traditions and Humanitarian Law: Similarities and differences,* (Geneva: International Committee of the Red Cross (ICRC), 1976).

[2] Håvard Hegre, Gudrun Østby and Clionadh Raleigh, "Poverty and civil war events: A disaggregated study of Liberia," *Journal of Conflict Resolution* (2009): 1-26; Charles Call, "Liberia's war recurrence: Grievance over greed," *Civil Wars* 12 (4), (2010): 347-369.

[3] O.B.C. Nwolise, "The fate of women, children and the aged in contemporary Africa's conflict theatres: The urgent need to revive Africa's code of honour." Lecture delivered at the 2001 Public Annual Lecture of the National Association of Political Science Students (NAPSS), University of Ibadan Chapter, at the Lady Bank Anthony Hall, University of Ibadan, August 15, 2001; Romeo Dallaire, *They fight like soldiers, they die like children,* (London: Hutchinson, 2010).

[4] The first phase of the Liberian civil war took place between 1989 and 1996. Failure by the parties to the conflict to effectively disarm and demobilise their combatants paved the way for the second phase between 1997 and 2003.

years old) served as soldiers within various warring factions.[5] It was estimated that 21,000 child-soldiers, including 8,500 girl-soldiers, were actively involved in the war.[6] Some child-soldiers were as young as seven years old.[7] After the Comprehensive Peace Agreement (CPA), out of the 21,000 child-soldiers who were to be officially demobilised, only 8,771 boy-soldiers and 2,511 girl-soldiers underwent the process. Before the formal end of the war, almost half of the child-soldiers self-demobilised, while 8,771 boy-soldiers and 2,511 girl-soldiers went through the official Disarmament Demobilisation and Reintegration (DDR)[8] process.[9] During the DDR project some child-soldiers, after turning in their guns, and staying for approximately three days to one week in the cantonment site for counselling and recreational activities, were allowed to go back to their communities. Although this was the general demobilisation procedure for all combatants, there were also cases of child-soldiers taken to transit centres and Interim Care Centres (ICCs) to allow humanitarian Non-Governmental Organisations (NGOs) to trace their family members for reunification.[10] Whether these former child-soldiers passed through cantonment sites or transit centres and ICCs, their final destination was the same: post-war society. Some young veterans returned to their communities of origin while others chose to settle in different receiving communities. As part of the reintegration process, and similar to adult former combatants, young veterans were predominantly asked to choose between mainstream education and a series of vocational training projects.

---

[5] Thomas Jaye, *Transitional Justice and DDR: The Case of Liberia,* (New York: International Center for Transitional Justice, 2009).

[6] Save the Children Fund, *Forgotten Casualties of War: Girls in Armed Conflict,* (London: Save the Children, 2005).

[7] Coalition to Stop the Use of Child Soldiers, *Child Soldiers: Global Report 2004,* (London: Coalition to Stop the Use of Child Soldiers, 2004).

[8] The United Nations-backed programme through which most African post-war governments ensure the shift of fighters from soldiers to civilians is Disarmament, Demobilisation (DD) and Rehabilitation, Reinsertion, Reintegration (Rs). While the D-component usually remains unchanged, the number of Rs in the R-component may vary leading to three acronyms for the same programme: DDR, DDRR, and DDRRR. This is an indication of the complexities which characterise the programme. But for the purpose of this paper DDR (Disarmament, Demobilisation and Reintegration) has been adopted.

[9] Nelson Alusula, *Disarmament, Demobilisation, Rehabilitation and Reintegration (DDRR) in Liberia* (Centre for International Cooperation and Security, 2008).

[10] Guillaume Landry, *Child soldiers and disarmament, demobilization, rehabilitation and reintegration in West Africa: A survey of programmatic work on child soldiers in Côte d'Ivoire, Guinea, Liberia and Sierra Leone,* (Dakar: Coalition to Stop the Use of Child Soldiers, 2006).

Young veterans were expected to complete the apprenticeship schemes in a few months in order to become economically empowered. The flaws embedded in such schemes prevented some young veterans from creating an adequate survival space for themselves in their respective post-conflict communities. The complexities surrounding the implementation of these reintegration programmes can be explored in three categories of young veterans: a first category of young veterans that went through mainstream education successfully despite being subjected to stigmatisation; a second category of young veterans who went through the vocational training programmes successfully; a third category of young veterans who could neither go to school nor succeed through the skill acquisition programmes. Drawing on young veterans' experiential stories, collected through in-depth interviews in Monrovia in 2010 as part of a PhD project, and by way of document analysis, it became evident how, through agency, some young veterans were able to free themselves from the war chain of chaos in the post-conflict society. The available body of writing on the fate of children, particularly child-soldiers in post-conflict society, has been remarkably dominated by victimhood-centred debates which uphold a societal and scholarly apocalyptic view of young veterans. But there has been a shift in focus with new debates woven around the notion of agency. While the agency of child-soldiers during wars has been central to these new debates on a macro level, on a micro level, there seems to be a dearth of literature on young veterans' agency towards their reintegration. It has been established that during armed conflicts particularly in Africa, children, women and the aged generally are the most vulnerable categories that bear the brunt of the war.[11] But it seems child-soldiers suffer most as they are psychologically injured from both having been separated from their families and exposed to awful treatment. Liberia was no exception. Many child-soldiers who were associated with the warring factions during the war came out of the violent conflict with both psychological and physical scars.[12]

Some former girl-fighters continually nurtured an inner pain often aggravated by the mere presence of a rape-induced child.[13] Other young veterans, as a result of their jungle-inherited assertiveness, were unwilling to submit to authori-

---

[11] Nwolise, *The fate of women, children and the aged in contemporary Africa's conflict theatres*; Charli R. Carpenter, "Women, children and other vulnerable groups: Gender, strategic frames and the protection of civilians as a transnational issue," *International Studies Quarterly* 49(2), (2005): 295–334.

[12] Human Rights Watch, *How to fight, how to kill: Child soldiers in Liberia,* (London: Human Rights Watch, 2004).

[13] Dallaire, *They fight like soldiers.*

ties in their post-war communities. Consequently, it was generally assumed that young veterans were in dissonance with members of their immediate families and the larger society. Young veterans were regarded as individuals unhinged by war. These negative attributes and labels combined to depict young veterans as shiftless and dispirited human beings or simply as social misfits. In addition, owing to the widespread poverty and corruption which characterise war-affected countries, one could conclude that the pre-war patron-client relationship which existed between child-soldiers and their commanders would be fully reproduced in the post-conflict situation, a situation wherein young veterans might continue to depend on their former bosses. But this chapter establishes how through an agency, young veterans rose to power in the post-conflict society. It specifically seeks to bring to the fore the mechanisms through which the pre-war patron-client relationship has been altered, paving the way for a change in power relations. The chapter highlights how, through their own stories, agency, jungle ties and instrumental coalitions in the damaged post-conflict society, former child-soldiers negotiated their civilian identity, social acceptance and created comfortable and conformable spaces for themselves, amid stigmatisation and marginalisation. The chapter uses Herbert Blumer's symbolic interactionism,[14] Joel M. Charon's human action,[15] Margaret S. Archer's internal conversation[16] and the notion of instrumental coalition to tease out the agency embedded in the young veterans' actions.[17]

Methodology

The research leading to this article was conducted using an Interpretive Phenomenological Analysis (IPA) which encourages the use of a small cohort of research informants.[18] Consequently, the data collection was done through in-depth interviews of a dozen young veterans in 2010 in Monrovia, the capital city of Liberia. Research informants were interviewed on a one-on-one basis and face-to-face. The data analysis was done through first and second

[14] Herbert Blumer, *Symbolic Interactionism*, (Englewood Cliffs, NJ: Prentice Hall, 1969).

[15] Joel M. Charon, *Symbolic Interactionism: An introduction, an Interpretation, an Integration*, (Upper Saddle River, NJ: Prentice-Hall, 2001).

[16] Margaret S. Archer, *Structure, Agency and the Internal Conversation*, (Cambridge: Cambridge University Press, 2003).

[17] Lee A. Kirkpatrick and Bruce J. Ellis, "An Evolutionary-psychological Approach to Self-esteem: Multiple Domains and Multiple Functions," in Marilynn B. Brewer and Miles Hewstone (eds.), *Self and Social Identity*, (Malden, Mass: Blackwell Publishing, 2004), 52-77.

[18] Jonathan A. Smith, Paul Flowers and Michael Larkin, *Interpretative Phenomenological Analysis: Theory, Method and Research*, (London: SAGE, 2009).

cycle coding.[19] Document analysis was also used for additional information to develop certain points and to put some of the claims into perspective. Owing to the peculiar nature of the research participants, ethical measures such as a pre-research induction course on how to interview war-affected youths, and debriefing after interviews, were taken to ensure a smooth interview process and to vouch for the safety of the informants. This was done with the help of two NGOs involved in the rehabilitation of former combatants in Monrovia.

The Nexus between Instrumental Coalition, Symbolic Interactionism, Human Action, Internal Conversation and Agency

Symbolic interactionism emphasises social interactions, that is, actions with symbolic meanings, negotiation of definitions, and emphatic role-taking between humans.[20] Norman K. Denzin explains that interactionists investigate the relationships and nexuses of interaction, biography and social system in specific moments in history. The interactional experience which is organised in "terms of the motives and accounts that persons give themselves for acting" can be "learned from others and popular culture". Accordingly, "[t]hese motives, gendered and nongendered, explain past behaviour and are used to predict future behaviour.[21]

Specifically and briefly put, the Blumerian symbolic interactionism indicates that human beings are engaged in action; individuals are in interaction with one another; human beings should be perceived as active interpreters of the world. As Blumer puts it, a human being should be seen "as an organism that not only responds to others on the non-symbolic level but as one that makes indications to others and interprets their indications."[22] Blumer rejected any argument considering human beings as passive beings.

Similarly, Charon indirectly unveiled the importance of self-agency in determining individuals' behaviour;[23] it involves an internal deliberation for decision-making purposes. Charon pointed out that human actions are like streams of water. They constantly change directions. Human actions influence their lives to change directions frequently; the change in direction may

---

[19] Johnny Saldaña, *The Coding Manual for Qualitative Researchers*, (London: SAGE, 2009).

[20] B. L. Berg, *Qualitative Research Methods for the Social Sciences*, (Boston, Mass: Allyn and Bacon, 2007).

[21] Norman K. Denzin, *Symbolic Interactionism and Cultural Studies: The Politics of Interpretation*, (Oxford: Blackwell Publishers, 1992).

[22] Blumer, *Symbolic Interactionism*, 6-12.

[23] Archer, *Structure, agency and the internal conversation*; Günther Knoblich and Natalie Sebanz, "Agency in the face of error," *Trends in Cognitive Sciences* 9(6), (2005): 259-261.

occur in small or significant ways depending on the actions. Moreover, like streams of water whose directions change because of barriers, environment and weather, human directions change because of experience with new situations and factors in their lives. "Streams of water change because smaller brooks enter and cause a change in the direction. So too do other people – individuals and groups – enter our stream of action, and as we interact with them our directions are changed too".[24]

Beyond this analogy between the *stream of action* and the *stream of water*, Charon argued that human beings are engaged in a continuous *stream of covert action*. He therefore clearly pointed out that as human beings, "we are actively and continuously engaged in an ongoing conversation with ourselves about what we are encountering and doing in the situation."[25] Besides this inner interaction, Charon revealed that human beings are also engaged in an *overt stream of action* which describes plainly their external self-agency, that agency characterised by concrete actions, and perceived by other individuals.

Instrumental coalitions are "groups of two or more individuals who coordinate their effort to achieve shared, valued objectives"; and participation in an instrumental coalition "involves interdependence and subordination of individual interests to shared goals that cannot be achieved alone".[26] Young veterans used such coalitions in the post-conflict society to express their agency. A combination of the aforementioned notions contributes to bringing to the fore the agency of young veterans.

From Decoys to Change Agents

During the Liberian civil war, about 80% of child-soldiers were directly involved in combat.[27] Within the warring factions where they served, child-soldiers were forced into unholy alliances, pacts and related dehumanising roles. Although the term "boys" generally refers to foot soldiers, for child-soldiers, it connotes foot soldiers and submissiveness to commanders. During the war, one of the notorious rebel leaders in the person of "General Butt Naked"[28] referred to his subordinates as "boys". So the use of the term "boys" is not related to child-soldiers' age alone but stems from the degree of en-

---

[24] Charon, *Symbolic Interactionism*, 125.

[25] Ibid., 125.

[26] Kirkpatrick and Ellis, *An Evolutionary-psychological Approach*, 56.

[27] P.W. Singer, *Children at War*, (Berkeley, L.A.: University of California Press, 2006).

[28] This name stems from the fact that during the Liberian civil war, this rebel leader fought naked.

slavement, the treatment that put them in a situation of total dependence on warlords, whereby violence was considered a norm, a form of worship.[29] Child-soldiers were referred to as boys and girls for at least a couple of reasons. Firstly, most of them were foot soldiers, although some did emerge as commanders as the war continued. Secondly, by virtue of their immature physical appearance they were considered minors. Their duty was to serve their commanders. It must be noted that the word "boys" usually overshadows girl-soldiers. In African war-torn countries, females whether young, adult or old are generally regarded as "forgotten casualties of war".[30]

The roles played by child-soldiers vary. Within factions, child-soldiers were to carry out any instructions they received from commanders without questioning. As a young veteran puts it, "the military order is obey, obey and obey" (Venunye 2010).[31] Child-soldiers served under a "harsh disciplinary code"[32] and were involved in a full range of egregious acts including murder, rape and executions. As a young female veteran pointed out, "some children, mostly the boys, they just get that wicked mind. In my presence, during the war, some children raped their great grannies" (Perfecto 2010). It must be noted that traditionally, in Liberia as in many African countries, "children raping grannies (grandmothers) in the presence of other children" is a taboo and perceived as an abomination.

Young veterans did not have pleasant experiences within their respective warring factions. Not only were they exposed to sickening scenes, but they were also forced to show what was supposedly regarded as incredible bravery by committing dreadful acts. Simply put, it was a multifaceted bondage. What other forms did this servitude of child-soldiers take? Slavery was deeply entrenched within armed groups and forces in a range of ways. One way was to be trained in small-scale theft. As a young veteran pointed out:

When they tried to reunite me with my family, they found that my father was dead. They could not find my mother. Now I live on my own. I sleep in the waterside area of Monrovia with some other boys. We hus-

---

[29] Hans G. Kippenberg, *Violence as worship: Religious wars in the age of globalization,* trans., Brian McNeil, (Stanford: Stanford University Press, 2011).
[30] Save the Children Fund, *Forgotten Casualties of War,* i.
[31] The names of some of the young veterans interviewed (Enfant, Flaviano, Fleur, Frero, Gracias, Jardin, Martine, Perfecto, Petit, Philemon, Venunye) are pseudonyms.
[32] Karen Wells, *Childhood in a Global Perspective,* (Cambridge: Polity Press, 2009).

tle for food. We go on chicken missions. We go into the community and when we see a chicken, we just grab it.[33]

Some of the units within which child-soldiers served, determined their status. The name of the unit itself described soldiers as boys. For instance, a young veteran revealed that: "because I had to go to look for food for my mother that is what made me be a "small soldier"[34] [child-soldier] until I grew big and I became SBU[35] Commander, Small Boys commander, junior bodyguard commander under General Buffalo [General's real name withheld]" (Fleur 2010). Notwithstanding his rank as commander, Fleur was categorised as one of the boys. He was in command, but he was still considered a small soldier, a boy. He was not a commander of adult soldiers, but a commander of a platoon or company made up of foot soldiers as young as himself. No adult soldier was a member of the SBU. So, physical immaturity was also a determining factor of who should be called boys or girls within particular factions.

The transition from war to post-conflict society did not immediately change young veterans' demeaning designations. As one interviewee revealed, "in the bush people were calling me 'small soldier'. When I came in my community that name was still behind me . . . but after a while people started calling my real name. When I came first they were calling me 'small soldier'" (Jardin 2010). Another young veteran echoed this: "I was picked up and they taught me how to fire pistol and they were calling me 'small soldier, small soldier'" (Martine 2010). The age at which child-soldiers were recruited meant they would be perceived as boys and girls by all cultural standards. A young veteran stated that, "the war started in 1990 . . . you can't leave, you are forced to join the war, so I joined . . . I was at the age of 10" (Philemon 2010). Gregarious behaviour, a hallmark of peer pressure, was also an indication of child-soldiers' immaturity. During an interview session, a young veteran in trying to answer the question, "What do we say about your tattoo?" stated that:

When I put this mark on me my father disliked me because he is a bishop. But he knows we are in a team. After the war, I went to Bikenu I was immature at that time, I saw my other friends ex-combatants doing it and I joined them and they put this on me... There was a time a fellow called me and asked me 'do you know what this sign indicates' I

---

[33] Lori Grinker, *After War: Veterans from a World in Conflict,* (New York: De MO, 2004).
[34] "Small soldier" was another appellation for "child-soldier" in Liberia.
[35] SBU means Small Boys Unit.

said 'no I don't know,' and I was informed that anybody who has it is part of a society, but I didn't know at all. (Philemon 2010).

The degree of loyalty to commanders, or the identification with the aggressor syndrome through which child-soldiers were strongly attached to their commanders, who became their surrogate parents,[36] was another sign of immaturity. Referring to Charles Taylor[37] as a surrogate father, a young veteran stated that: "when I open my eyes I only know one man called Charles Taylor" (Martine 2010). The nature of the involvement of children in the war was indicative of how vulnerable they were.

Fallible Antidotes

The United Nations peacekeeping missions' Child Protection Units and the Disarmament, Demobilisation and Reintegration sections, UNICEF and other humanitarian organisations and agencies usually champion the cause of child protection. But such rescue operations are greatly influenced by strategic, political and economic calculations of donors, suggestive of the politics of humanitarianism.[38]

This defective nature of the reintegration process stems from the complexities surrounding peacekeeping and peacebuilding operations. The flaws embedded in the Liberian reintegration process illustrate what occurs at a macro level. Romeo Dallaire, a former insider of the United Nations system, a general who commanded the United Missions in Rwanda, in his book *They Fight Like Soldiers, They Die Like Children*, made an illuminating observation, which exposed the laxity and the obscurity that envelop the intervention of the majority of humanitarian organisations and agencies involved in postconflict recovery operations. With particular focus on the United Nations, Dallaire noted that key individuals and international strategic bodies like the

---

[36] Karsten Hundeide, "Becoming a Committed Insider," *Culture Psychology* 9(2), (2003): 107-127.

[37] Charles Taylor was the leader of the NPFL (National Patriotic Front for Liberia), one of the warring factions.

[38] Eric A. Belgrad, "The Politics of Humanitarian Aid," in Eric A. Belgrad and Nitza Nachmias (eds.), *The Politics of International Humanitarian Aid Operations,* (Westport: Praeger, 1997), 3-17; Leon Gordenker, "By way of conclusion", in Eric A. Belgrad and Nitza Nachmias (eds.), *The Politics of International Humanitarian Aid Operations,* (Westport: Praeger, 1997), 189-198; Eric A. Heinze, *Waging Humanitarian War: The Ethics, Law, and Politics of Humanitarian Intervention,* (Albany, NY: State University of New York Press, 2009); Elizabeth G. Ferris, *The Politics of Protection: The Limits of Humanitarian Action,* (Washington, DC: Brookings Institution Press, 2011).

United Nations Department of Peacekeeping Operations and the Security Council who get involved in post-conflict recovery operations with mandates and field missions often do not pay much attention to child-soldiers because they "regard child soldiers as an annoyance, a pain in the side, a social adjustment meriting a minimum of effort." However, if child-soldiers who may better access some basics like food and medicine with and inside their armed groups "are not a priority for those nation states, funding and resources for DDR programmes can be hard to maintain". [39]

Dallaire's observation implies the necessity to find other redemptive pathways to rescue these war-affected children. This chapter demonstrates how their agency has contributed to the change in their conditions and perceptions.

Freedom from the Chain of Chaos through Agency

Agency played a key role in young veterans' emergence as influential community members and their acceptance into the post-conflict society. Through constant, consistent and deliberate attempts to serve within organisations, schools and communities, some young veterans became role-models and even mentors to their comrades and former commanders. Their determination made in-roads into the generally perceived shiftlessness of former young fighters. The drive to become relevant in society captivated many of them to the extent that some reached upper echelons of leadership in their communities. It can be argued that their deliberate effort to emerge as leaders, especially within associations and organisations, gained impetus through a strong sense of motivation. Motivation is a key component of Victor H. Vroom's theory of expectancy.[40] In whatever organisations, associations or other groups such young veterans found themselves, they actively expected an improvement in their living conditions and hoped for an identity accepted by community members; they strove to build such active identities for themselves.[41] This allowed for the attainment of their goals. As a young veteran revealed about himself:

> In school, I put myself strongly in politics, I was part of the students' movements . . . I went to Don Bosco training school, I became a counsellor, talking to people . . . When I left Don Bosco, I went to another organisation . . . Buzzi college association. I even emerged to become youth chairman (Martine 2010).

---

[39] Dallaire, *They fight like soldiers*, 154.
[40] Victor H. Vroom, *Work and Motivation*, (New York: John Wiley, 1964).
[41] H. Bradley, *Fractured Identities: Changing Patterns of Inequality*, (Cambridge: Polity Press, 1997).

Ambition, motivation and focus propelled some young veterans to occupy leadership positions in their communities. For instance, to the question: "What are you studying in the University?", a young veteran answered "sociology"; and to the question "Why did you choose sociology?", he answered "I see myself in the field talking to people and socialising with small organisations and leading societies" (Martine 2010). It is clear that the motives behind the choice of sociology as a field of study were leadership-oriented. Martine who was a "small soldier" before, was studying not to impress but influence other people in the Liberian post-conflict society.

To be accepted by community members, young veterans make deliberate efforts through the presentation of the self. As Erving Goffman puts it, "when an individual appears before others he will have many motives for trying to control the impression they receive."[42] This is an expression of the individual's self-agency. For example, a young veteran disclosed the following:

> I went to Don Bosco Home for workshops so I took the initiative to go by their training. In the training, I saw people below my age presenting, aaah! I got stuck. I said ah! ah! so I was in the bush with the gun ... something continues to tell me you can be like them, do it. Then the director of the centre called me one day and asked me what my expectations are and I told him my expectations. After he called me and talked to me that I have seen you as a junior counsellor. So he took me to a school when I talked to girls and fear started leaving me ... and so forth I talked to many categories of people (Martine 2010).

The above interview excerpt reveals Martine's ability to discover his own retardation through the interactional situation he was involved in. But through deliberate confidence-building steps, he was able to overcome those challenges faced at the outset of his post-conflict civilian life. Such personal initiatives to enhance one's self-confidence became possible through a chain of actions upon the self. The realisation that one is lagging behind here occurred as a result of the interaction with the self. As it has been argued elsewhere, "conflicting features of the environment" shape the individual behaviour, but such behaviour finally stems from the "definition of the situation",[43] that is, the individual's internal deliberation; this notion is similar to Archer's

---

[42] Erving Goffman, *The Presentation of Self in Everyday Life*, (London: Allen Lane Penguin Press, 1969), 13.

[43] Bernard N. Meltzer, John W. Petras, and Larry T. Reynolds, *Symbolic Interactionism: Genesis, Varieties and Criticism*, (London: Routledge and Kegan Paul Ltd, 1975), 23.

internal conversation, Charon's stream of action, and Foucault's "technologies of the self", [44] which all help the individual young veterans to redefine themselves in the post-conflict social environment. Such active actions upon the self, allow for self-agency through which the individual presents to others a new "self". The excerpt which follows illustrates Martine's improvement:

> I started seeing myself progressing. When organisations were looking for people in the community, so I see they chose me. So I see myself going for other trainings, other trainings, I started seeing myself developing. At one point in time team manager and with that role, I could get to chairmen. I became mobilisation chairman to later become chairman for the youths. I started making football key letters and making citations (he was in charge of writing letters on soccer issues). At the end of the day, it was election time. So there was a deposit of LD1000 . . . Buzzi Quarters[45] needed a lot of things. I have worked with organisations before, so I can talk to them. At the end of the day, I emerged as the leader in that community (Martine 2010).

Some young veterans used instrumental coalitions to rise to power. A young veteran while explaining how he and other young veterans were able to set up a peacebuilding NGO together pointed to how situation analysis, motivation and action synergise to bring about change:

> So one day, I was sitting and I said how about we are plenty here, there is no coordination among us. I think it is good to put ourselves together, structure ourselves and in that kind of form if you are ... that is how we were able to put ourselves together we called that the National Assistance Veteran Programme and I became one of the leaders there. (Gracias 2010)

Some young veterans developed a sense of prominence which allowed for easy access to humanitarian organisations in the country, to learn and keep abreast of the latest developments in the NGO sector. Through such initial

---

[44] On Foucault's Technologies of the self, see Michel Foucault, "Technologies of the Self," in Luther H. Martin, Huck Gutman, and Patrick H. Hutton (eds.), *Technologies of the Self: A Seminar with Michel Foucault,* (London: Tavistock Publications, 1988), 16-49; "Technologies of the Self." Lectures at University of Vermont Oct. 1982, https://foucault.info/docu ments/foucault.technologiesOfSelf.en/. Accessed on September 18, 2018.

[45] Buzzi Quarters is a location within Monrovia where Martine was living in 2010 when the interview was conducted.

channels and contacts, they became active participants in the post-war reconstruction process.

One striking feature of these active young veterans was their awareness of the importance of their intelligence and ability in changing their dismal situations into success stories in the post-conflict society. In a damaged society, where individuals categorised as war victims become psychosocial counsellors and peacebuilding agents and peace campaigners, it can be concluded that the phenomenon which Charon termed "stream of action" and the experience which Foucault called "technologies of the self", played an important role in orienting and reorienting the behaviour of such individuals.

In addition, it can be argued that the fragile state of post-conflict societies allows for the speedy emergence of individual agency. In such societies, exogenous forces have less influence on individual agency, especially on individuals who embark on initiatives devoid of all self-deprecating thoughts and attitudes. In a war context, individual agency can be strong and lead to negative or positive consequences. The young veterans, in this case, took prosocial pathways. As one of them revealed, "we all contributed to the war, the destruction of lives and infrastructure, so there is a need to work hard for peace and not wait for other people to do it for us" (Venunye 2010).

This was a frequent theme for young veterans who believed that the reconstruction of their war-shattered country required their active participation instead of dependence on external donors to rescue it from its war-induced maladies. As another young veteran puts it:

> When we got in Monrovia, I actually got in contact with the Lutheran Church through the first awareness workshop. They got very much encouraged with my participation and my level of IQ and a lot of them did not actually believe that I have fought the war except when I showed some body bullet marks and ... that is when they think that I actually took part in the war. So I was also selected from that group to do a trainer of trainers training TOT [training of trainers]. When my period came, they called me I came and I was taken to Torota where I stayed for a long time doing the trainings there, peacebuilding training (Gracias 2010).

The ways in which some young veterans articulated their dreams and ambitions clearly placed them in a position of emergence among their fellow ex-fighters, a world usually considered to be an ill-omened community of vacuous war-casualties, particularly in the African context, who display eccentric behaviour and, accordingly, are capable of masterminding nefarious schemes.[46] A young veteran, a key management team member of an NGO, referred to this in the following terms:

> The next step actually besides self-actualisation is to contribute to a greater society and that could not only be in Liberia. So because of that, I am trying to see how best I can get myself equipped education- ally, do some studies in peace and conflict that will give me a broader concept that will help me look at other theories and concepts that have been used. For instance in Colombia, we saw that their system of con- flict resolution was completely different from what we have here [in Liberia] (Gracias 2010).

Some young veterans have progressed from local to global change agents. On the local level, they believed that they had gone through sufficient transfor- mation and could then be considered as role models in their communities. The organisations and associations they created focused not only on young veterans but on other categories of former fighters, regardless of their age, rank or warring parties during the war. This puts this category of young veter- ans in a position of authority and influence vis-à-vis their counterparts.

At an international level, some young veterans had the opportunity to travel abroad and attended workshops, conferences, fora, short-term courses and seminars. During such trips to foreign countries, they learned that war was a categorical enemy to development, and education was, without doubt, a fun- damental ingredient for the development of both the individual and the soci- ety. This also positively contributed to an improvement of their societal sta- tus. As a young veteran puts it:

> When I came in contact with LC-THRP [Lutheran Church-Trauma Healing and Reconciliation Programme] . . . one or two capacity- building workshops and because of my interest in the programme, I was taken for a TOT [Training of Trainers] programme for like a month. From there you know I had a change of mind, rehabilitation was going on and I had the desire to now be a transformer, see myself as a role model to see how I can bring more ex-coms into the arena of peace- building ... The three [interviewee and two other young veterans] of us came from there and we had a new mind-set, and that was how we thought of establishing an organisation called NEPI National Ex-coms

[46] IIEP, *Guidebook for Planning Education in Emergencies and Reconstruction,* (Paris: International Institute For Educational Planning, 2010).

Peace building Initiative, ex-combatants involved into peace work. So NEPI became a vibrant institution, we have been working with ex-combatants . . . see how we can bridge the gap between ex-coms and the larger community, those ex-coms rejected in the society to see how we can use ourselves as a role model to the family and to them to see, just to help the building process of Liberia. With the peace building work, I have been able to travel to Sweden in a peace building pro-gramme, where I spent like three months and three weeks in Uppsala. And I have also travelled to Cambodia for some training programme, that is, how the work has been (Petit 2010).

Some young veterans understood early on that formal education was funda-mental to an individual's success, a pedestal for one's development in life. As Petit disclosed, "I could have gone back [to war] . . . One motivation I had was, going to school, if it were not school, my brother, I am telling you I could have gone back". Another young veteran echoed this view, "I usually tell my friends that if you want to go far in life the medicine is 'going to school'. So far, I can see myself in school today, I can say that my dreams are fulfilled" (Martine, 2010).

A female young veteran who was once a wife to a rebel commander, and who had two children by the time she was being interviewed, placed empha-sis on "education" as being a cardinal component of children's development. Referring to lessons she intended to convey to her children about war, she clearly stated: "I will tell them not to go to war, and they have to go to school . . . I want to labour for a better future for my children . . . Because my future is spoilt. Children must be sent to school and not to go to war (Flaviano 2010).

Duties performed during the war by some young veterans laid the ground-work for their career ambitions. Even if the Liberian civil war was generally perceived as a source of most, if not all, post-conflict ills, it incidentally creat-ed an environment which some young veterans managed to produce some constructive life-shaping activities, aspirations and enterprises from. By vir-tue of their participation in the war, some young veterans were able to discov-er professional pathways for themselves. John Dewey pointed out in Paul Hart and colleagues' "Starting Points: Questions of Quality in Environmental Edu-cation" that "in directing the activities of the young, society determines its own future",[47] but there are situations whereby societal institutions responsi-ble for such orientation of the youth are weak or almost inexistent; countries ravaged by war typify such societies.

---

[47] Paul Hart, Bob Jickling and Richard Kool, "Starting Points: Questions of Quality in Envi-ronmental Education," *Canadian Journal of Environmental Education* 4, (1999): 105.

A combination of altruism and the technologies of the self, and the desire to help comrades correct their way of life and be accepted in their respective communities contributed to this shift in identity. Through various means, they wanted to let their disgruntled counterparts know that although war is a dispiriting experience, former fighters can become as clear-sighted as other members in their respective post-war communities. Despite all the atrocities committed during the war, young veterans can still be accepted into the society if only they could show conciliatory attitudes towards community members who bore the brunt of the war. As a young veteran pointed out:

> The next motive for setting up that organisation (an NGO he founded together with other young veterans) is to reach our colleagues that are out there and give them hope because most of those guys out there, males and females are hopeless . . . and that is the reason why they are staying on drugs and not doing anything meaningful. That is the reason why their lives have not made any change or impact. So it is not just to build peace but to give them hope, use our own lives as a model, as an example that we used to be like you, and the only reason why we are different from you right now is based on the fact that we had a different orientation, so need similar orientation, to take a different step and way of life . . . we are actually giving them encouragement, giving them hope, building up their own skills and making them understand that the war has taken effect, you must see yourself to be the worst killer, you must see yourself to be rejected and denied but however don't give up (Venunye 2010).

From Jungle Bosses to Post-War Mendicants: The Fall of the Demigods and the Shift in Power Relations

The fate of leaders of warring factions after the war differed. Through the co-optation of war spoilers, warlords and war financiers (those who committed atrocities and profited most from the war and yet have been officially promoted even as leaders), some gained some level of political leverage and were still "heroes".[48] In stark contrast, some became fallen heroes, putting to test the loyalty of their former subordinates, that is, the young veterans. Do former subordinates pay homage to former commanders whose luck has run out in

---

[48] K. M. Jennings, "Unclear ends, unclear means: Reintegration in postwar societies - The case of Liberia," *Global Governance* 14(3), (2008): 327-345; Truth and Reconciliation Commission of Liberia, *Truth and Reconciliation Commission Volume II: Consolidated final report*, (Monrovia: Truth and Reconciliation Commission of Liberia, 2009).

the post-war society? Some former rank and file soldiers, especially young veterans tried to show forms of respect, but deep inside of them, they knew that nobody could boss another person around after the war. It was clear that young veterans were not willing to pander to the wishes of their former jungle taskmasters anymore. Some young veterans disclosed the following:

> Sometimes, some of them (former jungle bosses) are fearful and you are forced to call them boss. But the reality is that, they have no right over me now. At times, when you are going to school all you see them doing is to be drinking and smoking. So all of us we are equal today. And if we want to give that respect, I can, but I must not be forced. We are equal (Perfecto 2010).

> When we meet, we greet one another. When you see them (command-ers) there is a kind of smile because these were people who had a kind of authority. When they say you are finished you are finished, if they say move here and do x y z, that is it. So when you see them today and you look at your own level, everyone at the same level, and everyone can . . . greet and pass . . . When we see our comrades they may say 'my man the other time I saw the former chief, very simple, in fact, he was smiling when he was going, so I don't know what the guy is doing'. At times we see some of them we wonder because of whom they are. . . we say that guy people don't know him oh but during the war he was very dangerous . . . what is the person's intention? I hope they are not recruiting or hav-ing another plan. Because these were commanders who trained in Libya, Burkina Faso . . . You see just a man moving around without any job or any place to be you wonder. So we can see once in a while. Some still recognise us. So ask man how are doing . . . we greet and continue our way . . . everyone on his business (Venunye, 2010).

The above two interview excerpts reveal that what counts in post-war socie-ty is not the military prowess during the war, but one's social status after the war. Former commanders were no exception; some of them became wretched beggars. They shifted from honour to ignominy; their former subordinates, particularly child-soldiers in this case, have, on occasion, become their redemptive figures.

In post-war societies, after the guns have been collected, only former fighters who exercise their agency for self-improvement will emerge posi-tively, and this indubitably leads to a shift in power relations. As two young veterans mentioned:

I can meet them everywhere. I see them we shake hands; we laugh . . . 'you big men now where are you working?' I say, 'I am not working I am going to school.' But at times, we try to talk to them for those who want to listen. I saw some of our bosses but they push wheel barrow today; you speak to them and they want five dollars [Liberian Dollars] from you . . . Oh my man! Most of them are there wasting totally (Martine 2010).

Sometimes we meet but not to discuss war, nobody is commanding anybody this time around. You have many of these jungle generals who are beggars today because they took nothing serious (Enfant 2010).

Young veterans acknowledged a drastic change in power relations with some of their former bosses who were plunged into a crisis of credibility in post-war society. As one young veteran puts it:

I see some of them but, you know stratification has taken place, some of them actually you know say . . . now they see me, I was their junior but today they see me because of my level in the society . . . they call me boss and I say you are the chief, they will say you are the boss . . . so these are jokes but you know I see a lot of them but, I will be true a lot of them are bad off [in other words they are wretched] (Petit 2010).

A power shift occurred during the transition from war to post-war society. Some of the fighters who dominated their subordinates in the jungle became paupers. As one young veteran pointed out, "people who bossed us around when they see us in the street they say buy scratch card (mobile phone airtime) for me and if I have the means, I can help, that is my attribute" (Gracias 2010).

Some young veterans boasted about their contributions in changing the behaviour of other former fighters. And in truth, some of the ex-combatants who participated in their training were originally their bosses in the jungle. These young veterans developed a sense of self-appraisal. The self-congratulation that stemmed from such appraisal gave a fresh impetus to their self-agency. A high self-esteem reinforces self-agency. They believed that they had significantly contributed to the peacebuilding process. There was a sense of self-perpetuating effort in everything they did. As a young veteran pointed out:

I am better than some of them because some of them what they did to the people, some of them ran away from this country and some of them ran away from where people are and settled in the bush because if people set their eyes on them, to them . . . they will be thinking that people will come to harm them so they don't want to be among group of people. . . . For me, I haven't gotten problem with anybody, I can move here, any part of this city, nobody will come to me to say, you— you did that one to me or you did that one to me (Frero, 2010).

Leaders Made in the Jungle

For some young veterans with leadership positions in post-war society, this was not their first leadership role. They held leadership positions within their respective warring factions during the war. Such jungle leadership positions set the stage for their post-war leadership roles. A young veteran who was the director of an NGO referred to such leadership roles in wartime: "I was again part of the reinforcement that came back to Kowe to take over. At that time I was the leader of a group called 'Dragon Force'" (Gracias 2010).

As young veterans began to uncover and interpret the political environment, they gradually and cleverly mapped out the civilian trajectories to follow, in order to escape the widespread misery that marred their post-conflict societies. Such pioneer initiatives, to some extent, derived from young veterans' conscious and deliberate efforts. The various layers of interaction they had with people during meetings provided them with experiences which they consequently translated into actions, and even built upon. It was a deliberate and pre-emptive interpretation of the political, social and economic situation prevailing in the country, which informed their actions. Change did not come to them but change came through them, and they were the principal actors of that change. As a young veteran noted:

> Gradually until when the [Charles] Taylor regime started phasing out, we knew that this organisation will not live. Even if any other president took over, they will not give support to the national veterans' programmes because all the support we got for veterans assistance were actually from Charles Taylor; supplying rice, giving Christmas package. We thought it wise that we cannot continue with (name of organisation withheld) but we have to think of what can be done (Gracias 2010).

Two striking expressions in the above statement are indicative of the agency of young veterans: "we thought it was wise" and "we have to think of what can be done". These thoughts were not initiated by others but by young veterans themselves. Such pre-emptive expressions reveal a deep sense of interaction with the self, which engenders innovative approaches to tackling issues, thus fostering leadership skills. This also refers to a combination of the Foucauldian technologies of the self and Charon's notion of stream of action.

Such pre-emptive measures are also as a result of reactions to the symbolic meaning of the probable end of a political regime and its aftermath.[49] In this case, young veterans in the National Veterans Programme realised that the end of Charles Taylor's regime meant the end of the benefits they were enjoying under that regime. This realisation strengthened their self-agency and they created an NGO. They transformed challenges into a rewarding opportunity; and for them, failure was an anathema. Through their acuity, they interpreted people's actions towards them and they realised that they needed to exercise agency to overcome war-induced difficulties, especially in a society under reconstruction. They understood that they were being side-lined in public debates related to their living conditions and social decision-making processes. As an interviewee puts it: "people were talking but we could not see anybody talking of veterans" (Gracias 2010). They, therefore, transformed this communal apathy towards their predicaments into rewarding initiatives.

A clear and growing realisation that social institutions were ruined, most importantly the weak and shapeless security parastatals, and the lack of clear programmatic security reforms, led young veterans not only to make a prognosis on the security situation of the country, but to join the humanitarian fray and actively contribute to improving the situation of their fellow citizens. This was possible because the young veterans understood, more than the ordinary civilians, the life-world of their unruly counterparts.[50] As a young veteran revealed:

> To be factual, we were very disgruntled at that time. Yeah! Veterans were disgruntled . . . Sometimes they could even clash with the police, police cannot handle the situation. Yes, they were terrible; they could do anything so a lot of people were actually afraid and because we came from that background, we actually decided to take on that task, yeah, people commended us for that bold step and in fact, they said they needed to know the driving force behind our idea to make it more work that is how we began to form the National Ex-combatants Peace building Initiative (Gracias 2010).

---

[49] Blumer, *Symbolic Interactionism.*
[50] Helmut R. Wagner, "The scope of phenomenological sociology: Considerations and suggestions," in George Psathas (ed.), *Phenomenological Sociology: Issues and Applications,* (New York: John Wiley & Sons, 1973), 61-87.

The earnest desire to be part of the reconstruction process and to become role-models made it possible for some young veterans to fully develop prosocial attitudes, which consequentially singled them out. This frame of reference made them different from the war veterans of "Santos Street"[51] who displayed more antisocial behaviour. As Gracias mentioned:

> As we were part of the war, the destruction of the war, we found out that it was necessary to contribute to the reconstruction of the country . . . so we can use ourselves as role model for other ex-coms to follow . . . We have gone through this level of transformation (Gracias 2010).

> I assisted people in the community to the extent that when I even told some people that I am an ex-combatant, they were saying I am lying . . . So we were not only there because we wanted money, we were there to learn in the process. . . . a lot of international donors . . . just called us by phone. Oh yes! I heard about you from that person; I have that piece of job to do and we only want to see you and discuss so that we can know what to do. So it is like if you are doing something well . . . it will serve as a form of recommendation. So, if you are not doing good thing that could attract our own community that could attract the recovery process of the nation, other people could not just sit down and call upon us because there are a lot of NGOs in Liberia; a lot of local NGOs and a lot of INGO (International Non-Governmental Organisations). So for local NGOs to be called, it means that you are doing something meaningful (Gracias, 2010).

Conclusion

Owing to the overwhelming rights-based and victimhood-centred characterisation of the fate of children in African war theatres, a discourse of the agency of children, particularly those associated with armed groups and forces, towards their post-conflict reintegration, appears to be a controversial issue. There is a need to highlight this neglected aspect of the agency of child-soldiers. This chapter has tried to do that. Admittedly, the chapter has not presented all the facets of this agency but has shown how children, in the midst of chaos, are able to reinvent themselves, create for themselves some survival spaces.

In post-conflict societies, power relations among former fighters, be they former child-soldiers or adult fighters, can shift to a certain degree. With ref-

---

[51] Santos Street is an area in Monrovia, the capital city of Liberia, where various clusters of former combatants could be found in 2010 when the author conducted interviews in Liberia.

erence to Liberia, through a co-optation of conspicuous war-profiteers in the name of peace and stability, some warlords and war financiers gained political leverage, while some young veterans were able to accede to leadership positions as well. These changes did not simply come to young veterans but were a result of their conscious efforts.

Young veterans followed many pathways to become "bosses". They developed cordial relationships with their communities, and through prosocial behaviour, they established themselves as examples to other former fighters. They were ready to learn, even during workshops they were asked to facilitate. All their activities were undertaken with care, which fostered the development of strong relationships with other peacebuilding partners.

Originally boys and girls in the bush during the civil war, some were able to overcome the laxity and idleness which commonly characterise former fighters escaping. Those who were able to change did so through conscious and painstaking interaction with the self, the technologies of the self, streams of action, human action after an interpretation of the day to day grim realities of their new world, and instrumental coalitions.

Accordingly, within their respective communities, young veterans were able to deviate from the generally presumed passivity and vulnerability of former child-soldiers, to move up the social ladder. Some occupied leadership positions in community associations, professional bodies and schools. But most importantly, the expression of the stream of action to coalesce with others and set the pace in creating NGOs used by international institutions to carry out research, and to assist former fighters, and even create jobs for others, made some of the young veterans celebrated figures in post-conflict society. Through their self-agency, young veterans successfully overcame individual and societal hurdles to get to leadership positions, turning their former bosses in the bush, into "boys" in town, thus altering power relations. Through their own stories, it became clear that some of these former jungle boys and girls became "bosses" in the post-conflict society. Some "deified" jungle commanders became paupers and mendicants; some jungle warlords, however, became key political figures.

Bibliography

"Technologies of the Self." Lectures at University of Vermont Oct. 1982. https://foucault.info/documents/foucault.technologiesOfSelf.en/.

Alusula, Nelson. *Disarmament, Demobilisation, Rehabilitation and Reintegration (DDRR) in Liberia.* Centre for International Cooperation and Security, 2008.

Archer, Margaret S. *Structure, Agency and the Internal Conversation.* Cambridge: Cambridge University Press, 2003.

Belgrad, Eric A. "The Politics of Humanitarian Aid." In *The Politics of International Humanitarian Aid Operations,* edited by Eric A. Belgrad and Nitza Nachmias. Westport: Praeger, 1997. 3-19.

Berg, B. L. *Qualitative Research Methods for the Social Sciences.* Boston, Mass: Allyn and Bacon, 2007.

Blumer, Herbert. *Symbolic Interactionism.* Englewood Cliffs, NJ: Prentice Hall, 1969.

Bradley, H. *Fractured Identities: Changing Patterns of Inequality.* Cambridge: Polity Press, 1997.

Call, Charles. "Liberia's war recurrence: Grievance over greed." *Civil Wars* 12 (4), (2010): 347-369.

Carpenter, Charli R. "Women, children and other vulnerable groups: Gender, strategic frames and the protection of civilians as a transnational issue." *International Studies Quarterly* 49, no. 2 (2005): 295-334.

Charon, Joel M. *Symbolic Interactionism: An introduction, an Interpretation, an Integration.* Upper Saddle River, NJ: Prentice-Hall, 2001.

Coalition to Stop the Use of Child Soldiers. *Child Soldiers: Global Report 2004.* London: Coalition to Stop the Use of Child Soldiers, 2004.

Dallaire, Romeo. *They fight like soldiers, they die like children.* London: Hutchinson, 2010.

Denzin, Norman K. *Symbolic Interactionism and Cultural Studies: The Politics of Interpretation.* Oxford: Blackwell Publishers, 1992.

Diallo, Yolande. *African traditions and Humanitarian Law: Similarities and differences.* Geneva: International Committee of the Red Cross (ICRC), 1976.

Ferris, Elizabeth G. *The Politics of Protection: The Limits of Humanitarian Action.* Washington, DC: Brookings Institution Press, 2011.

Foucault, Michel. "Technologies of the Self." In *Technologies of the Self: A Seminar with Michel Foucault,* edited by Luther H. Martin, Huck Gutman, and Patrick H. Hutton. London: Tavistock Publications, 1988. 16-49.

Goffman, Erving. *The Presentation of Self in Everyday Life.* London: Allen Lane Penguin Press, 1969.

Gordenker, Leon. "By way of conclusion." In *The Politics of International Humanitarian Aid Operations,* edited by Eric A. Belgrad and Nitza Nachmias. Westport: Praeger, 1997. 189-198.

Grinker, Lori. *After War: Veterans from a World in Conflict.* New York: De MO, 2004.

Hart, Paul, Bob Jickling, and Richard Kool. "Starting Points: Questions of Quality in Environmental Education." *Canadian Journal of Environmental Education* 4, (1999): 104-124.

Hegre, Håvard. Gudrun Østby and Clionadh Raleigh, "Poverty and civil war events: A disaggregated study of Liberia." *Journal of Conflict Resolution* (2009): 1-26.

Heinze, Eric A. *Waging Humanitarian War: The Ethics, Law, and Politics of Humanitarian Intervention.* Albany, NY: State University of New York Press, 2009.

Human Rights Watch. *How to fight, how to kill: Child soldiers in Liberia.* London: Human Rights Watch, 2004.

Hundeide, Karsten. "Becoming a Committed Insider." *Culture Psychology* 9(2), (2003): 107-127.

IIEP. *Guidebook for Planning Education in Emergencies and Reconstruction.* Paris: International Institute For Educational Planning, 2010.

Jaye, Thomas. *Transitional Justice and DDR: The Case of Liberia.* New York: International Center for Transitional Justice, 2009.

Jennings, K. M. "Unclear ends, unclear means: Reintegration in postwar societies - The case of Liberia." *Global Governance* 14(3), (2008): 327-345.

Kippenberg, Hans G. *Violence as worship: Religious wars in the age of globalization.* Translated by Brian McNeil. Stanford: Stanford University Press, 2011.

Kirkpatrick, Lee A., and Bruce J. Ellis. "An Evolutionary-psychological Approach to Self-esteem: Multiple Domains and Multiple Functions." In *Self and Social Identity,* edited by Marilynn B. Brewer and Miles Hewstone. Malden, Mass: Blackwell Publishing, 2004. 52-77.

Knoblich, Günther, and Natalie Sebanz, "Agency in the face of error," *Trends in Cognitive Sciences* 9(6), (2005): 259-261.

Landry, Guillaume. *Child soldiers and disarmament, demobilization, rehabilitation and reintegration in West Africa: A survey of programmatic work on child soldiers in Côte d'Ivoire, Guinea, Liberia and Sierra Leone.* Dakar: Coalition to Stop the Use of Child Soldiers, 2006.

Meltzer, Bernard N., John W. Petras, and Larry T. Reynolds. *Symbolic Interactionism: Genesis, Varieties and Criticism.* London: Routledge and Kegan Paul Ltd, 1975.

Nwolise, O.B.C. "The fate of women, children and the aged in contemporary Africa's conflict theatres: The urgent need to revive Africa's code of honour." Lecture delivered at the 2001 Public Annual Lecture of the National Association of Political Science Students (NAPSS), University of Ibadan Chapter, at the Lady Bank Anthony Hall, University of Ibadan, August 15, 2001.

Saldaña, Johnny. *The Coding Manual for Qualitative Researchers.* London: SAGE, 2009.

Save the Children Fund. *Forgotten Casualties of War: Girls in Armed Conflict.* London: Save the Children, 2005.

Singer, P.W. *Children at War.* Berkeley, L.A.: University of California Press, 2006.

Smith,,Jonathan A. Paul Flowers, and Michael Larkin. *Interpretative Phenomenological Analysis: Theory, Method and Research.* London: SAGE, 2009.

Truth and Reconciliation Commission of Liberia. *Truth and Reconciliation Commission Volume II: Consolidated final report.* Monrovia: Truth and Reconciliation Commission of Liberia, 2009.

Vroom, Victor H. *Work and Motivation.* New York: John Wiley, 1964.

Wagner, Helmut R. "The scope of phenomenological sociology: Considerations and suggestions." In *Phenomenological Sociology: Issues and Applications,* edited by George Psathas. New York: John Wiley & Sons, 1973. 61-87.

Wells, Karen. *Childhood in a Global Perspective.* Cambridge: Polity Press, 2009.

Chapter 7

White Poverty, State Paternalism and Educational Reforms in Southern Rhodesia in the 1930s

Ivo Mhike

Introduction

The Great Depression saw the emergence of a state recognised social problem of juvenile delinquency in the settler colony of Southern Rhodesia in southern Africa. White poverty and weakening parental authority engendered public disquiet and a "moral panic" over the emergence of a "delinquent" and reprobate class of juveniles who engaged in crime, profaned racial binaries and, therefore, undermined the "respectability" of the white race. In typical Social Darwinism, officials believed that economic penury was a harbinger of interracial associations and potential racial "contamination"; a threat to the racial binaries on which racial segregation and colonial white domination rested.[1] The 1930s also brought to the fore the inadequacies of white education because white youths swelled the ranks of the unemployed due, in part, to lack of job skills in the face of African competition for skilled occupations. This period spawned a precipitous trajectory of "white men and boys who lacked the education, discipline and diligence necessary to raise white families..." and these "were perceived as an internal threat to settler visions of multi-generational success" and a liability on the colonial fiscus.[2] Social planners were alarmed at the symbolic, socio-economic and political implications of the emergent calibre of white male youth to the future development of the colony.

---

[1] Saul Dubow, "Race, Civilisation and Culture: The Elaboration of Segregation Discourse in the Inter-War Years," African Studies Seminar Paper, University of the Witwatersrand, 1986, 5-8.

[2] Carrol Summers, "Boys, Brats and Education: Reproducing White Maturity in Colonial Zimbabwe, 1915–1935", *Settler Colonial Studies* 1 (1), (2011): 132-133.

This article examines the emergence of a new form of state paternalism in the 1930s with a particular focus on the development of a social model of male youth education in juvenile rehabilitation institutions in Southern Rhodesia. The study argues that juvenile rehabilitation institutions became instruments of state social engineering which advanced the new model of emphasising productive masculinity in skills training for blue collar jobs for lower class whites. St. Pancras Home became key to the production of breadwinning patriarchs through fostering a "rural mindedness" in youth for agriculture sector jobs, providing instruction in elementary engineering, woodwork and metalwork. The new educational model was also enmeshed with the colony's long-term goal to build a white skills base for future industrial development as well as establishing an artisanal class that would serve as a bulwark against the economic mobility of Africans to the higher echelons of the colonial economy. Indeed, Southern Rhodesia attempted a similar social model of youth education which focused on practical skills from around 1915 albeit with little success.[3] However, white anxiety over economic collapse in the 1930s reignited the urgency for educational reforms to alleviate an increasingly precarious white position. Invariably, the new model of education reinforced the normative gender roles of colonial white society and reaffirmed the "white men" as breadwinners and paladins of imperial values.

The emergence of "delinquent" juveniles in the 1930s was one of many signs, but perhaps the most ominous one of the cataclysmic rapture of white social fabric and white values. Delinquency and unemployment refracted conceptions of social (dis)order and marked the thoroughgoing convergence between colonial state power and narratives of behaviour. The right to citizenship was predicated on youths' ability to embrace or (re)embrace their ascribed role in the colonial racial and social order. In Southern Rhodesia, white youths were imbued with a sense of mission and "manifest destiny" towards the rightness of white dominance and attendant civilisation. The demarcation of social boundaries for young people was, therefore, inextricably intertwined with the unflinching discourse of white hegemony in a colonial context. Those who transgressed officially sanctioned forms of behaviour or did not conform to "white standards" undermined the edifice of white racial superiority and were typically labelled deviant and delinquent. Allison Shutt demonstrates how the idea of "proper" social conduct for both Blacks (Africans) and non-Black colonisers (Europeans) was central to the sustenance of colonial social order. She argues that manners did not only pertain to

---

[3] Ibid., 132-153.

individual behaviour but also to a corporate but often discursive lifestyle which each race was prescribed.[4]

The "moral panic" over the condition and conduct of white male youths was more than just a knee-jerk reaction to the crisis. Constructs of deviance and delinquency among the youth were an accomplishment of modern state-making because the colonial state capitalised on the moral outrage that infected society to shape a new form of state paternalism that defined the 1930s and 1940s. Identification and treatment of delinquency became part of a wider scheme to plot the shifting moral centres of white society where increasing numbers of whites were making the poverty bracket and failing to uphold "white standards". As the effects of the depression began to bite, under the Moffat administration and more decisively Huggins, after 1933, the state extended control and regulation of Rhodesian society through legislation such as the Land Apportionment Act (LAA) 1930, Compulsory Education Act of 1930, Maize Control Act (1931 and 1934) and the Industrial Conciliation Act 1934 (ICA) among other pieces of legislation. The LAA divided the colony into White and African areas and secured whites' access to the most productive land in the colony and the Education Act compelled white children between 6 and 15 years to attend school. The ICA removed the African from the definition of employee and disqualified him/her from labour processes such as conciliation, arbitration and the right to go on strike.[5] More importantly, it preserved industrial apprenticeship for whites and limited African access to skilled jobs. Further, the state employed extra market measures to secure employment for white school leavers under the Juvenile Affairs Boards instituted in 1932 and encouraged some form of economic nationalism which prioritised Rhodesian-born whites over immigrants in job openings. The 1930s, therefore, witnessed some of the most radical legislation aimed at securing white economic interests by legally setting the settlers at an economic advantage against Africans, articulated under Huggins' "two pyramid" policy or separate development of the races.

White Education and Maturity

In Southern Rhodesia, formal school-type education was one of the foremost pillars of whiteness, white rule, and was central to the reproduction of white maturity.[6] Rhodesian colonial officials appreciated the importance of white

---

[4] Allison Shutt, *Manners Make a Nation: Race Etiquette in Southern Rhodesia, 1910-1963,* (New York: University of Rochester Press, 2015).

[5] Government of Southern Rhodesia, *Industrial Conciliation Act 1934.*

[6] Summers, "Boys, Brats and Education,"134-135.

education and believed that all whites should be educated in order for them to have an advantage over the numerically "superior" African race. A lack of education, skills training and resources would place whites into competition with Africans, thus disrupting the colonial correlation between white race and superior social roles. In 1915, Legislator Lionel Cripps affirmed that "The white men were the aristocrats of this country and it behoved them to keep that position for themselves" and education was key to in achieving this goal.[7] In colonial white societies "respectability" and maturity (productive masculinity) were the dominant norms and values and the colonial narrative was shaped by men of "gentlemanly background" of the public-school system in Britain or "men-of-the-officer-class".[8] According to Ann Stoler, twentieth-century colonials were "men of class" and "men of character" who advanced a modernised colonial rule and protected the colony against physical weakness, moral decay and "degeneracy".[9] Such societies viewed as anathema non-productive men (impoverished and unemployed). Indeed, "colonial discourse of degeneracy and social reform enforced middle-class conventions of respectability which became the personal and public boundaries of race".[10]

The educational policy of Southern Rhodesia was couched in segregationist thinking in which the curriculum for whites offered a general education with a view to preparing white children for the civil service and other white colour jobs while practical education for Africans prepared them for manual labour. In addition, a good education was designed to nurture Southern Rhodesia's international image as a conducive destination for would be settlers and their families in its quest to increase the settler population through immigration.[11] By the 1920s Southern Rhodesia had a relatively well-structured system of schools involving state-aided, state-controlled and denominational schools. In 1923, some 6.000 white pupils were in school at an average attendance of

---

[7] National Archives of Zimbabwe (hereafter NAZ) SRG 3, Government of Southern Rhodesia, *Southern Rhodesia Legislative Council Debates*, 09 August 1915, Column 198.
[8] William Jackson, *Madness and Marginality: The lives of Kenya's White Insane*, (Manchester: Manchester University Press, 2013), 15; Paul John Rich, *Chains of Empire: English Public Schools, Masonic Cabalism, Historical Causality, and Imperial Clubdom*, (London: Regency Press, 1991).
[9] Ann Stoler, "Making Empire respectable: the politics of race and sexual morality in 20th-century colonial cultures," *American Ethnologist* 16 (4), (1989): 645.
[10] Ibid., 634.
[11] Southern Rhodesia competed to attract settlers with other British territories like Australia, Canada, New Zealand and South Africa. See Alois S. Mlambo, "'Some are more White than others': Racial Chauvinism as a factor of Rhodesian Immigration Policy, 1890-1963," *Zambezia* 27 (2), (2000): 139-160.

88.14 percent.[12] The Compulsory Education Act of 1930 settled the issue of access to education by making education compulsory for all white children.

Rhodesian White maturity and identity were also guided by principles of muscular Christianity (life of bravery, "manliness" and cheerful physical activity).[13] Officials emphasised Bible reading and moral teaching in schools as essential for white children's ethical foundations. After the First World War, the Boy Scouts and Girl Guide movements gained popularity because they were perceived as ways of facilitating discipline and bushcraft among children.[14] In the early 1920s, Southern Rhodesia's Medical Inspector recommended physical drill and gymnasium as fundamental to child health and character.[15] In addition, the Southern Rhodesia Cadet Corps programme which was founded in 1900 for boys in school epitomised the brutal, violent and militaristic nature of white masculinity. Cadet Corps taught boys from twelve years weapons handling, signals, and musketry among other military skills designed to cultivate vigour in youths.[16] In particular, the Cadet system was central to the military recruitment during the World War One. Cadet Corps were meant to create a reserve force from which the state could recruit in case of an African uprising. Under the auspices of the Defence Department, the junior cadets passed through senior cadetship (15 years) to the Rifles Club and it formed the nucleus of the citizen (voluntary) forces and usually reinforced the colony's semi-military policy. The 1918 and 1926 Defence Acts stipulated compulsion military call-up to all white Rhodesian males from the age of 18 years. These pieces of legislation linked well with the Cadet system in militarising white Rhodesian youths.[17] The inter-war years also saw the introduction of Navy and Airforce corps.[18] Furthermore, Rhodesian school hymns evoked the exploits of pioneers such as Jameson and Blakiston as pal-

---

[12] Lewis H. Gann and Michael Gelfand, *Huggins of Rhodesia: The Man and His Country*, (London: George Allen and Unwin, 1964), 136.

[13] For a discussion on the concept see Nick J Watson, Stuart Weir, and S. Friend, "The Development of Muscular Christianity in Victorian Britain and Beyond," *Journal of Religion and Society* 7, (2005):1-21.

[14] The Scout Movement was founded by Robert Baden-Powell in 1907 to assist young men to utilize military and colonial frontier discipline in peacetime and renew white middle class manliness.

[15] Ethel Tawse Jollie, *The Real Rhodesia*, (Bulawayo: Books of Rhodesia, 1971), 237.

[16] NAZ S726/SW3/1-2, Government of Southern Rhodesia Cadets Policy 1926.

[17] *Southern Rhodesia Defence Act 1918.*

[18] NAZ S726/W36/8 -14, Cadets Policy 1933-1939.

adins of early Rhodesia.[19] In relation to the Kenyan case, as John Lonsdale notes, mastery required military, legal, and personal force to ensure prestige.[20] In this respect, white "values" of masculinity were inculcated in various ways including recreation and through formal channels.

State, Youth and Economic Crisis, Depression and State 'discovered' Juvenile Delinquency

As the effects of the Great Depression set in, white unemployment and increased poverty infringed on the sustenance of so-called "white standards". In 1932, of the 21,500 settler wage earners in Southern Rhodesia, eight percent or 1,720 were unemployed.[21] Male unemployment caused disillusionment because they were breadwinning patriarchs. Deprivation perforated white social fabric and family life was riddled with patterns of neglect, moral degradation, and disregard for law. Such an environment engendered a disaffected youth some of whom were involved in crime in a society whose shifting moral boundaries violated the sustenance of racial binaries and "respectability" of the white race. Poverty among Rhodesian whites also evoked the spectre of the South African "poor white problem".[22] In Southern Rhodesia, the term "Poor White" was adopted albeit in reference to "men accustomed to and content with a very low standard of living, that appear to be incapable, for various reasons, of keeping employment or maintaining themselves without

---

[19] Donal Lowry, "Rhodesia 1890-1980: 'The Lost Dominion'," in Robert Bickers (ed.), *Settlers and Expatriates: Britons over the Seas*, (Oxford: Oxford University Press, 2010), 140-141.

[20] John Lonsdale, "Kenya: Home Country and African Frontier," in Robert Bickers (ed.), *Settlers and Expatriates: Britons over the Seas*, (Oxford: Oxford University Press, 2010), 90.

[21] *Report of Select Committee to Investigate the Problem of Unemployment in the Colony*, 1932, 3.

[22] White poverty in South Africa developed in the wake of the economic and social processes wrought by the minerals revolution and became a problem for politicians and social planners for the greater part of the twentieth century; Colin Bundy, "Vagabond Hollanders and Runaway Englishmen: White Poverty in the Cape Before Poor Whiteism," in William Beinart, Peter Delius, and Stanley Trapido (eds.), *Putting a Plough to the Ground: Accumulation and Dispossession in Rural South Africa 1850-1930*, (Johannesburg: Ravan, 1986), 101-128; Robert Morell (ed.), *White but Poor: Essays on the History of Poor Whites in Southern Africa 1880–1940*, (Pretoria: University of South Africa, 1992); Charles van Onselen, *Studies in the Social and Economic History of the Witwatersrand, 1886–1914*, Volume 2 (Johannesburg: New Nineveh, 1982).

assistance from the state or charitable organisations".[23] The depression years enlarged this group due to lack of employment opportunities.

Social planners framed white poverty as the harbinger of racial contamination. Through the influences of Social Darwinism, inferior races were believed to have a contaminating effect on superior ones and, in particular, poor whites had to be rescued to preserve the purity and superiority of the white race.[24] The Southern Rhodesia Criminal Investigation Department (CID) were solicitous about an increase in the number of white children from economically deprived families who mixed with Africans during their play time. For example, in 1931 the CID at Que Que recommended that Douglas (13) and Ronald (9) be considered for the proposed Industrial School largely because, "it is well known that these children mix with natives in play, and are not cared for as they might by their parents who are in receipt of government rations and are in a very poor way (sic)".[25] Similarly, juveniles Peter and James Quinn were deemed "out of control".[26] However, what worried the authorities most was that "they frequent native compounds and return with 'Bicycles Cigarettes' (An African Brand) and other articles".[27] In addition, "they beg or steal these from natives as they have no money to buy them".[28] Acts of misdemeanour in themselves did not cause much anxiety as did the fact that these juveniles risked "contamination". In this regard, poverty and delinquency became two sides of the same coin.

Colonial racial binaries were as ideological as they were physical, and ungoverned child development created a most undesirable situation. Even more worrying for colonial officials was the fact that some of the criminal behaviours committed by white children, like petty theft, were conducted in full view of Africans or had Africans as victims. These acts transgressed the legal and cultural boundaries of white colonial society and undermined the edifice of perceived white infallibility and self-proclaimed obligation to civilise the Black subject

---

[23] Government of Southern Rhodesia, *Report on the Unemployment and the Relief of Destitution in Southern Rhodesia*, 1934, 24. However, poverty was not peculiar to the 1930s; Morell, *White but Poor.*
[24] Dubow, "Race, Civilisation and Culture," 5-8.
[25] NAZ S824/345/1, Government of Southern Rhodesia, Institutions for Juvenile Delinquents, July 20 1931-February 01 1934, CID Detective Sergeant, Que Que to Assistant Magistrate, Que Que, 01 October 1931.
[26] NAZ S824/345/1, Government of Southern Rhodesia, Institutions for Juvenile Delinquents, July 20 1931-February 01 1934, Sergeant, Bulawayo Police Station to Chief Superintendent CID, 16 October 1933.
[27] Ibid.
[28] Ibid.

race. Stealing from Africans by a member of a "superior" white race had a double meaning; it broke the law and embarrassed the white race. Similarly, the 1960s triggered a "moral panic" in sections of South African white society because some white youths fraternised across colour lines at the peak of youth popular culture in violation of ideals of apartheid.[29] The newly acquired youth tastes were viewed by sections of white society as an affront to Afrikaner morals and Calvinist values.[30] In this respect, racial contamination was a serious concern in South Africa and Southern Rhodesia albeit under different circumstances. The development of the social problem of juvenile delinquency could not have come at a worse time for Southern Rhodesia. In the first three decades of the twentieth century, white society was threatened by degeneration and loss of civilisation.[31] After the First World War, imperial authorities noted with concern the low birth rate and poor health of children, particularly amongst the white middle class.[32] There was a worry in the British Empire about efficiency and decline marked by the South African War (1899-1902) and to a degree the ravages of World War One and Spanish Influenza. Although degeneracy was not defined in physical terms but in terms of astuteness of character and qualities to sustain imperial control, the ravages of war and disease were a debilitating factor. The emergence of delinquent youths in a young colony like Southern Rhodesia worsened the fears over the nascent development of whites who were unable to inherit and defend the empire and its values.

Youth poverty justified state paternalism was rationalised to perform the function of guardian in place of "failed parents". In 1928 Legislator Tawse Jollie charged; "we cannot rely on parents of this country to do their duty invariably in regard to these children".[33] Consequently, the Southern Rhodesia Children's Protection and Adoption Act of 1929 empowered government to transfer legal guardianship in order to protect white children and the white race. The Quinn boys, as well as Douglas and Ronald's guardianship, were transferred to the state. Practically, the state assumed total control over poor children because it judged the parents unable to bring them up in a proper way that upheld "white standards". Similarly, British and South African social reformers believed that economic deprivation and dysfunctional families

---

[29] Albert Grundlingh, "'Are We Afrikaners Getting too Rich?' Cornucopia and Change in Afrikanerdom in the 1960s," *Journal of Historical Sociology* 21(2/3), (2008): 155-156.
[30] Ibid.
[31] Lowry, "Rhodesia 1890-1980," 124.
[32] Fiona Praisley, "Childhood and Race: Growing Up in The Empire", in Philippa Levine (ed.), *Gender and Empire*, (Oxford: Oxford University Press, 2004), 240-241.
[33] Quoted in Summers, "Boys, Brats and Education," 137.

were the principal causes of juvenile delinquency. This social theory became the bedrock of state paternalism and carte blanche intervention in working-class families to determine guardianship and the future of the children.[34]

Table 7.1 shows the nature of juvenile crime between 1935 and 1938. Theft offences were in the majority and these, largely, involved petty theft of small amounts of money or articles.[35] There was a sharp rise in the number of cases in 1936, a trend which can be attributed to the renewed impetus for more effective juvenile crime record keeping in light of the appointment of the Probation and School Attendance Officer in the same year. Overall, the juvenile figures were small but for Southern Rhodesia, it was not a question of numbers as for the implications of the development a reprobate class of white juveniles to the overall colonial designs.

Table 7.1. Offences committed by white Juveniles and Juvenile Adults, 1935-1938.

Year	1935	1936	1937	1938
Theft	42	39	34	42
Malicious Damage to Property	-	2	-	2
Assault	-	4	1	2
Rape and Indecency	1	3	2	1
Culpable Homicide	-	2	-	-
Fraud	2	4	-	1
Forgery	1	-	2	1
Other Offences	-	18	6	1
Total Number of Offences	46	72	45	50

Source: NAZ S824/345/3 Probation Officer Report, 1938.

---

[34] Victor Bailey, *Delinquency and Citizenship: Reclaiming the Young Offender, 1914-18,* (Oxford: Clarendon, 1987); Linda Chisholm, "Reformatories and Industrial Schools in South Africa: A Study in Class, Colour and Gender, 1882-1939," (PhD Thesis, University of the Witwatersrand, 1989), 77.

[35] Ibid.

White Education and Unemployment

The Great Depression also revealed the limitations of Southern Rhodesia's educational model. The question was no longer about whites' access to education but whether or not a general education was suitable and desirable when the civil service, the traditional employer, proved inelastic. Youths had to prepare for blue collar jobs if they were to keep the mantle of safeguarding white civilisation and carry the settler's mission in colonised lands.[36] The competitive edge of white youths over the Africans was compromised by their lack of practical skills. Statistically, about 369 pupils left school at the end of 1931 and this figure was far less than the annual average of 700.[37] The Director of Education speculated that the 1931 figure was lower than the usual on account that parents kept their children in school because there were no job openings.[38] In 1932, some 341 white youths left school and 247 required work.[39] The remaining 94 (28 %) went to higher education or left the colony. By May of 1933, some 91 white youths still required employment.[40] Such statistics vindicated Legislator Thompson's 1928 suggestion that there should be a "weeding out" of children who did not have the capacity to proceed to higher education and fill posts requiring such an education in order to avoid state wasting resources on a general higher education.[41] The 1934 report of the Labour Commissioner further emphasised that the school system was producing insufficiently equipped youths and this was reflected in the data relating to unemployed adults.[42] Sections of the white society blamed this development on the calibre of the Rhodesian teacher who was a product of England's public school system who found a rural life and the challenges of mining unattractive.

Low educational qualifications and limited skills training exposed whites to African competition. In 1934, the Labour Commissioner compiled information on 71 young jobs seekers and classified them into three distinct groups. Of the lot, 15 were deemed suitable for the usual avenues of employment, 45 were ill

---

[36] Stephanie Olsen, "Adolescent Empire: Moral Dangers for Boys in Britain and India, c.1800 to 1914", in Heather Ellis (ed.), *Juvenile Delinquency and the Limits of Western Influence, 1850-2000,* (Hampshire: Palgrave Macmillan, 2014), 20.

[37] NAZ S824/42/2, Government of Southern Rhodesia, Juvenile Affairs Boards, 1932-1934; Director of Education, Southern Rhodesia to the Secretary, Department of the Colonial Secretary, 03 February 1932.

[38] Ibid.

[39] Government of Southern Rhodesia, *Report on Unemployment and The Relief of Destitution in Southern Rhodesia,* 1934, 8

[40] Ibid.

[41] *Southern Rhodesia Legislative Assembly Debates,* 1928, 849.

[42] Ibid., 10.

equipped for employment owing to a low standard of education and could, with much difficulty, find employment as lorry drivers, unskilled artisans, or handymen.[43] The remaining 11 were classified as youths of the peasant type brought up and educated on farms and were unlikely to follow successfully any occupation but farming.[44] Technically, categories 2 and 3 constituted the "unemployable" youths. Of the 71 youths, 62 were assessed regarding their level of education of which 33 had reached Standard V or less, 14 (Standard VI), 12 (Standard VII) and only 3 had reached a higher level of education.[45] Effectively, 53 percent of the youths had reached Standard V and below and given the growing appetite for education among Africans from the 1920s, this group of white youths came into direct competition with the better educated Africans,[46] who, by virtue of colour, could be paid less than a white person in job opening.[47] By the 1920s the government policy thrust of providing Africans with practical skills for manual labour[48] was having an adverse effect on the economic security of whites as the economic situation made it counterintuitive to employ whites over equally if not better qualified Africans.

The demand for African trades and other businesses and the number of African service providers increased from 864 to 3545 between 1930 and 1938.[49] The job colour bar system, the quintessential weapon of the white worker and his existence became his Achilles' heel during the depression years. The 1930s gave paramountcy to economic factors and undermined the elimination of African competition through legislative means. Meanwhile, the white population increased from 39,470 in 1926 to 55,570 in 1936 at a time when white economic interests were eroding.[50] The 1930s job colour bar crisis in Rhodesia evoked the ghost of the Rand Revolt of 1922 when the economic recession of the early 1920s forced South African mining companies to substitute white workers for Africans in order to cut costs.

---

[43] NAZ S824/43/2, Government of Southern Rhodesia, Juvenile Affairs Boards, 1932-1934; Bulawayo Juveniles Affairs Board Second Annual Report, 1934, 4.
[44] Ibid.
[45] Ibid.
[46] Ibid.
[47] NAZ S824/43/2, Government of Southern Rhodesia, Juvenile Affairs Boards, 1932-1934; Bulawayo Juvenile Affairs Board Second Annual Report 1934, 4-5.
[48] Government of Southern Rhodesia, *Report on the Suggested Industrial Development of Natives*, 1920.
[49] Ian Phimister, *An Economic and Social History of Zimbabwe, 1890-1948: Capital Accumulation and Class Struggle*, (London: Longman, 1988), 190.
[50] Gann and Gelfand, *Huggins of Rhodesia*, 110.

Beyond the inadequate educational curriculum, social planners pinned the youth labour crisis on the character of the Rhodesian lad. Appraising the character and stamina of Rhodesian youth as a candidate for employment, Captain W.H. Kimpton of the Motor Traders' Association described the average youth as "indolent and imputed, without initiative or ambition", faults he ascribed to "lack of parental control, poor physique and undue native assistance."[51] Although A.J. Somerville, representing Principals of Salisbury Schools vehemently disagreed with this view, it was endorsed by the representative of the Salisbury Municipality, M.E. Cleveland, who perceived the youths as "lacking manners".[52] The Rhodesia Agricultural Union (RAU) also alleged that the 1930s labour shortages were, to some degree, artificial and expressed disappointment at the fact that offers of permanent employment on tobacco farms at £10 per month with lodgings had been turned down by white youths on the ground that "this was no suitable reward for the sacrifice of the attraction of town life which it entailed."[53] Similarly, Salisbury and Bulawayo experienced difficulty in getting youths to accept work on the mines.[54] In view of this fact, white youth were ill equipped and unwilling to respond to the demands of the changing colonial economy and the business community did not have confidence in them.

Social planners were also concerned about unemployed youths who drifted into government relief works in road construction and in European Labour Afforestation Operations (ELAO) in Mtao and Stapleford. [55] The basic daily rate of pay in these camps was 3s. 6d., with efficiency pay at 6d. and 1d. per day as bonus.[56] Some made up to 6s. 9d. per day against the cost of meals which ranged between 1s. 6d. and 1s. 9d.[57] However, the government did not consider the money paid in relief works as a wage but a token given to enable the men to maintain themselves. Barring the social stigma associated with being in a Relief Camp, relief works were an attractive option for youths who did not have any

---

[51] NAZ S824/42/2, Government of Southern Rhodesia Juvenile Affairs Boards, 1932-1934: Minutes of the Inaugural Meeting for the formation of a Juvenile Affairs Board, Salisbury, 04 March 1932, 12.

[52] Ibid., 13.

[53] Ibid.

[54] Government of Southern Rhodesia, *Report on Unemployment and The Relief of Destitution in Southern Rhodesia*, 1934, 9.

[55] Ibid.

[56] NAZ S1194/1660/1 Government of Southern Rhodesia, White Labour Afforestation Camp: Mtao Report, Memorandum from Minister of Agriculture to the Department of the Colonial Secretary, 10 December 1930, 1.

[57] Ibid., 2.

family to support. However, officials viewed the youths who were unwilling to take up proper jobs for relief work as running the risk of developing a dependency on the state. For example, a young man under 20 years at Stapleford refused an offer of employment at five pounds a month and "all round" and another left work at ten pounds per month, plus a free servant, vegetables and fruit, as he "preferred the life" at Stapleford.[58] This was exacerbated by the fact that some men were pulling their children, some as young as 16 years of age, from school to join them in relief work to supplement the family income.[59] At Umvuma School, it became a habit for youths to leave school to wait age and submission into relief camps. Such youths could never be relied upon to sustain an industrious life, become breadwinners and maintain family. Relief schemes, therefore, caused idleness and bred indolence.

Between 1934 and 1938 the colony implemented educational reform which had a bias for skills training to accommodate the needs of industry and agriculture.[60] The Fox Commission (1936) on education upheld the new educational thrust which Huggins characterised as an education for "a finer training for life".[61] The 1934 report on unemployment relief noted that in the post-1923 period, the fields of white employment were narrowing to skilled professions.[62] The Education Commission (1929) noted, with concern, the inefficiency and unsuitability of the education system in meeting the needs of those entering the professions, industries, commerce, agriculture and mining.[63] Huggins sought to stir educational reforms away from the philosophy of producing civil servants which the colony could no longer absorb towards producing a more grounded and technical cast mind in children.[64] In addition, the philosophy was driven by the capitalist labour needs of Southern Rhodesia and government policy aimed at expanding the class of white artisans, and the lower ranks of white society provided the ideal candidates. A strong aristocratic youth was needed and unlike in the period before the 1930s, where the government sought to explain and convince white parents

---

[58] Government of Southern Rhodesia, *Report on Unemployment and The Relief of Destitution in Southern Rhodesia*, 1934, 16.

[59] Ibid.

[60] Rungano J. Zvobgo, *Colonialism and Education in* Zimbabwe, (Harare: SAPES Books, 1994), 30-31.

[61] Ibid.

[62] Government of Southern Rhodesia, *Report on Unemployment and the Relief of Destitution in Southern Rhodesia*, 1934, 31.

[63] NAZ S824/43: Government of Southern Rhodesia, Juvenile Affairs Boards 1928-1947: Copy of evidence to the 1929 Education Committee, HD Sutherns, 1-2.

[64] Gann and Gelfand, *Huggins of Rhodesia*, 137.

about the need for a practical education,[65] in the 1930s the emergent form of state paternalism was marked by coercion.

Huggins was unapologetic about his vision of colonial economic development centred around white artisans. He viewed them as the bulwark against Black economic advancement in skilled professions and without whom white society was vulnerable.[66] Premier Huggins also recognised that Southern Rhodesia's industrial development was set on a shaky foundation because the colony heavily relied on external labour markets, mainly South Africa and the United Kingdom, for its skilled personnel. He would be vindicated by the outbreak of the Second World War and its concomitant labour shortages.

The Establishment and Pedagogy of St. Pancras, 1936-1939

St. Pancras Home was established in July 1936 with a dual mandate for industrial training and character reformation. Social planners equated poverty to delinquency and believed that an Industrial School was a panacea to all social ills associated with poor childhoods which found a remedy in skills training for the cultivation of a productive masculinity. Indeed, many "poor white" families were recipients of government rations and the concept of industrial education at St. Pancras was designed to break the chain of the perceived cyclical poverty among working-class families and sustain white dominance. White poverty was a source of angst at two distinct levels. First, the socio-political implications of poverty were too heavy for a young colony and its small white population. Second, poor whites would be a burden on the fiscus through welfare programmes and even more so under the economic depression.

The institution became the first certified institution in Southern Rhodesia under the Children's Protection and Adoption Act (1929) with a maximum enrolment capacity of 12 inmates between the ages of 12 and 17 years. Built on a 6000-acre farm donated by the Church of England at West Acre junction near Figtree, west of Bulawayo town, the institution was, however, ran on a non-denominational basis.[67] Although the government was initially averse to collaborating with church bodies over the establishment of the institution, the Anglican church's offer was attractive because it considerably cut the cost of establishing a juvenile institution from £5000 to £1750.[68] For its part, the

---

[65] Summers, "Boys, Brats and Education," 135.

[66] *Rhodesia Herald*, 1 April 1938.

[67] NAZ ORAL/CA 1 Frederick Sydney Caley, 5.

[68] NAZ S824/345/3, Institutions for Juvenile Delinquents, 1937-1939; Department of Internal Affairs, Minute dated 31 March 1936. Events in South African indicated that Juvenile Institutions run by churches were not very successful in achieving government

government provided a classroom, a workshop and farm training while the spiritual and recreational elements were the responsibility of the Home Committee and staff. The Education Department paid salaries of the administrators and gave an annual grant of £50 per child.[69]

The nebulous definition of delinquency delayed the establishment of a rehabilitation institution. Identification and recommendation for committal was done by Inspectors of Schools, even though the task was legally outside their ambit. Statistical data on indigent children and those deemed to be under "evil" home influences was gathered in preparation for the establishment of an Industrial School.[70] In 1932, the Bulawayo Inspector of Schools recommended 36 cases of white children for certification to the proposed school, but only six of them showed delinquent tendencies.[71] Given the nature of investigations into delinquency, school heads and School Inspectors, and not the courts, played a leading role. Such a situation obtained because there were no functional juvenile courts, notwithstanding provisions of the 1929 Act, and the majority of cases identified did not involve pure juvenile crime which the courts would handle, but involved indigence, truancy and other forms of school-based misdemeanours. The majority of delinquency cases involved socially constructed meanings of deviance and not necessarily the legal and technical definitions as enshrined in law. This extra-judicial imposition of labels rendered legal recourse ineffective. Under law, juvenile candidates to the proposed Industrial School were supposed to be committed by the authority of the Magistrate. Consequently, in 1932 officials from the Education Department in consultation with the Department of Justice indefinitely shelved the idea of establishing an Industrial School before the idea of a juvenile rehabilitation home was finally implemented in 1936.

---

set goals. The South African government alleged that church run institutions ended up operating on denominational lines much to the detriment of the juvenile reform process. By the mid-1930s the South African government had taken over seven of the nine denominational institutions. The two remaining were Langlaate Orphanage Industrial School, Witwatersrand (Dutch Reformed Church) and the Silesian Institute, Cape Town, (Roman Catholic). The argument was that church run institutions lacked adequate resources to provide for qualified staff and had a tendency to carry out work likely to be self-supporting rather than to equip the children for a life in society.

[69] NAZ S824/345/2, Institutions for Juvenile Delinquents, 1934-1937; Secretary of the Treasury to Director of Education, 25 July 1936.

[70] Evil home influences referred to homes where the parents were poor or were either drunkards and/ involved in prostitution.

[71] NAZ S824/345/1, Institutions for Juvenile Delinquents, July 20 1931-February 01 1934, Inspector of Schools Bulawayo to Director of Education, 01 May 1932.

St. Pancras harmonised the legal and social definitions of delinquency. It became a hybrid institution that combined training and character reformation. Ironically, the Government was invoking models of socially controlled education initially developed to train and contain Africans in order to adequately respond to the changing structure of the economy. It was a practical step at separating the lower class and redefining its role in colonial economic development. Lower class white male youths who were perceived to be gravitating towards indigence and were at risk of falling into delinquent were the ideal candidates for the school. The institution reflected the broader state programmes of social engineering in the wake of the Great Depression. Its curriculum was designed to instil a sense of responsibility and a work ethic in its inmates. Since officials strongly believed in the correlation between delinquency and poverty, the philosophy of rehabilitation was designed to instil a productive maturity in children from poor backgrounds and enable them to become "breadwinning patriarchs" as was expected of white males.[72]

Rehabilitation started with the very location of St. Pancras. The Director of Education opposed it being set up in an urban area. He recommended a country location as the ideal environment for juvenile rehabilitation and effective control of delinquents. The urban environment and the working class culture were believed to have a morally corrupting influence on children; the country environment was envisioned as the most ideal in the process of rehabilitating the delinquent.[73] In the case of Victorian Britain, Steadman Johns argues that years of exposure to the decaying urban environment gave rise to a degenerate populace unfit to reach maturity and reproduce its kind.[74] Indeed, images of social pathology, poverty and deviance in the Empire were linked with theories of urban degeneracy. In addition, the rural location of the rehab institution could well have been a way to break urban delinquency networks. Exposing urban juveniles to an alien country environment would put them "out of their groove" of misdemeanour. In this respect, the rural location of the new institution was believed to have a therapeutic effect on juvenile rehabilitation.

Practical subjects were a particular focus at St. Pancras because "the boys proved backward in the three 'Rs', expressed a loathing for school and they

---

[72] Summers, "Boys, Brats and Education," 132.
[73] Chisholm, "Reformatories and Industrial Schools in South Africa: A Study in Class, Colour and Gender, 1882-1939," 92.
[74] Gareth Stedman Johns, *Outcast London: A Study in the Relationship between Classes in Victorian Society,* (Oxford: Clarendon, 1971), 285.

required much patience in teaching".[75] Secondary education was thrown out
the window and agriculture was a prime subject. In 1938, the institution purchased 14 cows and 1 bull at the cost of £111 and pig runs were constructed
with a view to teaching animal husbandry.[76] Inmates were also engaged in
chicken projects and a dozen animal books were purchased for the library.[77]
In addition, some 25 acres of land were put under the plough for the production of maize, potatoes, beans, corn, cowpeas and sweet potatoes. When T.W.
Stead from Natal was appointed as School Master in 1938, the Superintendent
of St. Pancras Home wrote, "He is enthusiastic and reliable and the right man
for the job. With his influence, there will be an added emphasis on physical
fitness and the practical side of Agriculture."[78] There was deliberate effort to
hire people with experience in reformatory work from South Africa which had
a longer history of Industrial School. In this respect, the Superintendent's
enthusiasm about the new appointment indicated the core values of the government programme at St. Pancras. The fostering of a "rural mindedness" in
white youths was central rehabilitation.

The emphasis on agriculture was informed by a number of factors. The 1927
Education Inspectorate Conference and the Education Committee (1929)
emphasised the need to cultivate a rural mindedness in certain classes of
whites at primary school level because many among the "poor whites"
shunned weeding and hoeing as "Kaffir work".[79] Youths' attitude towards
agriculture had to be altered because it was the second largest economic
pillar after mining and the future of the industry depended on the development of a class of young farmers. In addition, the industry provided one of the
quickest and, perhaps, the cheapest way out of the colony's unemployment
quagmire. However, the agricultural industry had taken a battering with the
fall in agricultural commodity prices, starting with the recession of the early
1920s and the devastating effects of the 1930s depression. Perceptions around
agriculture had to change for future economic development, and inculcating
the requisite values as part of juvenile rehab was one of many strategies to

[75] NAZ S824/345/3, Institutions for Juvenile Delinquents, 1937-1939; St. Pancras Superintendent report for the period 01 July 1936 to 31 September 1937, 3.
[76] NAZ S824/345/3, Institutions for Juvenile Delinquents, 1937-1939; Minutes of Meeting of
the St. Pancras Home Committee Held at Southern Life Offices, 07 October 1938, 1.
[77] NAZ S824/345/3, Institutions for Juvenile Delinquents, 1937-1939; St. Pancras Superintendent, PC Sykes report to the St. Pancras Home Committee, 19 May 1938, 1.
[78] NAZ S824/345/3, Institutions for Juvenile Delinquents,1937-1939; St. Pancras Superintendent's report to the St. Pancras Home Committee, 18 May 1938, 1.
[79] NAZ S824/43: Juvenile Affairs Boards 1928-1947: Copy of evidence to the 1929 Education Committee, HD Sutherns, 1-2.

achieve that goal. To the extent that white youths were averse to taking up agricultural jobs, St. Pancras gave the state the room to develop the ideal calibre of white youth. The failure of Matopos Farm School in the 1920s showed that parents were generally averse to having their children pursue farming and looked upon Matric as the goal of a liberal education.[80] Consequently, St. Pancras became a convenient tool of social engineering in Southern Rhodesia. Like in South Africa, Compulsory and Industrial Schools were a long-term strategy for the capture of children of white working class and unskilled lower classes respectively.[81]

The lack of interest in agricultural related work among white youths also undermined the goal of securing a larger white population on the land, which was the basis of white immigration and settlement in Rhodesia after 1908. As a result, the Rhodesia Agricultural Union proposed placement of youths under apprenticeship with farmers and training on government farms in animal husbandry, tobacco growing, cutting and grading, brick laying and rough carpentry.[82] As was the case with many other policies in Southern Rhodesia, the idea of youth apprenticeship with farmers was borrowed from the South African experience. For example, the Farm Lads Bureau of the Witwatersrand Central Juvenile Affairs Board instituted this programme to curb youth unemployment and it was also adopted by the Orange Free State.[83] In the apprenticeship proposal, Southern Rhodesia was targeting youths in relief camps who ran the risk of becoming indolent. Despite the incentives which included the prospect of acquiring farms on extended purchase terms after training, the programme never took off because the youths were either too few or unwilling to take farm training. Similar programmes at Hillside Experimental Station and Matopos School of agriculture with free tuition were discontinued because of low enrolment numbers averaging between 9 and 15 per annum, forcing the institutions to close down.[84] The high costs of running these institutions became a financial burden in the 1930s. With so much failing in the development of a rural mindedness in white youth, St. Pancras provided one of the few avenues open to social planners in influencing youth education with a bias towards

---

[80] For the Matopos Farm School experiment, see Summers, "Boys, Brats and Education".

[81] Chisholm, "Reformatories and Industrial Schools in South Africa: A Study in Class, Colour and Gender, 1882-1939," 55.

[82] NAZ S1194/198/1 Farm Training for Youths at Mtao and Stapleford, Secretary Rhodesia Agricultural Union to the Secretary Department of Agriculture and Lands, 30 July 1934.

[83] Minutes of meeting of the Juvenile Affairs Board, Salisbury, 15 January 1934.

[84] NAZ S824/345/3, Institutions for Juvenile Delinquents, 1937-1939.

agriculture. Policy changes could be propagated in this captive institution among youth who needed life skills and whose citizenship depended on it.

The curriculum at St. Pancras also included elementary engineering, building and woodwork to feed into the wider trajectory of industrial training.[85] As already mentioned, lower class youths were earmarked for artisanal jobs as a buffer against African advancement, and the Industrial Conciliation Act (1934) gave priority to industrial apprenticeship for whites. As part of this new policy, secondary schools like Allan Wilson School in Salisbury began to cater largely for artisan classes.[86] At the tertiary level, the Southern Rhodesia government introduced new technical and commercial courses at the Bulawayo, Salisbury and Que Que Technical Colleges.[87] Industrial apprenticeship for the youth and opportunities were further enhanced by the establishment of Juvenile Affairs Boards in 1932. These Boards were mandated

> ... to deal with matters affecting the employment, training, welfare and further education of juveniles, including advice to juveniles and their parents, placement, the investigation of fresh avenues of employment and the collection of statistics bearing on these problems. It is further suggested that part of the duty of the Board will be to bring to the notice of Government and of the public generally the existence of any such evils, with suggested remedies, in all matters concerning the training and welfare of juveniles.[88]

The new model of education at St. Pancras was couched in the emergent sentiments of economic nationalism in the 1930s. "Rhodesianisation" of the civil service was, partly, conceived to accommodate youths. In line with the Public Service Regulations (1929), the Commissioner of Labour charged that "Whenever possible in Government Departments every facility be given for the employment of [Rhodesian born] white youths, even if it might entail in some cases the retrenchment of native employees."[89] An exclusionary immigration policy also emerged to limit the immigration of the economically active groups who would

---

[85] Ibid.

[86] Lowry, "Rhodesia 1890-1980", 140.

[87] Norman Joseph Atkinson, *Teaching Rhodesians: A History of Educational Policy in Rhodesia*, (London: Longman, 1977), 80-82.

[88] NAZ S824/42/2, Juvenile Affairs Boards, 1932-1934; Inspector of Schools, Salisbury District, H.D Sutherns to Employers (Chamber of Mines, Builders, Engineering Trades, Motor Trades, etc.) 26 February 1932.

[89] *Report of the Select Committee to Investigate the Problem of Unemployment in the Colony, 1932*, 6.

compete for jobs with locals. In addition, the enduring label of Afrikaners as "poor whites" became the focal point of white fear and an ample justification to secure white economic interests and exclude Afrikaners from the future of Southern Rhodesia. Huggins adopted a more candid approach in denouncing white poverty. He remarked that the "the good Dutchman is as good as anybody else in the world, but it is the poor whites...that we do not want".[90] As a result, by the late 1930s, a new immigration policy stipulated that competency in reading and writing English was a pre-requisite for would-be immigrants to Southern Rhodesia. This policy was designed to eliminate non-English speakers, particularly Afrikaners. Prior to the 1930s, immigration policy favoured whites of British origin but this was not written down. The 1930s, therefore, represented a radical shift in immigration policy. The approach to solving the youth crisis assumed both skills training and various other extra-market measures to secure the future of sections of the white race.

The Collapse of St. Pancras

However, the impact of St. Pancras as a social engineering measure was severely limited by the small number of inmates it could carry. It struggled to justify its relevance and remained a financial liability to government during its four-year existence. When the institution was opened in July 1936, there were no inmates until January 1937, yet there were some 13 juvenile boys in prison receiving "special treatment".[91] According to Sydney Caley, the first Probation and Schools Attendance Officer for Southern Rhodesia from 1936, "there were never more than eight or nine at a time."[92] During an Inspection in 1938, there were only five inmates on the books of whom two were absent at the time of inspection.[93] Caley recalled one occasion at a meeting with Bishop Paget of the Anglican Church and the St. Pancras Home Committee when "one member who was very peeved asked why I hadn't supplied St. Pancras

---

[90] Quoted in Gann and Gelfand, *Huggins of Rhodesia*, 136.
[91] NAZ S824/345/3, Institutions for Juvenile Delinquents, 1937-1939; Probation and Schools Attendance Officer, Caley, to Chief Education Officer, 05 May 1939, 1.
[92] In 1936 F.S. Caley was appointed as Southern Rhodesia's first Probation and Schools Attendance Officer in the Education Department with an initial salary of £500-£600 per annum with a £50 marriage allowance. Caley's appointment signalled the antecedence of what would become the Department of Social Welfare in the 1940s. Prior to his appointment Caley worked in England as Probation Officer at New-le-Willows, Lancashire, and in 1929 he was appointed Probation Officer at Stratford Police Court in London.
[93] NAZ S824/345/3, Institutions for Juvenile Delinquents, 1937-1939; Notes by Supervisor of School Boarding Houses on St. Pancras, 03 January 1938.

Home with the necessary inmates".[94] In June of 1939, the Minister of Justice suggested that the history of St. Pancras was not particularly pleasing maybe because it was established at a time when there were no sufficient numbers of delinquents available.[95] For its own part, St. Pancras earned the reputation of being extravagant and for demanding too much money from the government. In its four-year history, St. Pancras had several of its financial requests turned down by the government. For example, in the 1936/37 financial year, its claims for additional catering funds were outrightly rejected by Treasury.[96] The Home had been allocated £600 for twelve delinquents at fifty pounds each, yet its full enrolment for that year would not exceed eight.[97] Furthermore, the per capita financial requirements of St. Pancras were higher than all other European Boarding hostels in the colony.[98]

The industrial training policy thrust also weighed too heavily on a juvenile reform system which was in its infancy. Initiatives proved incapable of achieving a balance between instilling juveniles with a work ethic and producing psychologically rehabilitated youths who could be reintegrated into society. Skills training for white productive masculinity were pursued at the expense of disciplinary reform. Discipline training did not go beyond the boys being required to make their own beds, sweep their rooms and Christian moral teaching.[99] Although St. Pancras was a reformatory, its pedagogy was closer to one for an industrial school than that of a juvenile delinquent's home. Consequently, difficult delinquency cases found little remedy at St. Pancras. For example, in 1938, one boy, William Laurent (17), became troublesome and authorities at the institution labelled him an "evil influence" and danger to others only a year into his four-year committal period at St. Pancras.[100] "Willie" was found in possession of stolen goods including an automatic firearm.[101] In addition, he had sold stolen clothes to Africans on the school prem-

---

[94] NAZ ORAL/CA 1 Frederick Sydney Caley, 5.
[95] NAZ S824/345/4, Institutions for Juvenile Delinquents, 1940-1947; St Josephs' Report of Proceedings of Conference on the Treatment of Delinquent Children in Southern Rhodesia, Salisbury, 06 June 1939.
[96] Ibid.
[97] NAZ S824/345/3, Institutions for Juvenile Delinquents,1937-1939; Secretary of the Treasury to Director of Education, 25 July 1937.
[98] Ibid.
[99] NAZ S824/345/3, Institutions for Juvenile Delinquents,1937-1939; Proceedings of the Conference on Juvenile Delinquency, 06 June 1939, 12.
[100] NAZ S824/345/3, Institutions for Juvenile Delinquents, 1937-1939; St. Pancras Superintendent, PC Sykes report to the St. Pancras Home Committee, 18 May 1938, 1.
[101] Ibid.

ises and attempted to poison the Superintendent with cattle dip.[102] He also
bullied and cheated other inmates at games. At their wits' end, the St. Pancras
Committee and administration sent the boy home to be supervised by his
parents until such a time when the Ministry of Internal Affairs found an alternative for him.[103] Although this was one isolated case in the institution's four-
year history, to a degree it may prove that, overall, the institution was not fully
equipped for juvenile character reform.

In addition, contrary to official views about the therapeutic effects of a
country location, St. Pancras' location undermined rehabilitation efforts. The
majority of the inmates were taken from urban centres into an isolated institution sited in the rural location. The removal of children from their home
environments negatively impacted on character reform and societal reintegration. In Foucauldian discourse, discipline sometimes requires confine-
ment "a specification of a place ... closed upon itself ... a protected place of
disciplinary monotony".[104] However, the implementation of this form of discipline had problems because juveniles were robbed of their sense of community which was a fundamental element of their rehabilitation in a place
where numbers hardly exceeded half a dozen at any given time. In addition,
by 1939 there were growing negative reports about the failures of St. Pancras
engendering a lack of confidence within the Department of Justice, and Mag-
istrates became increasingly reluctant to commit juveniles at the institution.[105] This development kept the numbers at the institution very low. The
isolated location of St. Pancras and its inability to provide a sense of community for the inmates undermined effective rehabilitation of inmates.

St. Pancras' failures were partly a reflection of the lack of trained personnel
in juvenile rehabilitation within its administrative structures. For example,
Mr. Donkin, the first Superintendent at the institution, was seconded from
the Post Office Engineering Branch albeit on a short-term basis.[106] His work
experience was not in any way related to his new job at St. Pancras. In 1938,
the Department of Education advertised for the post of Superintendent and of
the applications, eight were short-listed for interviews. All the candidates had

[102] Ibid.
[103] NAZ S824/345/3, Institutions for Juvenile Delinquents, 1937-1939; Superintendent
of St. Pancras to Minister of Internal Affairs, 29 May 1938.
[104] Michel Foucault, *Discipline and Punish: The Birth of the Prison,* (New York: Vintage
Books, 1995), 141.
[105] NAZ S824/345/3, Institutions for Juvenile Delinquents,1937-1939; Proceedings of the
Conference on Juvenile Delinquency, 06 June 1939, 8.
[106] Ibid.

some teaching qualification and experience, and some had youth organisation experience on an informal basis. However, from the total number of candidates, only three candidates had either attended a juvenile court or visited a prison, but none had a qualification in juvenile rehabilitation.[107] As a last-ditch measure, the Government appointed Major A.I. Rice from St. George Home in Johannesburg to take over St. Pancras as its Principal in 1939.[108] He was a man with some experience in juvenile rehabilitation. However, at this stage, the fate of the institution was virtually sealed. Financial mismanagement and increasing allegations that the institutional was becoming denominational with aspects of the Anglican Church doctrine being forced on inmates left the government with little choice but to close the institution at the end of 1939.[109] The outbreak of the Second World War opened a convenient avenue for government where delinquents were enlisted into the army under the Defence Act of 1926.[110] It is not clear whether the closure of St. Pancras was influenced by the war or merely coincided with it. Either way, it signified the brutal and militaristic masculinities of Rhodesian white youths.

Conclusion

Although St. Pancras was not a very successful experiment into state social engineering, its operations serve as a prism into the nature of state policy for the youth during periods of economic uncertainty and social strife. The youth crisis shook the foundation of white society and the colonial project, prompting the state to embark on an aggressive state paternalism to secure the future of white society. Despite its relatively small population and deeply entrenched racial segregation policies, Southern Rhodesia was haunted by the possibility of the development of a poor class of whites. The overarching anxiety over the "poor white problem" affected policy in both South Africa and Southern Rhodesia. The new educational policy shaped industrial policy through the development of a white artisanal class, largely based on Victorian England and South African pathologies of delinquency and degeneracy within the working class. The new policy effectively separated lower class whites and redefined their role in colonial economic development. The emergent model of youth education in the 1930s

---

[107] NAZ S824/345/3, Institutions for Juvenile Delinquents, 1937-1939; Government of Southern Rhodesia, Educational Appointment: Superintendent, St. Pancras Juvenile Delinquency School, 1937.

[108] NAZ ORAL/CA 1 Frederick Sydney Caley, 6.

[109] Ibid.

[110] Files in the National Archives of Zimbabwe on juvenile delinquency run cold after 1939 and only re-surface around 1947.

also narrowed the difference between African education and education for lower class whites. In South Africa, the Industrial School became the quintessential institution for the children of the white working class, and character reform was sacrificed at the altar of the overarching imperatives of industrial training. The new policies of the 1930s which segregated the emergent "white underclass" for artisanal jobs were predicated on the same philosophy as the one that oppressed Africans. The 1930 decade was a period of state rejuvenation where the white elite had to preserve their position by removing from within their ranks those that were likely to overburden the state and undermine the status quo. In addition, agriculture provided one of the quickest and cheapest ways of dealing with youth unemployment and dovetailed with settler ideology of settlement and land occupation.

Bibliography

Atkinson, Norman Joseph. *Teaching Rhodesians: A History of Educational Policy in Rhodesia*. London: Longman, 1977.

Bailey, Victor. *Delinquency and Citizenship: Reclaiming the Young Offender, 1914-18*. Oxford: Clarendon, 1987.

Bundy, Colin. "Vagabond Hollanders and Runaway Englishmen: White Poverty in the Cape Before Poor Whiteism." In *Putting a Plough to the Ground: Accumulation and Dispossession in Rural South Africa 1850-1930*, edited by William Beinart, Peter Delius, and Stanley Trapido. Johannesburg: Ravan, 1986. 101-128.

Chisholm, Linda. "Reformatories and Industrial Schools in South Africa: A Study in Class, Colour and Gender, 1882-1939." PhD Thesis. University of the Witwatersrand, 1989.

Dubow, Saul. "Race, Civilisation and Culture: The Elaboration of Segregation Discourse in the Inter-War Years." African Studies Seminar Paper. University of the Witwatersrand, 1986.

Foucault, Michel. *Discipline and Punish: The Birth of the Prison*. New York: Vintage Books, 1995.

Gann, Lewis H., and Michael Gelfand. *Huggins of Rhodesia: The Man and His Country*, London: George Allen and Unwin, 1964.

Government of Southern Rhodesia. *Industrial Conciliation Act 1934*.

Government of Southern Rhodesia. *Report on the Suggested Industrial Development of Natives*, 1920.

Government of Southern Rhodesia. *Report on the Unemployment and the Relief of Destitution in Southern Rhodesia*, 1934.

Grundlingh, Albert. "'Are We Afrikaners Getting too Rich?' Cornucopia and Change in Afrikanerdom in the 1960s." *Journal of Historical Sociology* 21(2/3), (2008): 143-165.

Jackson, William. *Madness and Marginality: The lives of Kenya's White Insane*. Manchester: Manchester University Press, 2013.

Johns, Gareth Stedman. *Outcast London: A Study in the Relationship between Classes in Victorian Society.* Oxford: Clarendon, 1971.

Jollie, Ethel Tawse. *The Real Rhodesia.* Bulawayo: Books of Rhodesia, 1971.

Lonsdale, John. "Kenya: Home Country and African Frontier." In *Settlers and Expatriates: Britons over the Seas,* edited by Robert Bickers. Oxford: Oxford University Press, 2010. 74-111.

Lowry, Donal. "Rhodesia 1890-1980: 'The Lost Dominion'." In *Settlers and Expatriates: Britons over the Seas,* edited by Robert Bickers. Oxford: Oxford University Press, 2010. 112-149.

Minutes of meeting of the Juvenile Affairs Board, Salisbury, 15 January 1934.

Mlambo, Alois S. "'Some are more White than others': Racial Chauvinism as a factor of Rhodesian Immigration Policy, 1890-1963." *Zambezia* 27 (2), (2000): 139-160.

Morell, Robert (ed.) *White but Poor: Essays on the History of Poor Whites in Southern Africa 1880–1940.* Pretoria: University of South Africa, 1992.

National Archives of Zimbabwe (hereafter NAZ) S824/42/2. Government of Southern Rhodesia. Juvenile Affairs Boards, 1932-1934, Director of Education, Southern Rhodesia to the Secretary, Department of the Colonial Secretary, 03 February 1932.

NAZ SRG 3. Government of Southern Rhodesia. *Southern Rhodesia Legislative Council Debates,* 09 August 1915, Column 198.

NAZ ORAL/CA 1. Frederick Sydney Caley.

NAZ S1194/1660/1. Government of Southern Rhodesia. White Labour Afforestation Camp: Mtao Report, Memorandum from Minister of Agriculture to the Department of the Colonial Secretary, 10 December 1930.

NAZ S1194/198/1. Farm Training for Youths at Mtao and Stapleford, Secretary Rhodesia Agricultural Union to the Secretary Department of Agriculture and Lands, 30 July 1934.

NAZ S726/SW3/1-2. Government of Southern Rhodesia Cadets Policy 1926.

NAZ S726/W36/8 -14. Cadets Policy 1933-1939.

NAZ S824/345/1. Government of Southern Rhodesia. Institutions for Juvenile Delinquents, July 20 1931-February 01 1934, CID Detective Sergeant, Que Que to Assistant Magistrate, Que Que, 01 October 1931.

NAZ S824/345/1. Government of Southern Rhodesia. Institutions for Juvenile Delinquents, July 20 1931-February 01 1934, Sergeant, Bulawayo Police Station to Chief Superintendent CID, 16 October 1933.

NAZ S824/345/1. Institutions for Juvenile Delinquents, July 20 1931-February 01 1934, Inspector of Schools Bulawayo to Director of Education, 01 May 1932.

NAZ S824/345/2. Institutions for Juvenile Delinquents, 1934-1937; Secretary of the Treasury to Director of Education, 25 July 1936.

NAZ S824/345/3. Institutions for Juvenile Delinquents, 1937-1939.

NAZ S824/345/3. Institutions for Juvenile Delinquents, 1937-1939; Department of Internal Affairs, Minute dated 31 March 1936.

NAZ S824/345/3. Institutions for Juvenile Delinquents, 1937-1939; St. Pancras Superintendent report for the period 01 July 1936 to 31 September 1937.

NAZ S824/345/3. Institutions for Juvenile Delinquents, 1937-1939; Minutes of Meeting of the St. Pancras Home Committee Held at Southern Life Offices, 07 October 1938.

NAZ S824/345/3. Institutions for Juvenile Delinquents, 1937-1939; St. Pancras Superintendent, PC Sykes report to the St. Pancras Home Committee, 19 May 1938.

NAZ S824/345/3. Institutions for Juvenile Delinquents, 1937-1939; Probation and Schools Attendance Officer, Caley, to Chief Education Officer, 05 May 1939.

NAZ S824/345/3. Institutions for Juvenile Delinquents, 1937-1939; Notes by Supervisor of School Boarding Houses on St. Pancras, 03 January 1938.

NAZ S824/345/3. Institutions for Juvenile Delinquents, 1937-1939; St. Pancras Superintendent, PC Sykes report to the St. Pancras Home Committee, 18 May 1938.

NAZ S824/345/3. Institutions for Juvenile Delinquents, 1937-1939; Superintendent of St. Pancras to Minister of Internal Affairs, 29 May 1938.

NAZ S824/345/3. Institutions for Juvenile Delinquents, 1937-1939; Government of Southern Rhodesia, Educational Appointment: Superintendent, St. Pancras Juvenile Delinquency School, 1937.

NAZ S824/345/3. Institutions for Juvenile Delinquents, 1937-1939; St. Pancras Superintendent's report to the St. Pancras Home Committee, 18 May 1938.

NAZ S824/345/3. Institutions for Juvenile Delinquents,1937-1939; Secretary of the Treasury to Director of Education, 25 July 1937.

NAZ S824/345/3. Institutions for Juvenile Delinquents,1937-1939; Proceedings of the Conference on Juvenile Delinquency, 06 June 1939.

NAZ S824/345/3. Institutions for Juvenile Delinquents,1937-1939; Proceedings of the Conference on Juvenile Delinquency, 06 June 1939.

NAZ S824/345/4. Institutions for Juvenile Delinquents, 1940-1947; St Josephs' Report of Proceedings of Conference on the Treatment of Delinquent Children in Southern Rhodesia, Salisbury, 06 June 1939.

NAZ S824/42/2. Government of Southern Rhodesia. Juvenile Affairs Boards, 1932-1934: Minutes of the Inaugural Meeting for the formation of a Juvenile Affairs Board, Salisbury, 04 March 1932.

NAZ S824/42/2. Juvenile Affairs Boards, 1932-1934; Inspector of Schools, Salisbury District, H.D Sutherns to Employers (Chamber of Mines, Builders, Engineering Trades, Motor Trades, etc.) 26 February 1932.

NAZ S824/43. Government of Southern Rhodesia. Juvenile Affairs Boards 1928-1947: Copy of evidence to the 1929 Education Committee, HD Sutherns.

NAZ S824/43. Juvenile Affairs Boards 1928-1947: Copy of evidence to the 1929 Education Committee, HD Sutherns.

NAZ S824/43/2. Government of Southern Rhodesia. Juvenile Affairs Boards, 1932-1934. Bulawayo Juvenile Affairs Board Second Annual Report, 1934.

Olsen, Stephanie. "Adolescent Empire: Moral Dangers for Boys in Britain and India, c.1800 to 1914." In *Juvenile Delinquency and the Limits of Western Influence, 1850-2000*, edited by Heather Ellis. Hampshire: Palgrave Macmillan, 2014). 19-41.

Onselen, Charles van. *Studies in the Social and Economic History of the Witwatersrand, 1886–1914.* Volume 2. Johannesburg: New Nineveh, 1982.

Phimister, Ian. *An Economic and Social History of Zimbabwe, 1890-1948: Capital Accumulation and Class Struggle.* London: Longman, 1988.

Praisley, Fiona. "Childhood and Race: Growing Up in The Empire." In *Gender and Empire,* edited by Philippa Levine. Oxford: Oxford University Press, 2004). 240-259.

Report of the Select Committee to Investigate the Problem of Unemployment in the Colony, 1932.

Rhodesia Herald. 1 April 1938.

Rich, Paul John. *Chains of Empire: English Public Schools, Masonic Cabalism, Historical Causality, and Imperial Clubdom.* London: Regency Press, 1991.

Shutt, Allison. *Manners Make a Nation: Race Etiquette in Southern Rhodesia, 1910-1963.* New York: University of Rochester Press, 2015.

Southern Rhodesia Defence Act 1918.

Southern Rhodesia Legislative Assembly Debates, 1928.

Stoler, Ann. "Making Empire respectable: the politics of race and sexual morality in 20th-century colonial cultures." *American Ethnologist* 16 (4), (1989): 634-660.

Summers, Carrol. "Boys, Brats and Education: Reproducing White Maturity in Colonial Zimbabwe 1915–1935." *Settler Colonial Studies* 1 (1), (2011): 132-153.

Watson, Nick J., Stuart Weir, and S. Friend. "The Development of Muscular Christianity in Victorian Britain and Beyond." *Journal of Religion and Society* 7, (2005):1-21.

Zvobgo, Rungano J. *Colonialism and Education in Zimbabwe.* Harare: SAPES Books, 1994.

Chapter 8

Childhoods Rooted in Land: Connecting Child Development to Land Using Cultural Practices of the IsiXhosa Speaking People of South Africa

Zethu Cakata

An Ethical Point of Departure

I am guided by Professor Mogobe Ramose's counsel to treat the epistemicide which was engineered by colonialism as an ethical matter. Contributing in such projects as this publication is evidence that an atrocity was committed and it continues to undermine African ethics. These types of projects are often a response to knowledge gaps created by the inferiorisation and attempted erasure of African knowledge by colonialists. It is crucial therefore to constantly remind our readership that African epistemologies did not just disappear but were brutally taken off the face of the mainstream by those who have dominated what Africans know and how they should know it. By destroying African education systems and devaluing African languages, the colonizer was imposing its ways of knowing and existing in the world. It imposed its education so that Africans appear as less knowing, unintellectual and in need of rescue. I participate in knowledge disseminating exercises such as this publication with an aim of making African children see themselves in book pages and appearing as they have known and experienced themselves. I, however, find myself in a paradoxical position because of the contrasting ethos of knowledge dissemination between African and Western education systems. Most African knowledge are rooted in spirituality, thus they possess their own tools of dissemination. This is the dilemma I am treading carefully around in my attempts to elucidate what it means to be a child in a traditional IsiXhosa[1] speaking community.

---

[1] Although, a variation of the spelling is isiXhosa, the author prefers to spell it IsiXhosa.

IsiXhosa Conceptualization of Child-Human Development

To have a language is to have the knowledge and therefore Africa has always had knowledge. That knowledge is currently in the margins because the languages that transmit it are not national languages in almost all African nations. Efforts to revitalise language thus need to be taken seriously as they could help in reclaiming the ways of knowing of the speakers of those languages. As it will be demonstrated in this chapter, cultural practices used to ensure a healthy and well-adjusted childhood are named in ways that communicate their epistemologies. The language roots the practice in its context and communicates its significance. The colonial re-languaging of IsiXhosa practices, which happened with the introduction of missionary "education" in what is today known as the Eastern Cape province of South Africa, eroded the cultural meaning of these practices. Such a meaning was rooted in people's spiritual understanding of themselves and the land on which the practices have to take place. For example, one of the rites of passage discussed in this chapter is ulwaluko. The English translation of the concept is circumcision and that reduces the practice to be only about the biological aspect. The knowledge that ulwaluko was transmitting is lost and that has led to the practice of this rite of passage outside its spiritual context. In this chapter, I, therefore, argue that language is a vital site for the task of re-membering and reclaiming the meaning of being an African which begins with childhood.

In all cultures, life begins with childhood and there is no society which has not produced children. This, therefore, means that every culture has its understanding of child development. Human development for every culture begins with a new life entering the world. The new life is left in the hands of those equipped with knowledge and skills for survival. Each culture has its ways of ensuring that proper guidance is given for the new life to be well adjusted and to thrive in the world. Unfortunately, colonial invasion of African lands interrupted the various understanding of ushering a new life into the world that existed. Psychology (which is a discipline concerned with human development and behaviour) is mainly dominated by a single-lensed understanding of Western human development theories which simply consider what is important about childhood constructions in westernized societies. A mention of other ways of being a child is done so very minimally and through a colonized eye of othering. For example, "Introduction to Psychology" textbooks which are profusely used in South African universities minimally mention experiences from non-western societies and do so in an othering manner.[2] These kinds of textbooks are used despite calls from African scholars such as Augustine Bame Nsamenang to produce context relevant ways of understanding child development.[3] In this chapter, I shall look at what the speakers of IsiXhosa language in South Africa[4] consider as important features of childhood. The three important stages that will guide the focus of this paper are: ukuqatywa komntwana, intonjane and ulwaluko. I am weary of providing English translations to these concepts because translation tends to erode the meaning. This chapter will not provide in-depth details of these practices but what they signify and how their significance is rooted in land.

Ukufukamela usana

After the child is born, the AmaXhosa[5] keep the mother in seclusion for about ten days. This process is referred to as ifuku or imfukamo (seclusion). During this period experienced women assist her with critical aspects of parenting such as breastfeeding, child care and self maintenance. When it is deemed fit for the baby to be introduced to the rest of the family, the mother would come out of ifuku/imfukamo. This is after the falling of the umbilical cord (ukuwa kwe nkaba) which together with the mother's placenta are buried within the family yard (usually inside the kraal or under a tree). This is an important symbolic practice and it marks the very first crucial ritual performed for the child. Significantly, burying the umbilical cord and the placenta is perceived as re-rooting or returning the child to the source which is umhlaba (the soil, the land). The place where the umbilical cord is buried becomes a child's ancestral home as it has the child's roots. A sheep will be sacrificed when the mother leaves ifuku/imfukamo and the hide of the animal will be woven into a blanket called imbeleko. It is the imbeleko that the mother will use to ukubelaka (carry the child on her back). N. Mndende has observed that in recent times people mistake this phase with the practice of ukuqatywa komntwana. She states that the actual ceremony happens after a child has been out of

---

[2] Michael W. Passer, Ronald E Smith, Nigel Holt, Andy Bremner, Ed Sutherland, and Michael Vliek, *Psychology: The Science of Mind and Behaviour*, (Berkshire: McGraw-Hill Education, 2009); W. Weiten, *Psychology: Themes and Variations*, (Belmont, California: Wadsworth, 2006).

[3] A.B. Nsamenang, "A critical peek at early childhood care and education in Africa," *Child Health and Education* 1(1), (2007):14–26.

[4] IsiXhosa is one of the Nguni Bantu languages of southern Africa.

[5] The Xhosa people refer to themselves and language as AmaXhosa and IsiXhosa respectively.

ifuku/imfukamo for a while and this is when the child is properly introduced to the family (physical and spiritual family) and the community.[6]

Ukuqatywa komntwana

This is the practice which Mndende explains as an introduction of a child to the living, those in the spiritual world and to the community.[7] Although we see it among the AmaXhosa, it clearly demonstrates the common philosophical and spiritual notion in indigenous African societies that life is an interconnection of various states of being, that is, the physical and spiritual. This is why it becomes important for the AmaXhosa to mark the child's entry into the world by a ceremonial introduction to invite everyone involved in the child's life to cast blessings upon the child's mortal journey. This reflects and falls in line with the philosophy and social aspiration that the widespread African proverb: "it takes a whole village to raise a child", which exists in different forms in many African languages, conveys. The fundamental meaning is that things that are to be done and efforts that are to be made to bring up a child and protect it and make it part of society are communal endeavours because children are a blessing from the Supreme Being (God-Goddess) for the whole community. Thus, the responsibility is shared by the family, not just the nuclear but the extended family, and community, made up of neighbours and friends. This communal responsibility is also articulated by the Sukuma (Tanzania) proverb that "One knee does not bring up a child" and the Swahili (East and Central Africa) proverb that "One hand does not nurse a child."[8]

Ukuqatywa komntwana is a ceremony that is marked by the sacrificing of a goat. It is the family that decides when this ceremony should happen. If the child is too small when the ceremony is performed, she or he will be made to sit inside a hut with her mother and they will both cover their faces with red ochre. The goat will be brought to the house and the child will be told what is happening and blessings will be sought from the ancestors through prayer. Various members of the family take turns in addressing the gathering. The goat is then taken to the kraal where it is laid on the ground and further communication with the ancestors and those in attendance is made. Importantly, the purpose of the ceremony is announced to those present because of ukunizimasa (to bear witness) so that all will know exactly what brought them to the home of the

---

[6] N. Mndende, *Umthonyama*, (Cape Town: Icamagu, 2006), 20.

[7] Ibid., 21.

[8] See, for example, Marilize Schoeman, "African Concept of Ubuntu and Restorative Justice" in Theo Gavrielides and Vasso Artinopoulou (eds.), *Reconstructing Restorative Justice Philosophy*, (London/New York: Routledge, 2016), 291-310.

child's family. The goat will then be sacrificed and part of the meat will be given to the child to taste as umshwamo (a piece of meat used to connect the living and the ancestors). It is necessary for the child to eat that piece of meat for the ceremony to be complete. If the child is too young, the mother would eat it on the child's behalf. In this way, the child becomes a welcomed and accepted member of the family and the community. This is the first aspect of the construction and formalisation of the child's sense of belonging. A child first belongs to her or his family and is known by her or his ancestors. The community at large also gets to be introduced to the child.

Without Land Children will not be Children

As illustrated above, the first ritual a child is given by the speakers of IsiXhosa is to root her/him to the soil, the land, that is, the mother of all life. Within indigenous cosmologies in Africa, land is an integral part of African existence; without land life and existence are incomplete for Africans. African life as stated by M. Motsei requires that human beings live in harmony with nature.[9] This interconnectedness with the cosmos according to Motsei [10] is governed by three principles that are common in indigenous African cosmologies. Firstly, the land is seen as the mother of all life, hence, neglecting and not caring for her mean that humans – the individual and community – are "killing" themselves. Secondly, a crucial part of wellbeing is for humans to find ways to maintain an essential balance between earth, air and fire. The third principle is for humans to respect the laws of the land which govern how nature should be wisely and naturally used. These laws refer to the conscientious usage of nature's plants, sacrifice of animals, and treatment of water. By disrespecting these laws, nature becomes endangered and, consequently, humans too become unwell and ruined. The relational lifestyle of the African community is this interconnectedness. This relational life, according to Motsei, does not just relate to human beings and their communities but to nature as well.[11] Identities of people are tied to animals where each clan has its own totem as an integral part of the family. Children learn from an early age about their totems and how they should treat them and their habitat. In this way, they get a grasp of respecting nature.

It is around these principles that IsiXhosa speakers would socialize a child. Children start interacting with nature from a very young age. Being a child, therefore, means being free to interact with nature. Gradually industriousness

---

[9] M. Motsei, *Reweaving the Soul of the Nation*, (Pretoria: Afrika Ikalafe, 2017), 100.
[10] Ibid.
[11] Ibid., 101.

is introduced by giving a child age-appropriate responsibilities such as minding domestic animals within the household. Only when a child is older will they be allowed to attend to responsibilities outside the household such as herding cattle in the forest, collecting water or fire wood. During the pre-teen stage of life, there are no distinctive gender roles assigned to children. Children perform similar chores and are treated equally.

Nature-based industriousness produces knowledgeable children. The fact that children's identities are tied to animals in the form of totems makes learning about nature easy to comprehend. From an early age, children get familiarized to laws and principles of nature. In early childhood, domestic animals such as dogs and chickens become useful learning sites for children. They get introduced to concepts such as imfukamo which are an integral part of their cultural practices through observing animal behaviour. Hens, for example, go into seclusion when they are hatching and would emerge during certain times of the day for food and water. These are lessons which help children to easily comprehend aspects of their cultural practices later in life. When they are old enough to be allowed to take on tasks outside the homestead, they graduate to study nature outside of home. This industriousness is coupled with play, thus, there is no separation between learning and leisure. This shows that an overarching thread in African life observed and imbibed during childhood among the AmaXhosa is the importance of interconnection. This is a form of schooling which does not separate a child from herself/himself and family, community, land and nature as a whole.

Rites of Passage

Childhood, like many non-recurrent phases of a person's life, is marked by a rite of passage in almost all African cultures. The rite of passage differs depending on one's positioning in the order of life. For girls, the rite of passage happens when they enter into puberty. Conversely, the ritual welcoming young boys to adulthood happens in their late teens or early twenties.

Intonjane

Intonjane can be explained as the coming of age observance of a girl child. It is a ceremony which happens when a girl enters puberty. It is a school where girls learn about their changing bodies, sex, their identity and spiritual aspects of their being. This instruction would be led by knowledgeable female members of the family such as the child's great mothers who are siblings of the child's parents. According to Mndende, this ritual comprises some key segments which are ukungena (entering of the hut), ukutshatela (celebration), ukuphindela (going back to the hut) and ukuphuma (returning to normal life).[12]

The first segment involves choosing a house in the homestead where the girl would be kept in seclusion. This house would be prepared by her sisters ensuring that it is hidden by reeds. Numerous processes take place when the girl is taken to seclusion and all the procedures are led by an informed female member of the family who is well versed in family tradition. Within a day of seclusion, a goat will be sacrificed to provide umshwamo for the initiate. This is done to welcome the girl into seclusion. The second major stage of inton-jane, which is ukutshatela, happens after a week in seclusion and this time an ox will be sacrificed for the rite of ukushwama (tasting of the meat as an act of connecting with the spiritual world). During all this time the girl is taught and prayers are offered to strengthen her connection with the ancestors. A few days after ukutshatela the girl returns to seclusion and another goat is slaugh-tered. On her final day, the elders who cared for her take her to the main house and report back to her parents and other family members. This ritual marks the end of childhood for the young girl.

Noteworthy, intonjane has become a very rare practice. The colonial disrup-tions that disorganised African communities have made it impossible for many to engage in this practice. The forceful removal of African people from their natural habitats meant that they no longer had land for space and live-stock to ensure the continuation of many cultural practices. The capitalist re-organisation of the society took away people's ownership of their time. Or-ganised Western-style of schooling and working make it very difficult, if not impossible, for people to have time to observe the practice of intonjane. What happens as Mndende has observed is that some people get called back by their ancestors to this practice even if they get older through sickness or dreams. When divination reveals that a sickness or dream of a person is a reminder from the ancestors that they still require the performance of the ritual by the person, even when she is old, the ritual often gets performed.[13]

Isiko ulwaluko

For males, the rite of passage to manhood is marked by a ritual called ulwalu-ko. The English translation reduces it to circumcision, however, as Dr. Neo Ramoupi said in a conversation I had with him, ulwaluko is more than just the biological aspect. It is an epistemology on its own. Just like intonjane, ulwalu-

---

[12] Mndende, *Umthonyama*, 21.
[13] Ibid., 22.

ko is another site of learning which prepares boys for manhood. The word ulwaluko is derived from luka which means weaving. This makes ulwaluko a process of weaving boys into manhood. It is a centre of learning where boys (with guidance from the elders) become citizens of the forest (their seclusion happens in the forest). They become one with nature and learn from both their guardians and nature.[14]

As in the case of intonjane, ulwaluko involves seclusion but unlike intonjane, this seclusion happens away from the homestead. The practice is also separated into three segments; ukungena (entering seclusion), ukojiswa (re-introduction to food), nokuphuma (returning to normal life). During all these three phases a goat will be sacrificed for for the custom of ukushwama. It is during seclusion that the counsel of older men is received; during this period the boys will be in the care of young men who have undergone the process. What is emphasized during this counsel is the importance of respect, dignity, leaving behind child-hood habits and focusing on the importance of building a home in accordance with the principles of the family and ancestors. This phase is marked by ukuzila where certain foods are forbidden until the process of umojiso has taken place. During umojiso a goat is sacrificed to mark the end of ukuzila ukutya (abstaining from certain foods). After this phase the initiates will wait for ukuphuma (rejoining normal life) when it is deemed fit for the young men to go home.

Even though this rite of passage has refused to die, the capitalist demands of Western-type of schooling and employment leave people little time to fully apply the concept. It is nowadays squeezed into a four weeks' period of summer break. This new arrangement forgets to take cognisant of the fact that the time of the year had everything to do with the practice in the olden days. Being attuned to nature informed the time of the year suitable for this practice. The food and the herbs of the appropriate season allowed for a smooth transition of the rite.

Concluding Thoughts

My intention in this chapter has been to demonstrate that land is at the centre of African existence. It is to land that life of the community, which is made up of persons, is owed and it is to land that it is returned; thus land ownership by a people is a necessary aspect of being in the world on their own terms. I have tried to show that childhood for the AmaXhosa of Africa

---

[14] Personal interview with Neo Ramoupi in Zethu Cakata, "In search of the absent voice: The status of indigenous languages in post-apartheid South Africa," (PhD Thesis, Pretoria: University of South Africa 2015).

emphasizes a continuous connection among people, ancestors, land and by extension nature. The issue of how Africans learn and who is qualified to teach them became evident in the discussion about the AmaXhosa when the concepts of seclusion and elder education kept re-occurring. Below I try to explain the significance of those concepts.

Seclusion

The key feature among the three rites of passage discussed above is an aspect of seclusion. The learning far removed from the realities of daily life was something that was revered when these practices were still conducted in uninterrupted settings. Seclusion provided those undergoing the rite an uninterrupted space to learn from experts who were usually the elders from the family and community and well versed in the ways of being of a particular lineage. Seclusion also served a spiritual function where children were given age-appropriate introduction to their ancestors. The sacrifice of animals to mark various segments of the rituals meant that a connection was being made with the spiritual world. Again, it is in the context of the notion and practice of seclusion that the ethics of knowledge dissemination come to play. The critical feature of seclusion is to preserve the sacredness of the practice. It is important for those who are yet to partake in it to be uninformed about it. Among IsiXhosa speakers there is an emphasis on the importance of knowing things at the right time. In the olden days, communities were able to uphold the ethics of knowledge dissemination.

The Importance of Education by the People who Know You

Another common feature in the practices highlighted above is an integral role that family members play. It points to the importance of being educated by people who understand your lineage. The objective of marking passage to the next phase of life is to impart self-knowledge. To be a well-integrated member of the society requires that one is in possession of self-knowledge. The important information about one's maternal and paternal clans is necessary as it provides guidance about how to be in relation to others and nature. Important information about one's roles in life can be known and extracted from his or her clan praises. The totem, which is something every clan has, conveys a message about one's responsibility to the habitat of his or her totem. From this emanates the concept and attitude of humility around nature which offers and enforces the understanding that existence on planet earth is not due to human brilliance, but to the sacrifices of other planetary creatures; consequently, the human being needs to be mindful of how he or she takes "food" from the environment and uses natures gifts of flora and fauna in his or her interest. There has to be harmony between humans and totems and the land that they dwell on together. This explains the widespread African indigenous philosophical, cosmological and pragmatic concept of relationality of life. The ideas that support and clarify this concept constitute the teachings that are instilled during various stages of child development among IsiXhosa speakers of Africa.

Bibliography

Cakata, Zethu. "In search of the absent voice: The status of indigenous lan-guages in post- apartheid South Africa." PhD Thesis. Pretoria: University of South Africa 2015.

Mndende, N. *Umthonyama*. Cape Town: Icamagu, 2006.

Motsei, M. *Reweaving the Soul of the Nation*. Pretoria: Afrika Ikalafe, 2017.

Nsamenang, A.B. "A critical peek at early childhood care and education in Africa." *Child Health and Education* 1(1), (2007):14–26.

Passer, Michael W., Ronald E Smith, Nigel Holt, Andy Bremner, Ed Sutherland, and Michael Vliek. *Psychology: The Science of Mind and Behaviour*. Berk-shire: McGraw-Hill Education, 2009.

Schoeman, Marilize. "African Concept of Ubuntu and Restorative Justice." In *Reconstructing Restorative Justice Philosophy*, edited by Theo Gavrielides and Vasso Artinopoulou. London/New York: Routledge, 2016. 291-310.

Weiten, W. *Psychology: Themes and Variations*. Belmont, California: Wadsworth, 2006.

Chapter 9

"Adults are just obsolete children . . ."[1]: Child Fancy Dress Parades as a Carnivalesque Suspension of Adultism in Winneba, Ghana

Awo Sarpong and De-Valera N.Y.M Botchway

Introduction

This work is about Child Fancy Dress in Ghana, West Africa. It, however, takes a detour from the traditional themes that have dominated popular scholarship on the subject of the masquerade act of Fancy Dress in Ghana.[2] It observes the manifestation of abuse of adult power against children and demonstration of a spirit of creative and resilient resistance by children in response to the former, in an African town through the lens of Fancy Dress, a community-owned art expression – an African masquerade culture of the people of the historical town of Winneba, Ghana. It explores a dominantly patriarchal town

---

[1] This is part of a profound satirical statement by Theodor Seuss "Ted" Geisel, alias Dr. Seuss (1904-1991), a famous children's author, political cartoonist, poet, animator, screenwriter, filmmaker, and artist.

[2] See Herbert Cole and Doran Ross, *The Arts of Ghana*, (California: University of California, 1977), 179-186; Courtney Micots, "Fancy Dress: African Masquerade in Coastal Ghana," in Joanne B. Eicher and Doran H. Ross (eds.), *Berg Encyclopaedia of World Dress and Fashion*, Vol.1 – Africa, (Oxford: Berg Publishers, 2010) online, http://dx.doi.org/10.2752/BEWDF/EDch1511. Accessed on September 29, 2018; Courtney Micots, "Carnival in Ghana: Fancy Dress Street Parades and Competition," *African Arts*, 47 (1), (2014): 30-41, online, doi:10.1162/AFAR_a_00120. Accessed on September, 29, 2018; John Kedjanyi, "Masquerade Societies in Ghana," *Research Review*, 3 (2), (1967): 51-57; Simon Ottenberg and David A. Binkley, *Playful Performers: African Children's Masquerades*, (New Brunswick, N.J: Transaction Publishers, 2006); Henrietta Sarpong, "The Humanistic Values of the Dance in the Akan Society," (Master Thesis, University of Science and Technology, Kumasi, 1990):79-80; Carol Beckworth and Angela Fisher, *African Ceremonies*, Vol.1, (New York: Harry N. Abrams, Inc. 1999).

life shaped by adultism, and the paradoxical role which the town's masquerade art parade – the Winneba Fancy Dress masquerade art expression – plays in enforcing dominance of adults within the town, on one hand, and on the other breaking the hold and power of this dominant group over the town through the practices of the masquerade culture and public performances by the town's children. The paper examines the critical role played by the children maskers in mediating a carnivalesque descending of the power imbalance in Winneba through their masked performances. It explores how the child-led performances in Winneba challenge an adult-biased town and reconfigure the cultural space from one that is dominantly adult-centred to one that is co-created and co-owned by both adults and children and, as an extension to this, redefine the character of childhood for children in the town.

A Preliminary Observation about the Place of Masks and Masquerading in Africa

Masks and masquerade societies have existed in different parts of Africa since antiquity. Among their many religio-political, social and therapeutic functions,[3] Africa's masks, masking societies and masquerade performances exist and function as unique and powerful artistic expressions that create and maintain relationships within the African society. These relationships and their dynamics, and their outcomes lend to community life a vibrant, creative mental and spiritual energy that acts as a core force by which the physical and psychosocial structures and systems of the African village, town or city are continually and generationally raised and built up, or dismantled, and managed, sustained, or discontinued, for the good of society.[4] The fates of negative yet dominant cultures and values impacting community and national wellbeing in many African communities are intimately connected with masquerade performances. Masquerade acts, being unique community art expressions, have the power to spawn vital relationships which build a healthy and strong community; it also sensitises the people in community relationship to the aspects of their collective culture that are detrimental to the group and therefore must be done away with.

---

[3] See Sarpong, "The Humanistic Values of the Dance in the Akan Society". For greater expositions on this subject see Awo Sarpong and De-Valera N.Y.M. Botchway "Freaks in Procession? The Fancy Dress Masquerade as Haven for Negotiating Eccentricity During Childhood. A Study of Child Masqueraders in Cape Coast, Ghana," in Markus P.J. Bohlmann (ed.), *Misfit Children: An Inquiry into Childhood Belongings,* (Lanham, Maryland: Lexington Books, Rowman and Littlefield, 2017), 175-198.
[4] See Sarpong, "The Humanistic Values of the Dance in the Akan Society," 79-80 for an exposition on the use of masquerade to energise community unity.

Dramatic public masquerade performances and parades held at the request of chiefs, community leaders and the governing body in charge of the community illuminate characters and relationships in society and explain how their politics influence the village, town or city; they also expose system boons as well as flaws in community ideology which had fashion and continue to shape culture and lifestyles. Club membership and politics manifest and uncover ideological and political power plays and struggles in community-building relationships. They unveil power players involved in these tussles and confrontations behind the scenes of society, whose activities, being largely unseen, do impact greatly on the inner and outer form and shape of the African town, as well as on the living realities of the humans who inhabit and animate it. The masquerade art expression, the societies that create and perform this art and the artistic performance itself are carriers of culture and mirrors of the inner and outer workings of society. The mask culture of a masquerade-performing town shares an integral bond with its history, identity and cultural self-expression. Performances and the structure of masking societies afford a microcosmic view and insight into the nature and structure of the bigger society of that town, and with a blend of vivid factual storytelling and carnivalesque humour in dramatic performance helps observers conceive mental images of the building blocks, joints and atmosphere of town life.

Africa thinks and reflects through its arts and artistic expression, and hides its most valuable knowledge in its arts. The arts are oracles in Africa. They are employed in vision casting and are the visions in the African experience. They are the senses, meaning makers and media of thought, speech reasoning, conceiving and creating the life reality. There is no interpretation of life, and cosmology, no imagining or re-imagining, no reasoning that happens in Africa in absentia of its art, symbols, symbolism and art forms. The masquerading act and its symbolism and politics serve as an important conduit through which understandings of social life in African village and town communities could be reached.

The observer of the drama of African society and community life is, therefore, presented with a unique perspective of people and their core beliefs whenever its masquerade culture and arts become the lens through which observations are made and interpreted. The emotional states these arts evoke in an observer are many and varied; an unfolding drama may be humorous one minute, evoking loud laughter only to turn serious, drawing one into a meditative state as he or she ponders the events unfolding in a living drama performance; yet never once does a performance lie in its representation of community truths. It is for this reason that the masquerade cultures of Africa present research and researchers with a treasure trove of information about African lifeways, even a means of drawing out the subliminal into the open, catching a piece of a community story that escapes the eye and ear of the majority and making the micro a macro that it may be studied and appreciated. The researcher always stands at a greater advantage of witnessing vivid and life-coloured truths presented with masquerade performance. We, therefore, deem any attempt on our part to view, comprehend, imagine and re-imagine any aspect of a masquerade performing African town without due acknowledgment of its masquerade culture and unique artistic expression, and appreciation of its shaping and defining influence over the developing fabric of society through the relationships, bonds, connexions and disconnections, and power struggles between the young and the old, male and female, rich and poor, engendered through club membership and public performances, as vain. Thus, in this paper the Fancy Dress culture and performances of Winneba are used as a lens for viewing and making meaning of the power struggles that children have had to engage in, as they consciously, or unconsciously, carve new paths for their childhood reality and psychosocial wellbeing in the town.

What is Fancy Dress in Ghana? A Note on the State and Trajectory of a Study

The map of the origins, history and development of Fancy Dress in Ghana (formerly the Gold Coast), is rather complex to read because of the variations in accounts about the chronology of dates and events and the names of persons whose creativity birthed this tradition. Created by Gold Coast Africans through an ingenious merger of local and foreign cultural idioms of masking, fashion, music, symbols, choreographic and organisational inventiveness, and having thrived into the present period, it does not only mark continuity within the performance project of the colonial and post (neo) colonial Ghana but it is a sign of memory; its habitus is the imagination, and it holds keys for understanding the historicity, contemporariness and continuity of Ghanaian popular performance. By performance, we mean the movement, the drama, the cultural work of enacting one's identity.

So what is this Fancy Dress? Is it a music, or a dance, or a social movement, or a space, or a profile, or an attitude, or a philosophy? It is a mixture of all. Fancy Dress culture evolved from the interaction between the Fante culture of the Gold Coast and Euro-Caribbean masking cultures in the colonial period. It is believed to have evolved on the coast. It is a secular counterpart to the spiritually-oriented performances of longstanding traditional masking and secret societies in Africa.[5] Cole and Ross aptly describe it as "neither wholly Europe-an nor wholly African, but inspired from both sources."[6]

Although its epicentre is Ghana's littoral areas, Fancy Dress has spread to other parts of the country as a lively performance art in contemporary Ghana. Surviving in contemporary times as a known feature of popular festive occa-sions like Christmas, New Year's Day and indigenous festivals, and within the entertainment package of Ghana's Tourism industry, Fancy Dress is largely considered to be an ongoing performance practice to indigenous Ghana, and which is centred on music and dance masquerade parades. Some persons familiar with Fancy Dress might remember a sound, a dance rhythm; others might visualise stilt walkers and feet stomping dancers clad in colourful rag-tag costumes. Still, others may imagine the dancers, their movement, space, and bodily fashioning. Others may want to hear the history of such a practice. Thus, Fancy Dress can be analyzed as historical, geographical (that is taking account of the limited space available for the execution of movement) and performance instances.

Curiously, with available texts, studies on Fancy Dress have emphasised the music and the dance – their performers and production, and the entertainment. They also pay attention to themes that rather focus on the status and develop-ment of Fancy Dress within Ghana and its place within the context of Ghanaian popular culture. This is reflected in the scholarship on Fancy Dress.[7] The wider context of the social, spatial and cultural topographies of Fancy Dress remains under-exposed. Recently in 2107 Sarpong and Botchway explored the interest-ing dimension of children's participation as a way to showcase their eccentricity.

---

[5] See Kedjanyi, "Masquerade Societies in Ghana"; Cole and Ross, *The Arts of Ghana*; Judith Bettelheim, "Afro-Jamaican Junkanoo Festival: Playing the Forces and Operating the Cloth," (PhD Dissertation, Yale University, 1979); Judith Bettelheim, "Jonkonoo and other Christmas Masquerades," in John Nunley and Judith Bettelheim (eds.), *Caribbean Festival Arts: Each and Every Bit of Difference*, (Seattle: St. Louis Museum and University of Washington Press 1988), 39-83; Sarpong, "The Humanistic Values of the Dance in the Akan Society"; Keith Nicklin and Jill Salmons, "Hippies of Elmina," *African Arts* 38 (2), (2005): 60-95; Ottenberg and Binkley, *Playful Performers: African Children's Masquer-ades*; Carol and Fisher, *African Ceremonies*.

[6] Cole and Ross, *The Arts of Ghana*, 182.

[7] For example, see Cole and Ross, *The Arts of Ghana*, 179-186; Micots, "Fancy Dress: African Masquerade in Coastal Ghana"; Micots, "Carnival in Ghana: Fancy Dress Street Parades and Competition"; Bettelheim, "Afro-Jamaican Junkanoo Festival"; Bettelheim, Jonkonoo and other Christmas Masquerades"; Robert Wyndham Nicholls, *The Jumbies' Playing Ground: Old World Influence on Afro-Creole Masquerades in the Eastern Carib-bean*, (Mississippi: University of Mississippi Press, 2012).

The children's sphere is just one of the several facets of Fancy Dress. In this work we intend to press deeper into the child's sphere in the Fancy Dress art expression, but in a different way: to explore how children have used and continue to use performance as a challenge to adultism, and as a medium for reconfiguring child-adult power relations and redefining the nature of their childhood reality in the town of Winneba. Several theories exist to explain why Fancy Dress was created. These revolve around three main notions: (a) local attempt by colonised peoples to copy a European masquerade party, (b) local attempt to dress up like European officials and satirise their manners, and (c) local colonised people's simple attempt to create something for their entertainment. Amidst the theories about its genesis and beyond the focus on the performative aspect, Botchway and Sarpong argues that there is something else to the Fancy Dress "social movement", a particular "philosophy of redemption, a liberation ethos of self expression" controlled by child participants, that is overlooked but which lies beneath it. When they studied Fancy Dress in the coastal city of Cape Coast, they found that Fancy Dress became a safe haven that children creatively used to exhibit eccentricity. The intellectual purchase occasioned by the engagement of the artistic performance and more importantly the expression it gives to the children section of the social collective and figurative Ghanaian body performing today is that it gives a space for the children to use that cultural performance as a venue for "engaging" some critical issues central to their being and communities.

For Winneba town this popular art expression can become a social and redemptive movement, whose performance challenges the power, space and people politics of age discrimination apartheid against children and childhood expression in the town. It is the defiance to age discrimination apartheid aspect of Fancy Dress in its social context and performative aspects in the historical town of Winneba that this paper engages. We want to read this expanded conception of Fancy Dress performance as it opens up space for excavation of new knowledge about children's use of this community art as a devise for transforming living conditions that work against their experience of healthy childhoods and childhood wellbeing within the urban space of Winneba, which is considered as one of the main powerhouses of Fancy Dress and an early region where the culture started in Ghana.

Winneba: Profile of the Historical Town

Lying along the Gulf of Guinea, Winneba spans an area of about 95 square kilometres. Its population, which was about 68,597, in 2010, and about 70,000 in 2012, represents about 3.1% of the population of Central Region of Ghana.[8] Winneba is the administrative capital of the Effutu District in that region. Winneba is multi-ethnic now, however, it is the hometown of the Effutu, which is an ancillary group of the Guan major ethnic group. Effutu is widely spoken there, but Fante is also popular there because of Winneba's longstanding demographic and cultural interactions with the neighbouring coastal Fante (Akan) communities, especially Cape Coast, which was the first colonial capital of Ghana until Accra became the capital in the 1870s.

Simpa is the original name that the Effutu ancestors gave to the area when they settled after migrating from a parent Guan community in the northern part of the country. Osimpan, the name of the royal hunter who navigated the migrants to the area circa 1400 AD, was the root of Simpa. [9] The "Guan Research Papers" and research of Kwame Ampene, Organising Secretary of the Guan Congress 1981-1995, reveal that Simpa existed before the appearance of European imperialism in the country in the second part of the 15th century.[10] European sailing adventurers, especially the traders, found that Simpa had a bay, which served as a natural harbour. Because of its cool refreshing and sailing aiding winds, the English named it Windy Bay. Somehow, this became locally corrupted as Winneba. The Effutu still call their home Simpa. Under British colonial rule, it became a district administrative capital within the Central Province of the Gold Coast colony. In its heyday as a colonial port for the exportation of local products and importation of European merchandise, it was a lively market centre for thousands of people in its hinterland. Prominent chiefs, traders, local scholars and prosperous fishermen were among its population. With the building of the grand Takoradi Habour in 1928 and increase in the number of motor roads and railway facilities, the economic importance of the small coastal ports, including Winneba, began to dwindle, while Takoradi took on the vastly increased tonnage of exports and imports. The cocoa boom in the hinterland relocated major trading companies in the 1940s to neighbouring Agona Swedru. Port activities shut down in Winneba when another big harbour was constructed in Tema in the 1950s and commissioned in 1962, near Accra. Most commercial activities shifted to Tema and Accra. Today, oceanic fishing, salt production, pottery, roofing tiles produc-

---

[8] Republic of Ghana, *Composite Budget of the Effutu Municipal Assembly for 2014 Fiscal Year*, (Central Region: Effutu Municipal Assembly, 2014), 6.
[9] Kwame Ampene, *History of the Guan-Speaking Peoples of Ghana*, (Philadelphia, Penn,: StarSpirit, 2011), 22.
[10] Ibid., 20-25.

tion and trade provide livelihood for many residents of Winneba. A number of
government civil service jobs and a university of education exist there.

Winneba society of contemporary times still retains the culture of the indigenous Guan society that spawned it and continues to be adult-centred and
patriarchal in its socio-politico-religious setup. It has adapted itself to the
cultures of neighbouring groups; yet the dominance of a patriarchal culture
amongst the neighbouring settlements and some of the non-indigenous peoples that have made contact with Winneba, even in those that profess matri-
archal systems of group life, prevails strongly as a powerful shaper of relationships and power dynamics in the town. The traditional setting and hegemony
of the adult, and especially the healthy male figure over less powerful groups
such as children, girls and women, and people living with disabilities has
defied significant change despite the current mixed population of residents,
drawn from many different ethno-cultural and international backgrounds.
Unequal power relations among adults and children and other groups of persons deemed "weak" manifest as healthy-adult-male biased community activities, and socio-cultural and economic policies in Winneba. Noteworthy,
Aboakyer (lit. animal catching), the annual indigenous festival of the Effutu in
which indigenous martial groups (Asafo) go to the forest and catch a deer and
bring it as sacrifice for the state tutelary deity Penkye Otu for blessings and
protection, and a large number of community ceremonies in the town are not
only healthy-male dominated but adult-centred. The input and presence of
children, women and people with disabilities are often unwelcome through
bans on their free movement and involvement in the planning of the hunt
and other hunt-related rituals. Such attitudes towards non-healthy male and
non-adult serve largely to perpetuate the healthy adult male dominance and
control over less empowered members of the community, the unfortunate
class within which children fall. The arts and artistic institutions in Winneba
town reflect and are viewed in this paper as enforcers of this dominance in
the town. While very few arts – one prominent being the Fancy Dress Parade
competition in Winneba, a cultural event, which brings a lot of national and
international visitors to Winneba annually – portray the child and childness,
as a prominent feature of the town, there is an almost suffocating over representation of the healthy male and adult and his world through visual, performed and literary arts performances and productions that drive creativity
and define the character of the town. Music, dance, drum language, dramatic
plays and performances and spoken word delivered during ceremonies such
as burials and funerals usually avoid themes related to children and especially
persons with disabilities. Proverbs, riddles and wise sayings are bloated with
references to the virtues of the healthy male and adult. Even animals, plants
and non-living things that portray adult, adult male characteristics of

strength, virility and power in performance make the roll call. While naivety, innocence and folly are often spoken of as the characteristic nature of the child and of childhood, weakness is the commonly assumed character of females, and pity seeking is the extensively perceived character of the person with disability. With almost all socio-religious and economic institutions in Winneba town residing under the sway of the domination of the healthy adult male, one may conclude that Winneba as a town is faced with the monumental task of mediating balance of power of the different people groups that energise the spirit and soul of the town and its social, economic and political relations.

The Reality of Adultism in Winneba; An Indigenous Notion and Practice

We broadly deem adultism as the conscious creation of the social categories of power and roles between a demarcated section of persons of which one group is designated as adults and another as children by the section that calls itself adults. Adultism includes the attitude and effort of the adult elements to ensure and secure the existence of this duality and dichotomy. It contains the actions, methods and ideas of the adults to institutionalise this binary arrangement in the society in order for the adults to control and guide and direct the child/children category without the consent of the child group.

The Winneba locale has largely functioned with Effutu indigenous concepts of social relations. From our analyses of textual evidence of various kinds, interviews with persons in Winneba, and ethnographic observations and inquiries in homes, workplaces and communities across Winneba, we found that a demarcation between the category called "adults" and the other called "children" exists in Winneba. The Effutu society largely enforces the worldview that it is the adult category that must bestow citizenship and nurturance and sponsorship. Children, arbitrarily being persons ranging between the ages of 8 days to about 14 years old, are to be socialised for obedience, respect and technical training through hard work, and they are to be guided on this training by adults, which first starts with their parents, and then all adult members of the community. Although they were expected to grow naturally to become adults, and socially succeed the older generation in carrying the society ahead, children, according to the traditional social arrangement and notion, must derive the right to full citizenship from the adults. It is the adults that must confer this right so that the child can now "play" with the adults. Children are to be educated by adults. Traditionally, there were often threats of divine retribution if children disobeyed adults. Adults, being elders, were therefore like demi-gods to the children. For example in the instance of sending a child an adult could spit on the ground and tell a child that if he/she did not complete the errand before the drying of the spittle their navel would rot or their mother would die. This and other several threats, though mythical, were apparently to show children that they were children and had to obey adults, including their parents, who possessed a certain almost defied position in society. However, children were told that those who saw themselves as children and young and obeyed the adults and put up proper behaviour and demeanour and patiently received instructions from the adults would be allowed to jump the social chasm between them and the adults. Hence, a Fante proverb like *Abofra hu ne nsa hohor a, onye mpanyinfo dzidzi* (A child who knows how to wash his/her hands well qualifies to eat with the adults/elder) which is popular in Winneba attest to this chasm and the supreme values of patience and comportment for children. Thus, the relations between children and parents, adults in general, although affectionate in infancy, are usually on a pattern of social distance. The acquisition of knowledge was to be undertaken in stages. Peers were to converse with peers. The proverb that *Nkontrofi hwe hon kesi do na wodzi dzi agor* (Monkeys look at their sizes and play according to their sizes) attest to the idea that children must not freely play or interact with adults. Thus, children are held and treated to be children, first and foremost. Almost invariably whenever in the worst case scenario a child quarrelled with an adult, the child was adjudged guilty, not necessarily because of the true nature of the case, but because it was deemed improper for a child to dare challenge an adult openly.

When adults met to talk children must leave the premises, even if a child remained there he or she should be mute, because *Mmofra ntsie mpanyin nkomo* (children don't listen to the conversation of adults). Although a chasm was to be maintained, children were also expected to be circumspective and observe the ways of the adults and maintain some closeness to them in order to learn and acquire the licence, at times an expedited jump, to join the adults conversations and certain activities, hence the existence of a proverb like *Akoko a oben ni na na odi abebe ne sre* (A chick that keeps a closeness to the mother hen is the one that eats the thigh (better part) of a dead grasshopper). Basically, the children group, according to tradition, was not to make itself a nuisance to the adult population. Children had their spaces and activities and had to remain there. They could joke with their peers, but could not joke with their adults, who by traditional lore were their parents. To the traditional adult mind, a breach of this hierarchy was dangerous to their power and respect, positions which their well created gerontocratic notions and space enforced. The Fante proverb *wo woo panyin, ansa wo re wo ohen* (meaning "elder is born before a chief") emphasised the relevance of age, a value which has furthered the creation a chasm between adults and children by a prevailing adultism in the Winneba social terrain and Ghanaian indigenous societies in general.

A Brief History of the Origins of the Fancy Dress Art Form in Winneba, and the Power Struggles that Characterise and Animate the Performance Culture.

The town's annual Fancy Dress competition started in 1957/58 when a federation of Fancy Dress Clubs was established in Winneba. 1957 was the year that the Gold Coast became independent and Ghana was born. The Fancy Dress competition of 1958 in Winneba thus formed part of the different activities that celebrated the attainment of independence in the country. However, it must be said that Fancy Dress had flourished for many years in colonial Winneba, which, being a trans Atlantic trade port and a cosmopolis of European traders, settlers and colonisers and an African population, had been an early junction of contest, interaction and hybrisation of African and European cultural items, idioms and practices. The meeting of African and European cultures produced cultural tension and cooperation and assimilation concurrently. Tensions emanated when the colonial administration perceived aspects of local lifeways as backward and sought to ban them and superimpose Western worldviews on the Gold Coast local cultural terrain. Certain local festivals were condemned as unwholesome. For example, in 1897 the colonial administrator, H.T. Ussher, wrote: "[T]he time has come for us to get rid of . . . old institutions which . . . conflict with the modern idea of civilisation . . . A list should be made of all . . . which should be abolished".[11] Shortly Ussher enacted the Native Customs Regulation Ordinance to prohibit the yam festival and other processions and festivals involving musketry and drumming in Cape Coast in 1868. Few months later he became intolerant of the "silly custom" of deer-catching at Winneba because the competing hunting factions had a brawl. The affair was however dismissed by the Secretary of State as "Precisely similar to an Irish faction fight".[12] Conversely, Winneba assimilated aspects of Western culture such as European style of dressing, music, dance, architecture, Christianity, formal schooling, and English language. For example, it was a taste for Victorian style of dressing that developed the Kabasrotu, the prototype of the now popular Ghanaian Kaba and Slit for women, in the 1860s. The Kabasrotu (corruption of cover shoulder) a sort of loose jumper for the upper

---

[11] *Gold Coast Express*, 28 September, 1897, cited in David Kimble, *A Political History of Ghana: The Rise of Gold Coast Nationalism 1850-1928* (Oxford: Clarendon, 1963), 133.
[12] Dispatch No. 119 of 20 April, 1880, from Ussher to Hicks Beach, and Minuted on by Kimberly; CO/96/130 as cited by Kimble, *A Political History of Ghana:*, 132.

part of the body) was introduced by R.J. Ghartey of Winneba, for use among the women of his household.[13]

Generally, different facets of the local society of the Gold Coast became westernised. Regardless of what clothes some people wore, and the language they spoke, and their architectural preference, an alien culture had come to stay in the Gold Coast since the second part of the 15th century. This culture could neither be wholly accepted nor wholly rejected. It was within this cultural environment of the Gold Coast that Fancy Dress masquerade evolved. It flourished particularly in the coastal areas of Saltpond, Winneba, Cape Coast, Sekondi-Takoradi and Axim. Agona Swedru, Nyakrom, Breman Esikuma, Abakrampa and Tarkwa Aboso, which are near the coastal areas, also came to show remarkable Fancy Dress consciousness.[14]

Winneba took masking customs and practices that were strange, alien, even eccentric, and reworked them to create the alternate universe of Fancy Dress where at given times of the year, Winneba people could with dance, music and mask go and become creatures that defied the normal and engaged in the novel and the eccentric in an unrestrained and unbarred way. Fancy Dress originally started in Winneba as an all adults affair. The four main clubs that kept it alive and competed annually did not accept children. Today they do because over the years children expressed interest in participating in Fancy Dress. The Fancy Dress display and culture in Winneba's urban space is not just an entertaining masquerading act and a provider of memory only, but an item and haven that children have managed to secure to contest adultism.

The tradition of organising Fancy Dress spectacles, and institutionalising Association Fancy Dress into clubs and rules of engagement, long street processions, flamboyant costumes and masks, group choreographed and performed street dance and drama, and prize-tagged competitions, reached Winneba from Saltpond in the 1920s.[15] It is possible that information about it as a culture which had started in Saltpond around the late nineteenth century had filtered to some people in Winneba. Saltpond, a Fante town, was another major colonial trading outpost between Winneba and Cape Coast. It is also believed that Cape

---

[13] EJP Brown, *Gold Coast and Asianti Reader*, London, 1929, bk. I, 165-6, cited in Kimble, *A Political History of Ghana:*, 134.

[14] Samuel Ofori Amissah, "The Masquerade Tradition at Winneba," Long Essay, Diploma of Art Education, (Institute of Education, University of Cape Coast, 1988), 9.

[15] Personal interview with Anthony Abbam, Lecturer of University of Education, Winneba, and Charles Walker, an indigene of Winneba, 23 January 2016.

Coast's Fancy Dress culture was largely inspired by Saltpond's in the 1930s.[16] It started as all adult male performance in Saltpond and so when it reached Winneba it remained as an exclusive all adult male activity, although it is now open to all sexes. By 1933 the last of the four main clubs in Winneba, which are still operational today, had been established. The traditional clubs are: Number 1, alias Nobles, Number 2, alias Egyaa, Number 3, alias Tumus, which is a corruption of *Tun bo rusu* (which means the blacksmith's anvil is crying (chiming) in the Fante language), and Number 4, alias Red Cross. The clubs were formed by some very prominent people in Winneba. These included chiefs and businessmen. For example, the first patron of the Number 2 was Nana Ayirebi Acquah III, the paramount chief of Winneba. As an adult cum elitist association, children were not allowed to join the clubs. Currently, children, some as young as 4 years, are members of either one of the four clubs or the "rogue nation" of freelance and ad hoc groups and participate in spectacles. [17]

The originators in Saltpond included some chiefs and economically prosperous men. Indigenous social decorum did not permit chiefs to engage in public and popular spectacles and have close vulgar association with the general public. They could not go out and walk through town unescorted by royal aides and so the idea of disguising and joining the other circle of trusted adult maskers who had started to do the Fancy Dress for entertainment and to satirise the colonial administrators became attractive to them. But because the chiefs and royals and other notables and fathers and husbands felt that their identities should be protected, especially from children, for the sake of preserving "their social integrity" children were not allowed to join. Thus, behind the masks of the early masquerade spectacles and outings in Saltpond were prominent persons who *in cognito* danced to the music, especially the brass band music, joked and caroused in public. Over time the culture became democratised and different clubs emerged and the culture obtained more members. Some of the notable early clubs were Chinese, Tumbus, Justice, Anchor, Red Indian and Cosmos. So it was the desire to maintain the tradition of keeping the "integrity" and gravitas of adults that made adults to not allow a democratic acceptance of children into it when it reached Winneba around 1923. Thus, in Winneba the rule of excluding children from the Fancy Dress community was enforced from the 1920s to the 1980s, and for years, even though children, designated as persons below 12 years, persistent-

---

[16] Personal interview with Charles Kweku Aidoo, Opanyin Sam N.M. Afful, and Alhassan Yaya (elderly Fancy Dressers of Winneba), Winneba, 30 January 2016.
[17] Personal interview with Charles Kweku Aidoo, Opanyin Sam N.M. Afful, Alhassan Yaya, William Ebo Kittoe, Winneba, 30 January 2016.

ly requested clubs and parents to be allowed to join, parades in Winneba did not include children. Nevertheless, the exception to the rule was that a "specially" selected child below that age could be made to replace a dead or incapacitated adult relative in a club.

This was an exercise and exhibition of the practice of adultism. This display of bias against children in the context of Fancy Dress was spawned by the larger local traditional notions of adult superiority in Winneba, where indigenously the arbitrary relegation of persons to the state of children and therefore to a place where such persons were to be dictated to and decisions made for them by adults existed.

The Parades Tell Tales: Age Apartheid in Fancy Dress as a Reflection and Enforcement of Adultism in Winneba Society

A careful examination of the history, club lore and performance of the Fancy Dress art expression at Winneba reveals children in the Fancy Dress celebrations, from its emergence in the 1920s to the late 1990s when the first child led a club to victory in the New Year competition. Opanyin (elder) Sam, retired/veteran leader of the Tumus Fancy Dress Club describes the type of spirit that defined and drove the performance of Winneba town Fancy Dress masquerades prior to the child masker revolution in the late 1990s as "excluding children", "ostracising and punishing children caught imitating the ways of the adult masquerader" and "enforcing the notion of adult exclusive ownership of the art expression, and by extension of all community activities within the Winneba town". The age apartheid model that defined and gave form to the organisation, performance and appreciation of the Winneba Fancy Dress masquerade followed the pattern of society and was not simply a reflection of the culture of adultism in the town; it was also a medium by which the aspirations of the adults in the town to be the dominant and controlling force over the culture of the town were achieved. There was a certain psychological effect which the sight of an adult-only league of masqueraders had on the collective consciousness of the people of Winneba town. A powerful message was etched into the collective consciousness of the people, both adults and children, whenever children were "whipped for imitating adult ways through child-led masquerades in the nooks and crannies of the town"[18]. This message was simply: "Adults rule. Adults own the society. Adults define what our community life is. This community is for adults. Let the status quo remain". As long as the adult population controlled

---

[18] Personal interview with Charles Kweku Aidoo, Winneba 30 January 2016.

the annual *puei,*[19] that is, "emergence" of the clubs in street music and drama-
tized shows and their performances in the big competition, and as long as the
adult embodied the spirit of this annual celebration of creativity and emergence
of new culture in the town and punished all that is undesirable in Winneba, the
town remained one whose culture and identity was perceived by all ages, both
the young and the old as formed, defined and controlled by the adult. This perception will go on to define who possessed power to continue determining the
shape and form of the arts and arts expression, history, and socio-economics
and commerce, as well as the townscape, in the years preceding the chain of
events, which resulted in what we term the *ragtag wars* – the carnivalesque,
child-led descending of adult power within the Fancy Dress institution and the
town's power struggle terrain.

Breaking Out: From the Nooks to the Frontlines, and the Descending of Adult Power in the Winneba Fancy Dress Parades

We deem the inclusion of children in the Winneba Fancy Dress masquerade
performances as a lawful act of social "violence" and engineering that is sending ripples of potential change and transformation through the fabric of Winneba town life. Since the introduction of child-led performances in the Winneba parades, child maskers have been and continue to be more than a mere
ceremonial feature of the masquerade ritual and performance; they are symbols of a democratising and power-balancing force sweeping through the
town, by means of the Fancy Dress art performance. The visual and psychological impact of their appearances at the frontlines of performance on the
collective consciousness of the town has been a powerful challenge to attitudes and mindsets and tendencies favouring adultism and has gradually
mediated new ways of viewing the child and adult relationship in the town.

Paradoxically, the incitement to the democratisation of Fancy Dress clubs to
include the child in its parades began as a ploy by adult masqueraders to "win
first place in the annual competitions."[20] "The children can dance better and
they are very creative, and they can produce powerful choreographies for the
clubs to win"[21] was how one adult masker put that notion. Year after year
masquerade clubs sought to portray that special quality of "wonderful" aston-
ishment" that could win them the trophy. Combining skilful dance, outland-

---

[19] *Puei* means to "come out," a "coming out" or "emergence" in the language of the
Fante people. It describes the maskers' intent to perform the Fancy Dress carnival. It
also describes the performative act itself.
[20] Personal interview with Alhassan Yaya, Winneba, 30 January 2016.
[21] Personal interview with Charles Kweku Aidoo, Winneba, 30 January 2016.

ish outfits and brass-band renditions of the most popular top-of-the-charts songs on the market, backed by mystical charms to draw attention and turn the favour of the judges to their acts, these groups battled each other for the ultimate prize. When these attractions became inadequate to satisfy the enormous appetite of the spectators and the judges for that one element of surprise that had so long eluded them, the clubs devised an unthinkable scheme: to let a child lead its league of adult-only performers to the battlefront. The first child performance was a risky move aimed at adult profit. It was not an act purposed to balance power; if anything, it was a decision made in the true spirit of adultism, which often objectified the child and its childness for adult profit. We note, with humour, the paradox of a surprise descending of a vice that had sought to use that which descended it to entrench itself in the minds and culture of the people of Winneba.

For the Tumus Club, Kojo Akyen was the first child to lead an all-adult masquerade procession in Winneba, in 1998. According to Opanyin Sam, he was

> barely five years when we picked him up and set him at the forefront of our parade. He was a young child we had secretly observed perform together with a few other children, hidden away in a nook, shielded from the eyes of the adults, for fear of adult punishment for partaking in the dance of secret societies. . . He danced so well, and we marvelled. We thought, 'This is the one who will lead us to victory'. Our club won that year; that incited more clubs to search for dancing children to use as their flagship performers in the years that followed our win[22].

The years following 1998 marked revolutionary years in the history of Winneba Fancy Dress celebrations, as well as in the history of adultism and its influence within and over the town. From the nooks and backyards where young faint-hearted child masqueraders dared to express their shared legacy of the Fancy Dress performance with the adults, in their own private competitions, emerged a force never before imagined by the people of the town, who had long been "hypnotised" by their bias towards the desirability and dominating power of the male adult masquerader. The adult masqueraders were themselves pleasantly impressed by the influx of freshness and new ideas into performances, with the arrival of the first few child maskers. Opanyin Sam N. M. Afful confessed that:

> We discovered that the young ones were far better. They danced well, had fresh ideas and brought more eccentricity and sense of wonder-

---

[22] Personal interview with Opanyin Sam N.M. Afful, Winneba, 30 January 2016.

ment, which is the spirit of masquerade, to the competitions. How could we have kept such wealth suppressed and hidden for so long?[23]

Furthermore,

> [the] children performed their own parades in the corners, out of the way, for they feared the anger of the adults, expressed through the cane. But in their segregation, they developed their own ideas and culture of dance and art expression, which, when tested, proved to be an overwhelming force against which none could contest or put down. Child performances had to move from the backyards to the frontline; they were too good, too precious not to be in the limelight. They were teaching us something new, which we had hardened ourselves against – perhaps out of fear?[24]

By 2003, child masqueraders had become a norm in Winneba. Children brought something extra to parades: a zest and freedom of spirit that resonated with the spirit of masquerade, and the spirits of the spectators that watched from the sidelines. Their membership gave hope for the two critical gains the clubs coveted: future wins and the attainment of the rewards that came with first place in the competitions. Thus, as long as their parents could afford to pay their membership dues and buy their costumes, the universe of the Fancy Dress was an open and welcoming haven for them: Children could join in the fun of Fancy Dress, anytime and any day. No child was barred. Membership rules differed from club to club, however there were some standard themes concerning legibility: children had to love dancing and be able to dance; children had to be willing to keep club secrets as a secret; children had to have sponsorship; and intellectually, they had to be sound, with a record of good performance in school (if they had reached school-going age). Moral uprightness was a basic requirement: they had to love truth, be disciplined, and well-behaved, and genuinely interested in increasing their moral value through good deeds in society. If a child met these criteria, he qualified as a candidate for club membership. He could dance and enjoy all the privileges of a group member of any of the four major clubs in Winneba.

For a shot at a win, the adults pushed children from the peripheries into the centre. So, miniature costumes were made and became popular. Clothes for

---

[23] Personal interview with Opanyin Sam N.M. Afful, Winneba, 30 January 2016.
[24] Personal interview with Charles Kweku Aidoo, Winneba, 30 January 2016.

children became a concern for the clubs. Choreographed dances considered child's strengths and abilities, and not only admitted but also sought children's suggestions for dance movements and themes for dramatizations. The norm for performances by the clubs soon altered from a frontline packed with skilful adult dancers to a vast array of children, as crowd demand for the antics by children filtered from the sidelines to talent scouts: "The children are better! More of them!" Corroborated by the wins accumulating to clubs that had more dancing children occupying helm positions in their processions, adult resistance to children in the clubs melted. From the frontlines, and amidst the exciting and riotous carnival of music, dance, sweat of determination and innocent zeal, and masterful control over the Fancy Dress art expression by the child performers, the adult hegemony over performance was being toppled. Something was happening, which the adults had never factored into their quest for wins: children were overturning adult control over Fancy Dress! And as the community in the town fixed their gaze and hearts onto the children, their mindsets were being challenged too. No more could the adult public comfortably look upon and imagine children as occupants of a powerless position, and a town periphery, but able and capable performers at its centre. The evidence danced right before their eyes. Rather, the adults took mental steps backwards, in their bewilderment.

A Far Reaching Impact on Children's Perceptions of their Childness and Childhood

We note the fact that amongst the town's children, the child-led parades radically transformed their collective self-image and posturing in the town. As they gazed upon their peers at the front lines, their interpretations of their position in a social hierarchy and social space, as well as their understandings of the state of being a child and the definitions of what is considered "childness" were no doubt challenged. The structure of power ownership – power as co-owned by children and adults – demonstrated in the parades was something other than what their minds had become accustomed to over the years – power as owned and exercised only by adults. The idea of *child* being an outsider to power, to agency, to community-transformation responsibility, over time, shattered; the idea of themselves as "muted", voiceless and speechless beings huddling at the peripheries of society, over time, splintered; their idea of childness being silence, furtive movements, and being dominated by the adult shadow figuratively and literally, over time, developed fractures; childhood as a period of one's life where you owned and controlled little and nothing save one's breath and continence of bodily functions would, over time, started to become a fossil memory for most children in Winneba who managed to bring themselves to trust in the spectacle and the process of transformation their fellows were birthing in the town. Children could now move from the outer circle of society to the centre of it. During all the child-led performances witnessed by the authors in the months and years of their study of child masqueraders and their parades and child audienc-es/spectators of these parades, they noted that child spectators of these pa-rades, perhaps without real consciousness of their body language and its implications for understanding the thoughts and attitudes that were taking shape and flowering in their minds, always inching forward in parade side-lines, separating themselves from the peripheries and moving towards the centre. The sheer number of children that have been abandoning the periph-ery of the spectators and onlooking crowd and boldly pushing their way to stand in front of adults, even fearlessly treading adult feet in the process, has been overwhelming. From this observed phenomenon, one can comfortably say that the effect of these parades on children's new understanding of their transforming position in Winneba society have been more than ideological; they have been literal. In fact, few children today hide behind the scenes and move furtively in the town, for fear of the adult. Few children shy from the centre in favour of the periphery. This is no more their childhood experience; being a child of going through the period described as childhood is one that is no more characterised by unhealthy fear and timidity due to a perverse bal-ance of power. The powerful presence of children at the forefront of an im-portant cultural item of the town, once owned by adults but currently relent-lessly charged by the spirit and energy of children, has given the whole town a new boldness to challenge adultism – adult-centeredness and –bias – in the town and its rule over the collective consciousness. It has also released chil-dren mentally, to consider remaking, redefining and renegotiating the terms of their childhood states and social statuses in Winneba.

Pressure, Resistance and Enduring Struggle: Ramifications of the Ragtag Wars for the Adult-Child Power Struggle Culture and Terrain in Winneba

The novelty of child masqueraders as well as the powers of their skilful perfor-mance, popularity and reputation as facilitators of winnings make them most indispensable to the Fancy Dress community in Winneba. From all indications, the child performer has come to stay and Winneba Fancy Dress is changed for-ever. A child masker's status as child sharing space with the Winneba adult, and perhaps assuming a complementary position, however, has and continues to pose a complexity of challenges that still remain to be completely resolved. The desire of adults to maintain dominance within the new configuration of the Fancy Dress as a space accommodating children for specific adult-dictated and controlled purposes resists the desire of children to be more than a winning charm for adults, to prove themselves and their creative expressions as complementary to that of adults; this creates an internal power struggle between the two groups. Masking children and adults reveal rather divergent understandings of child presence in the performance parades and outings, roles played by the different groups and power-sharing within the clubs. Children believe the Fancy Dress is a co-owned endeavour and power must be shared equally.[25] Some even radically claim that Fancy Dress in now for the persons known as children, for it is they who now dominate the clubs in terms of membership, and they also largely serve as the main attraction to spectators.[26]

On the other hand, adults, especially the maskers, while they agree that children help the work of Fancy Dress in the town – which is to entertain, and maintain group cohesion, however maintain that the organisation of clubs, the masquerade art expression and the town itself should be kept as the sole prerogative of adults and not a co-owned effort with children. The struggle for absolute control of the powers of society prevail, and children and adults engage a silent struggle for power; adults through resistance to the idea of loss of all power and control over their entrenched positions in Fancy Dress and the town, and children through mounting pressure for access to more power in their clubs and within the town. Among club circles and at the Winneba Fancy Dress Clubs Association level there are whispers of organising separate competitions and outings for children and adults.[27] Adults seem to be brooding over the imposition of a type of segregation, again. Is this a desperate attempt by a cultural status quo that finds itself descended, challenged and at the brink of losing its hold, to maintain its hegemony over a town?

Despite the fact that the Fancy Dress culture and terrain contains a subtle love-detest relationship between adults and children, and energised by the somehow tension-filled complementary roles that both groups play in Fancy Dress and the support they give to each other, the Fancy Dress art and act has continued to energise community and town unity. The performance of Fancy Dress which attracts participants and observers creates a feeling of wellness and foments solidarity among these sections of the town's populace.

More importantly when the performance takes place, and it features children, the sharp dichotomy between adults and children, men and women, political leaders and followers is temporarily removed. Implicitly, that dichotomy's very existence and the continuous perpetuation of it as part of the indigenous status

---

[25] Personal interview with William Ebo Kittoe, Ezekiel Dampson, Mohammed Bary, and Joseph Baidoo (young Fancy Dressers), Winneba, 30 January 2016.

[26] Personal interview with William Ebo Kittoe, Ezekiel Dampson, and Mohammed Bary, Winneba, 30 January 2016.

[27] Personal interview with Alhaji Yaya, Winneba, 30 January, 2016.

quo of social arrangement are questioned. Who knows what such a continuous questioning would ultimately yield? A final total abolishing of such duality, the removal of such a demarcation, and the eventual birth of a society without such categories that represent a powerful versus powerless power relations?

Child Fancy Dress is creating a vital relationship between adults and children, because it is making many adults to now know that the children are not just entities without agency who must be consigned to the backyard of the future and seen as only capable of becoming citizens who matter, and who, as the common saying goes, "the future belongs to", when they are adults. The revolutionarised children contesting and infused performance, therefore, is a signifier that the town's children, in fact, are part of and matter in the "present", because they perform with and find themselves in the same space of action with the adult category that traditionally has considered itself as the owner of the present.

The children performers easily slide into the adult category, even though, they are not adults, and that makes them and, by implication, confers of children in the town, the status and right to be co-owners of the present and not just a mass of persons whom traditionally adults have dismissively thought and said of as future leaders. The right to perform and the performance empower the child maskers and the town children as a whole with the notion and unspoken vim that the children collective matters, and that that collective is important, powerful, part of the present, and is not only meant to be on the periphery of society which is hijacked by adults. Children's view of themselves, and their conception of what they must be and do during the period of being a child has been challenged by the Fancy Dress act. From our perspective, this is positive, with positive implications for the development of a healthy selfhood by children during their childhoods. As the world experiences change, and moves towards a new age of awareness for mankind, the revelations of the fluid nature of the social reality of place, position and power to Winneba children through their brave engagement with and sharing in power with adults in the masquerade act, together their own bold challenge of their own perceptions of what is childness and childhood open the door to their courageous exploration of new possibilities in their childhood. No doubt, the change they have mediated for their own child and childhood status in these still-early days of the 21st century through the Fancy Dress performance is the beginning of greater changes that will inform more positive views of the "child", "childness" and "childhood experience" that will shape lives of their future children.

For the researchers, the single story of adults in control of Winneba society through the Fancy Dress act has been replaced with a new narrative of co-ownership and co-creation of power and the use of the latter by adults and children to bring new energy into their town. This opens new doors to research into power-sharing and power-struggles that involve children; in the beginning there was the struggle between adults and children, which still persists today but in a defused way, but can we expect a time where power struggles will be between children themselves, a time where they will triumph again by redesigning and redefining their understanding of their places and positions in community and unite in unique and presently unknown ways through the masquerade act to strengthen their town with newer energy? Excitingly, we are presented with new ways of viewing children, their childness and their assertion of their right to be "more living" and active members of society. The quest for sustainable "victory" of children in Winneba over adultism calls for more studies and creative development of new scholarly approaches for studying children in their struggle to access and embody justice in childhood.

Conclusion

The discussions made so far in this work have uncovered an urban space-based "power" politics between children and adult residents in the littoral town of Winneba in the Central Region of Ghana, through their shared artistic medium of Fancy Dress. Winneba, a town which harbours many Fancy Dress clubs, is nationally acclaimed as one of the six powerhouses and citadels of the Fancy Dress culture in Ghana. As the preceding discourse has shown, Fancy Dress was first an adult male only spectacle of dramatic merry-making parades in Winneba; however, by mid-20th century the adult monopoly had been dissolved by a revolutionary enrolment of children into clubs and a burgeoning wresting of the adult's control and sole ownership of artistic self-expression in the masquerade parades by children. Reasons for the rise of the child performer and the descent of adult centeredness in the parades have been explained. The cultural ramifications of these developments to the adult-child power relations terrain in the town life of Winneba have been explored. Thus, this study has discussed how children's use of the Fancy Dress art expression dissolves adultism and mediates a town that thrives on the input of children. What has become clear is how as an all-male adults affair, Fancy Dress in Winneba served as one of the numerous institutions of society, acting as an enforcing arm of adult hegemony over town life and cultural identity. Through its performance, the adult population successfully managed to keep lines drawn between adults and children, adulthood and childhood, and administered a society that thrived on adult domination over children. Adult-designed and dominated Fancy Dress performances in Winneba tipped power in favour of adults for decades and, being unchallenged, etched the notion of adult superiority and child inferiority in the psyche of the town. Furthermore, through the performance of this artistic expression, adultism maintained its power as the authoritative definer of the adult-child power relation in Winneba: powerful adulthood in the centre and "invisible" and "muted" childhood in the peripheries. The second part of the 20th century, however, witnessed the dissolution of adult monopoly over the performance of the masquerade street drama and the beginnings of a wresting of control over the artistic culture article from adult domination in Winneba. Children, in spite of adultism, demanded to be part of Fancy Dress. Through child-led performances, adult-centeredness of the art and its influence over the town have diminished, resulting in an ongoing dismantling of adultism in the town's culture.

The performance of children in a spectacle and membership in an organised institution that was created and monopolised by adults, it appears is a hopeful sign that the traditional terrain of the culture of adultism is being gradually reconsidered and its relevance tested. The traditional cliché idea that "children are the leaders of tomorrow" has been challenged in Winneba, for it seems that the adults' attitude of yielding space to child maskers as a result of the demand of children to be part of the Fancy Dress, is an indication that some adults have thought or began to rethink that notion, and have seen that the persons in society called children can provide various leadership services in different ways in the African town today. It is sensitising people in community relationship to see the masquerade acts as an aspect of their collective culture which should be shared by both adults and children. As one elder and key member of the Tumus Fancy Dress Club suggested, it is a sign which shows that certain long-standing traditions from early generations that do not benefit subsequent generations and contemporary eras cultural should be deemed detrimental to social progress and should be done away with.[28] The democratisation of Fancy Dress is one example and it is in itself a teacher and inspirer which would make and is making the town to rethink and to consider the need to bring reforms to different aspects of the traditions of certain social relations and social institutions and norms.

Bibliography

Abbam, Anthony. Interview by authors. Winneba, January 23, 2016.

Afful, Opanyin Sam N.M. Interview by authors. Winneba, January 30, 2016.

Aidoo, Charles Kweku. Interview by authors. Winneba, January 30, 2016.

Amissah, Samuel Ofori. "The Masquerade Tradition at Winneba." Diploma of Art Education Long Essay. Institute of Education. University of Cape Coast, 1988.

---

[28] Personal interview with Opanyin Sam N.M. Afful, Winneba, 30 January 2016.

Ampene, Kwame. *History of the Guan-Speaking Peoples of Ghana.* Philadelphia, Penn: StarSpirit, 2011.

Baidoo, Joseph. Interview by authors. Winneba, January 30, 2016.

Bary, Mohammed. Interview by authors. Winneba, January 30, 2016.

Beckworth, Carol, and Angela Fisher, *African Ceremonies.* Vol.1. New York: Harry N. Abrams, Inc. 1999.

Bettelheim, Judith. "Afro-Jamaican Junkanoo Festival: Playing the Forces and Operating the Cloth." PhD Dissertation. Yale University, 1979.

Bettelheim, Judith. "Jonkonoo and other Christmas Masquerades." In *Caribbean Festival Arts: Each and Every Bit of Difference,* edited by John Nunley and Judith Bettelheim. Seattle: St. Louis Museum and University of Washington Press, 1988. 39-83.

Brown, EJP. *Gold Coast and Asianti Reader.* Bk. I. London, 1929.

Cole, Herbert, and Doran Ross. *The Arts of Ghana.* California: University of California, 1977.

Composite Budget of the Effutu Municipal Assembly for 2014 Fiscal Year. Central Region: Effutu Municipal Assembly, 2014.

Dampson, Ezekiel. Interview by authors. Winneba, January 30, 2016.

Dispatch No. 119 of 20 April, 1880, from Ussher to Hicks Beach, and Minuted on by Kimberly. CO/96/130. Cited in David Kimble *A Political History of Ghana: The Rise of Gold Coast Nationalism 1850-1928.* Oxford: Clarendon, 1963.

Gold Coast Express. 28 September 1897. Cited in David Kimble, *A Political History of Ghana: The Rise of Gold Coast Nationalism 1850-1928.* Oxford: Clarendon, 1963.

Kedjanyi, John. "Masquerade Societies in Ghana." *Research Review* 3 (2), (1967): 51-57.

Kimble, David. *A Political History of Ghana: The Rise of Gold Coast Nationalism 1850-1928.* Oxford: Clarendon, 1963.

Kittoe, William Ebo. Interview by authors. Winneba, January 30, 2016.

Micots, Courtney. "Carnival in Ghana: Fancy Dress Street Parades and Competition." *African Arts* 47 (1), (2014): 30-41. doi:10.1162/AFAR_a_00120.

Micots, Courtney. "Fancy Dress: African Masquerade in Coastal Ghana." In *Berg Encyclopaedia of World Dress and Fashion,* edited by Joanne B. Eicher and Doran H. Ross. Vol 1 – Africa. Oxford: Berg Publishers. 2010. http://dx.doi.org/10.2752/BEWDF/EDch1511.

Nicholls, Robert Wyndham. *The Jumbies' Playing Ground: Old World Influence on Afro-Creole Masquerades in the Eastern Caribbean.* Mississippi: University of Mississippi Press, 2012.

Nicklin, Keith and Jill Salmons. "Hippies of Elmina." *African Arts* 38 (2), (2005): 60-95.

Ottenberg, Simon, and David A. Binkley. *Playful Performers: African Children's Masquerades.* New Brunswick, N.J: Transaction Publishers, 2006.

Sarpong, Awo, and De-Valera N.Y.M. Botchway. "Freaks in Procession? "The Fancy Dress Masquerade as Haven for Negotiating Eccentricity During Childhood. A Study of Child Masqueraders in Cape Coast, Ghana." In *Misfit*

Children: An Inquiry into Childhood Belongings, edited by Markus P.J. Bohlmann. Lanham, Maryland: Lexington Books (Rowman and Littlefield), 2017. 175-195.

Sarpong, Henrietta. "The Humanistic Values of the Dance in the Akan Society." Master Thesis. University of Science and Technology, Kumasi. 1990.

Walker, Charles. Interview by authors. Winneba, January 23, 2016.

Yaya, Alhaji. Interview by authors. Winneba, January 30, 2016.

Yaya, Alhassan. Interview by authors. Winneba, January 30, 2016.

Chapter 10

Mending the Broken Fences: A Study of the Socialized and De-socialized Child in Laye's *The African Child* and Kourouma's *Allah Is Not Obliged*

Mawuloe Koffi Kodah

Introduction

The presence of child-narrators in a narrative fiction cuts across cultural boundaries. Since the narrative fiction is a reflection of a society, its values and practices, its people and their way of life, and their relationship with nature, the child who is an integral part of the society cannot be denied existence in it. Considering the fact that existence is inextricably linked to thinking, as postulated in Descartes's philosophical axiom "I think, therefore I am"[1] which heralded the advent of Enlightenment in Western societies, some writers have given children a voice as narrators in their textual universe. Works such as Romain Gary's *The Life Before Us*[2], Jonathan Safran Foer's *Extremely Loud and Incredibly Close*[3], Ferdinand Oyono's *The Houseboy*[4], Mongo Beti's *Poor Christ of Bomba*[5], Camara Laye's *The African Child* and Ahmadou Kourouma's *Allah Is Not Obliged*, among many others, have child-narrators admirably demonstrating incredible wisdom and wit in adult literary worlds, in spite of their extremely young age. Literary authors' choice of child-narrators as the main voice in their textual universe depends on the signifi-

---

[1] R. Descartes, *Discourse on the Method of Rightly Conducting the Reason, and Seeking Truth in the Sciences*, (Cambridge: Cambridge University Press, 1637), 14 – 20.
[2] R. Gary, *The Life Before Us*, (New York: New Directions Books, 1978).
[3] J. Safran Foer, *Extremely Loud and Incredibly Close*, (London: Penguin Books, 2000).
[4] F. Oyono, *The Houseboy*, (London: Heinemann, 1956).
[5] M. Beti, *The Poor Christ of Bomba*, Digitized by RevSocialist for Socialist Stories, (1956), www.socialiststories.com/liberate/The Poor Christ of Bomba – Mongo Beti.pdf. Accessed on 2 November, 2017.

cance of the statement they want to make through their works, and also the aspect of society they want to mirror through such narrators.

There is no gainsaying that the child in every human society is defined primarily by two main processes as established by psychologists. These are "nature" and "nurture". "Nature Versus Nurture" concept was coined by the English polymath, Sir Francis Galton in 1859. In the words of L.D. Fernald and P.S. Fernald (2004), "Each of us is both the product of heredity and environment..."[6]. According to Galton (1875), "Nature is all that a man brings with himself into the world; nurture is every influence from without that affects him after his birth".[7] Whereas "nature" refers to the inborn and predetermined physical and biological characteristics of a being, "nurture" is the sum-total of all the external factors that contribute to the socialization of a being into the human society. "Nurture" is characterized by the environment, the norms and practices of a society, its values, rules and regulations, secular and religious institutions associated with child upbringing and training. The nature versus nurture debate within psychology is concerned with the extent to which particular aspects of behaviour are a product of either inherited (i.e., genetic) or acquired (i.e., learned) characteristics.

The quality, effectiveness and efficiency of nurturing in the life of a child determine the quality, effectiveness and efficacy of an adult. This reflection finds expression in the lives of the two authorial narrators, Camara and Birahima, in *The African Child* and *Allah Is Not Obliged* respectively. It should be noted that Laye's story is an adult narrator's reminiscence of his glorious childhood upbringing as a socialized-child. In the case of Kourouma, the authorial narrator is still a child recounting his horrendous and inglorious upbringing and life experiences as a de-socialized child.

This paper critically examines and compares the processes of "nurturing" which produced a socialized and responsible child in Laye's *The African Child,* and those that churned out a de-socialized, insolent, blood-thirsty, callous and murderous child in Kourouma's *Allah Is Not Obliged.* "Mending the broken fences" seeks to make a case for the significance of the African communal value-systems deployed in nurturing Laye's authorial narrator into his replica, as a successful adult, while drawing attention to how senseless and selfish adult behaviour produces a de-socialized child whose characteris-

---

[6] L. D. Fernald and P. S. Fernald, *Munn's Introduction to Psychology,* (India: A.I.T.B.S. Publishers & Distributors,2004) 74.

[7] F. Galton, *English Men of Science: Their Nature and Nurture,* (New York: D. Appleton and Company, 1875). 9.

tics deny Kourouma's text the designation of an autobiography. The study is posited within the theoretical framework of socio-critique. It reflects on the interplay between socio-cultural values and institution, and literary artistry through textual data collected from the two narrative texts. At this point, it is useful to give a background of the stories in the two narrative texts which are the primary sources of data for the study.

The African Child and Allah Is Not Obliged

The African Child is Laye's very first narrative text published in French as "*L'Enfant noir*" in 1953. It was reproduced in 1954.[8] The story in this narrative text is a vivid account of the author's own childhood experiences as he gets socialized into a prestigious African family, community and the larger society. Set in a hospitable family and communal home-setting from the rural area to the city in Guinea, and to Argenteuil in France, the story of Camara is, without doubt, inclined towards the tenets of Negritude[9] persuasion as he exaggeratedly paints a paradise-like environment within which the characters are in perfect harmony with nature while reflecting a great sense of belongingness and well-being. The story depicts the involving role of the entire community in the upbringing of a child, believing that, much as the child belongs to its immediate parents – biological father and mother – it is first and foremost the bona fide resource and asset of the entire community. What that child becomes has significant implications, not only for the biological parents but also for the entire community. In this regard, the entire community must ensure that the child is appropriately nurtured into a responsible adult who can positively contribute to the welfare and the sustainable development of the community. This gives credence to an African wise saying that "A cock belongs to one person, but the entire community wakes up at its crows". The authorial narrator successfully grows through the various phases of African child-socialization processes from the parental home in the town of Kouroussa, through the ancestral home in the village of Tindican, through formal European school-type education and training in Conakry, and later at Argenteuil in

---

[8] Published in 1953, it received the Charles Veillon literary prize in 1954. It was reproduced in 1954. In this paper, references however will be made to the following edition: Camara Laye, *L'Enfant Noir*, (Paris: Librairie Plon, 1954) and the translated English versions of the work.

[9] Negritude is a literary movement formed by Léon Damas, Aimé César and Léopold Sédar Senghor to project the sum-total of African traditional and cultural values. These literary luminaries used poetry as a medium of literary expression to project the beauty and pride of "Blackness" as a counter discourse to the long-held Western disrespect and repudiation of "Blackness" as a racial and cultural category.

France to become a worthy citizen of his country Guinea, when it gained its independence from French colonialists in 1958.

Kourouma's *Allah Is Not Obliged*, first published in French as *"Allah n'est pas obligé"* in 2000,[10] but translated in 2006,[11] can be read as a denunciative satirical narrative text built around an authorial child-narrator, Birahima, who has no resemblance with the real author. The story is, therefore, an elaborate account of lived-experiences of the authorial child-narrator from a sordid early life in a broken-home, through early introduction to Western formal school education, streetism, attempted-nurturing by a magnanimous African traditional priest as a step-son, his journey to Liberia to live with an aunt at the death of his mother, and his life as a child-soldier trapped in the confluence of a senseless fratricidal civil war engendered by selfish and inconsequential adults. Within the dysfunctional socio-cultural, economic and political setting evoked in the preceding sentences, Birahima passes for a de-socialized child, untutored and fashioned within the framework of the disorder associated with the broken social value-fences in Kourouma's *Allah Is Not Obliged*. The narrative is set partly in Côte d'Ivoire, and mainly in Liberia and Sierra Leone. It is a mixture of fiction and historically factual events associated with the Liberian and Sierra Leonean civil wars of the 1990s and beyond. Though Birahima claims no resemblance to Kourouma, the author of the narrative text, it is obvious that the text by its title *"Allah Is Not Obliged"* is evocative of Kourouma's aversion for irrational religious practices and the ungodly exploitation of the vulnerability of the poor and needy in the human society. Considering the despicable and contemptuous nature of the depreciative descriptive used in painting and evoking socio-cultural and religious norms and practices in Kourouma's text, it would not be far-fetched to consider it as an anti-negritude diatribe which frowns on the exaggerated servile attempts to project everything African as glamorous and noteworthy in the spirit of Negritude.

Going forward, the significance of the following concepts as factors of child socialization and de-socialization in the narratives will be examined: the home-setting, processes of socialization, and authorial narrative voice.

---

[10] Ahmadou Kourouma, *Allah n'est pas obligé*, (Paris: Seuil, 2000).
[11] Ahmadou Kourouma, *Allah is not obliged*, trans., F. Wynne, (London: Vintage Books, 2006).

Significance of the Home Space in Child Socialization and De-socialization

A home refers to a domicile or residential space which serves as a dwelling-place for an individual, a group of individuals, and a family. As a permanent or semi-permanent residence, the home space provides shelter, protection from harm, and comfort for its occupants. Beyond the physical structures, the home is characterized by the nature, hospitality, love and human warmth associated with the indwellers. In the case of the two stories, the home-setting expands beyond the four corners of a single physical structure. It encompasses the entire space available for the socialization of the characters, especially the narrators. The home-setting undoubtedly has a significant impact on the socialization and de-socialization processes of the narrators in the two texts.

The very first statements of Laye's narrator in the opening paragraph of the narrative present a home-setting defined by the father's hut, the mother and the workshop and customers:

> I was a little boy playing round my father's hut. How old[?] ...[F]ive, maybe six years old. My mother was in the workshop with my father, I could just hear their familiar voices and the ... customers.[12]

The presence of the father and mother defines the initial characteristics of a home for the security of a child. The reference to "the customers" begins the expansion of the home-setting here to the community dimension. That the child is a communal asset, begins to take shape in the subsequent paragraphs as Damany, one of the apprentices of the narrator's father comes out of the workshop to save the narrator, then a child, from a possible snake bite on the family compound whilst both parents were in the workshop. Remembering that episode of his childhood in his narration, the narrator intimates how he stopped playing when he found a snake slithering around his family's hut:

> I had ... a reed ...I thrust it into the reptile's mouth...and the snake's jaws were terribly close to my fingers. I was laughing...at that moment, Damany,... the apprentice shouted to my father, and ... I felt myself lifted ...: safe in the arms of one of my father's friends![13]

---

[12] C. Laye, *The African Child,*(Glasgow: Fontana Books, 1954), 11.
[13] C. Laye, *The Black Child,* (Glasgow: Fontana/Collins, 1954). 11.

The significance of the involvement of the entire community in securing the child is once more highlighted in the role the friend of the narrator's father plays in rescuing him from the danger of snakebite: "The apprentice shouted to my father, and almost at once I felt myself lifted off my feet: I was safe in the arms of one of my father's friends!" It is vividly clear from the aforecited portions from Laye's text that the narrator as a child is secured within a social fence provided by the presence of his father and mother, his father's customers and friends, and the apprentices. This home-setting serves as a positive nurturing milieu for his socialization into a responsible adult.

Contrary to this positive outlook of the home-setting and its impact on the growing child in Laye's text, Kourouma's child-narrator in *Allah Is Not Obliged* makes no reference to a home-setting. At the very onset of his narrative, he comes out as a de-socialized child, insolent and uncouth. His language is full of indecent words and expressions that project him as a fenceless and rascal self-made child. He refers to his story as "my bullshit story": "The full, final and completely complete title of my *bullshit story* is: *Allah is not obliged to be fair about all the things he does here on earth.*"[14] In a six-point self-introduction to establish his authorship of the story, Kourouma's child-soldier-narrator, Birahima defines himself as a "little nigger" per the rules of French colonial prejudice. He declares himself so because he "can't talk French for shit".

> [O]ne ... I'm a little nigger ... [B]e a grown-up, or old ... Arab, or Chinese, or white, or Russian – or even American – if you talk bad French, it's called *parler petit nègre* – little nigger talking – ... you a little nigger too ... [R]ules of French for you.[15]

Furthermore, Birahima states his identity as a school dropout. This explains why he is a little nigger by virtue of speaking bad French. He says: "Number two ... I didn't get very far at school; I gave up in my third year in primary school. I chucked it because everyone says education's not worth an old grandmother's fart anymore."[16] Using a parenthetical construct, Birahima explains further what is meant by education being "not worth an old grandmother's fart".

> In Black Nigger African Native talk, when a thing isn't worth much we say it's an old grandmother's fart, on account of how a fart from a

---

14 Kourouma, *Allah Is Not Obliged*, 1.
15 Ibid.
16 Ibid., 1-2.

fucked-up old granny doesn't hardly make any noise and it doesn't even smell really bad.[17]

Birahima again reaffirms his identity as a de-socialized child, calling himself a "bastard" who is disrespectful, vulgar in speech and "rude as goat's beard" in the third part of his self-introduction. He affirms that he swears a lot but not like what he calls "the civilised Black Nigger African Natives in their nice suits" who "say fuck! shit! bitch!". Rather, he declares that he swears in Malinké because he is from the Malinké ethnic group, which he, being uneducated, refers to as a "tribe" of "Black Nigger African Savages and there's a lot of us in the north of Cote d'Ivoire and Guinea, and … in other corrupt fucked-up banana republics like Gambia, Sierra Leone and up in Senegal".[18] Thus, he announces that he swears with "words like *faforo!* (my father's cock – your father's or somebody's father's), *gnamokodé!* (bastard), [and] *walahé!* (I swear by Allah). [19]

Kourouma's child-narrator is indeed insolent and unassumingly abusive. In his own concluding words of his six points self-introduction, he states: "So that's me – six points, no more no less, with my cheeky foul-mouthed attitude thrown in for good treasure […] So that's me, and it's not an edifying spectacle."[20]

Contrary to Laye's narrator, he makes no reference to any home, parents or friends up to this point. It is therefore difficult to even link him to any location at the start of the narrative. The first time Birahima mentions his mother is in the second paragraph on page 4 of the text. This is the last point of his six-point self-introduction. He states: "Number six … Don't go thinking that I'm some cute kid, 'cos I'm not. I'm cursed because I did bad things to my *maman.*"[21]

Whereas at the mention of "mother" in the very beginning, Laye's story is associated with the narrator's admiration and appreciation for his mother, Kourouma's Birahima mentions his mother in connection with his de-socialized status as a cursed ugly child.

According to Black Nigger African Native customs, if your mother is angry with you and she dies with all that anger in her heart, then she

---

[17] Ibid., 2.
[18] Ibid., 2-3
[19] Ibid.
[20] Ibid., 4-5.
[21] Ibid., 4.

curses you and you're cursed. And afterwards nothing ever goes right for you or anyone who knows you.[22]

Not only is Birahima not "some cute kid" owing to maternal curses, but also as a result of being haunted by the spirit of victims of his murderous adventures as a child-soldier. He explains that he is not "some cute kid" because he killed many innocent people in the war in Liberia and Sierra Leone; he did hard drugs to undertake such murderous activities and as a result he feels cursed because "*gnamas* of the innocent people I killed are stalking me, so my whole life and everything round me is fucked. *Gnamokodé!*"[23] He states that:

> (*Gnamas* is a complicated Black Nigger African Native word that I need to explain so French people can understand ... [I]t is the shadow of a person that remains after death ...an immanent malevolent force which stalks anyone who has killed an innocent victim.)[24]

Mothers' place in the lives of their children and their roles in caring for them and nurturing them into adulthood is affirmed in the two narratives. Human life begins in the mother and ends with her in most cases. The place and roles of mothers and mother-figures in the two narrative texts are quite significant. This is revealed in the lives of both narrators. As found in Birahima's lamentations in the above quotation, the conspicuous absence of a caring and loving mother from his life has contributed to his de-socialization as "not some cute kid".

In a sharp contrast to Birahima's inglorious status resulting from the marred relationship with his mother and the community through "the bad things he did" in *Allah Is Not Obliged*, Laye's narrator is an epitome of a positively socialized child within an elaborate social fence engineered primarily by a mother. Laye's narrator evokes the positive role of his caring and loving mother in a eulogistic poem: *To My Mother*, at the opening of his narrative. He refers to his mother as "Black woman, [a] woman of Africa ... the fields ... rivers ... great river banks" who gave him life and understanding. This woman, who was with him in his happy and sad moments as a child, he confesses he continues to think about. He, with admiration, recalls her mother's proud lineage to a family of blacksmiths and goldsmiths; and with nostalgic memories about the care that his mother gave him, he, while thanking her, yearns for her

---

[22] Ibid.
[23] Ibid., 4.
[24] Ibid.

loving warmth again, to be a little child beside you …

Black woman, woman of Africa, O my mother, let me thank you; thank you for all that you have done for me, your son, who though so far away, is still so close to you! [25]

The centrality of the role of the mother of Laye's narrator is forcefully highlighted in this poem. Indeed, this poem is the appreciative words of the narrator as he casts his mind back to reconstruct his glorious childhood experiences with the caring and loving mother in an orderly home-setting. This poem sets the harmonized family home-setting which provides a qualitative socialization for Camara, Laye's child-narrator. Sadly, this cannot be said about Kourouma's child-narrator in *Allah Is Not Obliged*.

Processes of African Child Socialization

The African Child resembles a statement on child socialization in an African social setting. The narrator as a child is raised at three different levels – parental, extended-family and community. He highlights the significant roles of his biological parents in the family concession. In doing so, the involvement of the community in his socialization is also evoked immediately. This is vividly captured in the opening paragraph[26] in Chapter One of the narrative, where he mentions his "father's hut" as a significant landmark in his upbringing. The narrator's mention of his "father's hut" brings to mind the role of the father as the provider of shelter, a sign of protection, of paternal stronghold and fortress within which the child is secure. It also gives the child a sense of pride in the architecture and the dexterity of his father as a responsible head of a functioning family in a harmonious community.

In *Allah Is Not Obliged*, Birahima abhors the mother's hut which has no sense of pride for him. Memories of this hut are bitter ones.

Well, the first thing inside me or in my mind when I think about maman's hut is the fire, the glow of the embers, the flicker of flame. I don't know how many months old I was when I grilled my arm.[27]

---

[25] Laye, *The Black Child*, 5.
[26] Ibid., 11.
[27] Kourouma, *Allah Is Not Obliged*, 6.

Besides this harrowing reminiscence, Birahima's repulsion for his mother's hut, despite Balla's admonishing that "no kid ever leaves his mother's hut because her farts stink",[28] is ironically stated in the following lines:

> Maman's smells never bothered me. The hut was full of all kinds of stink. Farts, shit, piss, ...infected ulcer, ... smoke, and the smells of Balla the healer...I was surrounded by these smells...a natural habitat ... every animal has one; maman's hut with her smells was my natural habitat.[29]

Birahima refers to his step-father Balla's hut too with mixed-feelings considering the fact that "Balla was a *kaffir* – that's what you call someone who refuses to believe in Islam and keeps his gris-gris."[30] Balla was therefore repulsed by the villagers who profess Islam, because he "was the only *kaffir* in the village."[31] All the villagers seemed to fear him. As a result of this,

> No one in the village was allowed near Balla's hut, but actually at night everyone went to his hut. Some even went during the day, because Balla practiced sorcery, native medicine, magic and a million of other extravagant customs ('extravagant' means 'unrestrained or recklessly wasteful')[32]

In spite of this, Birahima is grateful to have been tutored by Balla at a point in time. He confesses: "All the stuff I bullshit about ('bullshit' means 'to say stupid things'), I learned from Balla. A man should always thank the shea tree for the fruits gathered from beneath its branches. I will always be grateful to Balla. *Faforo! Gnamokodé!*"[33] Considering the unwholesome nature of the "shea fruits" gathered from Balla, Birahima's statement in this quotation is nothing but a despicable irony to depict the deconstructed socio-cultural setting he finds himself in as a child.

Unlike Camara Laye who is positively influenced by all the trustworthy adults around him in his story in *The African Child*, Birahima is suspicious of the insincerity of the adults' world in which he lives in *Allah Is Not Obliged*.

---

[28] Ibid.,10.
[29] Ibid., 10-11.
[30] Ibid., 8.
[31] Ibid.,
[32] Ibid.,
[33] Ibid., 8-9.

He is therefore very critical of their behaviour and their institutions. He believes nothing of theirs as he ridicules them and their "devalued values" through hyperbole, sarcasm, and denunciative irony. All the adults around him are dubious, corrupt, mischievous, and murderous. From the grandmother, Balla, the Imam[34] of the village, to Yacouba-alias-Tiécoura,[35] Sekou[36] the marabout, and Colonel Papa le Bon,[37] all who form the human capital around Birahima are fake. They are behind the dysfunctional state of the textual universe in which Birahima is. They contribute to his de-socialization. All these characters are good examples of irresponsible and selfish adults whose actions and inactions have led to the corruption and de-socialization of the unsuspecting youth in Kourouma's *Allah Is Not Obliged*. Table 10.1 which I have constructed below recapitulates the socialization stages of the narrators in the two narrative texts under study.

Table 10.1. Socialization stages of the narrators in the two narrative texts under study.

	The African Child	Page	*Allah Is Not Obliged*	Page
Birth	• The first born and son of parents	19	• The third child and first son of parents	24
Parenthood	• Family and friends ensure child's safety (from being bitten by a snake) • Mother ensures that he has enough to eat • Father fights headmaster over bullying of his son	1 14 76	• Lived with mother and grandmother and later step-father • Lived in the streets • Self/auto parenting • Growth by trial and error method • Imitation of irresponsible adults	5 23 20 20 123

---

[34] Kourouma, *Allah Is Not Obliged,* 24.

[35] Ibid., 34.

[36] Ibid., 35.

[37] Ibid., 54.

Informal education (African communal Socialization)	• First initiation on the family totem by his father • Initiation on communal farming activities during the time of harvest • Initiation to overcome fear during the ceremony of the lions • Initiation to manhood/circumcision • Consideration for other members of society as taught by Uncle Lansana	17 44 83 103 52	• Goes through initiation rites just to travel to Liberia • Writes-off lessons learnt during initiation as unimportant • Picks up inordinate attitudes and mannerisms from acquaintances • Has no yardstick of decorum with which to measure a behaviour to be adopted	29 30
Formal education (Western Socialization)	• Islamic school • French school • Technical College in Conakry • Argenteuil (France)	63 63 113	• Ended in the third year of primary school	1
Agents of socialization	• Both parents • Grandmother • Uncles (maternal and paternal) • Aunties • School authorities • Community elders • Family friends		• Mother • Grandmother • Step-father (Balla) • Marabout (Yacouba) • Colonel Papa le Bon • Adult soldiers • Warlords	
Implications of socialized child	• Respect for societal customs and practices • Desire for communal living and interdependence • Being able to adapt to alien environment without losing touch with indigenous beliefs and values		• Disregard for societal customs and practices • Preference for individualistic tendencies and independence • Out of touch/alienation from indigenous beliefs and values	

Credit: Author, Mawuloe Koffi Kodah, 2017.

As captured in the table above, the narrators' character as shown in the texts is shaped by the presence or absence of the identified stages of socialization. In *The African Child*, these stages retain their inherent values that make it relevant to sustainable social engineering. In *Allah Is Not Obliged*, on the contrary, there is a complete devaluation and degeneration of the socio-cultural institutions required for the security and safety of children as they grow. Therefore, Birahima is exposed to the vagary of the socio-cultural "weather" of degeneration which turns him into a renegade, fearless and callous child-soldier, as a de-socialized poor child. Indeed, his childhood has been truncated and he is forced into a precocious adulthood of greed and savagery of civil war in Liberia and Sierra Leone. How do these socio-cultural experiences impact the authorial perspectives of the two narrators in their textual universe? The last segment of the paper will seek to answer this question under the sub-heading "Authorial Narrative Voice".

Authorial Narrative Voice

The authorial narrative voice is that of the owner of the narrative in the narrative text. It is articulated within the framework of "a set of five criteria drawn from a study of the practice of a corporation of West African griots, historians and literary artists in the tradition of Mali, as represented in Djibril Tamsir Niane's translation of the 13th-century epic Sundiata."[38] These criteria are as follows: an affirmation of "the author's identity and craft credential; the author's subject; the author's purpose; the author's audience; and the author's method".[39] In a substantive justification of the validity of these criteria, Armah states that they are not "arbitrary" nor "exocentric", rather, they are:

> part of the professional code of competence governing the craft of griots in the esoteric tradition ... designed to ensure that persons who aspired to speak as explicators of African values first took the trouble to earn the right to do so, as craft initiates.[40]

The narrators in the two narrative texts reveal their identities as credible proprietors of their stories and the worldviews which they represent from the very onset in the texts. Whereas Laye's narrator's identity and craft credentials, subject, purpose, audience, and method are implicitly unveiled in the narrative discourse, Kourouma's child-narrator personally and explicitly discloses his authorial credentials in his six-point self-introduction. Laye's narrator introduces himself using the first-person personal pronoun "I" in the very opening sentence: "I was a little boy playing round my father's hut".[41] Without mentioning his name, the narrator maintains his anonymity as a first-person narrator identity through the combination of the first-person subject pronoun "I" and its corresponding possessive adjective "my" in noun phrases such as "my father's hut"; "My mother..."; "my whole attention..."; "my hand"; "my fingers"; "my feet"; "my father's friends" which are identifiable in the first

---

[38] Ayi Kwei Armah, *Remembering the Dismembered Continent. Seedtime Essays*, (Popenguine, Senegal: Per Ankh, The African Publishing Cooperative, 2010), 51.
[39] Ibid.
[40] Ibid., 51.
[41] Camara, *The African Child*, 11.

three paragraphs of the opening page of the text, page 11, to be precise. This identification establishes the autobiographical orientation of his story. In an autobiographical text, the authorial voice is identical to the presence of the author or writer in the narrative. This is the case of Laye's *The African Child* in which Laye recounts his own childhood experiences in a eulogistic fashion of African child socialization processes. Examining the new attitude towards tradition in French Africa in Laye's text, Jahnheinz Jahn says of him that "he did not consider his African childhood as something remote, primitive, something to be ashamed of."[42] In this spirit, the first-person narrator "I" in this text is equal to the author. The "I" in the narrative is the shadow image and a replica of Camara Laye himself. This committed "I" who is the owner and main character-narrator at the same time reveals the Negritude mood of the author and his text. "In this respect, Laye reflects the new affirmations of the negritude movement. He treats Africa with a tremendous affection. He does not mock his outgrown superstitions."[43] This, however, is not the case with Kourouma's authorial child-narrator in *Allah Is Not Obliged.*

Authorial narrative voice in Kourouma's text is however limited to the narrator in his own story and textual universe. Birahima is not, and can never be said to be the shadow image of Kourouma. Unlike Laye, the author, whose life is identical to that of the first-person narrator in *The African Child,* Kourouma has no record of partaking in "tribal warfare in Liberia and Sierra Leone" like Birahima has. There is, therefore, a kind of denunciative detachment from the character and personality of Birahima, the child-narrator. *Allah Is Not Obliged* can be conceived as the biography of Birahima, the child-soldier-narrator, as recorded and played by Kourouma, the writer. The authorial narrative voice here is that of an "intradiegetic" narrator recounting his own story in the writing of the author. In the opening paragraph, for instance, the narrator intimates: "The full, final and completely complete title of my bullshit story is: Allah is not obliged to be fair about all the things he does here on earth. Okay. Right. I better start explaining some stuff."[44] The highlighted first-person possessive determinant "my" and first-person subject pronoun "I" in the preceding quotation are in reference to the narrator who goes further to clarify his authorial identity and credentials in the subsequent paragraph[45].

[42] Jahnheinz Jahn, "Discussion on Camara Laye," *Black Orpheus,* 6, (1959), 35.
[43] Najaria Hurst Gray, *Introduction to the novels of Camara Laye,* (Montana: Scholar Works at University of Montana, 1970), 10. https://scholarworks.umt.edu/cgi/. Accessed on 18 October, 2018.
[44] Kourouma, *Allah Is Not Obliged,* 1.
[45] Ibid., 1.

Birahima, as self-identified in the above quotation is different from Kou-rouma, the writer of the story. In this situation, the writer is merely a recorder of the child-narrator's story told by himself. The text is, therefore, a kind of replay of Birahima's story in writing by Kourouma. In order to establish his full authorship of the story he is about to relate, Birahima goes further in the presentation of his full credentials in five additional points to mention in the second point of that self introduction that he dropped out of school in the third year of his primary education because he thought education had lost it true lustre and "not worth old grandmother's fart any more"; furthermore, he was disillusioned about the fact people had degrees but still faced unemployment problems in "some fucked-up French-speaking banana republic". However, he explains that his primary school education nevertheless puts him in the category of "what the Black Nigger African Natives called grilled on both sides" because he "knows a bit, but not enough". In that position of not being "an indigenous savage ...like the rest of the Black Nigger African Natives" one "can understand the civilised blacks and the *toubabs* (*a toubab* is a white person)" and be able to "work out what they're saying, except maybe English people and the American Blacks in Liberia." Nevertheless, he mentions that a "grilled on both sides" persons are handicapped because they

> don't know how to do geography or grammar or conjugation or long division or comprehension so you'll never get the easy money working as a civil servant in some fucked-up, crooked republic like Guinea, Côte d'Ivoire, etc.[46]

In the third point of his self-introduction, he talks about his character as a disrespectful, unclouth and rude person who was fond of swearing crudely in his mother tongue. [47]

Although Birahima claims in the previous point that his level of education does not put him in good stead to talk about geography, it is surprising to hear him talk with precision about the origin of the Malinkés in space across the West African region. This precision grounds his credential as a knowledgeable and credible author in the narrative.

In the fourth point, Birahima gives his family background and his identity as a de-socialized child, "a kid ... maybe ten, maybe twelve ... [who] talk too much" and has "been in Liberia and killed lots of guys with an AK-47 (we

---

[46] Ibid.,1-2.
[47] Ibid., 2.

called it a 'kalash') and got fucked-up on kanif and lots of hard drugs".[48] Consequently, he states: "Number four ... I suppose I should apologise for talking right at you like this ... Polite kids ... listen ... Talking is for old men ..., 'For as long as there's a head on your shoulders, you don't put your headdress on your knee.' That's village customs".[49] But he is quick to blatantly add that he does not "give two fucks about village customs ... any more"[50] because of his de-socialised personality.

To re-emphasize his subject, and define his audience while indicating his method, Birahima states further in his fifth point that he keeps four French dictionaries: "the *Larousse* and *Petit Robert*",...*Glossary of French Lexical Particularities in Black Africa*, and...the *Harrap's*", to aid him find and explain the right words to convey the story of his "fucked-up life" in French so that all sorts of people: "colonial *toubabs*, Black Nigger African Natives and anyone that can understand French" will be able "to read my bullshit".[51] Although he clarifies that *The Glossary of French Lexical Particularities in Black Africa* "explains African words to French *toubabs* from France" and the *Harrap's* explains "pidgin words to French people who don't know shit about pidgin",[52] he refuses to disclose the source of the dictionaries, "[b]ecause I haven't got time 'cos I don't want to get tied up in bullshit. That's why. *Faforo!*"[53]

Finally, Birahima unveils his identity as a social deviant living under maternal curses in the sixth point[54] of his humorous self-introduction as already cited earlier.

Birahima's personal profile as presented in his six-point self-introduction places him within a seeming Socratic prejudicial description of children which opined that children (we will say some children) "are now tyrants, not the servants of their households. They no longer rise when elders enter the room. They contradict their parents, chatter before company, gobble up dainties at the table, cross their legs, and tyrannize their teachers".[55] Such children, according to

---

[48] Ibid., 3.
[49] Ibid.
[50] Ibid.
[51] Ibid., 3-4.
[52] Ibid.
[53] Ibid.
[54] Ibid.
[55] A. Koth, "Socrates," Quotationsbook.com: http://quotationsbook.com/quote/44998/#ix zz1K9ef61bh. Accessed on 2 November 2017.

Socrates, "love luxury; they have bad manners, contempt for authority; they show disrespect for elders and love chatter in place of exercise".[56]

Birahima is a product of a dysfunctional society marked by broken-home, juvenile delinquency, unreliable system of education, irrational religious practices, civil strife, drug addiction, senseless homicide, corruption, sexual violence and child abuse. Though his family circumstances do not provide any luxury for him to love as a child, he evidently shows marks of the remaining Socratic characteristics of children in the afore-cited quotation. It is within the chattering framework that Birahima assumes his authorial authority in narrating his own story while displaying his arrogance and foul-mouthed attributes as a de-socialized child. To conclude his six-point authorial self-introduction, he says:

> So that's me – six points..., with my cheeky foul-mouthed attitude..., not an edifying spectacle. Anyway, now... I'm ...going to tell you the life story of my cursed, fucked-up life. Sit ...and listen...write everything down. *Allah is not obliged to be fair about everything he does. Faforo!* [57]

Birahima however, displays a great deal of witticism and makes thought-provoking statements that make him a procacious precocious child and project him into a kind of strange premature-adulthood. Indeed, some of these statements appear to articulate in a tacit manner Kourouma's ideological persuasions on the issues being exposed through his witty child-narrator's narrative. The child-narrator, just like Kourouma, presents a denunciative attitude towards irrational religious practices and human frustrations in the narrative. In what Mawuloe K. Kodah[58] calls "néo-négritude"[59] stance, Birahima rummages the socio-cultural and religious practices in his textual universe and exposes the irrationality embedded in such practices, while

---

[56] Ibid.

[57] Kourouma, *Allah Is Not Obliged,* 4-5.

[58] Mawuloe Koffi Kodah. "Ahmadou Kourouma: un romancier anti-négritude ou néo-négritude?," *Proceedings of the 9th Inter-University Conference on Coexistence of Languages in West Africa,* (Cape Coast: University of Cape Coast Press, 2015),237 -253.

[59] This concept is used by Mawuloe Koffi Kodah in a paper presented at the 9th Inter-University Conference on Coexistence of Languages in West Africa, held at University of Cape Coast, 12th-14th November, 2012. Néo-négritude refers to a literary orientation which seeks to proffer an objective assessment of African socio-cultural values so as to avoid a subjective promotion of these values as a counter-statement to West colonial discourse on Africa as a continent devoid of civilization and culture.

pointing out how detrimental they have become to the very survival of the characters in the text in their daily struggles in a dysfunctional society.

Conclusion

After examining Laye's narrator in *The African Child* as a socialized child vis-à-vis Kourouma's child-narrator in *Allah Is Not Obliged* as a de-socialized child, it is revealing to establish here that the social dimension of both narrators is intrinsically linked to the adult-engineered socio-cultural environment within which they are socialized. Whereas Laye's setting provides a paradise-like socio-cultural framework for a healthy nurturing of the child in *The African child*, Kourouma's child-narrator in *Allah Is Not Obliged* evolves in a hell-like setting marked by dysfunctional and discredited socio-cultural institutions and irrational practices. It is unthinkable for instance to hear Birahima at his age – ten or twelve – state that his dropping out of school is due to the fact that education has lost all its values and "was no more worth a grandmother's fart". This situation is the very opposite of what pertains to Laye's narrator. He is nurtured in a functional socio-cultural African communal setting which provides him with security, comfort, love and human warmth. The parental, family and community socio-cultural African socialization institutions, serving as a social fence, provide the spiritual, physical, intellectual and social needs of the child. This is significantly revealed in *The African Child*. This is, however, missing in *Allah Is Not Obliged*, owing to the broken socio-cultural fence. The broken fence has produced Birahima as a de-socialized child prone to violence and drugs. No wonder his story is an account of his "fucked-up life", whereas that of Laye's narrator is an account of a glorious African socialization of the child.

Notwithstanding the predominant use of hyperbole in both narrative texts, the message of valorisation of African customary child socialization systems and institutions is clearly established. The role of the mother and mother figures supported by the responsible father and father figures is key in defining the nature of the future adult. Both Laye and Kourouma appear to converge on this thesis. Laye extols the resilient and enduring character of African child socialization and value systems involving immediate parents, members of the extended family, and the community in its entirety in harmonized, caring and loving communal spirit. Such a setting abhors selfishness, unhealthy competitions, self-aggrandizement and the pursuit of inglorious ambitions which are the bane of conflicts and social strife akin to a dysfunctional community which produces de-socialized children and renegade adults.

Considering the positive impact of the socio-cultural African child-socialization systems and institutions on the healthy socialization of Camara Laye into a healthy and sound adult who sees the express need to codify reminiscences of his childhood experiences into a narrative text of autobiographical dimension, it is important to reexamine African socio-cultural values, so as to save what needs to be saved for the effective and efficient socialization of the African child. This call transcends the sordid and horrendous story of Birahima, the de-socialized child-soldier-narrator in Kourouma's *Allah Is Not Obliged*. The broken fences as depicted in Kourouma's text require express mending so as to ensure a sustainable socio-cultural development for contemporary African children in a fast globalizing and technologically driven world.

Bibliography

Armah, Ayi Kwei. *Remembering the Dismembered Continent. Seedtime Essays.* Popenguine, Senegal: Per Ankh, The African Publishing Cooperative, 2010.

Beti, M. *The Poor Christ of Bomba.* Digitized by RevSocialist for Socialist Stories, 1956. www.socialiststories.com/liberate/The Poor Christ of Bomba – Mongo Beti.pdf.

Descartes, R. *Discourse on the Method of Rightly Conducting the Reason, and Seeking Truth in the Sciences.* Cambridge: Cambridge University Press, 1637.

Fernald L. D., and P. S. Fernald. *Munn's Introduction to Psychology.* India: A.I.T.B.S. Publishers & Distributors, 2004.

Foer, J. Safran. *Extremely Loud and Incredibly Close.* London: Penguin Books, 2000.

Galton, F. *English Men of Science: Their Nature and Nurture.* New York: D. Appleton and Company, 1875.

Gary, R. *The Life Before Us.* New York: New Directions Books, 1978.

Gray, Najaria Hurst. *Introduction to the novels of Camara Laye.* Montana: Scholar Works at University of Montana. 1970. 10. https://scholarworks.umt.edu/cgi/.

Jahn, Jahnheinz. "Discussion on Camara Laye." *Black Orpheus*, 6, (1959): 35-39.

Kodah, Mawuloe Koffi. "Ahmadou Kourouma: un romancier anti-négritude ou néo-négritude?." *Proceedings of the 9th Inter-University Conference on Coexistence of Languages in West Africa.* Cape Coast: University of Cape Coast Press, 2015. 237-253.

Koth, A. "Socrates." Quotationsbook.com. http://quotationsbook.com/quote/44998/#ixzz1K9ef61bh.

Kourouma, Ahmadou. *Allah is not obliged.* Translated by F. Wynne. London: Vintage Books, 2006.

Kourouma, Ahmadou. *Allah n'est pas oblige.* Paris: Seuil, 2000.

Laye, Camara. *L'Enfant Noir.* Paris: Librairie Plon, 1954.

Laye, Camara. *The African Child.* Glasgow: Fontana Books, 1954.

Laye, Camara. *The Black Child.* Glasgow: Fontana/Collins, 1954.

Oyono, F. *The Houseboy.* London: Heinemann, 1956.

Epilogue

Charles Quist-Adade

Africa is the second largest continent but has the largest youth population in the world, and children make up a significant percentage of that demography. Yet, the "childhood condition" in Africa has received little critical attention from academic research. *New Perspectives on African Childhood: Constructions, Histories, Representations and Understandings* provides a timely and interesting focus on the time and activities, visions and aspirations, fears, triumphs, challenges, and worldviews of children in Africa as they live and journey through life, from their birthdays up to the threshold of crossing over into adulthood. Extant studies have largely been on children, not their childhoods. Additionally, the exploration of the life of children in Africa has mostly treated children as victims caught up in war, famine and refugee crises: distressed children, hungry children, exploited and victimised, needy, diseased, or children living in the shadows of failed democracies and states.

Unfortunately, and myopically, the allure and trap of sensationalism often lurk in the few studies that focus on Africa's children. They tend to follow the formula followed by corporate media built on the all too familiar mantras: "When it bleeds, it leads" and "When a dog bites a man, it's no news. But when a man bites a dog, that's news!" The script is all too common and tragically so: "Naked, emaciated children with protruding eyes, flies feasting in the gaping mouths; frail, half-clad, barefoot mothers barely able to look after their dying children. And a Westerner, well-fed, rosy-cheeked, well-dressed and apparently driven by compassion, helping out the poor African victims of one of Africa's many scourges — AIDS, famine or drought."[1] Furthermore, a good number of other such studies that purport to centre on the child in the African context are appendages to studies that focus on other aspects of society and the world of the adult.

This anthology, thus, attempts to remove this lacuna. It does so by piecing together a complex narrative that highlights both the seamy and brighter sides of the "African childhood story" and presents the African child as "a

---

[1] Charles Quist-Adade and Anita van Wyk, "The Role of NGOs in Canada and the USA in the Transformation of the Socio-Cultural Structures in Africa," *Africa Development / Afrique et Développement* 32 (2), (2007): 66-96.

captain of the ship of destiny, not merely as a victim of circumstances." By so doing, the anthology addresses one of the shortcomings of extant research in Childhood Studies in Africa by crafting a narrative that accounts for the intersection of structure and agency.

However, this volume has its limitations too. Some areas of African childhood studies are unexplored, including the areas of childhoods constructed around given names, the experience of coming to a family, sexual identification and confrontations with sex; childhoods constructed around secret societies and forbidden associations; as well as different conceptions of childhood, a diversity of aspects and ramifications of childhood, from purely African cosmological and ethnological points of view.

New Perspectives on African Childhood: Constructions, Histories, Representations and Understandings has accomplished two goals: (1) it has taken a diversion from the traditional examination of the child solely, to the exploration and rationalisation of childhood in Africa, congregating composite analyses and interpretations and stories and case studies about various aspects of childhood in Africa by scholars who focus on African society, culture, education and history; (2) it has provided a lucid lesson on the socio-cultural and historical construction of childhood in Africa.

It is invidious to make comparisons, especially when it comes to culturally-bound practices, but the childhood experiences, practices and ideas described and analysed in the volume are comparable to those in societies in the Global South. The volume, therefore, provides a useful basis for comparative study for scholars and researchers of childhood not only in the Global South, but also their colleagues in the Global North. Childhood has increasingly become a very fertile area of scholarly inquiry and this volume is a testament to this fact. *New Perspectives on African Childhood: Constructions, Histories, Representations and Understandings* provides new lenses through which childhood, as experienced by children in Africa, can be viewed. It offers the reader a unique access to divergent, new stories and narratives, as well as emergent discourses of experiences of childhood. The authors of the volume have challenged some of the fixed conclusions and assumptions that have been taken for granted, re-examined passed on and received views about childhood as experienced by the African child, and replaced inappropriate external frames of viewing childhood in Africa with African-derived ones. Moreover, they supply insights for shaping new and contemporary understandings, policies and praxis for engaging with Africa's children, to support their growth, improvement and wellness.

The goal is not only to debunk the Eurocentric underpinnings of inquiry into aspects of childhood, such as childhood belongings and the cultures of childhood in the Global North of Europe and North America, but present new, more nuanced and complex analyses. The authors do not shy away from the sordid practices and experiences of the "childhood condition" in Africa. They weave a complex account juxtaposing excesses and abuses and sublime and benign practices and ideologies of childhood in Africa.

New Perspectives on African Childhood: Constructions, Histories, Representations, and Understandings adds to the stock of knowledge of Childhood Studies. It does so by setting the parameters and socio-scientific theoretical and preliminary empirical grounding for scholars from Africa and the international community to build on and further interrogate and fashion and share alternative viewpoints, ideas and perspectives about the lived experiences of African children and childhood in Africa. Additionally, the volume provides a chief conceptualizing point and intellectual and epistemological fodder for Childhood Studies scholars and researchers to renew, rethink, correct and even overturn traditional, fixed and conventional understandings and "wisdom" regarding childhood in Africa.

It is a truism, if trite and threadbare, that children are the future of any society. They are also society's valued untapped and fertile asset. Thus, the best investment of a society is that in children. This volume is premised on these truisms. It sheds the spotlight on African children and lays the groundwork for further research and a new emphasis on an area that still requires serious academic attention. We posit that all socio-scientific research must begin with the childhood condition. By privileging Childhood Studies, we arm ourselves with the knowledge and tools for the exploration of the life-cycle, just as learning to walk begins with the proverbial baby steps. *New Perspectives on African Childhood: Constructions, Histories, Representations, and Understandings* is, we are convinced, a firm "baby step" in the exciting, but a woefully under-studied area of socio-scientific study—Childhood Studies in Africa.

Work Cited

Quist-Adade, Charles, and Anita van Wyk. "The Role of NGOs in Canada and the USA in the Transformation of the Socio-Cultural Structures in Africa." *Africa Development / Afrique et Développement* 32 (2), (2007):66-96.

About the Editors and Contributors

Editors

De-Valera N.Y.M. Botchway (PhD) is an Associate Professor of History (Africa and the African Diaspora) at the University of Cape Coast (UCC), Ghana. His interdisciplinary researches and teaching expertise converge within the social and cultural history of Africa and the African and global historic and cultural exchanges and experiences. He has interest in the history of Black Religious and Cultural Nationalism(s), West Africa, African Indigenous Knowledge Systems, Sports (Boxing) in Ghana, Children in Popular Culture, World Civilisations, Regionalism and Integration in Africa, and Africans in Dispersion. He was a Fellow of the Centre of African Studies, University of Cambridge, England (2006-2007), a Visiting Scholar at the University of South Florida (2010), Exchange Faculty at Grand Valley State University, Michigan (2012), and received the AHP Fellowship award (2013/2014) from the American Council of Learned Societies, and a postdoctoral experience at the University of the Western Cape, South Africa. He edits three journals—*Drumspeak, Asemka* and *Abibisem*—in UCC, and belongs to the Historical Society of Ghana. He has authored books and several articles in different refereed journals and books. He co-authored "Freaks in Procession? Fancy Dress Masquerade as a Haven for Negotiating Eccentricity during Childhood. A study of child masqueraders in Cape Coast, in *Misfit Children: An Enquiry into Childhood Belongings,* (Lexington Books, 2017) and co-edited the new book *Africa and the First World War: Remembrance, Memories and Representations after 100 Years,* (Cambridge Scholars Publishing, 2018).

Awo Sarpong (PhD) is an early career academic and a lecturer at the Department of Basic Education, at the University of Cape Coast, Ghana, where she teaches courses that draw on her research in Art Education and Childhood Studies. Her publications include "Freaks in Procession? Fancy Dress Masquerade as a Haven for Negotiating Eccentricity during Childhood. A study of child masqueraders in Cape Coast, in *Misfit Children: An Enquiry into Childhood Belongings,* (Lexington Books, 2017), and "Bo Me Truo": A Female-Centred Sun Fire Nudity Dance Ritual of Fertility of the Sehwi People of Ghana, an article in *Chronica Mundi* (2014).

Charles Quist-Adade (PhD) is a faculty member and immediate past chair and former co-chair of the Sociology Department at Kwantlen Polytechnic University. He is the founder and convener of the Kwame Nkrumah International Conference series. His research and teaching interests are Social justice, Globalization, Racialization and Anti-racism, Social Theory, Pan-Africanist and Global South issues. Before joining the Department of Sociology, Dr. Quist-Adade was Assistant Professor at Department of Sociology, Anthropology and Social Work at Central Michigan University. He has previously held positions at the University of Windsor, Wayne State University, Madonna University, Michigan State University, Simon Fraser and the University of British Columbia. He is the author and co-author of several books such as *In the Shadows of the Kremlin and the White House: Africa's Media, Social Justice in Local and Global Contexts, From Colonization to Globalization The Political and Intellectual* (with Vincent Dodoo), *An Introduction to Critical Sociology: From Modernity to Postmodernity* (with Amir Mirfakhraie), *Africa's Many Divides and Africa's Future, Re-engaging the African Diasporas* (with Wendy Royal) and *From the Local to the Global: Theories and Key Issues in Global Justice.* He has also authored several chapters in books as well as scores of scholarly and popular press articles. Dr. Quist-Adade has won several teaching awards and accolades, including being cited twice in the Academic Edition of Canada's premier newsmagazine Maclean's as the top three most popular and one of 10 best professors at the University of Windsor. In 2013, he was Kwantlen Polytechnic University Faculty of Arts Dean's Teaching Award Finalist.

Contributors

Andrea Y. Adomako is a PhD student in the Department of African American Studies and a Mellon Cluster Fellow in Gender and Sexuality at Northwestern University. Adomako holds a B.A. from the Department of Africana Studies and Human Rights at Barnard College, Columbia University and M.A. from the American Studies programme at Purdue University. Her work examines Black childhood as a site of theorization. Her interdisciplinary scholarship spans the fields of Black girlhood studies, Black Feminism, children's literature, and Black political thought. Centring Black children's literature, Adomako emphasizes the genre's role in the aftermath of social movements. She critiques questions of citizenship, nation building and belonging relative to children throughout the African diaspora. As a child of Ghanaian immigrant parents, Adomako considers Ghana a particularly fruitful site to discuss issues and representations concerning childhood. In December of 2016 Adomako received a grant from Purdue University and the Social Science Research Council to travel to Ghana for her research project entitled "From the Shadows: Childhood while Black in the Age of Black Lives Matter and Globalization."

Adomako has presented at several conferences throughout the US including the Society for the History of Children and Youth Ninth Biennial Conference, the National Women's Studies Association Annual Conference, and the College Language Association Annual Conference. Through her scholarship and teaching, Adomako hopes to encourage future scholars to critically engage with the role of childhood as a site of influence. Adomako's work continues to be supported by the Social Science Research Council, the Mellon Mays Fellowship program, Purdue University and the Graduate School at Northwestern University. In 2017 she received the Paul and Eslanda Robeson International Studies Award from Purdue University for her work on Black Lives Matter in Ghana. Adomako currently lives in Chicago, Illinois.

Debbie Olson (PhD), is Assistant Professor of English at Missouri Valley College. Her research is located in the socio-economic, historical, political, and cultural intersections of race, gender, and images of African and African American children in cinema, television, video games, and digital media. She takes a critical look at Western notions of childhood and interrogates the junctures where Western ideas about childhood meet non-Western notions of childhood, specifically (though not exclusively), African and African American children. She is particularly interested in the way discourse functions in the intersections of race, gender, and cultural notions of innocence. Debbie Olson examines images of the child in West African cinema, in diaspora and exilic cinemas, Hollywood cinema, in video games, advertising, and in/on material objects for children. She is the Editor-in-Chief of *Red Feather Journal: an International Journal of Children's Popular Culture*, author of *Black Children in Hollywood Cinema: Cast in Shadow* (2017) and editor of *The Child in Post-apocalyptic Cinema* (2015), co-editor of *Children in the films of Steven Spielberg* (2016), *Lost and Othered Children in Contemporary Cinema* (2012), and *Portrayals of Children in Popular Culture: Fleeting Images* (2012). She is the editor of *The Child in the Films of Alfred Hitchcock* (2014) and the upcoming *Child in World Cinema* (2018) collection. Her articles appear in such works as *The Black Imagination: Science Fiction and Futurism* (2011), *The Tube Has Spoken: Reality TV as Film and History* (2009) and *Facts, Fiction, and African Creative Imaginations* (2009) edited by Toyin Falola and Fallou Ngom. She is the series editor for Lexington Books' Children and Youth in Popular Culture Series.

Ivo Mhike is a Postdoctoral Fellow with the International Studies Group at the University of the Free State in South Africa. His PhD thesis focused on the state constructs of childhood, deviance and delinquency in colonial Zimbabwe. His research interests include youths and the postcolonial state, youth and political cultures, youth and violence and economic change and the transformation of the family unit. His forthcoming publications include "Youth Violence in the Zimbabwe National Youth Service, 2001-2007" in Elina Oinas, Henri Onodera, and Leena Suurpää (eds.), *What politics? Youth and political engagement in Africa*, (Brill, Leiden, 2017).

Komlan Agbedahin is currently a postdoctoral Research Fellow at the Institute for Reconciliation and Social Justice (IRSJ) at the University of the Free State (South Africa). He holds an M.Sc. in Sociology from the University of Lomé (Togo), an MHRS/Peace and Conflicts Studies from the University of Ibadan (Nigeria), and a Ph.D. in Sociology from Rhodes University. He also earned a certificate on Strengthening Postgraduate Supervision Course at the Centre for Higher Education Research, Teaching and Learning, Rhodes University. In 2010, he was a DAAD visiting fellow at the Bremen International Graduate School of Social Sciences (Jacobs University/ Bremen University), Germany. He was a visiting fellow at the Centre for African Studies and the Division of Global Affairs of Rutgers University, USA, in 2013 and at the International Institute for the Advanced Study of Cultures, Institutions and Economic Enterprise, University of Ghana, (Ghana) in 2013. He was a postdoctoral Research Fellow under the African Humanities Programme (AHP/ACLS) in 2012, and a 2013 Presidential Fellow of the African Studies Association, USA. He taught social research methods, general sociology and industrial and economic sociology courses at Rhodes University. He is an active member of the South African Sociological Association, an assessor and mentor of the African Humanities Programme. He has also presented papers at local and international conferences. The following are some of his research interests: Armed conflict and Post-conflict Reconstruction, Child-soldiering, Militarism and Terrorism in Africa Transformation of Higher Education Systems in Africa, South-South Migration and Social Cohesion, Knowledge Production Politics, Border Studies, Empirical Research Methods, Civil-military Relations and African Democracy, Political Economy of African States. The following are two of his publications: "From control to parasitism: Interrogating the roles of border control agencies of the" in *African Security Review* (2014) and "Interrogating the Togolese historical sex strike" in *International Journal on World Peace* (2014). Before joining Rhodes University to study towards his PhD degree, he worked in the war-torn North Kivu region of the Democratic Republic of Congo as Protection/Field Officer with UNHCR, and as Monitoring and Reporting Officer with MINUSTAH in Haiti.

Mawuloe Koffi Kodah (PhD) is a Senior Lecturer of French, Francophone African Literature and Civilisation in the Department of French, Faculty of Arts, College of Humanities and Legal Studies, University of Cape Coast, Ghana. He is currently Head of the Department. Dr. Kodah is a product of the University of Cape Coast (Ghana), Université Cheick Anta Diop de Dakar (Senegal), and The Institute of Social Studies, The Hague (The Netherlands). His research interest is in Literary Critique, African Literature, and Governance. Dr. Kodah, by his academic and professional training is involved in interdisciplinary research spanning between literary criticism, postcolonial studies and Governance fields. He, therefore, has a good number of peer-reviewed publications in these disciplines. As a bilingual (English and French), Dr. Kodah publishes in both English and French languages in which he is very fluent. A good number of his publications in both English and French can, therefore, be easily accessed online.

Mofeyisara Oluwatoyin Omobowale earned a PhD in Anthropology from University of Ibadan, Nigeria. Her doctoral research was on Space, Sexuality and Power at Bodija Market, Ibadan, Nigeria. She is a recipient of the American Council of Learned Societies-African Humanities Programme(ACLS-AHP) Doctoral Fellowship (2012-2013) and Postdoctoral Fellowship (2016), and the Cadbury Fellowship (Department of Anthropology and African Studies, Birmingham University) in 2014. Dr. Mofeyisara Oluwatoyin Omobowale is a Research Fellow/Lecturer at the Institute of Child Health, College of Medicine, University of Ibadan, Nigeria.

Natalie A. Drozda is a PhD student in the counsellor education and supervision programme at Duquesne University. She has been working as a graduate assistant for Dr. Waganesh A. Zeleke on numerous research projects on autism as well as mental health professional development in Africa. Her research interests include autism, trauma, post-traumatic growth, gender, and multicultural counselling.

Olukemi K. Amodu (PhD) works as a Senior Research Fellow at the Institute of Child Health, University of Ibadan, Nigeria. She obtained her Bachelors and Masters from the University of Ibadan, Nigeria. She also obtained a PhD in Molecular Biology/Genetics from the same University. She has been involved in several research studies such as childhood infectious diseases (malaria) relevant to public health research. She has worked and collaborated with experts in Nigeria, and in International laboratories in malaria research, including the Malaria Genetic Epidemiology Network (MalariaGEN) and the EU-funded Network,

Biology of the Malaria Parasite (Biomalpar). Since her employment at the University of Ibadan, she has worked and deployed all efforts to establish a Genetics/Immunology laboratory from scratch at the Institute of Child Health. She has supervised several MPH/MPhil and MSc students. She recently developed the curriculum for the pioneering academic Master's programme in Public Health Biotechnology (Genetics/Molecular Sciences in the clear context or application in diseases of public health importance in Nigeria).

Richard Awubomu is a Senior Member of the Department of General and Liberal Studies, School of Basic and Biomedical Sciences of the University of Health and Allied Sciences (UHAS), Ho, Ghana. He obtained his B.A degree in African Studies at the University of Cape Coast, Ghana, and pursued further studies at the University of Ghana where he obtained a Master of Philosophy degree in African Studies. His varied research interests in African Studies include African belief systems and the environment, Female spirituality groups in West Africa, Traditional Societies and Health Delivery Services, Traditional (Land) Priests and Conflicts in Northern Ghana. He is the author of "Religion, Gender and Environment: The Case of Okule Cult in Ghana," *International Journal of Humanities and Social Sciences.*

Samuel Bewiadzi is a Senior Member at the Department of General and Liberal Studies, University of Health and Allied Sciences, Ho, Ghana. Prior to this position, he was a Teaching Assistant at the Institute of African Studies, University of Ghana. He holds a Bachelor of Arts degree in African Studies from the Centre for African and International Studies, University of Cape Coast, Ghana, and Master of Philosophy from the Institute of African Studies, University of Ghana. Samuel Bewiadzi's area of research is History, Politics and Governance, with special emphasis on African Traditional Governance structures (Chieftaincy) and community development initiatives in areas of health, education, sanitation, business/industry among others. He also focuses on contemporary governance issues such as elections, democracy, political songs and development in Ghana's Fourth Republic. Samuel is currently conducting a series of researches into areas of medical sociology, focusing on traditional orthopedic practice, children and health issues. His papers form part of nine (9) international conference proceedings. He is also the author of "Sustaining Good Governance and Development in Ghanaian Politics: The Role of Political Songs", in *Ghana Social Science Journal,* (2016).

Tammy L. Hughes is Professor and Chair of the Department of Counseling, Psychology and Special Education at Duquesne University. She is the recipient of numerous awards for her teaching (Trainers of School Psychologists), research (Fr. Martin A. Hehir, Endowed Chair for Scholarly Excellence), service to the discipline (American Psychological Association (APA), Pennsylvania Psychological Association), and service to children (National Association of School Psychologists) among others. Active on the national level, she is the immediate past Chair of APA's Board of Educational Affairs and is currently serving as a Council Representative at APA as well as the Co-Chair of the Diversity Strand for the first National High School Summit for Teachers of Psychology in Secondary Schools. Dr. Hughes is an Associate-Editor for *Journal of Early Childhood and Infant Psychology* and serves on the editorial boards of the *Journal of School Violence, International Journal of Offender Therapy and Comparative Criminology, International Journal of School & Educational Psychology* and the children's book series of Magination Press where she provides notes to parents and caregivers on how to help young children overcome adversity. The author and co-author of over 100 scholarly publications, chapters, and books, her writing is in the area of understanding the relationship between emotional dysregulation and conduct problems in children. Dr. Hughes is a licensed psychologist and certified school psychologist. Her clinical experience includes assessment, counselling and consultation services focusing on parent-school-interagency treatment planning and integrity monitoring. She is currently funded to work with families to help at-risk children stay in school; media interviews are available in print (CNN, ABA Journal) or on-line (Bullies, Victims and Bystanders: Tips for Teachers).

Waganesh A. Zeleke is an Assistant Professor in the Department of Counseling, Psychology, and Special Education at Duquesne University where she teaches different graduate level courses in the master's and doctoral programmes. She is a licensed clinical Mental Health counsellor and national certified counsellor. Her clinical experience includes counselling and consultation services focusing on autism, child-family relationship development, Post Traumatic Stress Disorder, parenting consultation, intercultural adoption, attachment, mental health issues among the immigrant population, and childhood mental disorders in the US and Africa. Dr. Zeleke has co-authored and authored more than 10 publications in topics related to children with special needs, clinical interviewing, autism, and family relational development, mental healthcare access and utilization of children with Autism Spectrum Disorders (ASDs) in Africa and the US. Dr. Zeleke's research focus primarily on two lines of inquiry: (1) Examining mechanisms that underlie the mental health development and psychological adjustment of African and African Diaspora communities who primarily experience migration and or international adoption; (2) Research leading to a better understanding and treatment methods of children and individuals with ASD in Africa.

Zethu Cakata (PhD) is an Associate Professor in Psychology at the University of South Africa. Her interest areas are indigenous ways of understanding psychology, coloniality of language, decolonizing through indigenous languages and understanding indigenous names and naming practices. She previously worked as a researcher and lecturer in institutions such as Statistics South Africa, Department of Psychology in the University of Pretoria, and Human Sciences Research Council. Some of her publications are: Review "The African University in the 21st Century", *South African Journal of Higher Education* (2007); "Obstacles to Post-Apartheid Language Policy Implementation: Insights from Language Policy Experts", (co-authored with P.J. Segalo) in *Southern African Linguistics and Applied Language Studies* (2017); "A Psychology in our own language: Redefining Psychology in an African context", *PINS* (2017) (co-authored with P.J. Segalo); and "ABPsi 2018-The 50th anniversary: A gathering of wounded and healing deers", *National Political Science Review* (2018).

Index

Y

Yoruba, xxix, xxx, 1, 2, 4, 5, 6, 8, 13
youth apprenticeship, 150

Z

Zimbabwe, xxvi, xxxiv

www.ingramcontent.com/pod-product-compliance
Lightning Source LLC
Chambersburg PA
CBHW072058020426
42334CB00017B/1557